The Collected Poetry of Paul Laurence Dunbar

Paul Laurence Dunbar

The Collected Poetry of
Paul Laurence Dunbar

Edited and with an Introduction by

JOANNE M. BRAXTON

University Press of Virginia

CHARLOTTESVILLE AND LONDON

THE UNIVERSITY PRESS OF VIRGINIA
Originally published in 1913 by Dodd, Mead and Company

Third printing 1996

Frontispiece: Paul Laurence Dunbar, courtesy of Ohio Historical Society

Library of Congress Cataloging-in-Publication Data

Dunbar, Paul Laurence, 1872–1906.
[Poems]
The collected poetry of Paul Laurence Dunbar / edited and with an introduction by Joanne M. Braxton.
p. cm.
Includes, in addition to added material, the text of the 1913 edition, The complete poems of Paul Laurence Dunbar, presumed to have been complete at the time.
Includes bibliographical references and indexes.
ISBN 0-8139-1454-X. — ISBN 0-8139-1438-8 (pbk.)
1. Afro-Americans—Poetry. I. Braxton, Joanne M. II. Title.
PS1556.A1 1993
811′.4—dc20 92-37190
CIP

Printed in the United States of America

Contents

Text of *The Complete Poems of Paul Laurence Dunbar* (1913 edition)

Acknowledgments

My best thanks go to my mother, Mary Ellen Weems Braxton, for reciting the poems of Paul Laurence Dunbar to me before I could read them to myself and for sharing her love of poetry. I am similarly indebted to the late Charles T. Davis for his Dunbar lectures and for his splendid reading of such favorites as "When Malindy Sings" and "The Party." Many thanks to Chris Carter, Bert Ashe, Amy Huesman, Jean Brown, Bonnie Chandler, Sandy Burr, and Julia Brazelton for their help with research and manuscript preparation, and again to Julia for her ongoing moral support.

I wish to express my thanks to the University of Illinois Press for granting permission to quote Michael Harper's poem "Paul Laurence Dunbar: 1872–1906" from the collection entitled *Images of Kin*. I am also grateful to Sally Scott of Columbus, Ohio, for permission to publish the heretofore unpublished poetry and to the Ohio Historical Society for granting me permission to use the cover photograph and to quote materials from the Paul Laurence Dunbar Collection. Archives associate Tauni Graham was very helpful, as was Gary J. Arnold, head of the research department in the archives. Likewise, the expertise of Stella Grant, of the Harvey Library of Hampton University, proved invaluable. I am also grateful to my colleague Elsa Nettels, of the Department of English at the College of William and Mary, for taking time to read an earlier version of this manuscript.

Finally, I would like to thank Cynthia Foote, my editor at the University Press of Virginia, for her attention to editorial detail and Nancy Essig, director of the press, for believing in this project.

Joanne M. Braxton

Introduction:
The Poetry of Paul Laurence Dunbar

He was a prophet of a new generation.

Robert Thomas Kerlin, quoted by Charles Eaton Burch
in *Southern Workman,* October 1921

Every artist, should he create long enough, will come full cycle again and again. The artist is a political animal as well as a sensitive being. Like any person the artist is a contradiction. Dunbar will speak of the good ole days, then say "We Wear the Mask." The message is clear and available to us if we invest in Dunbar the integrity we hope others will give us.

Nikki Giovanni, Afterword,
A Singer in the Dawn

Again, he did not inherit, he originated.

W. S. Scarborough in
A.M.E. Review, October 1914

Minstrel and mask:
a landscape of speech and body
burned in verbal space,
the match cinder unstandard:
double-conscious brother in the veil—
double-conscious brother in the veil:
double-conscious brother in the veil.

Michael S. Harper
"Paul Laurence Dunbar: 1872–1906"

PAUL LAURENCE DUNBAR achieved recognition as America's first professional black literary man. The author of six volumes of poetry—beginning with *Oak and Ivy* in 1893—as well as of novels, librettos, songs, and essays, Dunbar was known nationally at the turn of the century and accepted as a writer among both blacks and whites. He is remembered today chiefly as a poet.

As a black man and the son of former slaves, a survivor of the day-to-day oppression of both the spirit and the flesh, Paul Laurence Dunbar speaks from the particular to the universal. "I did once want to be a lawyer," Dunbar wrote his white friend Dr. Henry A. Tobey on July

13, 1895, "but that ambition has long since died out before the all-absorbing desire to be a worthy singer of the songs of God and nature. To be able to interpret my own people through song and story, and to prove to the many that after all we are more human than African."[1] This is the "Racial Mountain" that Dunbar confronted.[2]

An important transitional figure in black literature, Dunbar was a precursor of the Harlem Renaissance. Henry Louis Gates argues that the publication of Dunbar's *Lyrics of Lowly Life* in 1895 initiated a debate that occupied "the center of black aesthetic theory" for at least the next forty years; the issue, Gates asserts, is nothing less than that of "the absence and presence of the black voice in the text" (*Signifying,* 173–74). Dunbar evoked the black voice by interpreting the themes and images of the African-American experience two ways: through lyrical poetry written in standard English verse inspired by Shakespeare, Shelley, Keats, Tennyson, and the American romantics and in equally sophisticated dialect verse that located the black speaker, uniquely for Dunbar's time, at the center of experience.

During his lifetime, Dunbar's work appeared in the *New York Times* and such mainstream periodicals as *Century, Lippincott's Monthly,* and *Saturday Evening Post.* These establishment publications served to guide the tastes of an almost exclusively white readership. Hailed by the black literary lions of his day as well as the white—men like Frederick Douglass, Booker T. Washington, and W. E. B. Du Bois, as well as Eugene Field, James Whitcomb Riley, and William Dean Howells—Dunbar would be criticized beginning in the 1920s by some blacks for catering to an Anglo-Saxon audience. Despite this claim, however, Dunbar won the loyal admiration of a devoted black audience that read his volumes with pride and memorized his verses and shared them with their children; in his use of racialized cultural materials and his representation of black folk language, he also served as a model for some of the more liberated members of the Harlem Renaissance. Indeed, Dunbar's influence on the African-American literary tradition is so pervasive that, even today, American writers of African descent still feel it; his work also helped to shape mainstream American cultural and intellectual thought more generally through his popularized versions of the African-American experience.

Paul Laurence Dunbar was born at 311 Howard Street in Dayton, Ohio, on June 27, 1872.[3] His father, Joshua, had escaped from Kentucky via the Underground Railroad and joined the 55th Massachusetts Regiment of the Union army, serving in the Civil War. Joshua

Dunbar later married Matilda Murphy, a young widow with two children from her first marriage, who had moved to Dayton following the war to do laundry work. From this marriage two children were born, Paul and Elizabeth (who died at two years of age). Dunbar's parents separated before he was two years old, and his father went to live in the Soldiers' Home; they were divorced in 1876. Nevertheless, Dunbar's pride in his father's heroic achievements rivaled his love for his mother's stories, and it inspired poems like "Our Martyred Soldiers" and "Emancipation" and the short story "The Ingrate," based on his father's flight to Canada (Revell, *Dunbar,* 38–39). Dunbar learned to read from his mother, who recognized his talent for language when he was quite young and made many sacrifices so that he could be educated according to his ability. His first volume, *Oak and Ivy,* published in 1893, is dedicated "to her who has ever been my guide, teacher, and inspiration."

Like many other gifted adolescents, young Paul Dunbar possessed an inquisitive mind, keen powers of observation, a sense of the significant, and persistent, goal-directed behavior; he also had a sensitive ear for language, a large vocabulary, and a facility in written expression. One suspects that writing may have been as much an escape as a retreat for a lonely and introspective boy keenly aware of his racial as well as his intellectual difference. In any case, Paul Laurence Dunbar stood out. The only black in his class at Central High School, Dunbar was elected president of the Philomathean Society, a prestigious literary club. Charles T. Davis suggests that "Dunbar's primary literary conditioning in high school was one that gave importance to romantic verse" (130). Dunbar published three poems in the *Dayton Herald* in 1888; he also served as class poet and editor-in-chief of the school newspaper, and he wrote the class song sung at his high school graduation at the Dayton Opera House on June 16, 1891 (Revell, 41). The song included these words:

> The wind is fair, the sails are spread,
> Let hearts be firm, "God Speed" is said;
> Before us lies the untried way,
> And we're impatient at the stay.[4]

The sterling aspirations embodied in these lyrics were in keeping with Paul Dunbar's talent, but they would soon be dashed by his encounters with racism in his search for employment.

The trials and tribulations of Dunbar's life were many; these included the problem of earning a living, a thwarted desire for higher education, the failure of his marriage and his health, and increasing frustration with the critical reception of his work. Benjamin Brawley, perhaps the first true Dunbar scholar, refers to the period from 1891 to 1896 as "probably the most critical in the life of Paul Laurence Dunbar" (17). Young Dunbar found that physical labor and domestic service were the only forms of work available to an "unskilled" black boy, even a talented and educated one. Despite his dreams of attending Harvard to prepare for a career in law, Dunbar took a job at four dollars a week as an elevator boy at the Callahan Building in downtown Dayton, a position he would hold until 1893. Such frustrations would be repeated and magnified throughout Dunbar's career, and he would later give voice to his anger in the ironic and sometimes bitter tone of poems like "Sympathy," "Prometheus Bound," and "The Poet," as well as in short stories like "One Man's Fortunes," in which a black college graduate, similar to Paul Dunbar, is reduced to menial labor. In the two-year period when he worked at the Callahan Building, Dunbar sometimes wrote poetry on the job when there was little elevator traffic. Always at hand were his pen, notebook, dictionary, and thesaurus, and nearby was a set of law books. Perhaps it was during his employment there that Dunbar scribbled the unpublished lines:

> What's the use of dreaming all the time
> yes there's lots of hope a-beaming through your rhyme
> But the work you've got to do
> Dreams won't ever do for you
> Even if they did come true.[5]

Clearly, Dunbar never intended these rough lines for publication, but they are invaluable for what they reveal about the inner man and his private suffering. This is an aspect of the poet that rarely appears except in his personal correspondence, his unpublished manuscripts, and perhaps in some of the later verse such as that found in *Lyrics of Sunshine and Shadow* (1905).

Despite his hidden anguish during this important transitional period (1891–96) a turning point in Dunbar's career occurred in 1892, when a former teacher introduced him to Dr. James Newton Matthews, who invited Dunbar to read an original poem at the Western Association of Writers, which convened that year in Dayton. Dunbar awed the audience with his polished reading of "Welcome Address to the Western Association of Writers" (see the "Added Poems" section of this volume). Dunbar also completed his first volume of poems, *Oak and Ivy* (published in Dayton by the United Church of the Brethren in 1893), during this transitional period.

In 1893, when he was twenty-one, Dunbar traveled from his home in Ohio to the World's Columbian Exposition in Chicago, the first world's fair, carrying copies of his *Oak and Ivy* to sell at one dollar a copy. There he met Frederick Douglass, who was at that time U.S. minister to Haiti and the commissioner of the Haitian exhibition and who hired him as a clerk at the Haitian Building, paying Dunbar from his own funds at five dollars a week.[6] In a letter to his mother dated June 6, 1893, Dunbar describes his first meeting with Douglass. "The old man was just finishing dinner; he got up and came tottering into the room, 'and this is Paul Dunbar' he said shaking hands and patting me on the shoulder. 'Paul, how do you do? I've been knowing you for some time and you're one of my boys.' He said so much Ma that I must wait until I am with you before I can tell you all. He had me read to him my 'Ode to Ethiopia' and he himself read to us with much spirit 'The Ol' Tunes' with which he seemed delighted."[7] Douglass arranged for Dunbar to read his poems at the Colored American Day celebration held at the Haitian Building, and he introduced him to other black writers and artists, including Charlotte Forten Grimké, James Carrothers, James Campbell, and Will Marion Cook (Revell, *Dunbar,* 44). In this way, Douglass assumed a kind, fatherly role toward the young poet, but he was to live only two years after meeting Dunbar in 1893, and therefore did not play a continuing role in Dunbar's development. Nevertheless, Douglass's introduction on this occasion provided Dunbar with a wider audience, especially among black writers with whom he shared certain spiritual and aesthetic affinities. Douglass's interest also gave Dunbar increased confidence in his abilities.

Dunbar's correspondence with Alice Ruth Moore began in 1895. Alice Moore was born in New Orleans, Louisiana, on July 19, 1875; she was three years and one month younger than the man she would come to address as "husband" well before they were married (Fuller, 15). Although she had very little African blood, she, like Dunbar, identified completely with the African-American race and its struggle to survive and to create. She too was a writer, and Dunbar wrote to her after seeing her picture and reading some of her work published in a Boston magazine (Hull, 15): "You will pardon my boldness in addressing you,

I hope, and let my interest in your work be my excuse. . . . I am drawn to write you because we are both working along the same lines and a sketch of yours in the Monthly Review so interested me that I was anxious to know more of you and your work." In the same letter Dunbar solicited Miss Moore's opinion about the use of African-American folklore as a basis for written literature: "I want to know whether or not you believe in preserving by Afro-American—I don't like the word—writers these quaint old tales and songs of our fathers which have made the fame of Joel Chandler Harris, Thomas Nelson Page, Ruth McEnery Stuart and others! Or whether you like so many others think we should ignore the past and all its capital literary materials." [8]

Significantly, Dunbar attempted to elicit the thoughts of the woman who would become his wife on a point central to his career as a poet. He sought intellectual and spiritual support for his creative work in relation to the cultural dilemma he faced as a writer of dialect verse and a preserver of black folk traditions. "I should like to exchange opinions and work with you if you will agree. The counsel and encouragement of one who is striving toward the same end that I am would, I know, greatly help." In a later letter he would write, "I feel that the bond of a fellow-craft joins us together." [9] Indeed, the two had much in common. Each experimented with the use of folklore and folk language in both poetry and verse; the year before they were married, Alice Moore wrote to her "Dearest Paul" from Brooklyn, New York, where she was engaged as a teacher in the public schools, that she had given "a recitation in a concert" of "a monologue of my own composition in Creole dialect." [10] Well-educated and aspiring to participate in the creation of an authentic national literature that made use of both racial and regional materials, they did indeed share a bond. They loved early and deeply. Yet Alice was not above scolding her fiancé in a letter of October 21, 1897, when she disagreed with Dunbar's literary taste.[11] Overall, however, she adored him, and Dunbar seems to have appreciated his wife's abilities, as he told one writer from the *Philadelphia Times Book Review* in 1902: "She writes much better prose than I do, and is invaluable to me as a critic." [12] Dunbar published *Lyrics of Lowly Life,* which Charles T. Davis calls his "finest volume of poetry" (131), in 1896, during a period that included his courtship of Alice Ruth Moore and that was probably the most intensely optimistic time of his life.

Three years after initiating their often passionate and sometimes stormy correspondence, Paul Laurence Dunbar married Alice Ruth

Moore on Sunday March 6, 1898, in New York City.[13] They married in secret and over the objections of her family and many of her friends, who reportedly objected to Dunbar's "very dark skin color and his work with minstrel shows and musicals" (Hull, 123). Dunbar took his mother into his confidence, but his closest friends learned of his marriage only after announcements were mailed in mid-April (Arnold, 404). The newlyweds settled in a modest home at 1934 Fourth Street, N.W., in the Le Droit Park section of Washington, D.C., a mecca for the "Talented Tenth" of the educated scholars, intellectuals, and activists of the black middle class, as well as the light-skinned blue-veined members of the bourgeoisie, who identified with the genteel tradition and who frequently defined themselves by behavior critic Gloria Hull has characterized as "conservative, stiff, uptight and accommodationist" (23).

Although the young couple enjoyed their stimulating lives within their lively circle of artists and intellectuals, and although Dunbar was remarkably productive during the years immediately following their marriage, Washington, D.C., was a bastion of black respectability and middle-class convention that did not encourage experimentation. It is altogether probable that Dunbar might have felt freer to explore his strengths as an interpreter of black folk language and the oral tradition in a more cosmopolitan and perhaps a less color-conscious city, such as New York. During the first four years of their marriage, Alice and Paul were a loving though not a completely untroubled pair. Dunbar produced his first novel, *The Uncalled* (1898); a collection of short stories set in the antebellum South, *Folks from Dixie* (1898); and two collections of poetry, *Lyrics of the Hearthside* (1899) and *Poems of Cabin and Field* (1899). During this same four-year period, Dunbar also published a significant number of essays, stories, and articles and enjoyed wide popularity on the lecture circuit. This popularity, unfortunately, necessitated frequent separations from his wife and contributed to the deterioration of Dunbar's marriage. By 1902, Dunbar was becoming addicted to alcohol (which had been prescribed for tuberculosis), and his marriage was falling apart.

In 1902 Paul and Alice Dunbar separated permanently and by mutual consent; although the two remained friends, Dunbar was heartbroken. Following his separation from Alice, the mood of Dunbar's poetry changed dramatically. Dunbar—suffering terribly from tuberculosis, alcoholism, and the belief that he was a failure as a poet—now retreated to his study in the house at 219 North Summit Street in Dayton, where he would live his last days under the watchful eye of his mother. He died on February 9, 1906. By his mother's count, Dunbar's age at death was thirty-three years, seven months, and twelve days.[14] According to a contemporary account from the Dayton *Journal,* Dunbar's steel-gray casket was covered with two "handsome" floral blankets: one, "consisting of white lilacs and lillies," came from James Whitcomb Riley, "the other of American beauty roses" came from Dunbar's high school. Alice did not attend the services at the Eaker Street A.M.E. Church, but she did nothing publicly to tarnish the memory of her estranged husband and friend.[15] Indeed, she later published a laudatory essay, "The Poet and His Song," in the October 1914 issue of the *A.M.E. Review,* in which she illuminated plainly and sympathetically certain little-known and scantily understood aspects of Dunbar's life and work (Alice Dunbar, 135–43). She would continue to be known as the widow of Paul Laurence Dunbar even after her marriage in 1916 to Robert J. Nelson (Hull, 15).

The central debate concerning Dunbar's poetry had begun to emerge when his second collection, *Majors and Minors,* published in Dayton by Hadley and Hadley in 1895, was reviewed by William Dean Howells in the June 27, 1896, issue of *Harper's Weekly.* Howells's review drew wide attention to Dunbar, but it also limited the appreciation of the work of the twenty-four-year-old poet by declaring that the "Minors" (Dunbar's plantation-dialect poems, constituting about a third of the volume) were his real strength and that there was nothing "especially notable" in Dunbar's standard English verse "except for the Negro face of the author." "In his treatment of it," Howells wrote, "he has been able to bring us nearer to the heart of *primitive human nature* in his race than any one else has yet done" ("Life," 630; emphasis mine). With these words, Howells dismissed Dunbar's traditional verse and set the direction for future Dunbar criticism, "a line," in the words of Benjamin Brawley, "slavishly adhered to by reviewers and one about which the poet himself was not always enthusiastic" (*Dunbar,* 49). In time, it is true, Dunbar would come to sense the ways in which Howells's words limited him and his work, but in 1896 he was grateful for the notice that Howells's attention brought to his efforts. Elsa Nettels, writing about the "problem of Negro dialect," refers to "Dunbar's response to Howells's recognition" as "a good example of the debt of gratitude that becomes the burden of a grievance," for burden it did become (82). In 1897, Dunbar would write a friend from London, "One critic says a thing and the rest hasten to say the same things, in many cases using the identical words. I see very clearly that Mr. Howells has done me irrevocable harm in the dictum he laid down regarding my dialect verse. I am afraid it will even influence English criticism."[16] Indeed, Howells's comments helped to create an audience for Dunbar's dialect poetry while discouraging interest in his standard-English verse. Therefore it is not surprising that Dunbar grew to resent what he saw as the unfair trivialization of his "Minors" by Howells and other critics of his generation.

Dunbar's conflict with this well-meaning patron foreshadows the constraints imposed on the Harlem Renaissance artists of the 1920s by a white readership that insisted on stereotyped representations of black urban primitivism. For these later writers, the "old Negro" of plantation literature was supplanted by thematic treatment of the urban Negro of Seventh Street in Washington, D.C., and 125th Street in Harlem: views of black nightlife, dance and music, sexual freedom, and generally uninhibited behavior associated by many whites and some bourgeois blacks with a black urban underclass. However, although Rudolph Fisher, Langston Hughes, and Wallace Thurman all used black dialect quite deliberately in their work and each struggled with stereotypes in an attempt to create an original literature, none of them would be labeled as "just" a dialect writer as Dunbar was.

More than one critic has found Howells's assessment of Dunbar's dialect verse to be a fair one. While Dunbar protested what he saw as the unfair trivialization of his "Majors" by literary critics of his generation, Charles T. Davis argues that no American poet, black or white, has approached Dunbar's success in using "the spoken language of the people as medium" (164). According to Davis, Dunbar had formidable poetic options, including "high rhetoric about noble black themes," dialect verse, and the "white" romantic tradition as exemplified by Keats, Wordsworth, Coleridge, and the American romantics. Davis suggests that Dunbar's own use of the term *Minors* to describe his dialect verse suggests "problems about the poet's attitude about the use of dialect." One of Dunbar's failings, Davis suggests, is that he "never fully understood that he had to make a decision," that "the choice of voice is finally an act of will, and it requires a sense of where a poet's strength lies." Dunbar, Davis contends, lacked self-assurance where his dialect poems were concerned: "Dunbar does not make the decision that would enhance his stature as a poet." Because of his cultural ambivalence, Dunbar "could not bring himself to perform the act of will, to elect to concentrate upon his strengths and to create the geography, the psychology, and the imagery that must accompany a fundamental artistic decision of this kind" (134–35). This confusion distinguishes Dunbar from the generation of Negro artists who followed him, who were bold in their claims about the artistic value of racialized cultural materials where Dunbar remained apologetic.

For the reader of Paul Laurence Dunbar, the problem becomes one of demythologizing the text. According to Jay Martin and Gossie Hudson, writing in the *Paul Laurence Dunbar Reader,* the many myths surrounding Dunbar and his work include the belief "that Dunbar disliked his own work in dialect" and that "his dialect work, then, constituted a surrender to the racism so evident in the nation at the time" (261). While it is true that Dunbar's dialect poetry, much of it written in a comic and sometimes sentimental vein, was popular with whites, it was also popular with blacks of the post–World War I generation, who entertained each other with recitations of Dunbar's verse at slabtown conventions and at other all-black gatherings that excluded whites. According to Martin and Hudson, other myths surrounding Dunbar and his work include the beliefs that his "poetry avoided . . . racial issues," that it was simple, that Dunbar never revised his work, and that he did not grow as a poet (262–63).

They explode the first of these myths by referring to "The Haunted Oak," "Ode to Ethiopia," "To the South," and "We Wear the Mask"; these protest poems exhibit strong racial pride. Indeed, Benjamin Brawley, writing in the *Southern Workman* as early as 1930, defended Dunbar against the barbs of New Negro critics by pointing out that Dunbar's sonnet "Robert Gould Shaw" had been criticized on its appearance in the *Atlantic* for seeming "to give voice to restlessness rather than optimism." "When Dunbar sent 'The Haunted Oak' to the *Century,* there were those who were amazed that Mr. Gilder dared to print it" (191).

The myth that Dunbar did not grow as a poet might have been engendered, in part, by the fact that the *Lyrics of Lowly Life,* published by Dodd, Mead and Company in 1896 (Dunbar's first professionally published volume) reprinted much of the work from *Oak and Ivy* and almost everything from *Majors and Minors. Lyrics of Lowly Life* also included an Introduction by William Dean Howells based on his review of *Majors and Minors* that had appeared in *Harper's Weekly* two years earlier. In it Howells reiterated his sentiments about Dunbar's dialect poems: "there is a precious difference of temperament between the races which it would be a great pity ever to lose, and that . . . is . . . most charmingly suggested by Mr. Dunbar in those pieces of his where he studies the moods and traits of his race in its own accent of our English" (Howells, Intro., ix). Despite Howells's earlier devaluation of Dunbar's standard verse, Dunbar went on to include his poems on black heroic themes in *Lyrics of Lowly Life* as well as in successive volumes. These poems include ballads like "The Haunted Oak" and "The Colored Soldiers," both of which evince strong racial pride and a spirit of protest.

Dunbar's ballads are frequently overlooked and / or lumped together with other poems and dismissed as derivative or imitative. These fine poems deserve to be viewed alongside the better-known dialect poems as evidence of Dunbar's commitment to the black cause and as proof of his further accomplishment as a poet. Dunbar proclaimed his affection for the ballad in an early poem called "Songs" that appeared in *Oak and Ivy* (see "Added Poems"):

> I love the dear old ballads best,
> That tell of love and death,
> Whose every line sings love's unrest
> Or mourns the parting breath.

"The Colored Soldiers" praises the brave black men who, like Dunbar's father, had served in the Union army during the Civil War under the threat of immediate execution upon capture by rebel soldiers (who frequently killed black soldiers on capturing them or subsequently hanged them rather than taking black men as prisoners of war). Despite the widespread Confederate practice of intimidation and brutality and the atrocities routinely committed against Union troops of African descent at Fort Pillow and elsewhere, black soldiers acquitted themselves honorably in battle, often volunteering for the most dangerous assignments. Dunbar's "The Colored Soldiers" celebrates the heroism of these black men.

> And like hounds unleashed and eager
>   For the life blood of the prey,
> Sprung they forth and bore them bravely
>   In the thickest of the fray.
> And where'er the fight was hottest,
>   Where the bullets fastest fell,
> There they pressed unblanched and fearless
>   At the very mouth of hell.

(p. 51)

The style of "The Colored Soldiers" is reminiscent of the poetry of John Greenleaf Whittier, the antislavery poet Dunbar memorialized in the poem bearing his name ("Great poets never die, for Earth / Doth count their lives of too great worth"—p. 18). Dunbar's standard English models included not just the British and American romantics but the more popular American poets like Whittier and Longfellow. As a black man, Dunbar personalized the ballad form by treating racial topics; because of his use of this form and his popular appeal, many contemporary critics compared Dunbar to Robert Burns.

Although many associate Dunbar's verse with the plantation school of literature and the racist stereotypes of African-Americans prominent during the era when he wrote, Paul Laurence Dunbar himself was never complacent about racism; his quiet outrage is an aspect of his writing overlooked too frequently by contemporary critics of his work. Dunbar's eulogy "Frederick Douglass" (pp. 6–7) reveals his political stance; this poem celebrates Douglass's "straightforward, fearless" heroism and the spiritual strength of he who "dared the lightning in the lightning's track, / And answered thunder with his thunder back." "T'was for his race, not for himself he spoke," asserted Dunbar. Certainly, his private correspondence shows Dunbar to be a "race man" much more closely aligned with the W. E. B. Du Bois line of thinking than with the more accommodationist views of Booker T. Washington. In fact, Dunbar's published thoughts on suffrage, civil rights, and higher education for the Negro might be seen to *anticipate* those of Du Bois.[17]

The assertion that Dunbar did not continue to grow as a poet may be answered, in part, through a comparison of excerpts from two poems from different stages of Dunbar's career, each bearing the title "Sympathy." The first poem comes from Dunbar's debut collection, *Oak and Ivy,* but was not reprinted in any of the later collections. (It appears in full in the "Added Poems" section, below.)

A balm to bathe the wounded heart
    Where sorrow's hand hath lain,
The link divine from soul to soul
    That makes us one in pain,—

Sweet sympathy, benignant ray,
    Light of the soul doth shine;
In it is human nature giv'n
    A touch of the divine.

The language of this excerpt as well as that of the complete poem is stilted and archaic, and while its rigid form demonstrates the author's ability to conform to a European model, the poem itself doesn't breathe. The "Sympathy" written by the young elevator operator who had just graduated from high school might be thought of as a juvenile work or an apprentice piece for the later "Sympathy," which was written sometime during Dunbar's 1897–99 stint as an assistant at the Library of Congress, and which first appeared in *Lyrics of the Hearthside* (1899). The mature "Sympathy" opens with the unforgettable lines, "I know what the caged bird feels, alas!" By this time Dunbar, although still a young poet at twenty-seven, is nearing the end of his career and his life; he has published a total of four volumes of poetry, each showing a greater mastery of the poet's craft. He has become a more well-rounded individual as a result of his marriage and travel at home and abroad. Even so, Dunbar proclaims, "I know what the caged bird feels." In the powerful imagery of the "Sympathy" from *Lyrics of the Hearthside,* Dunbar finds the mature form for the sentiment of the earlier poem from *Oak and Ivy.*

> I know why the caged bird beats his wing
> Till its blood is red on the cruel bars;
> For he must fly back to his perch and cling
> When he fain would be on the bough a-swing;
> And a pain still throbs in the old, old scars
> And they pulse again with a keener sting—
> I know why he beats his wing!

(p. 102)

In this later "Sympathy," Dunbar moves away from the imitation of European models and toward a strong poetic voice of his own. Yet he displays his keen awareness of the limitations imposed on him by his culture, including anxiety about self-support, and the psychic injury he felt he had sustained from the abusive misreading of his work by critics following what Dunbar saw as Howells's "dictum" regarding his dialect verse, as well as from the general neglect of his protest ballads and standard English verse based on classical models. Well, then, might Dunbar have identified with the caged bird who sings "When his wing is bruised and his bosom sore."

Writing in the *A.M.E. Review* in 1914 the poet's widow argued that "a poet is a poet because he *understands;* because he is born with a divine kinship with all things, and he is a poet in direct ratio to his power of sympathy." She explained that:

> The iron grating of the book stacks in the Library of Congress suggested to him the bars of the bird's cage. June and July days are hot. All out of doors called and the trees of the shaded streets of Washington were tantalizingly suggestive of his beloved streams and fields. The torrid sun poured its rays down into the courtyard of the library and heated the iron grilling of the book stacks until they were like prison bars in more senses than one. The dry dust of the dry books (ironic incongruity!—a poet shut up with medical works), rasped sharply in his hot throat, and he understood how the bird felt when it beats its wings against its cage. (Alice Dunbar, 129)

Regarding Howells's "dictum," Alice (writing still as Alice M. Dunbar in 1914) went on to write: "Say what you will, or what Mr. Howells wills, about the 'feeling the Negro life esthetically, and expressing it lyrically,' it was in the pure English verse that the poet expressed *himself*" (Alice Dunbar, 124). Dead at thirty-three, Dunbar would always be a "young" poet who grew, but who never quite reached his fullest potential. Had he lived longer and perchance had he had the opportunity to realize his life's dream of attending college, he might have realized even more development than he did in his short lifetime.

Recent attempts by Henry Louis Gates and others to define the Dunbar canon have included a reconsideration of Dunbar's dialect verse as "mask in motion"; Dunbar often used humor as a mask, set in motion by dialect, to conceal his angriest messages.[18] "We Wear the Mask" (p. 71), one of Dunbar's most famous poems, has been read and reread by critics. I examine it here not only for what it shows of Dunbar's racial and aesthetic sensibility but for the way in which—potentially, at least—it unlocks the dialect poems.

> We wear the mask that grins and lies,
> It hides our cheeks and shades our eyes,—
> This debt we pay to human guile;
> With torn and bleeding hearts we smile,
> And mouth with myriad subtleties.

The "we" of the poem is the black folk collective, the speaker a Dunbar persona, or perhaps the real Dunbar lifting the mask from his danced language to speak plainly and unequivocally for just a moment about the double nature of the black experience. To put this another way, he draws aside the veil of the seventh son to give *the reader* second sight, if only briefly, into the inner circle of the black community and that other truth so often concealed behind Dunbar's comic drama, his witty lyricism, and his use of irony. In life, the mask covers the face and eyes, and the "torn and bleeding hearts" and the "myriad subtleties" that are mouthed are deliberately indirect and misleading; the speaker of this poem steps out from behind the mask, however, evincing briefly a consummate mastery of all the false "debts" that separate him from authentic wholeness. The mask is then replaced.

> Why should the world be overwise,
> In counting all our tears and sighs?
> Nay, let them only see us, while
> We wear the mask.

In the third verse, the race cries and even sings out to Christ in pain, but "the world dream[s] otherwise," unaware of the black man's struggle for equality in the world and for peace within. Martin and Hudson argue that "Dunbar was persuaded that the world was an affair of masks, that he could reveal himself only by the way he concealed himself, that the truths of his being were masked." In this way, they argue, Dunbar anticipated Robert Frost and W. B. Yeats, even though "he did not confront the nineteenth-century sensibility with the twentieth-century condition as they did" (267).

For Dunbar the masked language of black dialect was part and parcel of the larger American experience. Fascinated by the representation of regional language generally, Dunbar experimented with German-American, Irish-American, and Midwestern dialects. One such example of Dunbar's experimentation with German-American dialect is "Lager Beer," a humorous piece that appeared in the Dayton *Tattler* of December 13, 1890, signed with the Dunbar pseudonym Pffenberger Deutzelheim; the full text of this youthful effort is included in the "Added Poems" section.[19] Dunbar employed Western dialect in the short stories "The Tenderfoot" and "Little Billy," both published in 1891, and also in the poem "James Whitcomb Riley," dedicated to one he respected and viewed as a great poet and a man of the people.

> 'Tain't the words alone, but feelin's,
> That tech the tender spot.
> An' that's jest why I love him,—
> Why he's got sech human feelin',
> An' in ev'ry song he gives us,
> You kin see it creepin, stealin'

Through the core the tears go tricklin'
But the edge is bright an' smiley;
I never saw a poet
Like that poet Whitcomb Riley.

(p. 287)

Dunbar's experimentation with non-Negro dialects may represent a philosophical alignment with local-color writers of other regions and affirm a belief shared by Joel Chandler Harris, William Dean Howells, and others that "the writer of dialect helps to unite Americans by making the people of different parts of the country known to each other." [20]

More problematic than Dunbar's reverence for Riley is the poetic imagery he inherited from Irwin Russell, Thomas Nelson Page, Joel Chandler Harris, and Ruth McEnery Stuart, white writers in the plantation tradition who tended to perpetuate stereotypes of blackness.[21] According to Charles T. Davis, "the simplifying and reductive influence [in black dialect verse] came from the Plantation Tradition, the Southern wing of the Genteel, which was nourished in part by the efforts of many Southerners and Northerners too, to heal wounds inflicted by decades of conflict and a devastating Civil War" (123). To illustrate this problem further, Elsa Nettels notes that the black dialect speaker in the poems of Russell and Page was "more often than not an aged black man called Uncle, occasionally a preacher, sometimes blind, usually born in slavery—[who] recalls the happiness of life before the war with his 'master and mistress,' extols their virtues, and laments his freedom." Nettels argues that Negro dialect fashioned by post–Civil War writers of the dominant tradition is "itself a symbol of servitude, reflective of the white's desire, conscious or not, to enslave the Negro through language" (76).

For Henry Louis Gates, "even sympathetic characterizations of the black, such as Uncle Remus by Joel Chandler Harris, were far more related to a racist textual tradition that stemmed from minstrelsy, the plantation novel, and vaudeville than to representations of spoken language." Enslavement, then, is the "linguistic sign" of the origins of Dunbar's dialect poetry, but Dunbar exceeds his inheritance of racialized language, recharging and refocusing it, turning it to his own purpose (*Signifying*, 176).

For the purposes of my argument, we might compare Dunbar with Irwin Russell (1853–79), one of his white predecessors in the plantation tradition, a dialect poet who influenced not only Dunbar but also other white writers like Thomas Nelson Page and Joel Chandler Harris and perhaps Dubose Heyward and Julia Peterkin as well. Russell's "Christmas Night in the Quarters" is a fair example of his dialect verse. Russell's minstrel minister invokes a blessing on the slave's celebration, caricaturing the black celebrants in the crudest sort of comic dialect verse. By contrast, Dunbar's comic poem "The Party" (pp. 83–86)—which contains many of the same elements found in Russell's "Christmas Night"—though written in black dialect, is as much a parody of a white cotillion as it is a comment on black folk manners. So the white poet caricatured the black folk, and the black poet caricatured the white.

Dunbar was undeniably aware of Russell and other white poets who attempted to write black dialect. The existence in manuscript of an unpublished Dunbar poem that begins "Twas Christmas night, the quarters" underscores this fact.[22] But Dunbar did not accept the simplified views of black life expressed by Russell, Harris, and others in the plantation school, nor did he accept entirely their representations of black folk speech. He therefore would not publish his "Christmas night, the quarters" poem, which began very probably as an imitation of Russell's popular published work. Dunbar's "Christmas night" would remain, for him, an experiment in form—a private experiment from which he would gain artistic experience that he would put to use in other poems. Similarly, Dunbar's poem "At Night" (p. 254) serves as an apprentice piece for the well-known "In the Morning" (pp. 190–91), a masterpiece in dialect. In some sense, Dunbar would do what Russell had done, but he would do it more faithfully and with a different set of loyalties.

While it is difficult to overthrow the racial ideology associated with black dialect, Dunbar shared much of the humor and pathos of the slave experience without presenting the stereotypes of the plantation school. Charles T. Davis suggests that "Dunbar was saved, in general, from the excesses of the Plantation Tradition by his deep consciousness of being black. . . . It took a keen ear and a responsible sensibility to winnow a true voice out of the 'deses' and 'doses' of black dialect verse" (123). Dunbar possessed both of these gifts required to create an authentic black poetic diction; he succeeded admirably. Dunbar's dialect poems sometimes speak in two voices, one that is so subtle as to be almost incomprehensible to whites. Defending Dunbar in a 1914 issue of the *A.M.E. Review*, one critic wrote, "Every phase of Negro life has been caught by his pen as by a camera" (Scarborough, 140).

When reading Dunbar's dialect poems set on the plantation, one is reminded of a passage from *The Life of Frederick Douglass, an American Slave: Written by Himself.* Reflecting on songs he heard slaves sing when he was himself enslaved, Douglass wrote: "I did not, when a slave, understand the deep meaning of those rude and apparently incoherent songs. I was myself within the circle; so that I neither saw nor heard as those without might see and hear" (Douglass, 14). W. E. B. Du Bois would later articulate a similar sentiment in *The Souls of Black Folk*: "It is a peculiar sensation, this double-consciousness. . . . One ever feels his twoness,—an American, a Negro; two souls, two thoughts, two unreconciled strivings; two warring ideals in one dark body, whose dogged strength alone keeps it from being torn asunder" (Du Bois, 45). Although Dunbar himself was never a slave, he employed "double-consciousness" in his poetry and became a powerful interpreter of the slave experience. Like the slaves observed by Douglass in his 1845 *Narrative* and the caged bird of his own poem, Dunbar "would sometimes," to borrow Douglass's words, "sing the most pathetic sentiment in the most rapturous tone, and the most rapturous statement in the most pathetic tone" (Douglass, 14). Because of this sensitivity, "The Party" remains a comic poem devoid of the minstrel flavor of Russell's "Christmas Night."

Dunbar's dialect poetry is rich in drama, irony, understatement, hyperbole, and caricature. The dual voice of Dunbar's poems is a natural result of the double vision that Dunbar inherited as a black and an American and that threatened to tear him apart. His creation of a double voice in his poetry allowed him to speak to two distinct audiences at once. In fact, Dunbar's use of caricature often renders whites more comic than blacks. In "When Malindy Sings" (pp. 82–83), a poem written as a tribute to Dunbar's mother, Matilda, the dialect narrator addresses Miss Lucy.

> G'way an' quit dat noise, Miss Lucy—
> Put dat music book away;
> What's de use to keep on tryin'?
> Ef you practise twell you're gray. . . .
>
> You ain't got de nachel o'gans
> Fu' to make de soun' come right,
> You ain't got de tu'ns an' twistin's
> Fu' to make it sweet an' light. . . .

Easy 'nough fu' folk to hollah,
Lookin' at de lines an' dots,
When dey ain't no one kin sence it,
An' de chune comes in, in spots.

Using irony, caricature, and understatement, Dunbar here "signifies" on the whites' assumption of biological and intellectual superiority as well as their ability to read books and music. With all these supposed assets, Miss Lucy can't sing "right"; no amount of practice will render her singing "sweet an' light." And even her ability to "read" is suspect, with the tune coming in "in spots." Malindy may be the subject of the poem, but she is not the one being put down here. The comic use of dialect in "When Malindy Sings" cuts two ways, masking the speaker's critique of a white woman he is not free to criticize openly.

"The Deserted Plantation" (pp. 67–68) is a sentimental and somewhat oversimplified poem that must have appealed to white Southerners who wanted to see blacks back in their place.

So I'll stay an' watch de deah ole place an' tend it
Ez I used to in de happy days gone by.
'Twell, de othah Mastah thinks it's time to end it,
An' calls me to my gua'ters in de sky.

Anyone who wanted to restore the old ways could certainly take comfort from these lines. But this passing reference to the master is almost obligatory, and "the happy days gone by" are the ones shared with other slaves.

Whah's Aunt Doshy, Sam, an' Kit, an' all de res'?
Whah's ole Tom de da'ky fiddlah, how's he farin'?
Whah's de gals dat used to sing an' dance de bes'?

Still a group of singing, dancing black folk to be sure, but not stereotypes; none of the malevolence found by Brawley and Brown in the works of Page, Russell, and Harris is to be found here. These antebellum black folk are imagined on their own time and in an Afrocentric environment where they enjoy each other's company and where they are self-identified rather than focused on the master or the degree of their oppression: they are not bent under the driver's lash or bowing and scraping to the master.

Southern whites typically read such a poem from outside the circle of black culture, with a degree of unconscious indifference; black folks, on the other hand, read "The Deserted Plantation" or a poem like "The Party" from inside out, relishing the means by which their ancestors retained their humanity and their psychic wholeness to survive their enslavement. The narrator of "The Party" does not long for a return to the slave past; he *does* yearn for the binding ties of intraracial friendships forged in the heat of enslavement. The ex-slave speaker of "The Deserted Plantation" may indeed be "simple" in his ways and recollections, but he is complex in his outlook and faithful to himself and to his own, not to the master.

Another of Dunbar's most famous dialect poems, "Little Brown Baby," is likewise set in an Afrocentric environment, the slave cabin. In this poem, Dunbar refutes the popular myth that slave fathers did not love their children.

> Come to you' pallet now—go to yo' res';
> Wisht you could allus know ease an' cleah skies;
> Wisht you could stay jes' a chile on my breas'—
> Little brown baby wif spa'klin' eyes!
>
> (p. 135)

Here, in his own subtle way, Dunbar argues that the black family did survive enslavement and that black fathers bonded with their children and attempted to shield them from painful encounters with racist oppression, a notion that must seem novel to some outside the circle of the black experience, even today.

Some critics think that we have lost sight of what a dramatic innovation Dunbar's work represented in its day; Gates refers to Dunbar's "use of black dialect as a basis for poetic diction" as "startling." "Dunbar," claims Gates, "signified upon the received racist textual tradition and posited in its stead a black poetic diction which his more gifted literary heirs would, in their turn, signify upon, with often pathetic results." Because we "tend to read Dunbar backwards, as it were, through these often unfortunate poetic efforts" (of Dunbar's heirs), we tend to undervalue Dunbar's new language, and his attempt at a representation of authentic black poetic diction (*Signifying,* 176). As Arna Bontemps observes, we should remember that Frederick Douglass, Booker T. Washington, and W. E. B. Du Bois were "warmly drawn" to Paul Laurence Dunbar, and that none of them complained about Dunbar's poems and stories in dialect (*A Singer,* 51).

Dunbar's work began to decline in popularity during the 1920s after New Negro critics accused him of accommodating negative stereotypes of life in order to sell his poems to white readers, although Gates suggests alternatively that during the Harlem Renaissance "the issue of dialect as an inappropriate literary language seems to have been raised in order for a second poetic diction to be posited in its place" (*Signifying,* 177); this "second poetic diction" included the "standard English" representations of black folk language found in James Weldon Johnson's *God's Trombones,* a collection of "folk sermons" in verse. Johnson, always represented as a close friend of Dunbar's, actually went so far as to report that Dunbar himself became intensely dissatisfied with and perhaps even ashamed of his dialect verse. Thus Dunbar may have become—especially in the minds of "respectable" New Negroes like Johnson and others who were anxious to replace him as poet laureate of his race—a convenient symbol of the "Old Negro" and the "white man's burden" stereotype. Nevertheless, there were those who took issue with Johnson's view. In an article called "Old School of Negro 'Critics' Hard on Paul Laurence Dunbar" and published in the *Messenger* at the height of the Harlem Renaissance, Thomas Millard Henry suggested that Dunbar was more talented than Johnson and that Dunbar's work should be "read more and discussed less" (Henry, 310–11).

Throughout the Harlem Renaissance, Dunbar remained a model for writers as diverse as Countee Cullen and Langston Hughes, both of whom considered Dunbar a great poet. Langston Hughes wrote his first "Dunbar-style" folk poem when he was still in high school and published it later in his collection *The Dream Keeper.* Likewise, Cullen eulogized Dunbar with the poem "To Paul Laurence Dunbar," published in his first collection of poetry, *Color* (1925): Indeed, there was much to bind Dunbar's legacy with the spirit of what some would call "these bad New Negroes."[23] To begin with, there was what James A. Emanuel calls Dunbar's "racial fire," his pride in his blackness and his outcry against the oppression of his people, his well-directed if sometimes too understated anger (*A Singer,* 75). Then there is Dunbar's appreciation of the significance of his racial cultural heritage, his loving depiction of the black man and woman farthest down, and his musical rendition of black folk language: in short, his daring creation of something completely original, new, and unique—an Afrocentric poetic diction that transcended the racist heritage of the plantation tradition and did more than strive to imitate the Anglo-Saxon literary past. The more avant-garde of the Harlem Renaissance artists especially were to identify with and build upon these Dunbar innovations. Likewise, they would struggle with the demands of a predominantly white readership and its insistence on illustrations of black life that were at times more in keeping with its own taste than with the black writers' quest for artistic freedom and authenticity.

In the final analysis, it is difficult to answer the question of whether Dunbar *unconsciously* acquiesced to racist stereotypes. One could argue that because the dialect tradition Dunbar inherited was so completely and fully invested with negative and demeaning images of blackness, it was not possible for him to be successful, in every instance, in inverting these associations to "signify" on his received linguistic heritage. Perhaps what Dunbar attempted to do, in the words of contemporary black poet Audre Lorde, was "to dismantle the master's house using the masters tools," an extremely difficult if not impossible task (110–13). Despite Dunbar's success in writing dialect poetry, he was rightly uncomfortable with the approval he garnered from mainstream white critics, because he knew that they were deaf to his voice of protest and that they misread his work and praised it for the wrong reasons; they did not possess Dunbar's cultural background, his keen ear, or his sympathetic racial sensibility.

Paul Laurence Dunbar is not dead. In 1972 the University of California at Irvine held a "Centenary Conference" to mark the one-hundred-year anniversary of his birth. Participants included critics J. Saunders Redding, Arna Bontemps, Darwin Turner, and Addison Gayle, as well as poets Michael Harper, Raymond Patterson, Lorenzo Thomas, and Nikki Giovanni. Papers and poems from this conference were published as *A Singer in the Dawn: Reinterpretations of Paul Laurence Dunbar.* Despite this short-lived attempt at commemorating Dunbar's achievement, however, *The Complete Poems of Paul Laurence Dunbar,* the most popular volume of Dunbar's work, subsequently went out of print. This volume (originally published in 1913 with Howells's 1896 Introduction to *Lyrics of Lowly Life* serving as the Introduction to the whole) had been used consistently as the standard text of Dunbar's verse by teachers and scholars of Afro-American literature well into the seventies.

It is time to reclaim Paul Laurence Dunbar and *The Complete Poems* for a new generation of lovers of verse; he belongs to all who appreciate him. This new edition of the posthumously published *Complete Poems of Paul Laurence Dunbar* follows the order of the original, reproducing the text of the 1913 edition. However, sixty poems not included in the 1913 edition are found as a final section of poetry in this volume. Textual variants from the *Complete Poems* are listed in the Appendix. Thus this edition becomes the largest and the most authoritative collection of Dunbar's poetry ever published.

Poems added to the original *Complete Poems* in this edition fall into several categories. These include poems published in earlier volumes of Dunbar's work but omitted from the 1913 *Complete Poems,* poems published in magazines and periodicals but never collected—virtually all of Dunbar's published poetry—and a selection of unpublished works, some of them untitled fragments and probably never intended for publication. Most of the previously unpublished poems came from series 4, boxes 10–13, of the Paul Laurence Dunbar Collection at the Ohio Historical Society in Columbus, Ohio. A few were taken from MSS 659, which includes a box of material from the Dunbar papers that has not been microfilmed. Three poems to Alice Moore Dunbar are to be found among the correspondence of Alice Moore Dunbar and Paul Laurence Dunbar in series 5, 6, and 10, boxes 18–21, in the Paul Laurence Dunbar Collection at the Ohio Historical Society, and all are quoted by permission.[24]

While the present volume contains the largest collection of Dunbar's poetry ever published, it remains representative rather than inclusive. I did not, as an editor, set out to publish every poem that Dunbar ever wrote, but merely to reissue the original 1913 *Complete Poems* with a new introduction to replace the one written by Howells and an appendix containing variants of the poems published in that early posthumous edition. The more I learned about Dunbar and his work, however, the more I was amazed by the number of poems published by Dunbar during his lifetime that were excluded from the so-called *Complete Poems* after his death. From the work of Virginia Cunningham and of Jay Martin and Gossie Hudson, I learned that there was a sizable body of unpublished material too, but nothing actually prepared me for reading this material in Columbus. I went to the Ohio Historical Society in Columbus after trying in vain to read xeroxes of fading manuscripts in lead pencil from the mysterious MSS 659, a necessary supplement to the microfilm edition of Dunbar's work. Although the Ohio Historical Society has done an excellent job of preserving the Dunbar Collection through the efforts of pioneer Dunbar scholars Sara Fuller and Gossie Hudson, many of the manuscript poems had already begun to deteriorate when OHS acquired them in 1937 (Fuller, 10). Some of the poems, letters, and fragments are indistinct if not entirely impossible to read; a few have been nibbled by rodents. Although some of the deteriorated manuscripts may one day be enhanced by new methods, it is unlikely that there will ever be an edition of Dunbar's poetry that is truly complete.

Yet there are riches in the Paul Laurence Dunbar Collection. At the Ohio Historical Society I pored over Dunbar's high-school theme books, admiring the fine illustrations that accompany his chemistry experiments. The Paul Laurence Dunbar I came to know was artistic and intensely religious. When asked for an original design in one of his art notebooks, Dunbar drew a cross gushing the red blood of Christ. He paused in the middle of his accounting notes to record the following private reflection:

> The whole celestial concave was filled with the overflowing tides of the morning light which came pouring down from above in one great ocean of radiance.
>
> I do not wonder at the superstition [of] the ancient Magians [*sic*] who in the morning of the world went up to the hilltops of Central Asia and ignorant of the true God adored the most glorious work of his hand.[25]

Thus is Dunbar's poetic vision evident even in this schoolboy's awe-filled musing; similar sentiments are expressed in "God Reigns," included in the "Added Poems" section.

In the selection of the "Added Poems" I have tried to represent, as faithfully as possible, both the man we know as Paul Laurence Dunbar and the man whom perhaps nobody knew. The poems in this section are arranged in their probable chronological order. Again, virtually all of the poems published by Dunbar during his lifetime but excluded from the 1913 *Complete Poems* are here. These display obvious literary merit and require little justification; two of the technically less perfect are among my favorites. "My Best Girl" is a humorous poem about a girl with red hair, written in the voice of a young white man who is so smitten that he kneels on a pin. This poem, which appeared in a student publication called *Tomfoolery* in 1890 or 1891, was probably written to poke fun at one of Dunbar's adolescent friends. "Lager Beer," another juvenile poem, also demonstrates Dunbar's abundant humor. This poem in German-American dialect predates Dunbar's better-known and more sophisticated plantation verse, suggesting his larger interest in folk language and dialect as an artistic medium that might potentially have united Americans of disparate racial and ethnic backgrounds, as many other writers of his era believed was possible.

Making selections from among the unpublished poems proved difficult because of the uneven quality of the work and the lack of clues as to which Dunbar himself might have considered more finished and therefore suitable for publication. There were poems that started elegantly and boldly but that quickly became awkward and illegible, even to the most determined eye. Among the most brilliant of the unpublished poems is the roundeau "Love Is a Star," in which Dunbar demonstrates his mastery of that sophisticated form. "The Passage," translated from the German, and "Come and Kiss Me Sweet and Twenty" also demonstrate a level of sophistication in Dunbar's verse that may come as a surprise to some. Among my personal favorites of the unpublished poems are "Song" ("De bee hit sip some honey"), the beautiful love poems sent by Dunbar to his bride and never intended for publication, and "A Matter of Locality" and "Night on the Chesapeake." I found the latter two uncommon in the Dunbar canon for their reach toward modernism; these are real twentieth-century poems in which Dunbar takes off the mask of his essentially nineteenth-century self and puts it aside to sound surprisingly like a newborn Robert Frost.

Paul Laurence Dunbar's time has come again; it is time to reread Dunbar's poetry, investing in it the integrity that we want others to find in us, "to bring," in the words of Nikki Giovanni, "the sweet juice, not just the dried bones, alive to our young people" (244). The significance of the reissuing of Dunbar's *Complete Poems* today—after the Harlem Renaissance, after the Black Arts movement of the sixties, and amidst the excitement of the reclamation of lost works by black women writers of the nineteenth and early-twentieth centuries and the increasing diversity offered by the movement toward multiculturalism in American Studies and other disciplines throughout the university—is that of yet another rebirth.

We reclaim, in Paul Laurence Dunbar, a significant American author whose career transcends race and locality even while he makes use of racialized and regional cultural materials to create an African-American aesthetic and a unique black poetic diction. Returning the *Complete Poems* to the classroom will make it possible, once again, for teachers of literature to acquaint our students with the poetic works of one of America's best-loved authors. The "Added Poems" brings yet another dimension to both the reading and the scholarly consideration of the poetry and the life of Paul Laurence Dunbar.

Joanne M. Braxton
Frances L. and Edwin L. Cummings Professor
of American Studies and English
The College of William and Mary

NOTES

1. Paul Laurence Dunbar to Henry A. Tobey, July 13, 1895, Paul Laurence Dunbar Collection, series 1, box 1, Ohio Historical Society (OHS), Columbus. Quoted by permission.

2. The term *Racial Mountain* was first employed by Langston Hughes in his artistic manifesto "The Negro Artist and the Racial Mountain," in the *Nation,* June 28, 1926. Hughes outlines the dilemma of the black writer determined to create an authentic black aesthetic as he or she struggled with the innate conservatism of the black middle class and the problem of white patronage.

3. Handwritten note by Matilda Dunbar, Paul Laurence Dunbar Collection, MSS 659, series 1, box 1, OHS. This note is included in a box of manuscript papers that was removed from the Dunbar Collection prior to its being microfilmed.

4. Paul Laurence Dunbar, "Farewell Song," in *Class of 1891, Commencement Exercises of Central High School at Grand Opera House* (Tuesday evening, June 16, 1891, Dayton, Ohio), p. 4. The complete text of "Farewell Song" is included in the "Added Poems" section of this volume.

5. Excerpt from "What's the Use of Dreaming," unpublished poem fragment, Paul Laurence Dunbar Collection, series 4, box 10, OHS. Quoted by permission. (This fragment is not in the "Added Poems" section.)

6. Dunbar's "Worker's Pass" for the World's Columbian Exposition of 1893 may be found in Paul Laurence Dunbar Collection, MSS 659, series 1, box 1, OHS.

7. Paul Laurence Dunbar to Matilda Dunbar, June 6, 1893, Paul Laurence Dunbar Collection, series 1, box 1, OHS. Quoted by permission.

8. Paul Laurence Dunbar to Alice Ruth Moore, April 17, 1895, Paul Laurence Dunbar Collection, series 10, box 22, OHS. Quoted by permission.

9. Ibid.; Paul Laurence Dunbar to Alice Ruth Moore, May 23, 1895, Paul Laurence Dunbar Collection, series 6, box 20, OHS. Quoted by permission.

10. Alice Ruth Moore to Paul Laurence Dunbar, incomplete document circa 1897 [no date], Paul Laurence Dunbar Collection, series 6, box 20, OHS. Quoted by permission.

11. Alice Ruth Moore to Paul Laurence Dunbar, October 21, 1897, Paul Laurence Dunbar Collection, series 6, box 20, OHS.

12. Paul Laurence Dunbar, quoted by Gilberta S. Whittle in the *Philadelphia Times Book Review,* January 4, 1902.

13. Wedding announcement of Alice Ruth Moore and Paul Laurence Dunbar, Paul Laurence Dunbar Collection, MSS 659, series 1, box 1, OHS.

14. Calculation in the handwriting of Matilda Dunbar, Paul Laurence Dunbar Collection, MSS 659, series 1, box 1, OHS.

15. See Alice Dunbar, "In Keeping with the Life of the Dead Poet Laureate," Dayton, Ohio, *Journal,* February 13, 1906.

16. Paul Laurence Dunbar, quoted in Brawley, *Paul Laurence Dunbar*; see also Nettels, *Language, Race, and Social Class in Howells's America,* p. 82; quoted also in Jay Saunders Redding, "Portrait against Background," in Martin, ed., *A Singer in the Dawn,* p.42.

17. Even though he was publicly associated with both Du Bois and Washington and he actually wrote the "Tuskegee Song" (still the official school song of Tuskegee University), Dunbar adhered strongly to his own political analysis. He believed strongly in the value of a liberal arts education and the importance of educating black youth according to their ability. Although Dunbar was much admired by Washington and was even invited to Tuskegee to lecture, he rejected the notion of joining the faculty of Tuskegee Institute on a permanent basis because he did not agree with Washington's philosophy of education. This disagreement is underscored by an excerpt from a letter to his "Dear Wifling" dated September 3, 1898.

> Well I had a call this morning from Booker T. Washington, a gentleman from Tuskegee whom you probably know. He informs me that the editor of the New England Magazine is anxious for and is working up a meeting in the interest of Tuskegee at which are wanted DuBois, Washington and myself—the meeting to be held the 1st and fifteenth of December.
>
> "*Now what is their game?*" Is it to destroy any future power DuBois and I may have by bringing us before the public in the character of speakers for the very institution whose founder's utterances we cannot subscribe to? Am I too sagacious? It may be; but looking at the matter either synthetically or analytically, the same result appears to me.
>
> (Paul Laurence Dunbar to Alice Ruth Moore, September 3, 1898, Paul Laurence Dunbar Collection, series 6, box 20, OHS. Quoted by permission.)

Dunbar's published essays, such as "Recession Never" (Toledo, Ohio, *Journal,* December 18, 1898), "The Hapless Southern Negro" (Denver *Post,* September 17, 1899), "Is Higher Education for the Negro Hopeless?" (*Philadelphia Times,* June 10, 1900), and "The Negro as an Individual" (Chicago *Tribune,* October 12, 1902), present Dunbar's frank analysis of southern racial strife and his belief that the destiny of the black laborer lay in westward migration. While Dunbar admired and praised Booker T. Washington for his organizational skill and his ability to focus all of his energy on "one idea," Dunbar, like Du Bois, strongly believed that the individual black man or woman should not be limited to technical or industrial training and that he or she should be free to pursue a liberal education according to his or her ability. ("Recession Never," "The Hapless Southern Negro," "Is Higher Education for the Negro Hopeless?" "The Negro as an Individual," and "Representative American Negroes" are all reprinted in Martin and Hudson's *Paul Laurence Dunbar Reader.*)

18. See Henry Louis Gates, Jr., "Dis and Dat: Dialect and the Descent," pp. 88–117. See also Gates's discussion of Dunbar's poetic diction and black aesthetics in *The Signifying Monkey,* pp. 171–82.

19. Paul Laurence Dunbar Collection, series 3, box 9, OHS. The *Tattler* was published in Dayton by Wilber and Orville Wright, who were Dunbar's high school classmates. Dunbar served as its editor.

20. Joel Chandler Harris to E. L. Burlingame, November 14, 1888, quoted by Nettels in *Language, Race, and Social Class in Howells's America,* p. 77. Nettels argues that Harris anticipates Howells's "defense of regionalism." See also Nettels's discussion of "The Problem of 'Negro Dialect' in Literature," ibid., pp. 72–104.

21. In a January 4, 1904, article by Gilberta S. Whittle on Paul Laurence Dunbar in the *Philadelphia Times Book Review,* some of Dunbar's views on writers of dialect are quoted: "It is difficult to put any name before that of Ruth McEnery Stuart who depicts both the humorous and pathetic side of the race with such fidelity. There are, however, in the stories of Joel Chandler Harris intimate touches which are to me absolutely marvelous. He represents the negro in an aspect in which he would scarcely exhibit himself to a white man, repeating characteristic speeches which he would hardly give utterance to except to one of his own color."

22. The manuscript for the unpublished poem beginning "Twas Christmas night, the quarters" is cataloged under the title "The Colored Ball" in Sara Fuller's inventory of the Paul Laurence Dunbar Collection. "The Colored Ball" and "At Night" are in series 4, boxes 10 and 11 respectively of the Paul Laurence Dunbar Collection, Ohio Historical Society, Columbus. "The Colored Ball" is not reproduced in this volume.

23. Countee Cullen, "To Paul Laurence Dunbar," reprinted in *My Soul's High Song: The Collected Writings of Countee Cullen, Voice of the Harlem Renaissance* (New York: Anchor Books, 1991), p. 119; Langston Hughes, "These Bad New Negroes: A Critique on Critics," typescript draft, dated March 22, 1927, of an article written for the *Pittsburgh Courier* and inscribed to Carl Van Vechten (James Weldon Johnson Collection, Beinecke Library, Yale University, New Haven). In this essay, Hughes criticizes the black middle class for its pseudoculture, its assumption of Nordic standards, its snobbishness, its aloofness from the Negro masses, and its self-assumed superiority. He singles out for praise the work of Jean Toomer, Wallace Thurman, Countee Cullen, Zora Neale Hurston, and Edward Silvera.

24. In addition to selected letters, essays, and stories, Martin and Hudson's *Paul Laurence Dunbar Reader* offers a selection of Dunbar's poetry from the 1913 *Complete Poems* and other published sources. It also contains some of the poems from letters and other manuscript sources that appear in the "Added Poems" section of this volume.

25. Dunbar notebook, Paul Laurence Dunbar Collection, MSS 659, series 1, box 1, OHS. Quoted by permission.

LYRICS OF LOWLY LIFE

ERE SLEEP COMES DOWN TO SOOTHE THE WEARY EYES

Ere sleep comes down to soothe the weary eyes,
Which all the day with ceaseless care have sought
The magic gold which from the seeker flies;
Ere dreams put on the gown and cap of thought,
And make the waking world a world of lies,—
Of lies most palpable, uncouth, forlorn,
That say life's full of aches and tears and sighs,—
Oh, how with more than dreams the soul is torn,
Ere sleep comes down to soothe the weary eyes.

Ere sleep comes down to soothe the weary eyes,
How all the griefs and heartaches we have known
Come up like pois'nous vapors that arise
From some base witch's caldron, when the crone,
To work some potent spell, her magic plies.
The past which held its share of bitter pain,
Whose ghost we prayed that Time might exorcise,
Comes up, is lived and suffered o'er again,
Ere sleep comes down to soothe the weary eyes.

Ere sleep comes down to soothe the weary eyes,
What phantoms fill the dimly lighted room;
What ghostly shades in awe-creating guise
Are bodied forth within the teeming gloom.
What echoes faint of sad and soul-sick cries,
And pangs of vague inexplicable pain
That pay the spirit's ceaseless enterprise,
Come thronging through the chambers of the brain,
Ere sleep comes down to soothe the weary eyes.

Ere sleep comes down to soothe the weary eyes,
Where ranges forth the spirit far and free?
Through what strange realms and unfamiliar skies
Tends her far course to lands of mystery?

To lands unspeakable — beyond surmise,
Where shapes unknowable to being spring,
Till, faint of wing, the Fancy fails and dies
Much wearied with the spirit's journeying,
Ere sleep comes down to soothe the weary eyes.

Ere sleep comes down to soothe the weary eyes,
How questioneth the soul that other soul,—
The inner sense which neither cheats nor lies,
But self exposes unto self, a scroll
Full writ with all life's acts unwise or wise,
In characters indelible and known;
So, trembling with the shock of sad surprise,
The soul doth view its awful self alone,
Ere sleep comes down to soothe the weary eyes.

When sleep comes down to seal the weary eyes,
The last dear sleep whose soft embrace is balm,
And whom sad sorrow teaches us to prize
For kissing all our passions into calm,
Ah, then, no more we heed the sad world's cries,
Or seek to probe th' eternal mystery,
Or fret our souls at long-withheld replies,
At glooms through which our visions cannot see,
When sleep comes down to seal the weary eyes.

THE POET AND HIS SONG

A SONG is but a little thing,
And yet what joy it is to sing!
In hours of toil it gives me zest,
And when at eve I long for rest;
When cows come home along the bars,
And in the fold I hear the bell,
As Night, the shepherd, herds his stars,
I sing my song, and all is well.

There are no ears to hear my lays,
No lips to lift a word of praise;
But still, with faith unfaltering,
I live and laugh and love and sing.
What matters yon unheeding throng?
They cannot feel my spirit's spell,
Since life is sweet and love is long,
I sing my song, and all is well.

My days are never days of ease;
I till my ground and prune my trees.

When ripened gold is all the plain,
I put my sickle to the grain.
I labor hard, and toil and sweat,
While others dream within the dell;
But even while my brow is wet,
I sing my song, and all is well.

Sometimes the sun, unkindly hot,
My garden makes a desert spot;
Sometimes a blight upon the tree
Takes all my fruit away from me;
And then with throes of bitter pain
Rebellious passions rise and swell;
But — life is more than fruit or grain,
And so I sing, and all is well.

RETORT

"THOU art a fool," said my head to my heart,
"Indeed, the greatest of fools thou art,
To be led astray by the trick of a tress,
By a smiling face or a ribbon smart;"
And my heart was in sore distress.

Then Phyllis came by, and her face was fair,
The light gleamed soft on her raven hair;
And her lips were blooming a rosy red.
Then my heart spoke out with a right bold air:
"Thou art worse than a fool, O head!"

ACCOUNTABILITY

FOLKS ain't got no right to censuah othah folks about dey habits;
Him dat giv' de squir'ls de bushtails made de bobtails fu' de rabbits.
Him dat built de gread big mountains hollered out de little valleys,
Him dat made de streets an' driveways wasn't shamed to make de alleys.

We is all constructed diff'ent, d'ain't no two of us de same;
We cain't he'p ouah likes an' dislikes, ef we'se bad we ain't to blame.
Ef we 'se good, we need n't show off, case you bet it ain't ouah doin'
We gits into su'ttain channels dat we jes' cain't he'p pu'suin'.

But we all fits into places dat no othah ones could fill,
An' we does the things we has to, big er little, good er ill.
John cain't tek de place o' Henry, Su an' Sally ain't alike;
Bass ain't nuthin' like a suckah, chub ain't nuthin' like a pike.

When you come to think about it, how it 's all planned out it 's splendid.
Nuthin 's done er evah happens, 'dout hit 's somefin' dat 's intended;
Don't keer whut you does, you has to, an' hit sholy beats de dickens,—
Viney, go put on de kittle, I got one o' mastah's chickens.

FREDERICK DOUGLASS

A HUSH is over all the teeming lists,
And there is pause, a breath-space in the strife;
A spirit brave has passed beyond the mists
And vapors that obscure the sun of life.
And Ethiopia, with bosom torn,
Laments the passing of her noblest born.

She weeps for him a mother's burning tears—
She loved him with a mother's deepest love.
He was her champion thro' direful years,
And held her weal all other ends above.
When Bondage held her bleeding in the dust,
He raised her up and whispered, "Hope and Trust."

For her his voice, a fearless clarion, rung
That broke in warning on the ears of men;
For her the strong bow of his power he strung,
And sent his arrows to the very den
Where grim Oppression held his bloody place
And gloated o'er the mis'ries of a race.

And he was no soft-tongued apologist;
He spoke straightforward, fearlessly uncowed;
The sunlight of his truth dispelled the mist,
And set in bold relief each dark hued cloud;
To sin and crime he gave their proper hue,
And hurled at evil what was evil's due.

Through good and ill report he cleaved his way
Right onward, with his face set toward the heights,
Nor feared to face the foeman's dread array,—
The lash of scorn, the sting of petty spites.

He dared the lightning in the lightning's track,
And answered thunder with his thunder back.

When men maligned him, and their torrent wrath
In furious imprecations o'er him broke,
He kept his counsel as he kept his path;
'T was for his race, not for himself he spoke.
He knew the import of his Master's call,
And felt himself too mighty to be small.

No miser in the good he held was he,—
His kindness followed his horizon's rim.
His heart, his talents, and his hands were free
To all who truly needed aught of him.
Where poverty and ignorance were rife,
He gave his bounty as he gave his life.

The place and cause that first aroused his might
Still proved its power until his latest day.
In Freedom's lists and for the aid of Right
Still in the foremost rank he waged the fray;
Wrong lived; his occupation was not gone.
He died in action with his armor on!

We weep for him, but we have touched his hand,
And felt the magic of his presence nigh,
The current that he sent throughout the land,
The kindling spirit of his battle-cry.
O'er all that holds us we shall triumph yet,
And place our banner where his hopes were set!

Oh, Douglass, thou hast passed beyond the shore,
But still thy voice is ringing o'er the gale!
Thou 'st taught thy race how high her hopes may soar,
And bade her seek the heights, nor faint, nor fail.
She will not fail, she heeds thy stirring cry,
She knows thy guardian spirit will be nigh,
And, rising from beneath the chast'ning rod,
She stretches out her bleeding hands to God!

LIFE

A crust of bread and a corner to sleep in,
A minute to smile and an hour to weep in,
A pint of joy to a peck of trouble,
And never a laugh but the moans come double;
And that is life!

A crust and a corner that love makes precious,
With a smile to warm and the tears to refresh us;
And joy seems sweeter when cares come after,
And a moan is the finest of foils for laughter;
And that is life!

THE LESSON

My cot was down by a cypress grove,
And I sat by my window the whole night long,
And heard well up from the deep dark wood
A mocking-bird's passionate song.

And I thought of myself so sad and lone,
And my life's cold winter that knew no spring;
Of my mind so weary and sick and wild,
Of my heart too sad to sing.

But e'en as I listened the mock-bird's song,
A thought stole into my saddened heart,
And I said, "I can cheer some other soul
By a carol's simple art."

For oft from the darkness of hearts and lives
Come songs that brim with joy and light,
As out of the gloom of the cypress grove
The mocking-bird sings at night.

So I sang a lay for a brother's ear
In a strain to soothe his bleeding heart,
And he smiled at the sound of my voice and lyre,
Though mine was a feeble art.

But at his smile I smiled in turn,
And into my soul there came a ray:
In trying to soothe another's woes
Mine own had passed away.

THE RISING OF THE STORM

The lake's dark breast
Is all unrest,
It heaves with a sob and a sigh.
Like a tremulous bird,
From its slumber stirred,
The moon is a-tilt in the sky.

From the silent deep
The waters sweep,
But faint on the cold white stones,
And the wavelets fly
With a plaintive cry
O'er the old earth's bare, bleak bones.

And the spray upsprings
On its ghost-white wings,
And tosses a kiss at the stars;
While a water-sprite,
In sea-pearls dight,
Hums a sea-hymn's solemn bars.

Far out in the night,
On the wavering sight
I see a dark hull loom;
And its light on high,
Like a Cyclops' eye,
Shines out through the mist and gloom.

Now the winds well up
From the earth's deep cup,
And fall on the sea and shore,
And against the pier
The waters rear
And break with a sullen roar.

Up comes the gale,
And the mist-wrought veil
Gives way to the lightning's glare,
And the cloud-drifts fall,
A sombre pall,
O'er water, earth, and air.

The storm-king flies,
His whip he plies,
And bellows down the wind.
The lightning rash
With blinding flash
Comes pricking on behind.

Rise, waters, rise,
And taunt the skies
With your swift-flitting form.
Sweep, wild winds, sweep,
And tear the deep
To atoms in the storm.

And the waters leapt,
And the wild winds swept,
And blew out the moon in the sky,
And I laughed with glee,
It was joy to me
As the storm went raging by!

SUNSET

THE river sleeps beneath the sky,
And clasps the shadows to its breast;
The crescent moon shines dim on high;
And in the lately radiant west
The gold is fading into gray.
Now stills the lark his festive lay,
And mourns with me the dying day.

While in the south the first faint star
Lifts to the night its silver face,

And twinkles to the moon afar
Across the heaven's graying space,
Low murmurs reach me from the town,
As Day puts on her sombre crown,
And shakes her mantle darkly down.

THE OLD APPLE-TREE

There 's a memory keeps a-runnin'
Through my weary head to-night,
An' I see a picture dancin'
In the fire-flames' ruddy light;
'Tis the picture of an orchard
Wrapped in autumn's purple haze,
With the tender light about it
That I loved in other days.
An' a-standin' in a corner
Once again I seem to see
The verdant leaves an' branches
Of an old apple-tree.

You perhaps would call it ugly,
An' I don't know but it 's so,
When you look the tree all over
Unadorned by memory's glow;
For its boughs are gnarled an' crooked,
An' its leaves are gettin' thin,
An' the apples of its bearin'
Would n't fill so large a bin
As they used to. But I tell you,
When it comes to pleasin' me,
It 's the dearest in the orchard,—
Is that old apple-tree.

I would hide within its shelter,
Settlin' in some cosy nook,
Where no calls nor threats could stir me
From the pages o' my book.
Oh, that quiet, sweet seclusion
In its fulness passeth words!
It was deeper than the deepest
That my sanctum now affords.
Why, the jaybirds an' the robins,
They was hand in glove with me,
As they winked at me an' warbled
In that old apple-tree.

It was on its sturdy branches
That in summers long ago
I would tie my swing an' dangle
In contentment to an' fro,
Idly dreamin' childish fancies,
Buildin' castles in the air,
Makin' o' myself a hero
Of romances rich an' rare.
I kin shet my eyes an' see it
Jest as plain as plain kin be,
That same old swing a-danglin'
To the old apple-tree.

There 's a rustic seat beneath it
That I never kin forget.
It 's the place where me an' Hallie —
Little sweetheart—used to set,

When we 'd wander to the orchard
So 's no listenin' ones could hear
As I whispered sugared nonsense
Into her little willin' ear.
Now my gray old wife is Hallie,
An' I 'm grayer still than she,
But I 'll not forget our courtin'
'Neath the old apple-tree.

Life for us ain't all been summer,
But I guess we 've had our share
Of its flittin' joys an' pleasures,
An' a sprinklin' of its care.
Oft the skies have smiled upon us;
Then again we 've seen 'em frown,
Though our load was ne'er so heavy
That we longed to lay it down.
But when death does come a-callin',
This my last request shall be,—
That they 'll bury me an' Hallie
'Neath the old apple tree.

A PRAYER

O Lord, the hard-won miles
Have worn my stumbling feet:
Oh, soothe me with thy smiles,
And make my life complete.

The thorns were thick and keen
Where'er I trembling trod;
The way was long between
My wounded feet and God.

Where healing waters flow
Do thou my footsteps lead.
My heart is aching so;
Thy gracious balm I need.

PASSION AND LOVE

A maiden wept and, as a comforter,
Came one who cried, "I love thee," and he seized
Her in his arms and kissed her with hot breath,
That dried the tears upon her flaming cheeks.
While evermore his boldly blazing eye
Burned into hers; but she uncomforted
Shrank from his arms and only wept the more.

Then one came and gazed mutely in her face
With wide and wistful eyes; but still aloof
He held himself; as with a reverent fear,
As one who knows some sacred presence nigh.
And as she wept he mingled tear with tear,
That cheered her soul like dew a dusty flower,—
Until she smiled, approached, and touched his hand!

THE SEEDLING

As a quiet little seedling
Lay within its darksome bed,
To itself it fell a-talking,
And this is what it said:

"I am not so very robust,
But I 'll do the best I can;"
And the seedling from that moment
Its work of life began.

So it pushed a little leaflet
Up into the light of day,
To examine the surroundings
And show the rest the way.

The leaflet liked the prospect,
So it called its brother, Stem;
Then two other leaflets heard it,
And quickly followed them.

To be sure, the haste and hurry
Made the seedling sweat and pant;
But almost before it knew it
It found itself a plant.

The sunshine poured upon it,
And the clouds they gave a shower;
And the little plant kept growing
Till it found itself a flower.

Little folks, be like the seedling,
Always do the best you can;
Every child must share life's labor
Just as well as every man.

And the sun and showers will heip you
Through the lonesome, struggling hours,
Till you raise to light and beauty
Virtue's fair, unfading flowers.

PROMISE

I GREW a rose within a garden fair,
And, tending it with more than loving care,
I thought how, with the glory of its bloom,
I should the darkness of my life illume;
And, watching, ever smiled to see the lusty bud
Drink freely in the summer sun to tinct its blood.

My rose began to open, and its hue
Was sweet to me as to it sun and dew;
I watched it taking on its ruddy flame
Until the day of perfect blooming came,
Then hasted I with smiles to find it blushing red—
Too late! Some thoughtless child had plucked my rose and fled!

PAUL LAURENCE DUNBAR

FULFILMENT.

I GREW a rose once more to please mine eyes.
All things to aid it — dew, sun, wind, fair skies —
Were kindly; and to shield it from despoil,
I fenced it safely in with grateful toil.
No other hand than mine shall pluck this flower, said I,
And I was jealous of the bee that hovered nigh.
It grew for days; I stood hour after hour
To watch the slow unfolding of the flower,
And then I did not leave its side at all,
Lest some mischance my flower should befall.
At last, oh joy! the central petals burst apart.
It blossomed—but, alas! a worm was at its heart!

SONG

My heart to thy heart,
My hand to thine;
My lip to thy lips,
Kisses are wine
Brewed for the lover in sunshine and shade;
Let me drink deep, then, my African maid.

Lily to lily,
Rose unto rose;
My love to thy love
Tenderly grows.
Rend not the oak and the ivy in twain,
Nor the swart maid from her swarthier swain.

AN ANTE-BELLUM SERMON

WE is gathahed hyeah, my brothahs,
In dis howlin' wildaness,
Fu' to speak some words of comfo't
To each othah in distress.
An' we chooses fu' ouah subjic'
Dis — we 'll 'splain it by an' by;
"An' de Lawd said, 'Moses, Moses,'
An' de man said, 'Hyeah am I.'"

Now ole Pher'oh, down in Egypt,
Was de wuss man evah bo'n,
An' he had de Hebrew chillun
Down dah wukin' in his co'n;
'T well de Lawd got tiahed o' his foolin',
An' sez he: "I 'll let him know —
Look hyeah, Moses, go tell Pher'oh
Fu' to let dem chillun go."

"An' ef he refuse to do it,
I will make him rue de houah,
Fu' I 'll empty down on Egypt
All de vials of my powah."
Yes, he did — an' Pher'oh's ahmy
Was n't wuth a ha'f a dime;
Fu' de Lawd will he'p his chillun,
You kin trust him evah time.

An' yo' enemies may 'sail you
In de back an' in de front;
But de Lawd is all aroun' you,
Fu' to ba' de battle's brunt.
Dey kin fo'ge yo' chains an' shackles
F'om de mountains to de sea;
But de Lawd will sen' some Moses
Fu' to set his chillun free.

An' de lan' shall hyeah his thundah,
Lak a blas' f'om Gab'el's ho'n,
Fu' de Lawd of hosts is mighty
When he girds his ahmor on.
But fu' feah some one mistakes me,
I will pause right hyeah to say,
Dat I 'm still a-preachin' ancient,
I ain't talkin' 'bout to-day.

But I tell you, fellah christuns,
Things 'll happen mighty strange;
Now, de Lawd done dis fu' Isrul,
An' his ways don't nevah change,
An' de love he showed to Isrul
Was n't all on Isrul spent;
Now don't run an' tell yo' mastahs
Dat I 's preachin' discontent.

'Cause I is n't; I 'se a-judgin'
Bible people by deir ac's;
I 'se a-givin' you de Scriptuah,
I 'se a-handin' you de fac's.
Cose ole Pher'oh b'lieved in slav'ry,
But de Lawd he let him see,
Dat de people he put bref in,—
Evah mothah's son was free.

An' dahs othahs thinks lak Pher'oh,
But dey calls de Scriptuah liar,
Fu' de Bible says "a servant
Is a-worthy of his hire."
An' you cain't git roun' nor thoo dat,
An' you cain't git ovah it,
Fu' whatevah place you git in,
Dis hyeah Bible too 'll fit.

So you see de Lawd's intention,
Evah sence de worl' began,
Was dat His almighty freedom
Should belong to evah man,
But I think it would be bettah,
Ef I 'd pause agin to say,
Dat I 'm talkin' 'bout ouah freedom
In a Bibleistic way.

But de Moses is a-comin',
An' he 's comin', suah and fas'

We kin hyeah his feet a-trompin',
We kin hyeah his trumpit blas'.
But I want to wa'n you people,
Don't you git too brigity;
An' don't you git to braggin'
'Bout dese things, you wait an' see.

But when Moses wif his powah
Comes an' sets us chillun free,
We will praise de gracious Mastah
Dat has gin us liberty;
An' we 'll shout ouah halleluyahs,
On dat mighty reck'nin' day,
When we 'se reco'nised ez citiz'—
Huh uh! Chillun, let us pray!

ODE TO ETHIOPIA

O MOTHER RACE! to thee I bring
This pledge of faith unwavering,
This tribute to thy glory.
I know the pangs which thou didst feel,
When Slavery crushed thee with its heel,
With thy dear blood all gory.

Sad days were those — ah, sad indeed!
But through the land the fruitful seed
Of better times was growing.
The plant of freedom upward sprung,
And spread its leaves so fresh and young —
Its blossoms now are blowing.

On every hand in this fair land,
Proud Ethiope's swarthy children stand
Beside their fairer neighbor;
The forests flee before their stroke,
Their hammers ring, their forges smoke,—
They stir in honest labour.

They tread the fields where honour calls;
Their voices sound through senate halls
In majesty and power.
To right they cling; the hymns they sing
Up to the skies in beauty ring,
And bolder grow each hour.

Be proud, my Race, in mind and soul;
Thy name is writ on Glory's scroll
In characters of fire.
High 'mid the clouds of Fame's bright sky
Thy banner's blazoned folds now fly,
And truth shall lift them higher.

Thou hast the right to noble pride,
Whose spotless robes were purified
By blood's severe baptism.
Upon thy brow the cross was laid,

And labour's painful sweat-beads made
A consecrating chrism.

No other race, or white or black,
When bound as thou wert, to the rack,
So seldom stooped to grieving;
No other race, when free again,
Forgot the past and proved them men
So noble in forgiving.

Go on and up! Our souls and eyes
Shall follow thy continuous rise;
Our ears shall list thy story
From bards who from thy root shall spring,
And proudly tune their lyres to sing
Of Ethiopia's glory.

THE CORN-STALK FIDDLE

WHEN the corn 's all cut and the bright stalks shine
Like the burnished spears of a field of gold;
When the field-mice rich on the nubbins dine,
And the frost comes white and the wind blows cold;
Then it 's heigho! fellows and hi-diddle-diddle,
For the time is ripe for the corn-stalk fiddle.

And you take a stalk that is straight and long,
With an expert eye to its worthy points,
And you think of the bubbling strains of song
That are bound between its pithy joints —
Then you cut out strings, with a bridge in the middle,
With a corn-stalk bow for a corn-stalk fiddle.

Then the strains that grow as you draw the bow
O'er the yielding strings with a practised hand!
And the music's flow never loud but low
Is the concert note of a fairy band.
Oh, your dainty songs are a misty riddle
To the simple sweets of the corn-stalk fiddle.

When the eve comes on, and our work is done,
And the sun drops down with a tender glance,
With their hearts all prime for the harmless fun,
Come the neighbor girls for the evening's dance,
And they wait for the well-known twist and twid-dle —

More time than tune — from the corn-stalk fiddle.

Then brother Jabez takes the bow,
While Ned stands off with Susan Bland,
Then Henry stops by Milly Snow,
And John takes Nellie Jones's hand,
While I pair off with Mandy Biddle,
And scrape, scrape, scrape goes the corn-stalk fiddle.

"Salute your partners," comes the call,
"All join hands and circle round,"
"Grand train back," and "Balance all,"
Footsteps lightly spurn the ground.
"Take your lady and balance down the middle"
To the merry strains of the corn-stalk fiddle.

So the night goes on and the dance is o'er,
And the merry girls are homeward gone,
But I see it all in my sleep once more,
And I dream till the very break of dawn
Of an impish dance on a red-hot griddle
To the screech and scrape of a corn-stalk fiddle.

THE MASTER-PLAYER

An old, worn harp that had been played
Till all its strings were loose and frayed,
Joy, Hate, and Fear, each one essayed,
To play. But each in turn had found
No sweet responsiveness of sound.

Then Love the Master-Player came
With heaving breast and eyes aflame;
The Harp he took all undismayed,
Smote on its strings, still strange to song,
And brought forth music sweet and strong.

THE MYSTERY

I was not; now I am — a few days hence
I shall not be; I fain would look before
And after, but can neither do; some Power
Or lack of power says "no" to all I would.
I stand upon a wide and sunless plain,

Nor chart nor steel to guide my steps aright.
Whene'er, o'ercoming fear, I dare to move,
I grope without direction and by chance.
Some feign to hear a voice and feel a hand
That draws them ever upward thro' the gloom.
But I — I hear no voice and touch no hand,
Tho' oft thro' silence infinite I list,
And strain my hearing to supernal sounds;
Tho' oft thro' fateful darkness do I reach,
And stretch my hand to find that other hand.
I question of th' eternal bending skies
That seem to neighbor with the novice earth;
But they roll on, and daily shut their eyes
On me, as I one day shall do on them,
And tell me not the secret that I ask.

NOT THEY WHO SOAR

Not they who soar, but they who plod
Their rugged way, unhelped, to God
Are heroes; they who higher fare,
And, flying, fan the upper air,
Miss all the toil that hugs the sod.
'Tis they whose backs have felt the rod,
Whose feet have pressed the path unshod,
May smile upon defeated care,
Not they who soar.

High up there are no thorns to prod,
Nor boulders lurking 'neath the clod
To turn the keenness of the share,
For flight is ever free and rare;
But heroes they the soil who 've trod,
Not they who soar!

WHITTIER

Not o'er thy dust let there be spent
The gush of maudlin sentiment;
Such drift as that is not for thee,
Whose life and deeds and songs agree,
Sublime in their simplicity.

Nor shall the sorrowing tear be shed.
O singer sweet, thou art not dead!
In spite of time's malignant chill,
With living fire thy songs shall thrill,

And men shall say, "He liveth still!"

Great poets never die, for Earth
Doth count their lives of too great worth
To lose them from her treasured store;
So shalt thou live for evermore —
Though far thy form from mortal ken —
Deep in the hearts and minds of men.

TWO SONGS

A BEE that was searching for sweets one day
Through the gate of a rose garden happened to stray.
In the heart of a rose he hid away,
And forgot in his bliss the light of day,
As sipping his honey he buzzed in song;
Though day was waning, he lingered long,
For the rose was sweet, so sweet.

A robin sits pluming his ruddy breast,
And a madrigal sings to his love in her nest:
"Oh, the skies they are blue, the fields are green,
And the birds in your nest will soon be seen!"
She hangs on his words with a thrill of love,
And chirps to him as he sits above
For the song is sweet, so sweet.

A maiden was out on a summer's day
With the winds and the waves and the flowers at play;
And she met with a youth of gentle air,
With the light of the sunshine on his hair.
Together they wandered the flowers among;
They loved, and loving they lingered long,
For to love is sweet, so sweet.

BIRD of my lady's bower,
Sing her a song;
Tell her that every hour,
All the day long,
Thoughts of her come to me,
Filling my brain
With the warm ecstasy
Of love's refrain.

Little bird! happy bird!
Being so near,
Where e'en her slightest word
Thou mayest hear,
Seeing her glancing eyes,
Sheen of her hair,
Thou art in paradise,—
Would I were there.

I am so far away,
  Thou art so near;
Plead with her, birdling gay,
Plead with my dear.
Rich be thy recompense,
  Fine be thy fee,
If through thine eloquence
  She hearken me.

A BANJO SONG

Oh, dere 's lots o' keer an' trouble
  In dis world to swaller down;
An' ol' Sorrer 's purty lively
  In her way o' gittin' roun'.
Yet dere 's times when I furgit em,—
  Aches an' pains an' troubles all,—
An' it 's when I tek at ebenin'
  My ol' banjo f'om de wall.

'Bout de time dat night is fallin'
  An' my daily wu'k is done,
An' above de shady hilltops
  I kin see de settin' sun;
When de quiet, restful shadders
  Is beginnin' jes' to fall,—
Den I take de little banjo
  F'om its place upon de wall.

Den my fam'ly gadders roun' me
  In de fadin' o' de light,
Ez I strike de strings to try 'em
  Ef dey all is tuned er-right.
An' it seems we 're so nigh heaben
  We kin hyeah de angels sing
When de music o' dat banjo
  Sets my cabin all er-ring.

An' my wife an' all de othahs,—
  Male an' female, small an' big,—
Even up to gray-haired granny,
  Seem jes' boun' to do a jig;
'Twell I change de style o' music,
  Change de movement an' de time,
An' de ringin' little banjo
  Plays an ol' hea't-feelin' hime.

An' somehow my th'oat gits choky,
  An' a lump keeps tryin' to rise
Lak it wan'ed to ketch de water
  Dat was flowin' to my eyes;
An' I feel dat I could sorter
  Knock de socks clean off o' sin
Ez I hyeah my po' ol' granny
  Wif huh tremblin' voice jine in.

Den we all th'ow in our voices
  Fu' to he'p de chune out too,
Lak a big camp-meetin' choiry
  Tryin' to sing a mou'nah th'oo.
An' our th'oahts let out de music,
  Sweet an' solemn, loud an' free,
'Twell de raftahs o' my cabin
  Echo wif de melody.

Oh, de music o' de banjo,
  Quick an' deb'lish, solemn, slow,
Is de greates' joy an' solace
  Dat a weary slave kin know!

So jes' let me hyeah it ringin',
Dough de chune be po' an' rough,
It 's a pleasure; an' de pleasures
O' dis life is few enough.

Now, de blessed little angels
Up in heaben, we are told,
Don't do nothin' all dere lifetime
'Ceptin' play on ha'ps o' gold.
Now I think heaben 'd be mo' homelike
Ef we 'd hyeah some music fall
F'om a real ol'-fashioned banjo,
Like dat one upon de wall.

LONGING

If you could sit with me beside the sea to-day,
And whisper with me sweetest dreamings o'er and o'er;
I think I should not find the clouds so dim and gray,
And not so loud the waves complaining at the shore.

If you could sit with me upon the shore to-day,
And hold my hand in yours as in the days of old,
I think I should not mind the chill baptismal spray,
Nor find my hand and heart and all the world so cold.

If you could walk with me upon the strand to-day,
And tell me that my longing love had won your own,
I think all my sad thoughts would then be put away,
And I could give back laughter for the Ocean's moan!

THE PATH

There are no beaten paths to Glory's height,
There are no rules to compass greatness known;
Each for himself must cleave a path alone,
And press his own way forward in the fight.
Smooth is the way to ease and calm delight,
And soft the road Sloth chooseth for her own;
But he who craves the flower of life full-blown,
Must struggle up in all his armor dight!
What though the burden bear him sorely down
And crush to dust the mountain of his pride,
Oh, then, with strong heart let him still abide;
For rugged is the roadway to renown,
Nor may he hope to gain the envied crown,
Till he hath thrust the looming rocks aside.

THE LAWYERS' WAYS

I 'VE been list'nin' to them lawyers
In the court house up the street,
An' I 've come to the conclusion
That I'm most completely beat.
Fust one feller riz to argy,
An' he boldly waded in
As he dressed the tremblin' pris'ner
In a coat o' deep-dyed sin.

Why, he painted him all over
In a hue o' blackest crime,
An' he smeared his reputation
With the thickest kind o' grime,
Tell I found myself a-wond'rin',
In a misty way and dim,
How the Lord had come to fashion
Sich an awful man as him.

Then the other lawyer started,
An' with brimmin', tearful eyes,
Said his client was a martyr
That was brought to sacrifice.
An' he give to that same pris'ner
Every blessed human grace,
Tell I saw the light o' virtue
Fairly shinin' from his face.

Then I own 'at I was puzzled
How sich things could rightly be;
An' this aggervatin' question
Seems to keep a-puzzlin' me.
So, will some one please inform me,
An' this mystery unroll —
How an angel an' a devil
Can persess the self-same soul?

ODE FOR MEMORIAL DAY

DONE are the toils and the wearisome marches,
Done is the summons of bugle and drum.
Softly and sweetly the sky overarches,
Shelt'ring a land where Rebellion is dumb.
Dark were the days of the country's derangement,
Sad were the hours when the conflict was on,
But through the gloom of fraternal estrangement
God sent his light, and we welcome the dawn.
O'er the expanse of our mighty dominions,
Sweeping away to the uttermost parts,
Peace, the wide-flying, on untiring pinions,
Bringeth her message of joy to our hearts.

Ah, but this joy which our minds cannot measure,
What did it cost for our fathers to gain!
Bought at the price of the heart's dearest treasure,
Born out of travail and sorrow and pain;

Born in the battle where fleet
Death was flying,
Slaying with sabre-stroke bloody
and fell;
Born where the heroes and martyrs were dying,
Torn by the fury of bullet and
shell.
Ah, but the day is past: silent the
rattle,
And the confusion that followed
the fight.
Peace to the heroes who died in
the battle,
Martyrs to truth and the crowning of Right!

Out of the blood of a conflict fraternal,
Out of the dust and the dimness
of death,
Burst into blossoms of glory eternal
Flowers that sweeten the world
with their breath.
Flowers of charity, peace, and
devotion
Bloom in the hearts that are
empty of strife;
Love that is boundless and broad
as the ocean
Leaps into beauty and fulness
of life.
So, with the singing of pæans and
chorals,
And with the flag flashing high
in the sun,
Place on the graves of our heroes
the laurels
Which their unfaltering valor
has won!

PREMONITION

Dear heart, good-night!
Nay, list awhile that sweet voice
singing
When the world is all so bright,
And the sound of song sets the
heart a-ringing,
Oh, love, it is not right —
Not then to say, "Good-night."

Dear heart, good-night!
The late winds in the lake weeds
shiver,
And the spray flies cold and
white.
And the voice that sings gives a
telltale quiver —
"Ah, yes, the world is bright,
But, dearest heart, good-night!"

Dear heart, good-night!
And do not longer seek to hold
me!
For my soul is in affright
As the fearful glooms in their
pall enfold me.
See him who sang how white
And still; so, dear, good-night.

Dear heart, good-night!
Thy hand I 'll press no more forever,
And mine eyes shall lose the light;
For the great white wraith by the winding river
Shall check my steps with might.
So, dear, good-night, good-night!

RETROSPECTION

When you and I were young, the days
Were filled with scent of pink and rose,
And full of joy from dawn till close,
From morning's mist till evening's haze.
And when the robin sung his song
The verdant woodland ways along,
We whistled louder than he sung.
And school was joy, and work was sport
For which the hours were all too short,
When you and I were young, my boy,
When you and I were young.

When you and I were young, the woods
Brimmed bravely o'er with every joy
To charm the happy-hearted boy.
The quail turned out her timid broods;
The prickly copse, a hostess fine,
Held high black cups of harmless wine;
And low the laden grape-vine swung
With beads of night-kissed amethyst
Where buzzing lovers held their tryst,
When you and I were young, my boy,
When you and I were young.

When you and I were young, the cool
And fresh wind fanned our fevered brows
When tumbling o'er the scented mows,
Or stripping by the dimpling pool,
Sedge-fringed about its shimmering face,
Save where we 'd worn an ent'ring place.
How with our shouts the calm banks rung!

How flashed the spray as we plunged in,—
Pure gems that never caused a sin!
When you and I were young, my boy,
When you and I were young.

When you and I were young, we heard
All sounds of Nature with delight,—
The whirr of wing in sudden flight,
The chirping of the baby-bird.
The columbine's red bells were rung;
The locust's vested chorus sung;
While every wind his zithern strung
To high and holy-sounding keys,
And played sonatas in the trees —
When you and I were young, my boy,
When you and I were young.

When you and I were young, we knew
To shout and laugh, to work and play,
And night was partner to the day
In all our joys. So swift time flew
On silent wings that, ere we wist,
The fleeting years had fled unmissed;
And from our hearts this cry was wrung —
To fill with fond regret and tears
The days of our remaining years —
"When you and I were young, my boy,
When you and I were young."

UNEXPRESSED

Deep in my heart that aches with the repression,
And strives with plenitude of bitter pain,
There lives a thought that clamors for expression,
And spends its undelivered force in vain.

What boots it that some other may have thought it?
The right of thoughts' expression is divine;
The price of pain I pay for it has bought it,
I care not who lays claim to it —'t is mine!

And yet not mine until it be delivered;
The manner of its birth shall prove the test.
Alas, alas, my rock of pride is shivered —
I beat my brow — the thought still unexpressed.

SONG OF SUMMER

DIS is gospel weathah sho'—
  Hills is sawt o' hazy.
Meddahs level ez a flo'
  Callin' to de lazy.
Sky all white wif streaks o' blue,
  Sunshine softly gleamin',
D'ain't no wuk hit 's right to do,
  Nothin' 's right but dreamin'.

Dreamin' by de rivah side
  Wif de watahs glist'nin',
Feelin' good an' satisfied
  Ez you lay a-list'nin'
To the little nakid boys
  Splashin' in de watah,
Hollerin' fu' to spress deir joys
  Jes' lak youngsters ought to.

Squir'l a-tippin' on his toes,
  So 's to hide an' view you;
Whole flocks o' camp-meetin' crows
  Shoutin' hallelujah.
Peckahwood erpon de tree
  Tappin' lak a hammah;
Jaybird chattin' wif a bee,
  Tryin' to teach him grammah.

Breeze is blowin' wif perfume,
  Jes' enough to tease you;
Hollyhocks is all in bloom,
  Smellin' fu' to please you.
Go 'way, folks, an' let me 'lone,
  Times is gettin' dearah—
Summah's settin' on de th'one,
  An' I 'm a-layin' neah huh!

SPRING SONG

A BLUE-BELL springs upon the ledge,
A lark sits singing in the hedge;
Sweet perfumes scent the balmy air,
And life is brimming everywhere.
What lark and breeze and blue-bird sing,
  Is Spring, Spring, Spring!

No more the air is sharp and cold;
The planter wends across the wold,
And, glad, beneath the shining sky
We wander forth, my love and I.
And ever in our hearts doth ring
  This song of Spring, Spring!

For life is life and love is love,
'Twixt maid and man or dove and dove.
Life may be short, life may be long,
But love will come, and to its song
Shall this refrain for ever cling
  Of Spring, Spring, Spring!

TO LOUISE

OH, the poets may sing of their Lady Irenes,
And may rave in their rhymes about wonderful queens;
But I throw my poetical wings to the breeze,

And soar in a song to my Lady Louise.
A sweet little maid, who is dearer, I ween,
Than any fair duchess, or even a queen.
When speaking of her I can't plod in my prose,
For she 's the wee lassie who gave me a rose.

Since poets, from seeing a lady's lip curled,
Have written fair verse that has sweetened the world;
Why, then, should not I give the space of an hour
To making a song in return for a flower?
I have found in my life — it has not been so long —
There are too few of flowers — too little of song.
So out of that blossom, this lay of mine grows,
For the dear little lady who gave me the rose.

I thank God for innocence, dearer than Art,
That lights on a by-way which leads to the heart,
And led by an impulse no less than divine,
Walks into the temple and sits at the shrine.
I would rather pluck daisies that grow in the wild,
Or take one simple rose from the hand of a child,
Then to breathe the rich fragrance of flowers that bide
In the gardens of luxury, passion, and pride.

I know not, my wee one, how came you to know
Which way to my heart was the right way to go;
Unless in your purity, soul-clean and clear,
God whispers his messages into your ear.
You have now had my song, let me end with a prayer
That your life may be always sweet, happy, and fair;
That your joys may be many, and absent your woes,
O dear little lady who gave me the rose!

THE RIVALS

'T WAS three an' thirty year ago,
When I was ruther young, you know,
I had my last an' only fight
About a gal one summer night.
'T was me an' Zekel Johnson; Zeke
'N' me 'd be'n spattin' 'bout a week,
Each of us tryin' his best to show
That he was Liza Jones's beau.

We could n't neither prove the thing,
Fur she was fur too sharp to fling
One over fur the other one
An' by so doin' stop the fun
That we chaps did n't have the sense
To see she got at our expense,
But that 's the way a feller does,
Fur boys is fools an' allus was.
An' when they 's females in the game
I reckon men 's about the same.
Well, Zeke an' me went on that way
An' fussed an' quarrelled day by day;
While Liza, mindin' not the fuss,
Jest kep' a-goin' with both of us,
Tell we pore chaps, that 's Zeke an' me,
Was jest plum mad with jealousy.
Well, fur a time we kep' our places,
An' only showed by frownin' faces
An' looks 'at well our meanin' boded
How full o' fight we both was loaded.
At last it come, the thing broke out,
An' this is how it come about.
One night ('t was fair, you 'll all agree)
I got Eliza's company,
An' leavin' Zekel in the lurch,
Went trottin' off with her to church.
An' jest as we had took our seat
(Eliza lookin' fair an' sweet),
Why, I jest could n't help but grin
When Zekel come a-bouncin' in
As furious as the law allows.
He 'd jest be'n up to Liza's house,
To find her gone, then come to church
To have this end put to his search.
I guess I laffed that meetin' through,
An' not a mortal word I knew
Of what the preacher preached er read
Er what the choir sung er said.
Fur every time I 'd turn my head
I could n't skeercely help but see
'At Zekel had his eye on me.
An' he 'ud sort o' turn an' twist
An' grind his teeth an' shake his fist.
I laughed, fur la! the hull church seen us,
An' knowed that suthin' was between us.
Well, meetin' out, we started hum,
I sorter feelin' what would come.
We 'd jest got out, when up stepped Zeke,
An' said, "Scuse me, I 'd like to speak

To you a minute." "Cert," said I —
A-nudgin' Liza on the sly
An' laughin' in my sleeve with glee,
I asked her, please, to pardon me.
We walked away a step er two,
Jest to git out o' Liza's view,
An' then Zeke said, "I want to know
Ef you think you 're Eliza's beau,
An' 'at I 'm goin' to let her go
Hum with sich a chap as you?"
An' I said bold, "You bet I do."
Then Zekel, sneerin', said 'at he
Did n't want to hender me.
But then he 'lowed the gal was his
An' 'at he guessed he knowed his biz,
An' was n't feared o' all my kin
With all my friends an' chums throwed in.
Some other things he mentioned there
That no born man could no ways bear
Er think o' ca'mly tryin' to stan'
Ef Zeke had be'n the bigges' man
In town, an' not the leanest runt
'At time an' labor ever stunt.
An' so I let my fist go "bim,"
I thought I 'd mos' nigh finished him.
But Zekel did n't take it so.
He jest ducked down an' dodged my blow
An' then come back at me so hard,
I guess I must 'a' hurt the yard,
Er spilet the grass plot where I fell,
An' sakes alive it hurt me; well,
It would n't be'n so bad, you see,
But he jest kep' a-hittin' me.
An' I hit back an' kicked an' pawed,
But 't seemed 't was mostly air I clawed,
While Zekel used his science well
A-makin' every motion tell.
He punched an' hit, why, goodness lands,
Seemed like he had a dozen hands.
Well, afterwhile they stopped the fuss,
An' some one kindly parted us.
All beat an' cuffed an' clawed an' scratched,
An' needin' both our faces patched,
Each started hum a different way;
An' what o' Liza, do you say,
Why, Liza — little humbug — dern her,
Why, she 'd gone home with Hiram Turner.

THE LOVER AND THE MOON

A LOVER whom duty called over the wave,
With himself communed: "Will my love be true

If left to herself? Had I better not sue
Some friend to watch over her, good and grave?
But my friend might fail in my need," he said,
"And I return to find love dead.
Since friendships fade like the flow'rs of June,
I will leave her in charge of the stable moon."

Then he said to the moon: "O dear old moon,
Who for years and years from thy thrown above
Hast nurtured and guarded young lovers and love,
My heart has but come to its waiting June,
And the promise time of the budding vine;
Oh, guard thee well this love of mine."
And he harked him then while all was still,
And the pale moon answered and said, "I will."

And he sailed in his ship o'er many seas,
And he wandered wide o'er strange far strands:
In isles of the south and in Orient lands,
Where pestilence lurks in the breath of the breeze.
But his star was high, so he braved the main,
And sailed him blithely home again;
And with joy he bended his footsteps soon
To learn of his love from the matron moon.

She sat as of yore, in her olden place,
Serene as death, in her silver chair.
A white rose gleamed in her whiter hair,
And the tint of a blush was on her face.
At sight of the youth she sadly bowed
And hid her face 'neath a gracious cloud.
She faltered faint on the night's dim marge,
But "How," spoke the youth, "have you kept your charge?"

The moon was sad at a trust ill-kept;
The blush went out in her blanching cheek,
And her voice was timid and low and weak,
As she made her plea and sighed and wept.
"Oh, another prayed and another plead,

And I could n't resist," she answering said;
"But love still grows in the hearts of men:
Go forth, dear youth, and love again."

But he turned him away from her proffered grace.
"Thou art false, O moon, as the hearts of men,
I will not, will not love again."
And he turned sheer 'round with a soul-sick face
To the sea, and cried: "Sea, curse the moon,
Who makes her vows and forgets so soon."
And the awful sea with anger stirred,
And his breast heaved hard as he lay and heard.

And ever the moon wept down in rain,
And ever her sighs rose high in wind;
But the earth and sea were deaf and blind,
And she wept and sighed her griefs in vain.
And ever at night, when the storm is fierce,
The cries of a wraith through the thunder pierce;
And the waves strain their awful hands on high
To tear the false moon from the sky.

CONSCIENCE AND REMORSE

"Good-bye," I said to my conscience —
"Good-bye for aye and aye,"
And I put her hands off harshly,
And turned my face away;
And conscience smitten sorely
Returned not from that day.

But a time came when my spirit
Grew weary of its pace;
And I cried: "Come back, my conscience;
I long to see thy face."
But conscience cried: "I cannot;
Remorse sits in my place."

IONE

I

Ah, yes, 't is sweet still to remember,
Though 't were less painful to forget;
For while my heart glows like an ember,
Mine eyes with sorrow's drops are wet,
And, oh, my heart is aching yet.
It is a law of mortal pain

That old wounds, long accounted well,
Beneath the memory's potent spell,
Will wake to life and bleed again.

So 't is with me; it might be better
If I should turn no look behind,—
If I could curb my heart, and fetter
From reminiscent gaze my mind,
Or let my soul go blind — go blind!
But would I do it if I could?
Nay! ease at such a price were spurned;
For, since my love was once returned,
All that I suffer seemeth good.

I know, I know it is the fashion,
When love has left some heart distressed,
To weight the air with wordful passion;
But I am glad that in my breast
I ever held so dear a guest.
Love does not come at every nod,
Or every voice that calleth "hasten;"
He seeketh out some heart to chasten,
And whips it, wailing, up to God!
Love is no random road wayfarer
Who where he may must sip his glass.
Love is the King, the Purple-Wearer,
Whose guard recks not of tree or grass
To blaze the way that he may pass.
What if my heart be in the blast
That heralds his triumphant way;
Shall I repine, shall I not say:
"Rejoice, my heart, the King has passed!"

In life, each heart holds some sad story —
The saddest ones are never told.
I, too, have dreamed of fame and glory,
And viewed the future bright with gold;
But that is as a tale long told.
Mine eyes have lost their youthful flash,
My cunning hand has lost its art;
I am not old, but in my heart
The ember lies beneath the ash.

I loved! Why not? My heart was youthful,
My mind was filled with healthy thought.
He doubts not whose own self is truthful,

Doubt by dishonesty is taught;
So loved I boldly, fearing naught.
I did not walk this lowly earth;
Mine was a newer, higher sphere,
Where youth was long and life was dear,
And all save love was little worth.

Her likeness! Would that I might limn it,
As Love did, with enduring art;
Nor dust of days nor death may dim it,
Where it lies graven on my heart,
Of this sad fabric of my life a part.
I would that I might paint her now
As I beheld her in that day,
Ere her first bloom had passed away,
And left the lines upon her brow.

A face serene that, beaming brightly,
Disarmed the hot sun's glances bold.
A foot that kissed the ground so lightly,
He frowned in wrath and deemed her cold,
But loved her still though he was old.
A form where every maiden grace
Bloomed to perfection's richest flower,—
The statued pose of conscious power,
Like lithe-limbed Dian's of the chase.

Beneath a brow too fair for frowning,
Like moon-lit deeps that glass the skies
Till all the hosts above seem drowning,
Looked forth her steadfast hazel eyes,
With gaze serene and purely wise.
And over all, her tresses rare,
Which, when, with his desire grown weak,
The Night bent down to kiss her cheek,
Entrapped and held him captive there.

This was Ione; a spirit finer
Ne'er burned to ash its house of clay;
A soul instinct with fire diviner
Ne'er fled athwart the face of day,
And tempted Time with earthly stay.
Her loveliness was not alone
Of face and form and tresses' hue;

For aye a pure, high soul shone through
Her every act: this was Ione.
Go striding down the gory West,
When Day's long fight was fought and won.

II

'Twas in the radiant summer weather,
When God looked, smiling, from the sky;
And we went wand'ring much together
By wood and lane, Ione and I,
Attracted by the subtle tie
Of common thoughts and common tastes,
Of eyes whose vision saw the same,
And freely granted beauty's claim
Where others found but worthless wastes.

We paused to hear the far bells ringing
Across the distance, sweet and clear.
We listened to the wild bird's singing
The song he meant for his mate's ear,
And deemed our chance to do so dear.
We loved to watch the warrior Sun,
With flaming shield and flaunting crest,

And life became a different story;
Where'er I looked, I saw new light.
Earth's self assumed a greater glory,
Mine eyes were cleared to fuller sight.
Then first I saw the need and might
Of that fair band, the singing throng,
Who, gifted with the skill divine,
Take up the threads of life, spun fine,
And weave them into soulful song.

They sung for me, whose passion pressing
My soul, found vent in song nor line.
They bore the burden of expressing
All that I felt, with art's design,
And every word of theirs was mine.
I read them to Ione, ofttimes,
By hill and shore, beneath fair skies,

And she looked deeply in mine eyes,
And knew my love spoke through their rhymes.

Her life was like the stream that floweth,
And mine was like the waiting sea;
Her love was like the flower that bloweth,
And mine was like the searching bee —
I found her sweetness all for me.
God plied him in the mint of time,
And coined for us a golden day,
And rolled it ringing down life's way
With love's sweet music in its chime.

And God unclasped the Book of Ages,
And laid it open to our sight;
Upon the dimness of its pages,
So long consigned to rayless night,
He shed the glory of his light.
We read them well, we read them long,
And ever thrilling did we see
That love ruled all humanity,—
The master passion, pure and strong.

III

To-day my skies are bare and ashen,
And bend on me without a beam.
Since love is held the master-passion,
Its loss must be the pain supreme —
And grinning Fate has wrecked my dream.
But pardon, dear departed Guest,
I will not rant, I will not rail;
For good the grain must feel the flail;
There are whom love has never blessed.

I had and have a younger brother,
One whom I loved and love today
As never fond and doting mother
Adored the babe who found its way
From heavenly scenes into her day.
Oh, he was full of youth's new wine,—
A man on life's ascending slope,
Flushed with ambition, full of hope;
And every wish of his was mine.

A kingly youth; the way before him
Was thronged with victories to be won;

So joyous, too, the heavens o'er him
Were bright with an unchanging sun,—
His days with rhyme were overrun.
Toil had not taught him Nature's prose,
Tears had not dimmed his brilliant eyes,
And sorrow had not made him wise;
His life was in the budding rose.

I know not how I came to waken,
Some instinct pricked my soul to sight;
My heart by some vague thrill was shaken,—
A thrill so true and yet so slight,
I hardly deemed I read aright.
As when a sleeper, ign'rant why,
Not knowing what mysterious hand
Has called him out of slumberland,
Starts up to find some danger nigh.

Love is a guest that comes, unbidden,
But, having come, asserts his right;
He will not be repressed nor hidden.
And so my brother's dawning plight
Became uncovered to my sight.
Some sound-mote in his passing tone
Caught in the meshes of my ear;
Some little glance, a shade too dear,
Betrayed the love he bore Ione.

What could I do? He was my brother,
And young, and full of hope and trust;
I could not, dared not try to smother
His flame, and turn his heart to dust.
I knew how oft life gives a crust
To starving men who cry for bread;
But he was young, so few his days,
He had not learned the great world's ways,
Nor Disappointment's volumes read.

However fair and rich the booty,
I could not make his loss my gain.
For love is dear, but dearer duty,
And here my way was clear and plain.

I saw how I could save him pain.
And so, with all my day grown dim,
That this loved brother's sun might shine,
I joined his suit, gave over mine,
And sought Ione, to plead for him.

I found her in an eastern bower,
Where all day long the am'rous sun
Lay by to woo a timid flower.
This day his course was well-nigh run,
But still with lingering art he spun
Gold fancies on the shadowed wall.
The vines waved soft and green above,
And there where one might tell his love,
I told my griefs — I told her all!

I told her all, and as she hearkened,
A tear-drop fell upon her dress.
With grief her flushing brow was darkened;
One sob that she could not repress
Betrayed the depths of her distress.
Upon her grief my sorrow fed,
And I was bowed with unlived years,
My heart swelled with a sea of tears,
The tears my manhood could not shed.

The world is Rome, and Fate is Nero,
Disporting in the hour of doom.
God made us men; times make the hero —
But in that awful space of gloom
I gave no thought but sorrow's room.
All — all was dim within that bower,
What time the sun divorced the day;
And all the shadows, glooming gray,
Proclaimed the sadness of the hour.

She could not speak — no word was needed;
Her look, half strength and half despair,
Told me I had not vainly pleaded,
That she would not ignore my prayer.
And so she turned and left me there,
And as she went, so passed my bliss;
She loved me, I could not mistake —

But for her own and my love's sake,
Her womanhood could rise to this!

My wounded heart fled swift to cover,
And life at times seemed very drear.
My brother proved an ardent lover —
What had so young a man to fear?
He wed Ione within the year.
No shadow clouds her tranquil brow,
Men speak her husband's name with pride,
While she sits honored at his side —
She is — she must be happy now!

I doubt the course I took no longer,
Since those I love seem satisfied.
The bond between them will grow stronger
As they go forward side by side;
Then will my pains be jusfied.
Their joy is mine, and that is best —
I am not totally bereft;
For I have still the mem'ry left —
Love stopped with me — a Royal Guest!

RELIGION

I AM no priest of crooks nor creeds,
For human wants and human needs
Are more to me than prophets' deeds;
And human tears and human cares
Affect me more than human prayers.

Go, cease your wail, lugubrious saint!
You fret high Heaven with your plaint.
Is this the "Christian's joy" you paint?
Is this the Christian's boasted bliss?
Avails your faith no more than this?

Take up your arms, come out with me,
Let Heav'n alone; humanity
Needs more and Heaven less from thee.
With pity for mankind look 'round;
Help them to rise — and Heaven is found.

PAUL LAURENCE DUNBAR

DEACON JONES' GRIEVANCE

I 'VE been watchin' of 'em, parson,
An' I 'm sorry fur to say
'At my mind is not contented
With the loose an' keerless way
'At the young folks treat the music;
'T ain't the proper sort o' choir.
Then I don't believe in Christuns
A-singin' hymns for hire.

But I never would 'a' murmured
An' the matter might 'a' gone
Ef it was n't fur the antics
'At I've seen 'em kerry on;
So I thought it was my dooty
Fur to come to you an' ask
Ef you would n't sort o' gently
Take them singin' folks to task.

Fust, the music they 've be'n singin'
Will disgrace us mighty soon;
It 's a cross between a opry
An' a ol' cotillion tune.
With its dashes an' its quavers
An' its hifalutin style —
Why, it sets my head to swimmin'
When I 'm comin' down the aisle.

Now it might be almost decent
Ef it was n't fur the way
'At they git up there an' sing it,
Hey dum diddle, loud and gay.
Why, it shames the name o' sacred
In its brazen wordliness,
An' they 've even got " Ol' Hundred "
In a bold, new-fangled dress.

You 'll excuse me, Mr. Parson,
Ef I seem a little sore;
But I 've sung the songs of Isr'el
For threescore years an' more,
An' it sort o' hurts my feelin's
Fur to see 'em put away
Fur these harum-scarum ditties
'At is capturin' the day.

There 's anuther little happ'nin'
'At I 'll mention while I 'm here,
Jes' to show 'at my objections
All is offered sound and clear.
It was one day they was singin'
An' was doin' well enough —
Singin' good as people could sing
Sich an awful mess o' stuff —

When the choir give a holler,
An' the organ give a groan,
An' they left one weak-voiced feller
A-singin' there alone!
But he stuck right to the music,
Tho' 't was tryin' as could be;

An' when I tried to help him,
Why, the hull church scowled at me.

You say that 's so-low singin',
Well, I pray the Lord that I
Growed up when folks was willin'
To sing their hymns so high.
Why, we never had sich doin's
In the good ol' Bethel days,
When the folks was all contented
With the simple songs of praise.

Now I may have spoke too open,
But 't was too hard to keep still,
An' I hope you 'll tell the singers
'At I bear 'em no ill-will.
'At they all may git to glory
Is my wish an' my desire,
But they 'll need some extry trainin'
'Fore they jine the heavenly choir.

ALICE

KNOW you, winds that blow your course
Down the verdant valleys,
That somewhere you must, perforce,
Kiss the brow of Alice?
When her gentle face you find,
Kiss it softly, naughty wind.

Roses waving fair and sweet
Thro' the garden alleys,
Grow into a glory meet
For the eye of Alice;
Let the wind your offering bear
Of sweet perfume, faint and rare.

Lily holding crystal dew
In your pure white chalice,
Nature kind hath fashioned you
Like the soul of Alice;
It of purest white is wrought,
Filled with gems of crystal thought.

AFTER THE QUARREL

So we, who 've supped the selfsame cup,
To-night must lay our friendship by;
Your wrath has burned your judgment up,
Hot breath has blown the ashes high.
You say that you are wronged — ah, well,
I count that friendship poor, at best
A bauble, a mere bagatelle,
That cannot stand so slight a test.

I fain would still have been your friend,
And talked and laughed and loved with you;

But since it must, why, let it end;
The false but dies, 't is not the true.
So we are favored, you and I,
Who only want the living truth.
It was not good to nurse the lie;
'T is well it died in harmless youth.

I go from you to-night to sleep.
Why, what 's the odds? why should I grieve?
I have no fund of tears to weep
For happenings that undeceive.
The days shall come, the days shall go
Just as they came and went before.
The sun shall shine, the streams shall flow
Though you and I are friends no more.

And in the volume of my years,
Where all my thoughts and acts shall be,
The page whereon your name appears
Shall be forever sealed to me.
Not that I hate you over-much,
'T is less of hate than love defied;
Howe'er, our hands no more shall touch,
We 'll go our ways, the world is wide.

BEYOND THE YEARS

I

Beyond the years the answer lies,
Beyond where brood the grieving skies
And Night drops tears.
Where Faith rod-chastened smiles to rise
And doff its fears,
And carping Sorrow pines and dies —
Beyond the years.

II

Beyond the years the prayer for rest
Shall beat no more within the breast;
The darkness clears,
And Morn perched on the mountain's crest
Her form uprears —
The day that is to come is best,
Beyond the years.

III

Beyond the years the soul shall find
That endless peace for which it pined,
For light appears,
And to the eyes that still were blind
With blood and tears,
Their sight shall come all unconfined
Beyond the years.

AFTER A VISIT

I BE'N down in ole Kentucky
Fur a week er two, an' say,
'T wuz ez hard ez breakin' oxen
Fur to tear myse'f away.
Allus argerin' 'bout fren'ship
An' yer hospitality —
Y' ain't no right to talk about it
Tell you be'n down there to see.

See jest how they give you welcome
To the best that 's in the land,
Feel the sort o' grip they give you
When they take you by the hand.
Hear 'em say, "We 're glad to have you,
Better stay a week er two;"
An' the way they treat you makes you
Feel that ev'ry word is true.

Feed you tell you hear the buttons
Crackin' on yore Sunday vest;
Haul you roun' to see the wonders
Tell you have to cry for rest.
Drink yer health an' pet an' praise you
Tell you git to feel ez great
Ez the Sheriff o' the county
Er the Gov'ner o' the State.

Wife, she sez I must be crazy
'Cause I go on so, an' Nelse
He 'lows, "Goodness gracious! daddy,
Cain't you talk about nuthin' else?"
Well, pleg-gone it, I 'm jes' tickled,
Bein' tickled ain't no sin;
I be'n down in ole Kentucky,
An' I want o' go ag'in.

CURTAIN

VILLAIN shows his indiscretion,
Villain's partner makes confession.
Juvenile, with golden tresses,
Finds her pa and dons long dresses.
Scapegrace comes home money-laden,
Hero comforts tearful maiden,
Soubrette marries loyal chappie,
Villain skips, and all are happy.

THE SPELLIN'-BEE

I NEVER shall furgit that night when father hitched up Dobbin,
An' all us youngsters clambered in an' down the road went bobbin'
To school where we was kep' at work in every kind o' weather,
But where that night a spellin'-bee was callin' us together.
'Twas one o' Heaven's banner nights, the stars was all a glitter,
The moon was shinin' like the hand o' God had jest then lit her.

The ground was white with spotless snow, the blast was sort o' stingin';
But underneath our round-abouts, you bet our hearts was singin'.
That spellin'-bee had be'n the talk o' many a precious moment,
The youngsters all was wild to see jes' what the precious show meant,
An' we whose years was in their teens was little less desirous
O' gittin' to the meetin' so 's our sweethearts could admire us.
So on we went so anxious fur to satisfy our mission
That father had to box our ears, to smother our ambition.
But boxin' ears was too short work to hinder cur arrivin',
He jest turned roun' an' smacked us all, an' kep' right on a-drivin'.
Well, soon the schoolhouse hove in sight, the winders beamin' brightly;
The sound o' talkin' reached our ears, and voices laffin' lightly.
It puffed us up so full an' big 'at I 'll jest bet a dollar,
There wa'n't a feller there but felt the strain upon his collar.
So down we jumped an' in we went ez sprightly ez you make 'em,
But somethin' grabbed us by the knees an' straight began to shake 'em.
Fur once within that lighted room, our feelin's took a canter,
An' scurried to the zero mark ez quick ez Tam O'Shanter.
'Cause there was crowds o' people there, both sexes an' all stations;
It looked like all the town had come an' brought all their relations.
The first I saw was Nettie Gray, I thought that girl was dearer
'N' gold; an' when I got a chance, you bet I aidged up near her.
An' Farmer Dobbs's girl was there, the one 'at Jim was sweet on,
An' Cyrus Jones an' Mandy Smith an' Faith an' Patience Deaton.
Then Parson Brown an' Lawyer Jones were present — all attention,
An' piles on piles of other folks too numerous to mention.
The master rose an' briefly said: "Good friends, dear brother Crawford,
To spur the pupils' minds along, a little prize has offered.
To him who spells the best to-

night — or 't may be ' her '—
no tellin'—
He offers ez a jest reward, this
precious work on spellin'."
A little blue-backed spellin'-book
with fancy scarlet trimmin';
We boys devoured it with our
eyes — so did the girls an'
women.
He held it up where all could see,
then on the table set it,
An' ev'ry speller in the house felt
mortal bound to get it.
At his command we fell in line,
prepared to do our dooty,
Outspell the rest an' set 'em down,
an' carry home the booty.
'T was then the merry times be-
gan, the blunders, an' the
laffin',
The nudges an' the nods an' winks
an' stale good-natured chaf-
fin'.
Ole Uncle Hiram Dane was there,
the clostest man a-livin',
Whose only bugbear seemed to be
the dreadful fear o' givin'.
His beard was long, his hair un-
cut, his clothes all bare an'
dingy;
It was n't 'cause the man was
pore, but jest so mortal
stingy;
An' there he sot by Sally Riggs
a-smilin' an' a-smirkin',
An' all his children lef' to home a
diggin' an' a-workin'.
A widower he was, an' Sal was
thinkin' 'at she 'd wing him;
I reckon he was wond'rin' what
them rings o' hern would
bring him.
An' when the spellin'-test com-
menced, he up an' took his
station,
A-spellin' with the best o' them
to beat the very nation.
An' when he 'd spell some young-
ster down, he 'd turn to look
at Sally,
An' say: " The teachin' nowadays
can't be o' no great vally."
But true enough the adage says,
" Pride walks in slipp'ry
places,"
Fur soon a thing occurred that
put a smile on all our faces.
The laffter jest kep' ripplin' 'roun'
an' teacher could n't quell it,
Fur when he give out " charity "
ole Hiram could n't spell it.
But laffin' 's ketchin' an' it
throwed some others off their
bases,
An' folks 'u'd miss the very word
that seemed to fit their cases.
Why, fickle little Jessie Lee come
near the house upsettin'
By puttin' in a double " kay " to
spell the word " coquettin'."
An' when it come to Cyrus Jones,
it tickled me all over —
Him settin' up to Mandy Smith
an' got sot down on " lover."

But Lawyer Jones of all gone men
did shorely look the gonest,
When he found out that he 'd furgot to put the "h" in "honest."
An' Parson Brown, whose sermons were too long fur toleration,
Caused lots o' smiles by missin' when they give out "condensation."
So one by one they giv' it up — the big words kep' a-landin',
Till me an' Nettie Gray was left, the only ones a-standin',
An' then my inward strife began — I guess my mind was petty —
I did so want that spellin'-book; but then to spell down Nettie
Jest sort o' went ag'in my grain — I somehow could n't do it,
An' when I git a notion fixed, I 'm great on stickin' to it.
So when they giv' the next word out — I had n't orter tell it,
But then 't was all fur Nettie's sake — I missed so 's she could spell it.
She spelt the word, then looked at me so lovin'-like an' mello',
I tell you 't sent a hunderd pins a shootin' through a fello'.

O' course I had to stand the jokes an' chaffin' of the fello's,
But when they handed her the book I vow I was n't jealous.
We sung a hymn, an' Parson Brown dismissed us like he orter,
Fur, la! he 'd learned a thing er two an' made his blessin' shorter.
'T was late an' cold when we got out, but Nettie liked cold weather,
An' so did I, so we agreed we 'd jest walk home together.
We both wuz silent, fur of words we nuther had a surplus,
'Till she spoke out quite sudden like, "You missed that word on purpose."
Well, I declare it frightened me; at first I tried denyin',
But Nettie, she jest smiled an' smiled, she knowed that I was lyin'.
Sez she: "That book is yourn by right;" sez I: "It never could be —
I — I — you — ah —" an' there I stuck, an' well she understood me.
So we agreed that later on when age had giv' us tether,
We 'd jine our lots an' settle down to own that book together.

KEEP A-PLUGGIN' AWAY

I 'VE a humble little motto
That is homely, though it 's true,—
Keep a-pluggin' away.
It 's a thing when I 've an object
That I always try to do,—
Keep a-pluggin' away.
When you 've rising storms to quell,
When opposing waters swell,
It will never fail to tell,—
Keep a-pluggin' away.

If the hills are high before
And the paths are hard to climb,
Keep a-pluggin' away.
And remember that successes
Come to him who bides his time,—
Keep a-pluggin' away.
From the greatest to the least,
None are from the rule released.
Be thou toiler, poet, priest,
Keep a-pluggin' away.

Delve away beneath the surface,
There is treasure farther down,—
Keep a-pluggin' away.
Let the rain come down in torrents,
Let the threat'ning heavens frown,
Keep a-pluggin' away.
When the clouds have rolled away,
There will come a brighter day
All your labor to repay,—
Keep a-pluggin' away.

There 'll be lots of sneers to swallow,
There 'll be lots of pain to bear,—
Keep a-pluggin' away.
If you 've got your eye on heaven,
Some bright day you 'll wake up there,—
Keep a-pluggin' away.
Perseverance still is king;
Time its sure reward will bring;
Work and wait unwearying,—
Keep a-pluggin' away.

NIGHT OF LOVE

THE moon has left the sky, love,
The stars are hiding now,
And frowning on the world, love,
Night bares her sable brow.
The snow is on the ground, love,
And cold and keen the air is.
I 'm singing here to you, love;
You 're dreaming there in Paris.

But this is Nature's law, love,
Though just it may not seem,
That men should wake to sing, love,
While maidens sleep and dream.
Them care may not molest, love,
Nor stir them from their slumbers,

Though midnight find the swain,
love,
Still halting o'er his numbers.

I watch the rosy dawn, love,
Come stealing up the east,
While all things round rejoice,
love,
That Night her reign has
ceased.
The lark will soon be heard, love,
And on his way be winging;
When Nature's poets wake, love,
Why should a man be singing?

COLUMBIAN ODE

I

Four hundred years ago a tangled
waste
Lay sleeping on the west At-
lantic's side;
Their devious ways the Old
World's millions traced
Content, and loved, and la-
bored, dared and died,
While students still believed the
charts they conned,
And revelled in their thriftless
ignorance,
Nor dreamed of other lands that
lay beyond
Old Ocean's dense, indefinite
expanse.

II

But deep within her heart old Na-
ture knew
That she had once arrayed, at
Earth's behest,
Another offspring, fine and fair
to view,—
The chosen suckling of the
mother's breast.
The child was wrapped in vest-
ments soft and fine,
Each fold a work of Nature's
matchless art;
The mother looked on it with love
divine,
And strained the loved one
closely to her heart.
And there it lay, and with the
warmth grew strong
And hearty, by the salt sea
breezes fanned,
Till Time with mellowing touches
passed along,
And changed the infant to a
mighty land.

III

But men knew naught of this, till
there arose
That mighty mariner, the
Genoese,
Who dared to try, in spite of fears
and foes,
The unknown fortunes of un-
sounded seas.
O noblest of Italia's sons, thy
bark

Went not alone into that shrouding night!
O dauntless darer of the rayless dark,
  The world sailed with thee to eternal light!
The deer-haunts that with game were crowded then
  To-day are tilled and cultivated lands;
The schoolhouse tow'rs where Bruin had his den,
  And where the wigwam stood the chapel stands;
The place that nurtured men of savage mien
  Now teems with men of Nature's noblest types;
Where moved the forest-foliage banner green,
  Now flutters in the breeze the stars and stripes!

A BORDER BALLAD

Oh, I have n't got long to live, for we all
  Die soon, e'en those who live longest;
And the poorest and weakest are taking their chance
  Along with the richest and strongest.
So it 's heigho for a glass and a song,
  And a bright eye over the table,
And a dog for the hunt when the game is flush,
  And the pick of a gentleman's stable.

There is Dimmock o' Dune, he was here yester-night,
  But he 's rotting to-day on Glen Arragh;
'T was the hand o' MacPherson that gave him the blow,
  And the vultures shall feast on his marrow.
But it 's heigho for a brave old song
  And a glass while we are able;
Here 's a health to death and another cup
  To the bright eye over the table.

I can show a broad back and a jolly deep chest,
  But who argues now on appearance?
A blow or a thrust or a stumble at best
  May send me to-day to my clearance.
Then it 's heigho for the things I love,
  My mother 'll be soon wearing sable,
But give me my horse and my dog and my glass,
  And a bright eye over the table.

AN EASY-GOIN' FELLER

Ther' ain't no use in all this strife,
An' hurryin', pell-mell, right thro' life.
I don't believe in goin' too fast
To see what kind o' road you 've passed.
It ain't no mortal kind o' good,
'N' I would n't hurry ef I could.
I like to jest go joggin' 'long,
To limber up my soul with song;
To stop awhile 'n' chat the men,
'N' drink some cider now an' then.
Do' want no boss a-standin' by
To see me work; I allus try
To do my dooty right straight up,
An' earn what fills my plate an' cup.
An' ez fur boss, I 'll be my own,
I like to jest be let alone,
To plough my strip an' tend my bees,
An' do jest like I doggoned please.
My head 's all right, an' my heart 's meller,
But I 'm a easy-goin' feller.

A NEGRO LOVE SONG

Seen my lady home las' night,
  Jump back, honey, jump back.
Hel' huh han' an' sque'z it tight,
  Jump back, honey, jump back.
Hyeahd huh sigh a little sigh,
Seen a light gleam f'om huh eye,
An' a smile go flittin' by —
  Jump back, honey, jump back.

Hyeahd de win' blow thoo de pine,
  Jump back, honey, jump back.
Mockin'-bird was singin' fine,
  Jump back, honey, jump back.
An' my hea't was beatin' so,
When I reached my lady's do',
Dat I could n't ba' to go —
  Jump back, honey, jump back.

Put my ahm aroun' huh wais',
  Jump back, honey, jump back.
Raised huh lips an' took a tase,
  Jump back, honey, jump back.
Love me, honey, love me true?
Love me well ez I love you?
An' she answe'd, " 'Cose I do "—
  Jump back, honey, jump back.

THE DILETTANTE: A MODERN TYPE

He scribbles some in prose and verse,
  And now and then he prints it;
He paints a little,— gathers some
  Of Nature's gold and mints it.

He plays a little, sings a song,
  Acts tragic rôles, or funny;
He does, because his love is strong,
  But not, oh, not for money!

He studies almost everything
  From social art to science;
A thirsty mind, a flowing spring,
  Demand and swift compliance.

He looms above the sordid crowd —
  At least through friendly lenses;
While his mamma looks pleased and proud,
  And kindly pays expenses.

BY THE STREAM

By the stream I dream in calm delight, and watch as in a glass,
How the clouds like crowds of snowy-hued and white-robed maidens pass,
And the water into ripples breaks and sparkles as it spreads,
Like a host of armored knights with silver helmets on their heads.
And I deem the stream an emblem fit of human life may go,
For I find a mind may sparkle much and yet but shallows show,
And a soul may glow with myriad lights and wondrous mysteries,
When it only lies a dormant thing and mirrors what it sees.

THE COLORED SOLDIERS

If the muse were mine to tempt it
  And my feeble voice were strong,
If my tongue were trained to measures,
  I would sing a stirring song.
I would sing a song heroic
  Of those noble sons of Ham,
Of the gallant colored soldiers
  Who fought for Uncle Sam!

In the early days you scorned them,
  And with many a flip and flout
Said "These battles are the white man's,
  And the whites will fight them out."
Up the hills you fought and faltered,
  In the vales you strove and bled,
While your ears still heard the thunder
  Of the foes' advancing tread.

Then distress fell on the nation,
  And the flag was drooping low;
Should the dust pollute your banner?
  No! the nation shouted, No!
So when War, in savage triumph,
  Spread abroad his funeral pall —
Then you called the colored soldiers,
  And they answered to your call.

And like hounds unleashed and eager
For the life blood of the prey,
Sprung they forth and bore them bravely
In the thickest of the fray.
And where'er the fight was hottest,
Where the bullets fastest fell,
There they pressed unblanched and fearless
At the very mouth of hell.

Ah, they rallied to the standard
To uphold it by their might;
None were stronger in the labors,
None were braver in the fight.
From the blazing breach of Wagner
To the plains of Olustee,
They were foremost in the fight
Of the battles of the free.

And at Pillow! God have mercy
On the deeds committed there,
And the souls of those poor victims
Sent to Thee without a prayer.
Let the fulness of Thy pity
O'er the hot wrought spirits sway
Of the gallant colored soldiers
Who fell fighting on that day!

Yes, the Blacks enjoy their freedom,
And they won it dearly, too;
For the life blood of their thousands
Did the southern fields bedew.
In the darkness of their bondage,
In the depths of slavery's night,
Their muskets flashed the dawning,
And they fought their way to light.

They were comrades then and brothers,
Are they more or less to-day?
They were good to stop a bullet
And to front the fearful fray.
They were citizens and soldiers,
When rebellion raised its head;
And the traits that made them worthy, —
Ah! those virtues are not dead.

They have shared your nightly vigils,
They have shared your daily toil;
And their blood with yours commingling
Has enriched the Southern soil.

They have slept and marched and suffered
'Neath the same dark skies as you,
They have met as fierce a foeman,
And have been as brave and true.

And their deeds shall find a record
 In the registry of Fame;
For their blood has cleansed completely
 Every blot of Slavery's shame.
So all honor and all glory
 To those noble sons of Ham—
The gallant colored soldiers
 Who fought for Uncle Sam!

NATURE AND ART

TO MY FRIEND CHARLES BOOTH NETTLETON

I

THE young queen Nature, ever sweet and fair,
 Once on a time fell upon evil days.
 From hearing oft herself discussed with praise,
There grew within her heart the longing rare
To see herself; and every passing air
 The warm desire fanned into lusty blaze.
 Full oft she sought this end by devious ways,
But sought in vain, so fell she in despair.
For none within her train nor by her side
 Could solve the task or give the envied boon.
 So day and night, beneath the sun and moon,
She wandered to and fro unsatisfied,
 Till Art came by, a blithe inventive elf,
 And made a glass wherein she saw herself.

II

Enrapt, the queen gazed on her glorious self,
 Then trembling with the thrill of sudden thought,
 Commanded that the skilful wight be brought
That she might dower him with lands and pelf.
Then out upon the silent sea-lapt shelf
 And up the hills and on the downs they sought
 Him who so well and wondrously had wrought;
And with much search found and brought home the elf.
 But he put by all gifts with sad replies,
And from his lips these words flowed forth like wine:
 "O queen, I want no gift but thee," he said.
She heard and looked on him with love-lit eyes,
Gave him her hand, low murmuring, "I am thine,"
 And at the morrow's dawning they were wed.

PAUL LAURENCE DUNBAR

AFTER WHILE

A POEM OF FAITH

I THINK that though the clouds be dark,
That though the waves dash o'er the bark,
Yet after while the light will come,
And in calm waters safe at home
The bark will anchor.
Weep not, my sad-eyed, gray-robed maid,
Because your fairest blossoms fade,
That sorrow still o'erruns your cup,
And even though you root them up,
The weeds grow ranker.

For after while your tears shall cease,
And sorrow shall give way to peace;
The flowers shall bloom, the weeds shall die,
And in that faith seen, by and by
Thy woes shall perish.
Smile at old Fortune's adverse tide,
Smile when the scoffers sneer and chide.
Oh, not for you the gems that pale,
And not for you the flowers that fail;
Let this thought cherish:
That after while the clouds will part,
And then with joy the waiting heart
Shall feel the light come stealing in,
That drives away the cloud of sin
And breaks its power.
And you shall burst your chrysalis,
And wing away to realms of bliss,
Untrammelled, pure, divinely free,
Above all earth's anxiety
From that same hour.

THE OL' TUNES

YOU kin talk about yer anthems
An' yer arias an' sich,
An' yer modern choir-singin'
That you think so awful rich;
But you orter heerd us youngsters
In the times now far away,
A-singin' o' the ol' tunes
In the ol'-fashioned way.

There was some of us sung treble
An' a few of us growled bass,
An' the tide o' song flowed smoothly
With its 'comp'niment o' grace;
There was spirit in that music,
An' a kind o' solemn sway,
A-singin' o' the ol' tunes
In the ol'-fashioned way.

I remember oft o' standin'
In my homespun pantaloons —
On my face the bronze an' freckles
O' the suns o' youthful Junes —
Thinkin' that no mortal minstrel
Ever chanted sich a lay
As the ol' tunes we was singin'
In the ol'-fashioned way.

The boys 'ud always lead us,
An' the girls 'ud all chime in
Till the sweetness o' the singin'
Robbed the list'nin' soul o' sin;
An' I used to tell the parson
'T was as good to sing as pray,
When the people sung the ol' tunes
In the ol'-fashioned way.

How I long ag'in to hear 'em
Pourin' forth from soul to soul,
With the treble high an' meller,
An' the bass's mighty roll;
But the times is very diff'rent,
An' the music heerd to-day
Ain't the singin' o' the ol' tunes
In the ol'-fashioned way.

Little screechin' by a woman,
Little squawkin' by a man,
Then the organ's twiddle-twaddle,
Jest the empty space to span, —
An' ef you should even think it,
'T is n't proper fur to say
That you want to hear the ol' tunes
In the ol'-fashioned way.

But I think that some bright mornin',
When the toils of life air o'er,
An' the sun o' heaven arisin'
Glads with light the happy shore,
I shall hear the angel chorus,
In the realms of endless day,
A-singin' o' the ol' tunes
In the ol'-fashioned way.

MELANCHOLIA

Silently without my window,
Tapping gently at the pane,
Falls the rain.
Through the trees sighs the breeze
Like a soul in pain.
Here alone I sit and weep;
Thought hath banished sleep.

Wearily I sit and listen
To the water's ceaseless drip.
To my lip
Fate turns up the bitter cup,
Forcing me to sip;
'T is a bitter, bitter drink,
Thus I sit and think, —

Thinking things unknown and awful,
Thoughts on wild, uncanny themes,
Waking dreams.
Spectres dark, corpses stark,
Show the gaping seams
Whence the cold and cruel knife
Stole away their life.

Bloodshot eyes all strained and
staring,
Gazing ghastly into mine;
Blood like wine
On the brow — clotted now—
Shows death's dreadful sign.
Lonely vigil still I keep;
Would that I might sleep!

Still, oh, still, my brain is whirl-
ing!
Still runs on my stream of
thought;
I am caught
In the net fate hath set.
Mind and soul are brought
To destruction's very brink;
Yet I can but think!

Eyes that look into the future,—
Peeping forth from out my
mind,
They will find
Some new weight, soon or late,
On my soul to bind,
Crushing all its courage out,—
Heavier than doubt.

Dawn, the Eastern monarch's
daughter,
Rising from her dewy bed,
Lays her head
'Gainst the clouds' sombre
shrouds
Now half fringed with red.
O'er the land she 'gins to peep;
Come, O gentle Sleep!

Hark! the morning cock is crow-
ing;
Dreams, like ghosts, must hie
away;
'Tis the day.
Rosy morn now is born;
Dark thoughts may not stay.
Day my brain from foes will keep;
Now, my soul, I sleep.

THE WOOING

A YOUTH went faring up and
down,
Alack and well-a-day.
He fared him to the market town,
Alack and well-a-day.
And there he met a maiden fair,
With hazel eyes and auburn hair;
His heart went from him then and
there,
Alack and well-a-day.

She posies sold right merrily,
Alack and well-a-day;
But not a flower was fair as she,
Alack and well-a-day.
He bought a rose and sighed a
sigh,
"Ah, dearest maiden, would that I
Might dare the seller too to buy!"
Alack and well-a-day.

She tossed her head, the coy co-
quette,
Alack and well-a-day.

"I'm not, sir, in the market yet,"
Alack and well-a-day.
"Your love must cool upon a shelf;
Tho' much I sell for gold and pelf,
I 'm yet too young to sell myself,"
Alack and well-a-day.

The youth was filled with sorrow sore,
Alack and well-a-day.
And looked he at the maid once more,
Alack and well-a-day.
Then loud he cried, "Fair maiden, if
Too young to sell, now as I live,
You're not too young yourself to give,"
Alack and well-a-day.

The little maid cast down her eyes,
Alack and well-a-day.
And many a flush began to rise,
Alack and well-a-day.
"Why, since you are so bold," she said,
"I doubt not you are highly bred,
So take me!" and the twain were wed,
Alack and well-a-day.

MERRY AUTUMN

It's all a farce,— these tales they tell
About the breezes sighing,
And moans astir o'er field and dell,
Because the year is dying.

Such principles are most absurd,—
I care not who first taught 'em;
There 's nothing known to beast or bird
To make a solemn autumn.

In solemn times, when grief holds sway
With countenance distressing,
You'll note the more of black and gray
Will then be used in dressing.

Now purple tints are all around;
The sky is blue and mellow;
And e'en the grasses turn the ground
From modest green to yellow.

The seed burrs all with laughter crack
On featherweed and jimson;
And leaves that should be dressed in black
Are all decked out in crimson.

A butterfly goes winging by;
A singing bird comes after;

And Nature, all from earth to sky,
Is bubbling o'er with laughter.

The ripples wimple on the rills,
Like sparkling little lasses;
The sunlight runs along the hills,
And laughs among the grasses.

The earth is just so full of fun
It really can't contain it;
And streams of mirth so freely run
The heavens seem to rain it.

Don't talk to me of solemn days
In autumn's time of splendor,
Because the sun shows fewer rays,
And these grow slant and slender.

Why, it 's the climax of the year, —
The highest time of living! —
Till naturally its bursting cheer
Just melts into thanksgiving.

WHEN DE CO'N PONE'S HOT

Dey is times in life when Nature
Seems to slip a cog an' go,
Jes' a-rattlin' down creation,
Lak an ocean's overflow;
When de worl' jes' stahts a-spinnin'
Lak a picaninny's top,
An' yo' cup o' joy is brimmin'
'Twell it seems about to slop,
An' you feel jes' lak a racah,
Dat is trainin' fu' to trot —
When yo' mammy says de blessin'
An' de co'n pone 's hot.

When you set down at de table,
Kin' o' weary lak an' sad,
An' you 'se jes' a little tiahed
An' purhaps a little mad;
How yo' gloom tu'ns into gladness,
How yo' joy drives out de doubt
When de oven do' is opened,
An' de smell comes po'in' out;
Why, de 'lectric light o' Heaven
Seems to settle on de spot,
When yo' mammy says de blessin'
An' de co'n pone 's hot.

When de cabbage pot is steamin'
An' de bacon good an' fat,
When de chittlins is a-sputter'n'
So 's to show you whah dey 's at;
Tek away yo' sody biscuit,
Tek away yo' cake an' pie,
Fu' de glory time is comin',
An' it 's 'proachin' mighty nigh,
An' you want to jump an' hollah,
Dough you know you 'd bettah not,
When yo' mammy says de blessin'
An' de co'n pone 's hot.

I have hyeahd o' lots o' sermons,
An' I 've hyeahd o' lots o' prayers,
An' I've listened to some singin'
Dat has tuck me up de stairs
Of de Glory-Lan' an' set me
Jes' below de Mastah's th'one,
An' have lef' my hea't a-singin'
In a happy aftah tone;
But dem wu'ds so sweetly murmured
Seem to tech de softes' spot,
When my mammy says de blessin',
An' de co'n pone 's hot.

BALLAD

I KNOW my love is true,
And oh the day is fair.
The sky is clear and blue,
The flowers are rich of hue,
The air I breathe is rare,
I have no grief or care;
For my own love is true,
And oh the day is fair.

My love is false I find,
And oh the day is dark.
Blows sadly down the wind,
While sorrow holds my mind;
I do not hear the lark,
For quenched is life's dear spark,—
My love is false I find,
And oh the day is dark!

For love doth make the day
Or dark or doubly bright;
Her beams along the way
Dispel the gloom and gray.
She lives and all is bright,
She dies and life is night.
For love doth make the day,
Or dark or doubly bright.

THE CHANGE HAS COME

THE change has come, and Helen sleeps —
Not sleeps; but wakes to greater deeps
Of wisdom, glory, truth, and light,
Than ever blessed her seeking sight,
In this low, long, lethargic night,
Worn out with strife
Which men call life.

The change has come, and who would say
"I would it were not come to-day"?
What were the respite till tomorrow?
Postponement of a certain sorrow,
From which each passing day would borrow!
Let grief be dumb,
The change has come.

COMPARISON

The sky of brightest gray seems dark
To one whose sky was ever white.
To one who never knew a spark,
Thro' all his life, of love or light,
The grayest cloud seems over-bright.

The robin sounds a beggar's note
Where one the nightingale has heard,
But he for whom no silver throat
Its liquid music ever stirred,
Deems robin still the sweetest bird.

A CORN-SONG

On the wide veranda white,
In the purple failing light,
Sits the master while the sun is lowly burning;
And his dreamy thoughts are drowned
In the softly flowing sound
Of the corn-songs of the field-hands slow returning.

Oh, we hoe de co'n
Since de ehly mo'n;
Now de sinkin' sun
Says de day is done.

O'er the fields with heavy tread,
Light of heart and high of head,
Though the halting steps be labored, slow, and weary;
Still the spirits brave and strong
Find a comforter in song,
And their corn-song rises ever loud and cheery.

Oh, we hoe de co'n
Since de ehly mo'n;
Now de sinkin' sun
Says de day is done.

To the master in his seat,
Comes the burden, full and sweet,
Of the mellow minor music growing clearer,
As the toilers raise the hymn,
Thro' the silence dusk and dim,
To the cabin's restful shelter drawing nearer.

Oh, we hoe de co'n
Since de ehly mo'n;
Now de sinkin' sun
Says de day is done.

And a tear is in the eye
Of the master sitting by,
As he listens to the echoes low-replying
To the music's fading calls
As it faints away and falls
Into silence, deep within the cabin dying.

Oh, we hoe de co'n
Since de ehly mo'n;
Now de sinkin' sun
Says de day is done.

DISCOVERED

Seen you down at chu'ch las' night,
Nevah min', Miss Lucy.
What I mean? oh, dat 's all right,
Nevah min', Miss Lucy.
You was sma't ez sma't could be,
But you could n't hide f'om me.
Ain't I got two eyes to see!
Nevah min', Miss Lucy.

Guess you thought you 's awful keen;
Nevah min', Miss Lucy.
Evahthing you done, I seen;
Nevah min', Miss Lucy.
Seen him tek yo' ahm jes' so,
When he got outside de do' —
Oh, I know dat man 's yo' beau!
Nevah min', Miss Lucy.

Say now, honey, wha 'd he say? —
Nevah min', Miss Lucy!
Keep yo' secrets — dat 's yo' way —
Nevah min', Miss Lucy.
Won't tell me an' I'm yo' pal —
I'm gwine tell his othah gal, —
Know huh, too, huh name is Sal;
Nevah min', Miss Lucy!

DISAPPOINTED

An old man planted and dug and tended,
Toiling in joy from dew to dew;
The sun was kind, and the rain befriended;
Fine grew his orchard and fair to view.
Then he said: "I will quiet my thrifty fears,
For here is fruit for my failing years."

But even then the storm-clouds gathered,
Swallowing up the azure sky;
The sweeping winds into white foam lathered
The placid breast of the bay, hard by;
Then the spirits that raged in the darkened air
Swept o'er his orchard and left it bare.

The old man stood in the rain, uncaring,
Viewing the place the storm had swept;
And then with a cry from his soul despairing,
He bowed him down to the earth and wept.
But a voice cried aloud from the driving rain;
"Arise, old man, and plant again!"

PAUL LAURENCE DUNBAR

INVITATION TO LOVE

COME when the nights are bright with stars
Or when the moon is mellow;
Come when the sun his golden bars
Drops on the hay-field yellow.
Come in the twilight soft and gray,
Come in the night or come in the day,
Come, O love, whene'er you may,
And you are welcome, welcome.

You are sweet, O Love, dear Love,
You are soft as the nesting dove.
Come to my heart and bring it rest
As the bird flies home to its welcome nest.

Come when my heart is full of grief
Or when my heart is merry;
Come with the falling of the leaf
Or with the redd'ning cherry.
Come when the year's first blossom blows,
Come when the summer gleams and glows,
Come with the winter's drifting snows,
And you are welcome, welcome.

HE HAD HIS DREAM

HE had his dream, and all through life,
Worked up to it through toil and strife.
Afloat fore'er before his eyes,
It colored for him all his skies:
The storm-cloud dark
Above his bark,
The calm and listless vault of blue
Took on its hopeful hue,
It tinctured every passing beam —
He had his dream.

He labored hard and failed at last,
His sails too weak to bear the blast,
The raging tempests tore away
And sent his beating bark astray.
But what cared he
For wind or sea!
He said, "The tempest will be short,
My bark will come to port."
He saw through every cloud a gleam —
He had his dream.

GOOD-NIGHT

THE lark is silent in his nest,
The breeze is sighing in its flight,
Sleep, Love, and peaceful be thy rest.
Good-night, my love, good-night, good-night.

Sweet dreams attend thee in thy sleep,
To soothe thy rest till morning's light,
And angels round thee vigil keep.
Good-night, my love, good-night, good-night.

Sleep well, my love, on night's dark breast,
And ease thy soul with slumber bright;
Be joy but thine and I am blest.
Good-night, my love, good-night, good-night.

A COQUETTE CONQUERED

YES, my ha't 's ez ha'd ez stone —
Go 'way, Sam, an' lemme 'lone.
No; I ain't gwine change my min' —
Ain't gwine ma'y you — nuffin' de kin'.

Phiny loves you true an' deah?
Go ma'y Phiny; whut I keer?
Oh, you need n't mou'n an' cry —
I don't keer how soon you die.

Got a present! Whut you got?
Somef'n fu' de pan er pot!
Huh! yo' sass do sholy beat —
Think I don't git 'nough to eat?

Whut 's dat un'neaf yo' coat?
Looks des lak a little shoat.
'T ain't no possum! Bless de Lamb!
Yes, it is, you rascal, Sam!

Gin it to me; whut you say?
Ain't you sma't now! Oh, go 'way!
Possum do look mighty nice,
But you ax too big a price.

Tell me, is you talkin' true,
Dat 's de gal's whut ma'ies you?
Come back, Sam; now whah 's you gwine?
Co'se you knows dat possum's mine!

NORA: A SERENADE

AH, Nora, my Nora, the light fades away,
While Night like a spirit steals up o'er the hills;
The thrush from his tree where he chanted all day,
No longer his music in ecstasy trills.
Then, Nora, be near me; thy presence doth cheer me,
Thine eye hath a gleam that is truer than gold.

I cannot but love thee; so do not reprove me,
If the strength of my passion should make me too bold.

Nora, pride of my heart —
Rosy cheeks, cherry lips, sparkling with glee,—
Wake from thy slumbers, wherever thou art;
Wake from thy slumbers to me.

Ah, Nora, my Nora, there 's love in the air,—
It stirs in the numbers that thrill in my brain;
Oh, sweet, sweet is love with its mingling of care,
Though joy travels only a step before pain.
Be roused from thy slumbers and list to my numbers;
My heart is poured out in this song unto thee.
Oh, be thou not cruel, thou treasure, thou jewel;
Turn thine ear to my pleading and hearken to me.

OCTOBER

October is the treasurer of the year,
And all the months pay bounty to her store;
The fields and orchards still their tribute bear,
And fill her brimming coffers more and more.
But she, with youthful lavishness,
Spends all her wealth in gaudy dress,
And decks herself in garments bold
Of scarlet, purple, red, and gold.

She heedeth not how swift the hours fly,
But smiles and sings her happy life along;
She only sees above a shining sky;
She only hears the breezes' voice in song.
Her garments trail the woodlands through,
And gather pearls of early dew
That sparkle, till the roguish Sun
Creeps up and steals them every one.

But what cares she that jewels should be lost,
When all of Nature's bounteous wealth is hers?
Though princely fortunes may have been their cost,
Not one regret her calm demeanor stirs.
Whole-hearted, happy, careless, free,
She lives her life out joyously,
Nor cares when Frost stalks o'er her way
Aud turns her auburn locks to gray.

A SUMMER'S NIGHT

THE night is dewy as a maiden's mouth,
The skies are bright as are a maiden's eyes,
Soft as a maiden's breath the wind that flies
Up from the perfumed bosom of the South.
Like sentinels, the pines stand in the park;
And hither hastening, like rakes that roam,
With lamps to light their wayward footsteps home,
The fireflies come stagg'ring down the dark.

SHIPS THAT PASS IN THE NIGHT

OUT in the sky the great dark clouds are massing;
I look far out into the pregnant night,
Where I can hear a solemn booming gun
And catch the gleaming of a random light,
That tells me that the ship I seek is passing, passing.

My tearful eyes my soul's deep hurt are glassing;
For I would hail and check that ship of ships.
I stretch my hands imploring, cry aloud,
My voice falls dead a foot from mine own lips,
And but its ghost doth reach that vessel, passing, passing.

O Earth, O Sky, O Ocean, both surpassing,
O heart of mine, O soul that dreads the dark!
Is there no hope for me? Is there no way
That I may sight and check that speeding bark
Which out of sight and sound is passing, passing?

THE DELINQUENT

GOO'-BY, Jinks, I got to hump,
Got to mek dis pony jump;
See dat sun a-goin' down
'N' me a-foolin' hyeah in town!
Git up, Suke — go long!

Guess Mirandy 'll think I's tight,
Me not home an' comin' on night.
What 's dat stan'in' by de fence?
Pshaw! why don't I lu'n some sense?
Git up, Suke — go long!

Guess I spent down dah at Jinks'
Mos' a dollah fur de drinks.
Bless yo'r soul, you see dat star?
Lawd, but won't Mirandy rar?
Git up, Suke — go long!

Went dis mo'nin', hyeah it 's night,
Dah 's de cabin dah in sight.
Who 's dat stan'in' in de do'?
Dat must be Mirandy, sho',
    Git up, Suke — go long!

Got de close-stick in huh han',
Dat look funny, goodness lan',
Sakes alibe, but she look glum!
Hyeah, Mirandy, hyeah I come!
    Git up, Suke — go long!

Ef 't had n't a' b'en fur you, you slow ole fool, I 'd a' be'n home long fo' now!

DAWN

An angel, robed in spotless white,
Bent down and kissed the sleeping Night.
Night woke to blush; the sprite was gone.
Men saw the blush and called it Dawn.

A DROWSY DAY

The air is dark, the sky is gray,
  The misty shadows come and go,
And here within my dusky room
Each chair looks ghostly in the gloom.
  Outside the rain falls cold and slow —
Half-stinging drops, half-blinding spray.

Each slightest sound is magnified,
  For drowsy quiet holds her reign;
The burnt stick in the fireplace breaks,
The nodding cat with start awakes,
  And then to sleep drops off again,
Unheeding Towser at her side.

I look far out across the lawn,
  Where huddled stand the silly sheep;
My work lies idle at my hands,
My thoughts fly out like scattered strands
  Of thread, and on the verge of sleep —
Still half awake — I dream and yawn.

What spirits rise before my eyes!
  How various of kind and form!
Sweet memories of days long past,
The dreams of youth that could not last,
  Each smiling calm, each raging storm,
That swept across my early skies.

Half seen, the bare, gaunt-fingered boughs
  Before my window sweep and sway,
And chafe in tortures of unrest.

My chin sinks down upon my
 breast;
I cannot work on such a day,
But only sit and dream and
 drowse.

DIRGE

PLACE this bunch of mignonette
 In her cold, dead hand;
When the golden sun is set,
 Where the poplars stand,
Bury her from sun and day,
Lay my little love away
 From my sight.

She was like a modest flower
 Blown in sunny June,
Warm as sun at noon's high hour,
 Chaster than the moon.
Ah, her day was brief and bright,
Earth has lost a star of light;
 She is dead.

Softly breathe her name to me,—
 Ah, I loved her so.
Gentle let your tribute be;
 None may better know
Her true worth than I who weep
O'er her as she lies asleep —
 Soft asleep.

Lay these lilies on her breast,
 They are not more white
Than the soul of her, at rest
 'Neath their petals bright.
Chant your aves soft and low,
Solemn be your tread and slow,—
 She is dead.

Lay her here beneath the grass,
 Cool and green and sweet,
Where the gentle brook may pass
 Crooning at her feet.
Nature's bards shall come and
 sing,
And the fairest flowers shall spring
 Where she lies.

Safe above the water's swirl,
 She has crossed the bar;
Earth has lost a precious pearl,
 Heaven has gained a star,
That shall ever sing and shine,
Till it quells this grief of mine
 For my love.

HYMN

WHEN storms arise
And dark'ning skies
 About me threat'ning lower,
To thee, O Lord, I raise mine
 eyes,
To thee my tortured spirit flies
 For solace in that hour.

The mighty arm
Will let no harm
 Come near me nor befall me;
Thy voice shall quiet my alarm,
When life's great battle waxeth
 warm —
 No foeman shall appall me.

Upon thy breast
Secure I rest,
From sorrow and vexation;
No more by sinful cares oppressed,
But in thy presence ever blest,
O God of my salvation.

PREPARATION

The little bird sits in the nest and sings
A shy, soft song to the morning light;
And it flutters a little and prunes its wings.
The song is halting and poor and brief,
And the fluttering wings scarce stir a leaf;
But the note is a prelude to sweeter things,
And the busy bill and the flutter slight
Are proving the wings for a bolder flight!

THE DESERTED PLANTATION

Oh, de grubbin'-hoe 's a-rustin' in de co'nah,
An' de plow 's a-tumblin' down in de fiel',
While de whippo'will 's a-wailin' lak a mou'nah
When his stubbo'n hea't is tryin' ha'd to yiel'.

In de furrers whah de co'n was allus wavin',
Now de weeds is growin' green an' rank an' tall;
An' de swallers roun' de whole place is a-bravin'
Lak dey thought deir folks had allus owned it all.

An' de big house stan's all quiet lak an' solemn,
Not a blessed soul in pa'lor, po'ch, er lawn;
Not a guest, ner not a ca'iage lef' to haul 'em,
Fu' de ones dat tu'ned de latch-string out air gone.

An' de banjo's voice is silent in de qua'ters,
D' ain't a hymn ner co'n-song ringin' in de air;
But de murmur of a branch's passin' waters
Is de only soun' dat breks de stillness dere.

Whah 's de da'kies, dem dat used to be a-dancin'
Evry night befo' de ole cabin do'?
Whah 's de chillun, dem dat used to be a-prancin'
Er a-rollin' in de san' er on de flo'?

Whah 's ole Uncle Mordecai an' Uncle Aaron?

Whah 's Aunt Doshy, Sam, an' Kit, an' all de res'?
Whah 's ole Tom de da'ky fiddlah, how 's he farin'?
Whah 's de gals dat used to sing an' dance de bes'?

Gone! not one o' dem is lef' to tell de story;
Dey have lef' de deah ole place to fall away.
Could n't one o' dem dat seed it in its glory
Stay to watch it in de hour of decay?

Dey have lef' de ole plantation to de swallers,
But it hol's in me a lover till de las';
Fu' I fin' hyeah in de memory dat follers
All dat loved me an' dat I loved in de pas'.

So I 'll stay an' watch de deah ole place an' tend it
Ez I used to in de happy days gone by.
'Twell de othah Mastah thinks it 's time to end it,
An' calls me to my qua'ters in de sky.

THE SECRET

What says the wind to the waving trees?
What says the wave to the river?
What means the sigh in the passing breeze?
Why do the rushes quiver?
Have you not heard the fainting cry
Of the flowers that said "Good-bye, good-bye"?

List how the gray dove moans and grieves
Under the woodland cover;
List to the drift of the falling leaves,
List to the wail of the lover.
Have you not caught the message heard
Already by wave and breeze and bird?

Come, come away to the river's bank,
Come in the early morning;
Come when the grass with dew is dank,
There you will find the warning —
A hint in the kiss of the quickening air
Of the secret that birds and breezes bear.

PAUL LAURENCE DUNBAR

THE WIND AND THE SEA

I STOOD by the shore at the death of day,
As the sun sank flaming red;
And the face of the waters that spread away
Was as gray as the face of the dead.

And I heard the cry of the wanton sea
And the moan of the wailing wind;
For love's sweet pain in his heart had he,
But the gray old sea had sinned.

The wind was young and the sea was old,
But their cries went up together;
The wind was warm and the sea was cold,
For age makes wintry weather.

So they cried aloud and they wept amain,
Till the sky grew dark to hear it;
And out of its folds crept the misty rain,
In its shroud, like a troubled spirit.

For the wind was wild with a hopeless love,
And the sea was sad at heart
At many a crime that he wot of,
Wherein he had played his part.

He thought of the gallant ships gone down
By the will of his wicked waves;
And he thought how the churchyard in the town
Held the sea-made widows' graves.

The wild wind thought of the love he had left
Afar in an Eastern land,
And he longed, as long the much bereft,
For the touch of her perfumed hand.

In his winding wail and his deep-heaved sigh
His aching grief found vent;
While the sea looked up at the bending sky
And murmured: "I repent."

But e'en as he spoke, a ship came by,
That bravely ploughed the main,
And a light came into the sea's green eye,
And his heart grew hard again.

Then he spoke to the wind: "Friend, seest thou not
Yon vessel is eastward bound?
Pray speed with it to the happy spot

Where thy loved one may be found."

And the wind rose up in a dear delight,
And after the good ship sped;
But the crafty sea by his wicked might
Kept the vessel ever ahead.

Till the wind grew fierce in his despair,
And white on the brow and lip.
He tore his garments and tore his hair,
And fell on the flying ship.

And the ship went down, for a rock was there,
And the sailless sea loomed black;
While burdened again with dole and care,
The wind came moaning back.

And still he moans from his bosom hot
Where his raging grief lies pent,
And ever when the ships come not,
The sea says: " I repent."

RIDING TO TOWN

WHEN labor is light and the morning is fair,
I find it a pleasure beyond all compare
To hitch up my nag and go hurrying down
And take Katie May for a ride into town;
For bumpety-bump goes the wagon,
But tra-la-la-la our lay.
There 's joy in a song as we rattle along
In the light of the glorious day.

A coach would be fine, but a spring wagon's good;
My jeans are a match for Kate's gingham and hood;
The hills take us up and the vales take us down,
But what matters that? we are riding to town,
And bumpety-bump goes the wagon,
But tra-la-la-la sing we.
There 's never a care may live in the air
That is filled with the breath of our glee.

And after we 've started, there 's naught can repress
The thrill of our hearts in their wild happiness;
The heavens may smile or the heavens may frown,
And it 's all one to us when we 're riding to town.
For bumpety-bump goes the wagon,
But tra-la-la-la we shout,

For our hearts they are clear and there 's nothing to fear,
And we 've never a pain nor a doubt.

The wagon is weak and the roadway is rough,
And tho' it is long it is not long enough,
For mid all my ecstasies this is the crown
To sit beside Katie and ride into town,
When bumpety-bump goes the wagon,
But tra-la-la-la our song;
And if I had my way, I 'd be willing to pay
If the road could be made twice as long.

WE WEAR THE MASK

We wear the mask that grins and lies,
It hides our cheeks and shades our eyes,—
This debt we pay to human guile;
With torn and bleeding hearts we smile,
And mouth with myriad subtleties.

Why should the world be overwise,
In counting all our tears and sighs?
Nay, let them only see us, while
We wear the mask.

We smile, but, O great Christ, our cries
To thee from tortured souls arise.
We sing, but oh the clay is vile
Beneath our feet, and long the mile;
But let the world dream otherwise,
We wear the mask!

THE MEADOW LARK

Though the winds be dank,
And the sky be sober,
And the grieving Day
In a mantle gray
Hath let her waiting maiden robe her,—
All the fields along
I can hear the song
Of the meadow lark,
As she flits and flutters,
And laughs at the thunder when it mutters.
O happy bird, of heart most gay
To sing when skies are gray!

When the clouds are full,
And the tempest master
Lets the loud winds sweep
From his bosom deep
Like heralds of some dire disaster,

Then the heart alone
To itself makes moan;
And the songs come slow,
While the tears fall fleeter,
And silence than song by far seems sweeter.
Oh, few are they along the way
Who sing when skies are gray!

ONE LIFE

Oh, I am hurt to death, my Love;
The shafts of Fate have pierced my striving heart,
And I am sick and weary of
The endless pain and smart.
My soul is weary of the strife,
And chafes at life, and chafes at life.

Time mocks me with fair promises;
A blooming future grows a barren past,
Like rain my fair full-blossomed trees
Unburden in the blast.
The harvest fails on grain and tree,
Nor comes to me, nor comes to me.

The stream that bears my hopes abreast
Turns ever from my way its pregnant tide.
My laden boat, torn from its rest,
Drifts to the other side.
So all my hopes are set astray,
And drift away, and drift away.

The lark sings to me at the morn,
And near me wings her skyward-soaring flight;
But pleasure dies as soon as born,
The owl takes up the night,
And night seems long and doubly dark;
I miss the lark, I miss the lark.

Let others labor as they may,
I'll sing and sigh alone, and write my line.
Their fate is theirs, or grave or gay,
And mine shall still be mine.
I know the world holds joy and glee,
But not for me,—'t is not for me.

CHANGING TIME

The cloud looked in at the window,
And said to the day, "Be dark!"
And the roguish rain tapped hard on the pane,
To stifle the song of the lark.

The wind sprang up in the tree tops

And shrieked with a voice of death,
But the rough-voiced breeze, that shook the trees,
Was touched with a violet's breath.

DEAD

A KNOCK is at her door, but she is weak;
Strange dews have washed the paint streaks from her cheek;
She does not rise, but, ah, this friend is known,
And knows that he will find her all alone.
So opens he the door, and with soft tread
Goes straightway to the richly curtained bed.
His soft hand on her dewy head he lays.
A strange white light she gives him for his gaze.
Then, looking on the glory of her charms,
He crushes her resistless in his arms.

Stand back! look not upon this bold embrace,
Nor view the calmness of the wanton's face;
With joy unspeakable and 'bated breath,
She keeps her last, long liaison with death!

A CONFIDENCE

UNCLE JOHN, he makes me tired;
Thinks 'at he's jest so all-fired
Smart, 'at he kin pick up, so,
Ever'thing he wants to know.
Tried to ketch me up last night,
But you bet I would n't bite.
I jest kep' the smoothes' face,
But I led him sich a chase,
Could n't corner me, you bet—
I skipped all the traps he set.
Makin' out he wan'ed to know
Who was this an' that girl's beau;
So 's he 'd find out, don't you see,
Who was goin' 'long with me.
But I answers jest ez sly,
An' I never winks my eye,
Tell he hollers with a whirl,
" Look here, ain't you got a girl? "
Y' ought 'o seen me spread my eyes,
Like he 'd took me by surprise,
An' I said, " Oh, Uncle John,
Never thought o' havin' one."
An' somehow that seemed to tickle
Him an' he shelled out a nickel.
Then you ought to seen me leave
Jest a-laffin' in my sleeve.
Fool him — well, I guess I did;
He ain't on to this here kid.
Got a girl! well, I guess yes,
Got a dozen more or less,
But I got one reely one,

Not no foolin' ner no fun;
Fur I 'm sweet on her, you see,
An' I ruther guess 'at she
Must be kinder sweet on me,
So we 're keepin' company.
Honest Injun! this is true,
Ever' word I 'm tellin' you!
But you won't be sich a scab
Ez to run aroun' an' blab.
Mebbe 't ain't the way with you,
But you know some fellers do.
Spoils a girl to let her know
'At you talk about her so.
Don't you know her? her name 's
Liz,
Nicest girl in town she is.
Purty? ah, git out, you gilly —
Liz 'ud purt 'nigh knock you silly.
Y' ought 'o see her when she 's
dressed
All up in her Sunday best,
All the fellers nudgin' me,
An' a-whisperin', gemunee!
Betcher life 'at I feel proud
When she passes by the crowd.
'T 's kinder nice to be a-goin'
With a girl 'at makes some show-
in'—
One you know 'at hain't no snide,
Makes you feel so satisfied.
An' I 'll tell you she 's a trump,
Never even seen her jump
Like some silly girls 'ud do,
When I 'd hide and holler "Boo!"
She 'd jest laff an' say "Git out!
What you hollerin' about?"
When some girls 'ud have a fit
That 'un don't git skeered a bit,
Never makes a bit o' row
When she sees a worm er cow.
Them kind 's few an' far between;
Bravest girl I ever seen.
Tell you 'nuther thing she 'll do,
Mebbe you won't think it 's true,
But if she 's jest got a dime
She 'll go halvers ever' time.
Ah, you goose, you need n't laff;
That 's the kinder girl to have.
If you knowed her like I do,
Guess you 'd kinder like her too.
Tell you somep'n' if you 'll swear
You won't tell it anywhere.
Oh, you got to cross yer heart
Earnest, truly, 'fore I start.
Well, one day I kissed her cheek;
Gee, but I felt cheap an' weak,
'Cause at first she kinder flared,
'N', gracious goodness! I was
scared.
But I need n't been, fer la!
Why, she never told her ma.
That 's what I call grit, don't
you?
Sich a girl 's worth stickin' to.

PHYLLIS

PHYLLIS, ah, Phyllis, my life is a
gray day,
Few are my years, but my griefs
are not few,
Ever to youth should each day be
a May-day,

Warm wind and rose-breath and diamonded dew —
Phyllis, ah, Phyllis, my life is a gray day.

Oh for the sunlight that shines on a May-day!
Only the cloud hangeth over my life.
Love that should bring me youth's happiest heyday
Brings me but seasons of sorrow and strife;
Phyllis, ah, Phyllis, my life is a gray day.

Sunshine or shadow, or gold day or gray day,
Life must be lived as our destinies rule;
Leisure or labor or work day or play day —
Feasts for the famous and fun for the fool;
Phyllis, ah, Phyllis, my life is a gray day.

RIGHT'S SECURITY

What if the wind do howl without,
And turn the creaking weather-vane;
What if the arrows of the rain
Do beat against the window-pane?
Art thou not armored strong and fast
Against the sallies of the blast?
Art thou not sheltered safe and well
Against the flood's insistent swell?

What boots it, that thou stand'st alone,
And laughest in the battle's face
When all the weak have fled the place
And let their feet and fears keep pace?
Thou wavest still thine ensign, high,
And shoutest thy loud battle-cry;
Higher than e'er the tempest roared,
It cleaves the silence like a sword.

Right arms and armors, too, that man
Who will not compromise with wrong;
Though single, he must front the throng,
And wage the battle hard and long.
Minorities, since time began,
Have shown the better side of man;
And often in the lists of Time
One man has made a cause sublime!

IF

If life were but a dream, my Love,
And death the waking time;

If day had not a beam, my Love,
And night had not a rhyme,—
A barren, barren world were this
Without one saving gleam;
I 'd only ask that with a kiss
You 'd wake me from the dream.

If dreaming were the sum of days,
And loving were the bane;
If battling for a wreath of bays
Could soothe a heart in pain,—
I 'd scorn the meed of battle's might,
All other aims above
I 'd choose the human's higher right,
To suffer and to love!

THE SONG

My soul, lost in the music's mist,
Roamed, rapt, 'neath skies of amethyst.
The cheerless streets grew summer meads,
The Son of Phœbus spurred his steeds,
And, wand'ring down the mazy tune,
December lost its way in June,
While from a verdant vale I heard
The piping of a love-lorn bird.

A something in the tender strain
Revived an old, long-conquered pain,
And as in depths of many seas,
My heart was drowned in memories.
The tears came welling to my eyes,
Nor could I ask it otherwise;
For, oh! a sweetness seems to last
Amid the dregs of sorrows past.

It stirred a chord that here of late
I 'd grown to think could not vibrate.
It brought me back the trust of youth,
The world again was joy and truth.
And Avice, blooming like a bride,
Once more stood trusting at my side.
But still, with bosom desolate,
The 'lorn bird sang to find his mate.

Then there are trees, and lights and stars,
The silv'ry tinkle of guitars;
And throbs again as throbbed that waltz,
Before I knew that hearts were false.
Then like a cold wave on a shore,

Comes silence and she sings no more.
I wake, I breathe, I think again,
And walk the sordid ways of men.

SIGNS OF THE TIMES

Air a-gittin' cool an' coolah,
Frost a-comin' in de night,
Hicka' nuts an' wa'nuts fallin',
Possum keepin' out o' sight.
Tu'key struttin' in de ba'nya'd,
Nary step so proud ez his;
Keep on struttin', Mistah Tu'key,
Yo' do' know whut time it is.

Cidah press commence a-squeakin'
Eatin' apples sto'ed away,
Chillun swa'min' 'roun' lak ho'-nets,
Huntin' aigs ermung de hay.
Mistah Tu'key keep on gobblin'
At de geese a-flyin' souf,
Oomph! dat bird do' know whut 's comin';
Ef he did he 'd shet his mouf.

Pumpkin gittin' good an' yallah
Mek me open up my eyes;
Seems lak it 's a-lookin' at me
Jes' a-la'in' dah sayin' "Pies."
Tu'key gobbler gwine 'roun' blow-in',
Gwine 'roun' gibbin' sass an' slack;
Keep on talkin', Mistah Tu'key,
You ain't seed no almanac.

Fa'mer walkin' th'oo de ba'nya'd
Seein' how things is comin' on,
Sees ef all de fowls is fatt'nin' —
Good times comin' sho 's you bo'n.
Hyeahs dat tu'key gobbler brag-gin',
Den his face break in a smile —
Nebbah min', you sassy rascal,
He 's gwine nab you atter while.

Choppin' suet in de kitchen,
Stonin' raisins in de hall,
Beef a-cookin' fu' de mince meat,
Spices groun' — I smell 'em all.
Look hyeah, Tu'key, stop dat gobblin',
You ain' luned de sense ob feah,
You ol' fool, yo' naik 's in dangah,
Do' you know Thanksgibbin 's hyeah?

WHY FADES A DREAM?

Why fades a dream?
An iridescent ray
Flecked in between the tryst
Of night and day.
Why fades a dream? —
Of consciousness the shade
Wrought out by lack of light and made
Upon life's stream.
Why fades a dream?

That thought may thrive,
So fades the fleshless dream;

Lest men should learn to trust
  The things that seem.
  So fades a dream,
That living thought may grow
And like a waxing star-beam glow
  Upon life's stream —
  So fades a dream.

THE SPARROW

A LITTLE bird, with plumage brown,
Beside my window flutters down,
A moment chirps its little strain,
Ten taps upon my window-pane,
And chirps again, and hops along,
To call my notice to its song;
But I work on, nor heed its lay,
Till, in neglect, it flies away.

So birds of peace and hope and love
Come fluttering earthward from above,
To settle on life's window-sills,
And ease our load of earthly ills;
But we, in traffic's rush and din
Too deep engaged to let them in,
With deadened heart and sense plod on,
Nor know our loss till they are gone.

SPEAKIN' O' CHRISTMAS

BREEZES blowin' middlin' brisk,
Snow-flakes thro' the air a-whisk,
Fallin' kind o' soft an' light,
Not enough to make things white,
But jest sorter siftin' down
So 's to cover up the brown
Of the dark world's rugged ways
'N' make things look like holidays.
Not smoothed over, but jest specked,
Sorter strainin' fur effect,
An' not quite a-gittin' through
What it started in to do.
Mercy sakes! it does seem queer
Christmas day is 'most nigh here.
Somehow it don't seem to me
Christmas like it used to be,—
Christmas with its ice an' snow,
Christmas of the long ago.
You could feel its stir an' hum
Weeks an' weeks before it come;
Somethin' in the atmosphere
Told you when the day was near,
Did n't need no almanacs;
That was one o' Nature's fac's.
Every cottage decked out gay —
Cedar wreaths an' holly spray —
An' the stores, how they were drest,
Tinsel tell you could n't rest;
Every winder fixed up pat,
Candy canes, an' things like that;
Noah's arks, an' guns, an' dolls,
An' all kinds o' fol-de-rols.
Then with frosty bells a-chime,
Slidin' down the hills o' time,
Right amidst the fun an' din
Christmas come a-bustlin' in,
Raised his cheery voice to call
Out a welcome to us all;

Hale and hearty, strong an' bluff,
That was Christmas, sure enough.
Snow knee-deep an' coastin' fine,
Frozen mill-ponds all ashine,
Seemin' jest to lay in wait,
Beggin' you to come an' skate.
An' you 'd git your gal an' go
Stumpin' cheerily thro' the snow,
Feelin' pleased an' skeert an' warm
'Cause she had a-holt yore arm.
Why, when Christmas come in, we
Spent the whole glad day in glee,
Havin' fun an' feastin' high
An' some courtin' on the sly.
Bustin' in some neighbor's door
An' then suddenly, before
He could give his voice a lift,
Yellin' at him, "Christmas gift."
Now sich things are never heard,
"Merry Christmas" is the word.
But it 's only change o' name,
An' means givin' jest the same.
There 's too many new-styled ways
Now about the holidays.
I 'd jest like once more to see
Christmas like it used to be!

LONESOME

Mother 's gone a-visitin' to spend a month er two,
An', oh, the house is lonesome ez a nest whose birds has flew
To other trees to build ag'in; the rooms seem jest so bare
That the echoes run like sperrits from the kitchen to the stair.
The shetters flap more lazy-like 'n what they used to do,
Sence mother 's gone a-visitin' to spend a month er two.

We 've killed the fattest chicken an' we've cooked her to a turn;
We 've made the richest gravy, but I jest don't give a durn
Fur nothin' 'at I drink er eat, er nothin' 'at I see.
The food ain't got the pleasant taste it used to have to me.
They 's somep'n' stickin' in my throat ez tight ez hardened glue,
Sence mother 's gone a-visitin' to spend a month er two.

The hollyhocks air jest ez pink, they 're double ones at that,
An' I wuz prouder of 'em than a baby of a cat.
But now I don't go near 'em, though they nod an' blush at me,
Fur they 's somep'n' seems to gall me in their keerless sort o' glee
An' all their fren'ly noddin' an' their blushin' seems to say:
"You 're purty lonesome, John, old boy, sence mother 's gone away."

The neighbors ain't so fren'ly ez it seems they 'd ort to be;
They seem to be a-lookin' kinder sideways like at me,
A-kinder feared they 'd tech me off ez ef I wuz a match,
An' all because 'at mother 's gone an' I 'm a-keepin' batch!
I 'm shore I don't do nothin' worse 'n what I used to do
'Fore mother went a-visitin' to spend a month er two.

The sparrers ac's more fearsome like an' won't hop quite so near,
The cricket's chirp is sadder, an' the sky ain't ha'f so clear;
When ev'nin' comes, I set an' smoke tell my eyes begin to swim,
An' things aroun' commence to look all blurred an' faint an' dim.
Well, I guess I 'll have to own up 'at I 'm feelin' purty blue
Sence mother 's gone a-visitin' to spend a month er two.

GROWIN' GRAY

Hello, ole man, you 're a-gittin' gray,
An' it beats ole Ned to see the way
'At the crow's feet 's a-getherin' aroun' yore eyes;
Tho' it ought n't to cause me no su'prise,
Fur there 's many a sun 'at you 've seen rise
An' many a one you 've seen go down
Sence yore step was light an' yore hair was brown,
An' storms an' snows have had their way —
Hello, ole man, you 're a-gittin' gray.

Hello, ole man, you 're a-gittin' gray,
An' the youthful pranks 'at you used to play
Are dreams of a far past long ago
That lie in a heart where the fires burn low —
That has lost the flame though it kept the glow,
An' spite of drivin' snow an' storm,
Beats bravely on forever warm.
December holds the place of May —
Hello, ole man, you 're a-gittin' gray.

Hello, ole man, you 're a-gittin' gray —
Who cares what the carpin' youngsters say?
For, after all, when the tale is told,
Love proves if a man is young or old!
Old age can't make the heart grow cold

When it does the will of an honest mind;
When it beats with love fur all mankind;
Then the night but leads to a fairer day —
Hello, ole man, you 're a-gittin' gray!

TO THE MEMORY OF MARY YOUNG

God has his plans, and what if we
With our sight be too blind to see
Their full fruition; cannot he,
Who made it, solve the mystery?
One whom we loved has fall'n asleep,
Not died; although her calm be deep,
Some new, unknown, and strange surprise
In Heaven holds enrapt her eyes.

And can you blame her that her gaze
Is turned away from earthly ways,
When to her eyes God's light and love
Have giv'n the view of things above?
A gentle spirit sweetly good,
The pearl of precious womanhood;
Who heard the voice of duty clear,
And found her mission soon and near.
She loved all nature, flowers fair,
The warmth of sun, the kiss of air,
The birds that filled the sky with song,
The stream that laughed its way along.
Her home to her was shrine and throne,
But one love held her not alone;
She sought out poverty and grief,
Who touched her robe and found relief.

So sped she in her Master's work,
Too busy and too brave to shirk,
When through the silence, dusk and dim,
God called her and she fled to him.
We wonder at the early call,
And tears of sorrow can but fall
For her o'er whom we spread the pall;
But faith, sweet faith, is over all.

The house is dust, the voice is dumb,
But through undying years to come,
The spark that glowed within her soul
Shall light our footsteps to the goal.
She went her way; but oh, she trod
The path that led her straight to God.

Such lives as this put death to scorn;
They lose our day to find God's morn.

WHEN MALINDY SINGS

G'WAY an' quit dat noise, Miss Lucy —
Put dat music book away;
What 's de use to keep on tryin'?
Ef you practise twell you 're gray,
You cain't sta't no notes a-flyin'
Lak de ones dat rants and rings
F'om de kitchen to be big woods
When Malindy sings.

You ain't got de nachel o'gans
Fu' to make de soun' come right,
You ain't got de tu'ns an' twistin's
Fu' to make it sweet an' light.
Tell you one thing now, Miss Lucy,
An' I 'm tellin' you fu' true,
When hit comes to raal right singin',
'T ain't no easy thing to do.

Easy 'nough fu' folks to hollah,
Lookin' at de lines an' dots,
When dey ain't no one kin sence it,
An' de chune comes in, in spots;
But fu' real melojous music,
Dat jes' strikes yo' hea't and clings,
Jes' you stan' an' listen wif me
When Malindy sings.

Ain't you nevah hyeahd Malindy?
Blessed soul, tek up de cross!
Look hyeah, ain't you jokin', honey?
Well, you don't know whut you los'.
Y' ought to hyeah dat gal a-wa'b-lin',
Robins, la'ks, an' all dem things,
Heish dey moufs an' hides dey faces
When Malindy sings.

Fiddlin' man jes' stop his fiddlin',
Lay his fiddle on de she'f;
Mockin'-bird quit tryin' to whistle,
'Cause he jes' so shamed hisse'f.
Folks a-playin' on de banjo
Draps dey fingahs on de strings —
Bless yo' soul — fu'gits to move em,
When Malindy sings.

She jes' spreads huh mouf and hol-lahs,
"Come to Jesus," twell you hyeah
Sinnahs' tremblin' steps and voices,
Timid-lak a-drawin' neah;
Den she tu'ns to "Rock of Ages,"
Simply to de cross she clings,
An' you fin' yo' teahs a-drappin'
When Malindy sings.

Who dat says dat humble praises
Wif de Master nevah counts?

Heish yo' mouf, I hyeah dat music,
  Ez hit rises up an' mounts —
Floatin' by de hills an' valleys,
  Way above dis buryin' sod,
Ez hit makes its way in glory
  To de very gates of God!

Oh, hit 's sweetah dan de music
  Of an edicated band;
An' hit 's dearah dan de battle's
  Song o' triumph in de lan'.
It seems holier dan evenin'
  When de solemn chu'ch bell rings,
Ez I sit an' ca'mly listen
  While Malindy sings.

Towsah, stop dat ba'kin', hyeah me!
  Mandy, mek dat chile keep still;
Don't you hyeah de echoes callin'
  F'om de valley to de hill?
Let me listen, I can hyeah it,
  Th'oo de bresh of angels' wings,
Sof' an' sweet, "Swing Low, Sweet Chariot,"
  Ez Malindy sings.

THE PARTY

Dey had a gread big pahty down to Tom's de othah night;
Was I dah? You bet! I nevah in my life see sich a sight;
All de folks f'om fou' plantations was invited, an' dey come,
Dey come troopin' thick ez chillun when dey hyeahs a fife an' drum.
Evahbody dressed deir fines'— Heish yo' mouf an' git away,
Ain't seen no sich fancy dressin' sence las' quah'tly meetin' day;
Gals all dressed in silks an' satins, not a wrinkle ner a crease,
Eyes a-battin', teeth a-shinin', haih breshed back ez slick ez grease;
Sku'ts all tucked an' puffed an' ruffled, evah blessed seam an' stitch;
Ef you 'd seen 'em wif deir mistus, could n't swahed to which was which.
Men all dressed up in Prince Alberts, swaller-tails 'u'd tek yo' bref!
I cain't tell you nothin' 'bout it, y' ought to seen it fu' yo'se'f.
Who was dah? Now who you askin'? How you 'spect I gwine to know?
You mus' think I stood an' counted evahbody at de do.'
Ole man Babah's house-boy Isaac, brung dat gal, Malindy Jane,
Huh a-hangin' to his elbow, him a-struttin' wif a cane;
My, but Hahvey Jones was jealous! seemed to stick him lak a tho'n;

But he laughed with Viney Cahteh, tryin' ha'd to not let on,
But a pusson would 'a' noticed f'om de d'rection of his look,
Dat he was watchin' ev'ry step dat Ike an' Lindy took.
Ike he foun' a cheer an' asked huh: " Won't you set down? " wif a smile,
An' she answe'd up a-bowin', " Oh, I reckon 't ain't wuth while."
Dat was jes' fu' style, I reckon, 'cause she sot down jes' de same,
An' she stayed dah 'twell he fetched huh fu' to jine some so't o' game;
Den I hyeahd huh sayin' propah, ez she riz to go away,
" Oh, you raly mus' excuse me, fu' I hardly keers to play."
But I seen huh in a minute wif de othahs on de flo',
An' dah was n't any one o' dem a-playin' any mo';
Comin' down de flo' a-bowin' an' a-swayin' an' a-swingin',
Puttin' on huh high-toned mannahs all de time dat she was singin':
" Oh, swing Johnny up an' down, swing him all aroun',
Swing Johnny up an' down, swing him all aroun',
Oh, swing Johnny up an' down, swing him all aroun'
Fa' you well, my dahlin'."
Had to laff at ole man Johnson, he 's a caution now, you bet —
Hittin' clost onto a hunderd, but he 's spry an' nimble yet;
He 'lowed how a-so't o' gigglin', " I ain't ole, I 'll let you see,
D'ain't no use in gittin' feeble, now you youngstahs jes' watch me,"
An' he grabbed ole Aunt Marier — weighs th'ee hunderd mo' er less,
An' he spun huh 'roun' de cabin swingin' Johnny lak de res'.
Evahbody laffed an' hollahed: " Go it! Swing huh, Uncle Jim! "
An' he swung huh too, I reckon, lak a youngstah, who but him.
Dat was bettah 'n young Scott Thomas, tryin' to be so awful smaht.
You know when dey gits to singin' an' dey comes to dat ere paht:
" In some lady's new brick house,
In some lady's gyahden.
Ef you don't let me out, I will jump out,
So fa' you well, my dahlin'."
Den dey 's got a circle 'roun' you, an' you 's got to break de line;
Well, dat dahky was so anxious, lak to bust hisse'f a-tryin';

Kep' on blund'rin' 'roun' an' foolin' 'twell he giv' one gread big jump,
Broke de line, an lit head-fo'most in de fiah-place right plump;
Hit 'ad fiah in it, mind you; well, I thought my soul I 'd bust,
Tried my best to keep f'om laffin', but hit seemed like die I must!
Y' ought to seen dat man a-scramblin' f'om de ashes an' de grime.
Did it bu'n him! Sich a question, why he did n't give it time;
Th'ow'd dem ashes and dem cindahs evah which-a-way I guess,
An' you nevah did, I reckon, clap yo' eyes on sich a mess;
Fu' he sholy made a picter an' a funny one to boot,
Wif his clothes all full o' ashes an' his face all full o' soot.
Well, hit laked to stopped de pahty, an' I reckon lak ez not
Dat it would ef Tom's wife, Mandy, had n't happened on de spot,
To invite us out to suppah — well, we scrambled to de table,
An' I 'd lak to tell you 'bout it — what we had — but I ain't able,
Mention jes' a few things, dough I know I had n't orter,
Fu' I know 't will staht a hank'rin' an' yo' mouf 'll 'mence to worter.
We had wheat bread white ez cotton an' a egg pone jes like gol',
Hog jole, bilin' hot an' steamin' roasted shoat an' ham sliced cold —
Look out! What 's de mattah wif you? Don't be fallin' on de flo';
Ef it 's go'n' to 'fect you dat way, I won't tell you nothin' mo'.
Dah now — well, we had hot chittlin's — now you 's tryin' ag'in to fall,
Cain't you stan' to hyeah about it? S'pose you'd been an' seed it all;
Seed dem gread big sweet pertaters, layin' by de possum's side,
Seed dat coon in all his gravy, reckon den you 'd up and died!
Mandy 'lowed "you all mus' 'scuse me, d' wa'n't much upon my she'ves,
But I 's done my bes' to suit you, so set down an' he'p yo'se'ves."
Tom, he 'lowed: "I don't b'lieve in 'pologisin' an' perfessin',
Let 'em tek it lak dey ketch it. Eldah Thompson, ask de blessin'."

Wish you 'd seed dat colo'ed preachah cleah his th'oat an' bow his head;
One eye shet, an' one eye open,—dis is evah wud he said:
" Lawd, look down in tendah mussy on sich generous hea'ts ez dese;
Make us truly thankful, amen. Pass dat possum, ef you please!"
Well, we eat and drunk ouah po'tion, 'twell dah was n't nothin' lef,
An' we felt jes' like new sausage, we was mos' nigh stuffed to def!
Tom, he knowed how we 'd be feelin', so he had de fiddlah 'roun',
An' he made us cleah de cabin fu' to dance dat suppah down.
Jim, de fiddlah, chuned his fiddle, put some rosum on his bow,
Set a pine box on de table, mounted it an' let huh go!
He 's a fiddlah, now I tell you, an' he made dat fiddle ring,
'Twell de ol'est an' de lamest had to give deir feet a fling.
Jigs, cotillions, reels an' break-downs, cordrills an' a waltz er two;
Bless yo' soul, dat music winged 'em an' dem people lak to flew.
Cripple Joe, de old rheumatic, danced dat flo' f'om side to middle,
Th'owed away his crutch an' hopped it; what 's rheumatics 'ginst a fiddle?
Eldah Thompson got so tickled dat he lak to los' his grace,
Had to tek bofe feet an' hol' dem so 's to keep 'em in deir place.
An' de Christuns an' de sinnahs got so mixed up on dat flo',
Dat I don't see how dey 'd pahted ef de trump had chanced to blow.
Well, we danced dat way an' capahed in de mos' redic'lous way,
'Twell de roostahs in de bahnyard cleahed deir th'oats an' crowed fu' day.
Y' ought to been dah, fu' I tell you evahthing was rich an' prime,
An' dey ain't no use in talkin', we jes had one scrumptious time!

LYRICS OF THE HEARTHSIDE

LOVE'S APOTHEOSIS

Love me. I care not what the circling years
To me may do.
If, but in spite of time and tears,
You prove but true.

Love me — albeit grief shall dim mine eyes,
And tears bedew,
I shall not e'en complain, for then my skies
Shall still be blue.

Love me, and though the winter snow shall pile,
And leave me chill,
Thy passion's warmth shall make for me, meanwhile,
A sun-kissed hill.

And when the days have lengthened into years,
And I grow old,
Oh, spite of pains and griefs and cares and fears,
Grow thou not cold.

Then hand and hand we shall pass up the hill,
I say not down;
That twain go up, of love, who 've loved their fill,—
To gain love's crown.

Love me, and let my life take up thine own,
As sun the dew.
Come, sit, my queen, for in my heart a throne
Awaits for you!

THE PARADOX

I am the mother of sorrows,
I am the ender of grief;
I am the bud and the blossom,
I am the late-falling leaf.

I am thy priest and thy poet,
I am thy serf and thy king;
I cure the tears of the heartsick,
When I come near they shall sing.

White are my hands as the snowdrop;
Swart are my fingers as clay;
Dark is my frown as the midnight,
Fair is my brow as the day.

Battle and war are my minions,
Doing my will as divine;
I am the calmer of passions,
Peace is a nursling of mine.

Speak to me gently or curse me,
Seek me or fly from my sight;
I am thy fool in the morning,
Thou art my slave in the night.

Down to the grave will I take thee,
Out from the noise of the strife;
Then shalt thou see me and know me —
Death, then, no longer, but life.

Then shalt thou sing at my coming,
Kiss me with passionate breath,
Clasp me and smile to have thought me
Aught save the foeman of Death.

Come to me, brother, when weary,
Come when thy lonely heart swells;
I 'll guide thy footsteps and lead thee
Down where the Dream Woman dwells.

OVER THE HILLS

Over the hills and the valleys of dreaming
Slowly I take my way.
Life is the night with its dream-visions teeming,
Death is the waking at day.

Down thro' the dales and the bowers of loving,
Singing, I roam afar.
Daytime or night-time, I constantly roving,—
Dearest one, thou art my star.

WITH THE LARK

Night is for sorrow and dawn is for joy,
Chasing the troubles that fret and annoy;
Darkness for sighing and daylight for song,—
Cheery and chaste the strain, heartfelt and strong.
All the night through, though I moan in the dark,
I wake in the morning to sing with the lark.

Deep in the midnight the rain whips the leaves,
Softly and sadly the wood-spirit grieves.
But when the first hue of dawn tints the sky,
I shall shake out my wings like the birds and be dry;
And though, like the rain-drops, I grieved through the dark,
I shall wake in the morning to sing with the lark.

On the high hills of heaven, some morning to be,
Where the rain shall not grieve thro' the leaves of the tree,

There my heart will be glad for the pain I have known,
For my hand will be clasped in the hand of mine own;
And though life has been hard and death's pathway been dark,
I shall wake in the morning to sing with the lark.

IN SUMMER

OH, summer has clothed the earth
In a cloak from the loom of the sun!
And a mantle, too, of the skies' soft blue,
And a belt where the rivers run.

And now for the kiss of the wind,
And the touch of the air's soft hands,
With the rest from strife and the heat of life,
With the freedom of lakes and lands.

I envy the farmer's boy
Who sings as he follows the plow;
While the shining green of the young blades lean
To the breezes that cool his brow.

He sings to the dewy morn,
No thought of another's ear;
But the song he sings is a chant for kings
And the whole wide world to hear.

He sings of the joys of life,
Of the pleasures of work and rest,
From an o'erfull heart, without aim or art;
'T is a song of the merriest.

O ye who toil in the town,
And ye who moil in the mart,
Hear the artless song, and your faith made strong
Shall renew your joy of heart.

Oh, poor were the worth of the world
If never a song were heard,—
If the sting of grief had no relief,
And never a heart were stirred.

So, long as the streams run down,
And as long as the robins trill,
Let us taunt old Care with a merry air,
And sing in the face of ill.

THE MYSTIC SEA

THE smell of the sea in my nostrils,
The sound of the sea in mine ears;

The touch of the spray on my burning face,
Like the mist of reluctant tears.

The blue of the sky above me,
The green of the waves beneath;
The sun flashing down on a gray-white sail
Like a scimitar from its sheath.

And ever the breaking billows,
And ever the rocks' disdain;
And ever a thrill in mine inmost heart
That my reason cannot explain.

So I say to my heart, "Be silent,
The mystery of time is here;
Death's way will be plain when we fathom the main,
And the secret of life be clear."

A SAILOR'S SONG

Oh for the breath of the briny deep,
And the tug of the bellying sail,
With the sea-gull's cry across the sky
And a passing boatman's hail.
For, be she fierce or be she gay,
The sea is a famous friend alway.

Ho! for the plains where the dolphins play,
And the bend of the mast and spars,
And a fight at night with the wild sea-sprite
When the foam has drowned the stars.
And, pray, what joy can the landsman feel
Like the rise and fall of a sliding keel?

Fair is the mead; the lawn is fair
And the birds sing sweet on the lea;
But the echo soft of a song aloft
Is the strain that pleases me;
And swish of rope and ring of chain
Are music to men who sail the main.

Then, if you love me, let me sail
While a vessel dares the deep;
For the ship 's my wife, and the breath of life
Are the raging gales that sweep;
And when I 'm done with calm and blast,
A slide o'er the side, and rest at last.

THE BOHEMIAN

Bring me the livery of no other man.
I am my own to robe me at my pleasure.
Accepted rules to me disclose no treasure:

What is the chief who shall my garments plan?
No garb conventional but I 'll attack it.
(Come, why not don my spangled jacket?)

ABSENCE

GOOD-NIGHT, my love, for I have dreamed of thee
In waking dreams, until my soul is lost —
Is lost in passion's wide and shoreless sea,
Where, like a ship, unruddered, it is tost
Hither and thither at the wild waves' will.
There is no potent Master's voice to still
This newer, more tempestuous Galilee!

The stormy petrels of my fancy fly
In warning course across the darkening green,
And, like a frightened bird, my heart doth cry
And seek to find some rock of rest between
The threatening sky and the relentless wave.
It is not length of life that grief doth crave,
But only calm and peace in which to die.

Here let me rest upon this single hope,
For oh, my wings are weary of the wind,
And with its stress no more may strive or cope.
One cry has dulled mine ears, mine eyes are blind,—
Would that o'er all the intervening space,
I might fly forth and see thee face to face.
I fly; I search, but, love, in gloom I grope.

Fly home, far bird, unto thy waiting nest;
Spread thy strong wings above the wind-swept sea.
Beat the grim breeze with thy unruffled breast
Until thou sittest wing to wing with me.
Then, let the past bring up its tales of wrong;
We shall chant low our sweet connubial song,
Till storm and doubt and past no more shall be!

HER THOUGHT AND HIS

THE gray of the sea, and the gray of the sky,
A glimpse of the moon like a half-closed eye.
The gleam on the waves and the light on the land,

A thrill in my heart,— and — my sweetheart's hand.

She turned from the sea with a woman's grace,
And the light fell soft on her upturned face,
And I thought of the flood-tide of infinite bliss
That would flow to my heart from a single kiss.

But my sweetheart was shy, so I dared not ask
For the boon, so bravely I wore the mask.
But into her face there came a flame: —
I wonder could she have been thinking the same?

THE RIGHT TO DIE

I HAVE no fancy for that ancient cant
That makes us masters of our destinies,
And not our lives, to hold or give them up
As will directs; I cannot, will not think
That men, the subtle worms, who plot and plan
And scheme and calculate with such shrewd wit,
Are such great blund'ring fools as not to know
When they have lived enough.
Men court not death
When there are sweets still left in life to taste.
Nor will a brave man choose to live when he,
Full deeply drunk of life, has reached the dregs,
And knows that now but bitterness remains.
He is the coward who, outfaced in this,
Fears the false goblins of another life.
I honor him who being much harassed
Drinks of sweet courage until drunk of it,—
Then seizing Death, reluctant, by the hand,
Leaps with him, fearless, to eternal peace!

BEHIND THE ARRAS

As in some dim baronial hall restrained,
A prisoner sits, engirt by secret doors
And waving tapestries that argue forth
Strange passages into the outer air;
So in this dimmer room which we call life,
Thus sits the soul and marks with eye intent

That mystic curtain o'er the portal death;
Still deeming that behind the arras lies
The lambent way that leads to lasting light.
Poor fooled and foolish soul! Know now that death
Is but a blind, false door that nowhere leads,
And gives no hope of exit final, free.

WHEN THE OLD MAN SMOKES

In the forenoon's restful quiet,
When the boys are off at school,
When the window lights are shaded
And the chimney-corner cool,
Then the old man seeks his arm-chair,
Lights his pipe and settles back;
Falls a-dreaming as he draws it
Till the smoke-wreaths gather black.

And the tear-drops come a-trickling
Down his cheeks, a silver flow—
Smoke or memories you wonder,
But you never ask him,—no;
For there 's something almost sacred
To the other family folks
In those moods of silent dreaming
When the old man smokes.

Ah, perhaps he sits there dreaming
Of the love of other days
And of how he used to lead her
Through the merry dance's maze;
How he called her "little princess,"
And, to please her, used to twine
Tender wreaths to crown her tresses,
From the "matrimony vine."

Then before his mental vision
Comes, perhaps, a sadder day,
When they left his little princess
Sleeping with her fellow clay.
How his young heart throbbed, and pained him!
Why, the memory of it chokes!
Is it of these things he 's thinking
When the old man smokes?

But some brighter thoughts possess him,
For the tears are dried the while.
And the old, worn face is wrinkled
In a reminiscent smile,
From the middle of the forehead
To the feebly trembling lip,

At some ancient prank remembered
Or some long unheard-of quip.

Then the lips relax their tension
And the pipe begins to slide,
Till in little clouds of ashes,
It falls softly at his side;
And his head bends low and lower
Till his chin lies on his breast,
And he sits in peaceful slumber
Like a little child at rest.

Dear old man, there 's something sad'ning,
In these dreamy moods of yours,
Since the present proves so fleeting,
All the past for you endures.
Weeping at forgotten sorrows,
Smiling at forgotten jokes;
Life epitomized in minutes,
When the old man smokes.

THE GARRET

WITHIN a London garret high,
Above the roofs and near the sky,
My ill-rewarding pen I ply
To win me bread.
This little chamber, six by four,
Is castle, study, den, and more,—
Altho' no carpet decks the floor,
Nor down, the bed.

My room is rather bleak and bare;
I only have one broken chair,
But then, there 's plenty of fresh air,—
Some light, beside.
What tho' I cannot ask my friends
To share with me my odds and ends,
A liberty my aerie lends,
To most denied.

The bore who falters at the stair
No more shall be my curse and care,
And duns shall fail to find my lair
With beastly bills.
When debts have grown and funds are short,
I find it rather pleasant sport
To live " above the common sort "
With all their ills.

I write my rhymes and sing away,
And dawn may come or dusk or day:
Tho' fare be poor, my heart is gay,
And full of glee.
Though chimney-pots be all my views;
'T is nearer for the winging Muse,
So I am sure she 'll not refuse
To visit me.

PAUL LAURENCE DUNBAR

TO E. H. K.

ON THE RECEIPT OF A FAMILIAR POEM

To me, like hauntings of a vagrant breath
From some far forest which I once have known,
The perfume of this flower of verse is blown.
Tho' seemingly soul-blossoms faint to death,
Naught that with joy she bears e'er withereth.
So, tho' the pregnant years have come and flown,
Lives come and gone and altered like mine own,
This poem comes to me a shibboleth:
Brings sound of past communings to my ear,
Turns round the tide of time and bears me back
Along an old and long untraversed way;
Makes me forget this is a later year,
Makes me tread o'er a reminiscent track,
Half sad, half glad, to one forgotten day!

A BRIDAL MEASURE

Come, essay a sprightly measure,
Tuned to some light song of pleasure.
Maidens, let your brows be crowned
As we foot this merry round.

From the ground a voice is singing,
From the sod a soul is springing.
Who shall say 't is but a clod
Quick'ning upward toward its God?

Who shall say it? Who may know it,
That the clod is not a poet
Waiting but a gleam to waken
In a spirit music-shaken?

Phyllis, Phyllis, why be waiting?
In the woods the birds are mating.
From the tree beside the wall,
Hear the am'rous robin call.

Listen to yon thrush's trilling;
Phyllis, Phyllis, are you willing,
When love speaks from cave and tree,
Only we should silent be?

When the year, itself renewing,
All the world with flowers is strewing,
Then through Youth's Arcadian land,
Love and song go hand in hand.

Come, unfold your vocal treasure,
Sing with me a nuptial measure,—
Let this springtime gambol be
Bridal dance for you and me.

VENGEANCE IS SWEET

WHEN I was young I longed for Love,
And held his glory far above
All other earthly things. I cried:
" Come, Love, dear Love, with me abide; "
And with my subtlest art I wooed,
And eagerly the wight pursued.
But Love was gay and Love was shy,
He laughed at me and passed me by.

Well, I grew old and I grew gray,
When Wealth came wending down my way.
I took his golden hand with glee,
And comrades from that day were we.
Then Love came back with doleful face,
And prayed that I would give him place.
But, though his eyes with tears were dim,
I turned my back and laughed at him.

A HYMN

AFTER READING "LEAD, KINDLY LIGHT."

LEAD gently, Lord, and slow,
For oh, my steps are weak,
And ever as I go,
Some soothing sentence speak;

That I may turn my face
Through doubt's obscurity
Toward thine abiding-place,
E'en tho' I cannot see.

For lo, the way is dark;
Through mist and cloud I grope,
Save for that fitful spark,
The little flame of hope.

Lead gently, Lord, and slow,
For fear that I may fall;
I know not where to go
Unless I hear thy call.

My fainting soul doth yearn
For thy green hills afar;
So let thy mercy burn —
My greater, guiding star!

JUST WHISTLE A BIT

JUST whistle a bit, if the day be dark,
And the sky be overcast:
If mute be the voice of the piping lark,
Why, pipe your own small blast.

And it 's wonderful how o'er the gray sky-track
The truant warbler comes stealing back.
But why need he come? for your soul 's at rest,
And the song in the heart,— ah, that is best.

Just whistle a bit, if the night be drear
And the stars refuse to shine:
And a gleam that mocks the star-light clear
Within you glows benign.

Till the dearth of light in the glooming skies
Is lost to the sight of your soul-lit eyes.
What matters the absence of moon or star?
The light within is the best by far.

Just whistle a bit, if there 's work to do,
With the mind or in the soil.
And your note will turn out a talisman true
To exorcise grim Toil.

It will lighten your burden and make you feel
That there 's nothing like work as a sauce for a meal.
And with song in your heart and the meal in — its place,
There 'll be joy in your bosom and light in your face.

Just whistle a bit, if your heart be sore;
'Tis a wonderful balm for pain.
Just pipe some old melody o'er and o'er
Till it soothes like summer rain.

And perhaps 't would be best in a later day,
When Death comes stalking down the way,
To knock at your bosom and see if you 're fit,
Then, as you wait calmly, just whistle a bit.

THE BARRIER

The Midnight wooed the Morning-Star,
And prayed her: "Love come nearer;
Your swinging coldly there afar
To me but makes you dearer!"

The Morning-Star was pale with dole
As said she, low replying:
"Oh, lover mine, soul of my soul,
For you I too am sighing.

"But One ordained when we were born,
In spite of Love's insistence,
That Night might only view the Morn
Adoring at a distance."

But as she spoke the jealous Sun
Across the heavens panted.
"Oh, whining fools," he cried, "have done;
Your wishes shall be granted!"

He hurled his flaming lances far;
The twain stood unaffrighted —
And Midnight and the Morning-Star
Lay down in death united!

DREAMS

DREAM on, for dreams are sweet:
Do not awaken!
Dream on, and at thy feet
Pomegranates shall be shaken.

Who likeneth the youth
Of life to morning?
'Tis like the night in truth,
Rose-coloured dreams adorning.

The wind is soft above,
The shadows umber.
(There is a dream called Love.)
Take thou the fullest slumber!

In Lethe's soothing stream,
Thy thirst thou slakest.
Sleep, sleep; 't is sweet to dream.
Oh, weep when thou awakest!

THE DREAMER

TEMPLES he built and palaces of air,
And, with the artist's parent-pride aglow,
His fancy saw his vague ideals grow
Into creations marvellously fair;
He set his foot upon Fame's nether stair.
But ah, his dream,— it had entranced him so
He could not move. He could no farther go;
But paused in joy that he was even there!

He did not wake until one day there gleamed
Thro' his dark consciousness a light that racked
His being till he rose, alert to act.
But lo! what he had dreamed, the while he dreamed,
Another, wedding action unto thought,
Into the living, pulsing world had brought.

WAITING

THE sun has slipped his tether
And galloped down the west.
(Oh, it 's weary, weary waiting, love.)
The little bird is sleeping
In the softness of its nest.
Night follows day, day follows dawn,
And so the time has come and gone:
And it 's weary, weary waiting, love.

The cruel wind is rising
With a whistle and a wail.

(And it 's weary, weary waiting, love.)
My eyes are seaward straining
For the coming of a sail;
But void the sea, and void the beach
Far and beyond where gaze can reach!
And it 's weary, weary waiting, love.

I heard the bell-buoy ringing —
How long ago it seems!
(Oh, it 's weary, weary waiting, love.)
And ever still, its knelling
Crashes in upon my dreams.
The banns were read, my frock was sewn;
Since then two seasons' winds have blown —
And it 's weary, weary waiting, love.

The stretches of the ocean
Are bare and bleak to-day.
(Oh, it 's weary, weary waiting, love.)
My eyes are growing dimmer —
Is it tears, or age, or spray?
But I will stay till you come home.
Strange ships come in across the foam!
But it 's weary, weary waiting, love.

THE END OF THE CHAPTER

AH, yes, the chapter ends to-day;
We even lay the book away;
But oh, how sweet the moments sped
Before the final page was read!

We tried to read between the lines
The Author's deep-concealed designs;
But scant reward such search secures;
You saw my heart and I saw yours.

The Master,— He who penned the page
And bade us read it,— He is sage:
And what he orders, you and I
Can but obey, nor question why.

We read together and forgot
The world about us. Time was not.
Unheeded and unfelt, it fled.
We read and hardly knew we read.

Until beneath a sadder sun,
We came to know the book was done.
Then, as our minds were but new lit,
It dawned upon us what was writ;

And we were startled. In our eyes,

Looked forth the light of great surprise.
Then as a deep-toned tocsin tolls,
A voice spoke forth: "Behold your souls!"

I do, I do. I cannot look
Into your eyes: so close the book.
But brought it grief or brought it bliss,
No other page shall read like this!

SYMPATHY

I KNOW what the caged bird feels, alas!
When the sun is bright on the upland slopes;
When the wind stirs soft through the springing grass,
And the river flows like a stream of glass;
When the first bird sings and the first bud opes,
And the faint perfume from its chalice steals —
I know what the caged bird feels!

I know why the caged bird beats his wing
Till its blood is red on the cruel bars;
For he must fly back to his perch and cling
When he fain would be on the bough a-swing;
And a pain still throbs in the old, old scars
And they pulse again with a keener sting —
I know why he beats his wing!

I know why the caged bird sings, ah me,
When his wing is bruised and his bosom sore,—
When he beats his bars and he would be free;
It is not a carol of joy or glee,
But a prayer that he sends from his heart's deep core,
But a plea, that upward to Heaven he flings —
I know why the caged bird sings!

LOVE AND GRIEF

OUT of my heart, one treach'rous winter's day,
I locked young Love and threw the key away.
Grief, wandering widely, found the key,
And hastened with it, straightway, back to me,
With Love beside him. He unlocked the door
And bade Love enter with him there and stay.
And so the twain abide for evermore.

LOVE'S CHASTENING

Once Love grew bold and arrogant of air,

Proud of the youth that made him
fresh and fair;
So unto Grief he spake, "What
right hast thou
To part or parcel of this heart?"
Grief's brow
Was darkened with the storm of
inward strife;
Thrice smote he Love as only he
might dare,
And Love, pride purged, was chas-
tened all his life.

MORTALITY

ASHES to ashes, dust unto dust,
What of his loving, what of his
lust?
What of his passion, what of his
pain?
What of his poverty, what of his
pride?
Earth, the great mother, has called
him again:
Deeply he sleeps, the world's ver-
dict defied.
Shall he be tried again? Shall he
go free?
Who shall the court convene?
Where shall it be?
No answer on the land, none from
the sea.
Only we know that as he did, we
must:
You with your theories, you with
your trust,—
Ashes to ashes, dust unto dust!

LOVE

A LIFE was mine full of the close
concern
Of many-voiced affairs. The
world sped fast;
Behind me, ever rolled a preg-
nant past.
A present came equipped with lore
to learn.
Art, science, letters, in their turn,
Each one allured me with its
treasures vast;
And I staked all for wisdom,
till at last
Thou cam'st and taught my soul
anew to yearn.
I had not dreamed that I could
turn away
From all that men with brush
and pen had wrought;
But ever since that memorable
day
When to my heart the truth of
love was brought,
I have been wholly yielded to
its sway,
And had no room for any other
thought.

SHE GAVE ME A ROSE

SHE gave a rose,
And I kissed it and pressed it.
I love her, she knows,
And my action confessed it.
She gave me a rose,
And I kissed it and pressed it.

Ah, how my heart glows,
  Could I ever have guessed it?
It is fair to suppose
  That I might have repressed it:
She gave me a rose,
  And I kissed it and pressed it.

'T was a rhyme in life's prose
  That uplifted and blest it.
Man's nature, who knows
  Until love comes to test it?
She gave me a rose,
  And I kissed it and pressed it.

DREAM SONG I

Long years ago, within a distant clime,
Ere Love had touched me with his wand sublime,
I dreamed of one to make my life's calm May
The panting passion of a summer's day.
And ever since, in almost sad suspense,
I have been waiting with a soul intense
To greet and take unto myself the beams,
Of her, my star, the lady of my dreams.

O Love, still longed and looked for, come to me,
Be thy far home by mountain, vale, or sea.
My yearning heart may never find its rest
Until thou liest rapt upon my breast.
The wind may bring its perfume from the south,
Is it so sweet as breath from my love's mouth?
Oh, naught that surely is, and naught that seems
May turn me from the lady of my dreams.

DREAM SONG II

Pray, what can dreams avail
  To make love or to mar?
The child within the cradle rail
  Lies dreaming of the star.
But is the star by this beguiled
To leave its place and seek the child?

The poor plucked rose within its glass
  Still dreameth of the bee;
But, tho' the lagging moments pass,
  Her Love she may not see.
If dream of child and flower fail,
Why should a maiden's dreams prevail?

PAUL LAURENCE DUNBAR

CHRISTMAS IN THE HEART

THE snow lies deep upon the ground,
And winter's brightness all around
Decks bravely out the forest sere,
With jewels of the brave old year.
The coasting crowd upon the hill
With some new spirit seems to thrill;
And all the temple bells achime.
Ring out the glee of Christmas time.

In happy homes the brown oak-bough
Vies with the red-gemmed holly now;
And here and there, like pearls, there show
The berries of the mistletoe.
A sprig upon the chandelier
Says to the maidens, "Come not here!"
Even the pauper of the earth
Some kindly gift has cheered to mirth!

Within his chamber, dim and cold,
There sits a grasping miser old.
He has no thought save one of gain,—
To grind and gather and grasp and drain.
A peal of bells, a merry shout
Assail his ear: he gazes out
Upon a world to him all gray,
And snarls, "Why, this is Christmas Day!"

No, man of ice,—for shame, for shame!
For "Christmas Day" is no mere name.
No, not for you this ringing cheer,
This festal season of the year.
And not for you the chime of bells
From holy temple rolls and swells.
In day and deed he has no part—
Who holds not Christmas in his heart!

THE KING IS DEAD

AYE, lay him in his grave, the old dead year!
His life is lived—fulfilled his destiny.
Have you for him no sad, regretful tear
To drop beside the cold, unfollowed bier?
Can you not pay the tribute of a sigh?

Was he not kind to you, this dead old year?
Did he not give enough of earthly store?
Enough of love, and laughter, and good cheer?
Have not the skies you scanned sometimes been clear?

How, then, of him who dies, could
you ask more?

It is not well to hate him for the
pain
He brought you, and the sorrows
manifold.
To pardon him these hurts still I
am fain;
For in the panting period of his
reign,
He brought me new wounds, but
he healed the old.

One little sigh for thee, my poor,
dead friend —
One little sigh while my com-
panions sing.
Thou art so soon forgotten in the
end;
We cry e'en as thy footsteps down-
ward tend:
"The king is dead! long live the
king!"

THEOLOGY

There is a heaven, for ever, day
by day,
The upward longing of my soul
doth tell me so.
There is a hell, I 'm quite as sure; for pray,
If there were not, where would
my neighbours go?

RESIGNATION

Long had I grieved at what I
deemed abuse;
But now I am as grain within
the mill.
If so be thou must crush me for
thy use,
Grind on, O potent God, and
do thy will!

LOVE'S HUMILITY

As some rapt gazer on the lowly
earth,
Looks up to radiant planets,
ranging far,
So I, whose soul doth know thy
wondrous worth
Look longing up to thee as to a
star.

PRECEDENT

The poor man went to the rich
man's doors,
"I come as Lazarus came," he
said.
The rich man turned with humble
head,—
"I will send my dogs to lick your
sores!"

SHE TOLD HER BEADS

She told her beads with down-
cast eyes,
Within the ancient chapel dim;
And ever as her fingers slim

Slipt o'er th' insensate ivories,
My rapt soul followed, spaniel-wise.
Ah, many were the beads she wore;
But as she told them o'er and o'er,
They did not number all my sighs.
My heart was filled with unvoiced cries
And prayers and pleadings unexpressed;
But while I burned with Love's unrest,
She told her beads with downcast eyes.

LITTLE LUCY LANDMAN

Oh, the day has set me dreaming
In a strange, half solemn way
Of the feelings I experienced
On another long past day,—
Of the way my heart made music
When the buds began to blow,
And o' little Lucy Landman
Whom I loved long years ago.

It 's in spring, the poet tells us,
That we turn to thoughts of love,
And our hearts go out a-wooing
With the lapwing and the dove.
But whene'er the soul goes seeking
Its twin-soul, upon the wing,
I 've a notion, backed by mem'ry,
That it 's love that makes the spring.

I have heard a robin singing
When the boughs were brown and bare,
And the chilling hand of winter
Scattered jewels through the air.
And in spite of dates and seasons,
It was always spring, I know,
When I loved Lucy Landman
In the days of long ago.

Ah, my little Lucy Landman,
I remember you as well
As if 't were only yesterday
I strove your thoughts to tell,—
When I tilted back your bonnet,
Looked into your eyes so true,
Just to see if you were loving
Me as I was loving you.

Ah, my little Lucy Landman
It is true it was denied
You should see a fuller summer
And an autumn by my side.
But the glance of love's sweet sunlight
Which your eyes that morning gave
Has kept spring within my bosom,
Though you lie within the grave.

THE GOURD

In the heavy earth the miner
Toiled and laboured day by day,
Wrenching from the miser mountain
Brilliant treasure where it lay.

And the artist worn and weary
  Wrought with labour manifold
That the king might drink his nectar
  From a goblet made of gold.

On the prince's groaning table
  Mid the silver gleaming bright
Mirroring the happy faces
  Giving back the flaming light,
Shine the cups of priceless crystal
  Chased with many a lovely line,
Glowing now with warmer colour,
  Crimsoned by the ruby wine.

In a valley sweet with sunlight,
  Fertile with the dew and rain,
Without miner's daily labour,
  Without artist's nightly pain,
There there grows the cup I drink from,
  Summer's sweetness in it stored,
And my lips pronounce a blessing
  As they touch an old brown gourd.

Why, the miracle at Cana
  In the land of Galilee,
Tho' it puzzles all the scholars,
  Is no longer strange to me.
For the poorest and the humblest
  Could a priceless wine afford,
If they 'd only dip up water
  With a sunlight-seasoned gourd.

So a health to my old comrade,
  And a song of praise to sing
When he rests inviting kisses
  In his place beside the spring.
Give the king his golden goblets,
  Give the prince his crystal hoard;
But for me the sparkling water
  From a brown and brimming gourd!

THE KNIGHT

Our good knight, Ted, girds his broadsword on
  (And he wields it well, I ween);
He 's on his steed, and away has gone
  To the fight for king and queen.
What tho' no edge the broadsword hath?
What tho' the blade be made of lath?
  'T is a valiant hand
  That wields the brand,
So, foeman, clear the path!

He prances off at a goodly pace;
  'T is a noble steed he rides,
That bears as well in the speedy race
  As he bears in battle-tides.
What tho' 't is but a rocking-chair
That prances with this stately air?
  'T is a warrior bold
  The reins doth hold,
Who bids all foes beware!

PAUL LAURENCE DUNBAR

THOU ART MY LUTE

THOU art my lute, by thee I sing,—
My being is attuned to thee.
Thou settest all my words a-wing,
And meltest me to melody.

Thou art my life, by thee I live,
From thee proceed the joys I know;
Sweetheart, thy hand has power to give
The meed of love — the cup of woe.

Thou art my love, by thee I lead
My soul the paths of light along,
From vale to vale, from mead to mead,
And home it in the hills of song.

My song, my soul, my life, my all,
Why need I pray or make my plea,
Since my petition cannot fall;
For I 'm already one with thee!

THE PHANTOM KISS

ONE night in my room, still and beamless,
With will and with thought in eclipse,
I rested in sleep that was dreamless;
When softly there fell on my lips

A touch, as of lips that were pressing
Mine own with the message of bliss —
A sudden, soft, fleeting caressing,
A breath like a maiden's first kiss.

I woke — and the scoffer may doubt me —
I peered in surprise through the gloom;
But nothing and none were about me,
And I was alone in my room.

Perhaps 't was the wind that caressed me
And touched me with dew-laden breath;
Or, maybe, close-sweeping, there passed me
The low-winging Angel of Death.

Some sceptic may choose to disdain it,
Or one feign to read it aright;
Or wisdom may seek to explain it —
This mystical kiss in the night.

But rather let fancy thus clear it:
That, thinking of me here alone,
The miles were made naught, and, in spirit,
Thy lips, love, were laid on mine own.

COMMUNION

In the silence of my heart,
I will spend an hour with thee,
When my love shall rend apart
All the veil of mystery:

All that dim and misty veil
That shut in between our souls
When Death cried, "Ho, maiden, hail!"
And your barque sped on the shoals.

On the shoals? Nay, wrongly said.
On the breeze of Death that sweeps
Far from life, thy soul has sped
Out into unsounded deeps.

I shall take an hour.and come
Sailing, darling, to thy side.
Wind nor sea may keep me from
Soft communings with my bride.

I shall rest my head on thee
As I did long days of yore,
When a calm, untroubled sea
Rocked thy vessel at the shore.

I shall take thy hand in mine,
And live o'er the olden days
When thy smile to me was wine,—
Golden wine thy word of praise,

For the carols I had wrought
In my soul's simplicity;
For the petty beads of thought
Which thine eyes alone could see.

Ah, those eyes, love-blind, but keen
For my welfare and my weal!
Tho' the grave-door shut between,
Still their love-lights o'er me steal.

I can see thee thro' my tears,
As thro' rain we see the sun.
What tho' cold and cooling years
Shall their bitter courses run,—

I shall see thee still and be
Thy true lover evermore,
And thy face shall be to me
Dear and helpful as before.

Death may vaunt and Death may boast,
But we laugh his pow'r to scorn;
He is but a slave at most,—
Night that heralds coming morn.

I shall spend an hour with thee
Day by day, my little bride.
True love laughs at mystery,
Crying, "Doors of Death, fly wide."

MARE RUBRUM

In Life's Red Sea with faith I plant my feet,
And wait the sound of that sustaining word

Which long ago the men of Israel heard,
When Pharaoh's host behind them, fierce and fleet,
Raged on, consuming with revengeful heat.
Why are the barrier waters still unstirred?—
That struggling faith may die of hope deferred?
Is God not sitting in His ancient seat?

The billows swirl above my trembling limbs,
And almost chill my anxious heart to doubt
And disbelief, long conquered and defied.
But tho' the music of my hopeful hymns
Is drowned by curses of the raging rout,
No voice yet bids th' opposing waves divide!

IN AN ENGLISH GARDEN

In this old garden, fair, I walk to-day
Heart-charmed with all the beauty of the scene:
The rich, luxuriant grasses' cooling green,
The wall's environ, ivy-decked and gray,
The waving branches with the wind at play,
The slight and tremulous blooms that show between,
Sweet all: and yet my yearning heart doth lean
Toward Love's Egyptian flesh-pots far away.

Beside the wall, the slim Laburnum grows
And flings its golden flow'rs to every breeze.
But e'en among such soothing sights as these,
I pant and nurse my soul-devouring woes.
Of all the longings that our hearts wot of,
There is no hunger like the want of love!

THE CRISIS

A man of low degree was sore oppressed,
Fate held him under iron-handed sway,
And ever, those who saw him thus distressed
Would bid him bend his stubborn will and pray.
But he, strong in himself and obdurate,
Waged, prayerless, on his losing fight with Fate.

Friends gave his proffered hand their coldest clasp,
Or took it not at all; and Poverty,
That bruised his body with relentless grasp,
Grinned, taunting, when he struggled to be free.
But though with helpless hands he beat the air,
His need extreme yet found no voice in prayer.

Then he prevailed; and forthwith snobbish Fate,
Like some whipped cur, came fawning at his feet;
Those who had scorned forgave and called him great —
His friends found out that friendship still was sweet.
But he, once obdurate, now bowed his head
In prayer, and trembling with its import, said:

" Mere human strength may stand ill-fortune's frown;
So I prevailed, for human strength was mine;
But from the killing pow'r of great renown,
Naught may protect me save a strength divine.
Help me, O Lord, in this my trembling cause;
I scorn men's curses, but I dread applause!"

THE CONQUERORS

THE BLACK TROOPS IN CUBA

Round the wide earth, from the red field your valour has won,
Blown with the breath of the far-speaking gun,
Goes the word.
Bravely you spoke through the battle cloud heavy and dun.
Tossed though the speech toward the mist-hidden sun,
The world heard.

Hell would have shrunk from you seeking it fresh from the fray,
Grim with the dust of the battle, and gray
From the fight.
Heaven would have crowned you, with crowns not of gold but of bay,
Owning you fit for the light of her day,
Men of night.

Far through the cycle of years and of lives that shall come,
There shall speak voices long muffled and dumb,
Out of fear.
And through the noises of trade and the turbulent hum,
Truth shall rise over the militant drum,
Loud and clear.

Then on the cheek of the honester nation that grows,

All for their love of you, not for your woes,
There shall lie
Tears that shall be to your souls as the dew to the rose;
Afterward thanks, that the present yet knows
Not to ply!

ALEXANDER CRUMMELL — DEAD

BACK to the breast of thy mother,
Child of the earth!
E'en her caress can not smother
What thou hast done.
Follow the trail of the westering sun
Over the earth.
Thy light and his were as one —
Sun, in thy worth.
Unto a nation whose sky was as night,
Camest thou, holily, bearing thy light:
And the dawn came,
In it thy fame
Flashed up in a flame.

Back to the breast of thy mother —
To rest.
Long hast thou striven;
Dared where the hills by the lightning of heaven were riven;
Go now, pure shriven.
Who shall come after thee, out of the clay —
Learned one and leader to show us the way?
Who shall rise up when the world gives the test?
Think thou no more of this —
Rest!

WHEN ALL IS DONE

WHEN all is done, and my last word is said,
And ye who loved me murmur, "He is dead,"
Let no one weep, for fear that I should know,
And sorrow too that ye should sorrow so.

When all is done and in the oozing clay,
Ye lay this cast-off hull of mine away,
Pray not for me, for, after long despair,
The quiet of the grave will be a prayer.

For I have suffered loss and grievous pain,
The hurts of hatred and the world's disdain,
And wounds so deep that love, well-tried and pure,
Had not the pow'r to ease them or to cure.

When all is done, say not my day is o'er,

And that thro' night I seek a dimmer shore:
Say rather that my morn has just begun,—
I greet the dawn and not a setting sun,
When all is done.

THE POET AND THE BABY

How's a man to write a sonnet, can you tell,—
How 's he going to weave the dim, poetic spell,—
When a-toddling on the floor
Is the muse he must adore,
And this muse he loves, not wisely, but too well?

Now, to write a sonnet, every one allows,
One must always be as quiet as a mouse;
But to write one seems to me
Quite superfluous to be,
When you 've got a little sonnet in the house.

Just a dainty little poem, true and fine,
That is full of love and life in every line,
Earnest, delicate, and sweet,
Altogether so complete
That I wonder what 's the use of writing mine.

DISTINCTION

" I AM but clay," the sinner plead,
Who fed each vain desire.
" Not only clay," another said,
" But worse, for thou art mire."

THE SUM

A LITTLE dreaming by the way,
A little toiling day by day;
A little pain, a little strife,
A little joy,— and that is life.

A little short-lived summer's morn,
When joy seems all so newly born,
When one day's sky is blue above,
And one bird sings,— and that is love.

A little sickening of the years,
The tribute of a few hot tears
Two folded hands, the failing breath,
And peace at last,— and that is death.

Just dreaming, loving, dying so,
The actors in the drama go —
A flitting picture on a wall,
Love, Death, the themes; but is that all?

PAUL LAURENCE DUNBAR

SONNET

ON AN OLD BOOK WITH UNCUT LEAVES

Emblem of blasted hope and lost desire,
No finger ever traced thy yellow page
Save Time's. Thou hast not wrought to noble rage
The hearts thou wouldst have stirred. Not any fire
Save sad flames set to light a funeral pyre
Dost thou suggest. Nay,—impotent in age,
Unsought, thou holdst a corner of the stage
And ceasest even dumbly to aspire.

How different was the thought of him that writ.
What promised he to love of ease and wealth,
When men should read and kindle at his wit.
But here decay eats up the book by stealth,
While it, like some old maiden, solemnly,
Hugs its incongruous virginity!

ON THE SEA WALL

I sit upon the old sea wall,
And watch the shimmering sea,
Where soft and white the moonbeams fall,
Till, in a fantasy,
Some pure white maiden's funeral pall
The strange light seems to me.

The waters break upon the shore
And shiver at my feet,
While I dream old dreams o'er and o'er,
And dim old scenes repeat;
Tho' all have dreamed the same before,
They still seem new and sweet.

The waves still sing the same old song
That knew an elder time;
The breakers' beat is not more strong,
Their music more sublime;
And poets thro' the ages long
Have set these notes to rhyme.

But this shall not deter my lyre,
Nor check my simple strain;
If I have not the old-time fire,
I know the ancient pain:
The hurt of unfulfilled desire,—
The ember quenched by rain.

I know the softly shining sea
That rolls this gentle swell
Has snarled and licked its tongues at me
And bared its fangs as well;
That 'neath its smile so heavenly,
There lurks the scowl of hell!

But what of that? I strike my string
(For songs in youth are sweet);
I 'll wait and hear the waters bring
Their loud resounding beat;
Then, in her own bold numbers sing
The Ocean's dear deceit!

TO A LADY PLAYING THE HARP

THY tones are silver melted into sound,
And as I dream
I see no walls around,
But seem to hear
A gondolier
Sing sweetly down some slow Venetian stream.

Italian skies — that I have never seen —
I see above.
(Ah, play again, my queen;
Thy fingers white
Fly swift and light
And weave for me the golden mesh of love.)

Oh, thou dusk sorceress of the dusky eyes
And soft dark hair,
'T is thou that mak'st my skies
So swift to change
To far and strange;
But far and strange, thou still dost make them fair.

Now thou dost sing, and I am lost in thee
As one who drowns
In floods of melody.
Still in thy art
Give me this part,
Till perfect love, the love of loving crowns.

CONFESSIONAL

SEARCH thou my heart;
If there be guile,
It shall depart
Before thy smile.

Search thou my soul;
Be there deceit,
'T will vanish whole
Before thee, sweet.

Upon my mind
Turn thy pure lens;
Naught shalt thou find
Thou canst not cleanse.

If I should pray,
I scarcely know
In just what way
My prayers would go.

So strong in me
I feel love's leaven,
I 'd bow to thee
As soon as Heaven!

PAUL LAURENCE DUNBAR

MISAPPREHENSION

OUT of my heart, one day, I wrote a song,
With my heart's blood imbued,
Instinct with passion, tremulously strong,
With grief subdued;
Breathing a fortitude
Pain-bought.
And one who claimed much love for what I wrought,
Read and considered it,
And spoke:
"Ay, brother,—'t is well writ,
But where 's the joke?"

PROMETHEUS

PROMETHEUS stole from Heaven the sacred fire
And swept to earth with it o'er land and sea.
He lit the vestal flames of poesy,
Content, for this, to brave celestial ire.

Wroth were the gods, and with eternal hate
Pursued the fearless one who ravished Heaven
That earth might hold in fee the perfect leaven
To lift men's souls above their low estate.

But judge you now, when poets wield the pen,
Think you not well the wrong has been repaired?
'T was all in vain that ill Prometheus fared:
The fire has been returned to Heaven again!

We have no singers like the ones whose note
Gave challenge to the noblest warbler's song.
We have no voice so mellow, sweet, and strong
As that which broke from Shelley's golden throat.

The measure of our songs is our desires:
We tinkle where old poets used to storm.
We lack their substance tho' we keep their form:
We strum our banjo-strings and call them lyres.

LOVE'S PHASES

LOVE hath the wings of the butterfly,
Oh, clasp him but gently,
Pausing and dipping and fluttering by
Inconsequently.
Stir not his poise with the breath of a sigh;
Love hath the wings of the butterfly.

Love hath the wings of the eagle bold,
Cling to him strongly —
What if the look of the world be cold,
And life go wrongly?
Rest on his pinions, for broad is their fold;
Love hath the wings of the eagle bold.

Love hath the voice of the nightingale,
Hearken his trilling —
List to his song when the moonlight is pale,—
Passionate, thrilling.
Cherish the lay, ere the lilt of it fail;
Love hath the voice of the nightingale.

Love hath the voice of the storm at night,
Wildly defiant.
Hear him and yield up your soul to his might,
Tenderly pliant.
None shall regret him who heed him aright;
Love hath the voice of the storm at night.

FOR THE MAN WHO FAILS

The world is a snob, and the man who wins
Is the chap for its money's worth:
And the lust for success causes half of the sins
That are cursing this brave old earth.
For it 's fine to go up, and the world's applause
Is sweet to the mortal ear;
But the man who fails in a noble cause
Is a hero that 's no less dear.

'T is true enough that the laurel crown
Twines but for the victor's brow;
For many a hero has lain him down
With naught but the cypress bough.
There are gallant men in the losing fight,
And as gallant deeds are done
As ever graced the captured height
Or the battle grandly won.

We sit at life's board with our nerves highstrung,
And we play for the stake of Fame,
And our odes are sung and our banners hung
For the man who wins the game.
But I have a song of another kind

Than breathes in these fame-wrought gales,—
An ode to the noble heart and mind
Of the gallant man who fails!

The man who is strong to fight his fight,
And whose will no front can daunt,
If the truth be truth and the right be right,
Is the man that the ages want.
Tho' he fail and die in grim defeat,
Yet he has not fled the strife,
And the house of Earth will seem more sweet
For the perfume of his life.

HARRIET BEECHER STOWE

SHE told the story, and the whole world wept
At wrongs and cruelties it had not known
But for this fearless woman's voice alone.
She spoke to consciences that long had slept:
Her message, Freedom's clear reveille, swept
From heedless hovel to complacent throne.
Command and prophecy were in the tone
And from its sheath the sword of justice leapt.
Around two peoples swelled a fiery wave,
But both came forth transfigured from the flame.
Blest be the hand that dared be strong to save,
And blest be she who in our weakness came —
Prophet and priestess! At one stroke she gave
A race to freedom and herself to fame.

VAGRANTS

LONG time ago, we two set out,
My soul and I.
I know not why,
For all our way was dim with doubt.
I know not where
We two may fare:
Though still with every changing weather,
We wander, groping on together.

We do not love, we are not friends,
My soul and I.
He lives a lie;
Untruth lines every way he wends.
A scoffer he
Who jeers at me:

And so, my comrade and my brother,
We wander on and hate each other.

Ay, there be taverns and to spare,
Beside the road;
But some strange goad
Lets me not stop to taste their fare.
Knew I the goal
Toward which my soul
And I made way, hope made life fragrant:
But no. We wander, aimless, vagrant!

A WINTER'S DAY

Across the hills and down the narrow ways,
And up the valley where the free winds sweep,
The earth is folded in an ermined sleep
That mocks the melting mirth of myriad Mays.
Departed her disheartening duns and grays,
And all her crusty black is covered deep.
Dark streams are locked in Winter's donjon-keep,
And made to shine with keen, unwonted rays.

O icy mantle, and deceitful snow!
What world-old liars in your hearts ye are!
Are there not still the darkened seam and scar
Beneath the brightness that you fain would show?
Come from the cover with thy blot and blur,
O reeking Earth, thou whited sepulchre!

MY LITTLE MARCH GIRL

Come to the pane, draw the curtain apart,
There she is passing, the girl of my heart;
See where she walks like a queen in the street,
Weather-defying, calm, placid and sweet.
Tripping along with impetuous grace,
Joy of her life beaming out of her face,
Tresses all truant-like, curl upon curl,
Wind-blown and rosy, my little March girl.

Hint of the violet's delicate bloom,
Hint of the rose's pervading perfume!

How can the wind help from kissing her face,—
Wrapping her round in his stormy embrace?
But still serenely she laughs at his rout,
She is the victor who wins in the bout.
So may life's passions about her soul swirl,
Leaving it placid,—my little March girl.

What self-possession looks out of her eyes!
What are the wild winds, and what are the skies,
Frowning and glooming when, brimming with life,
Cometh the little maid ripe for the strife?
Ah! Wind, and bah! Wind, what might have you now?
What can you do with that innocent brow?
Blow, Wind, and grow, Wind, and eddy and swirl,
But bring her to me, Wind,—my little March girl.

REMEMBERED

She sang, and I listened the whole song thro'.
(It was sweet, so sweet, the singing.)
The stars were out and the moon it grew
From a wee soft glimmer way out in the blue
To a bird thro' the heavens winging.

She sang, and the song trembled down to my breast,—
(It was sweet, so sweet the singing.)
As a dove just out of its fledgling nest,
And, putting its wings to the first sweet test,
Flutters homeward so wearily winging.

She sang and I said to my heart "That song,
That was sweet, so sweet i' the singing,
Shall live with us and inspire us long,
And thou, my heart, shalt be brave and strong
For the sake of those words a-winging.

The woman died and the song was still.
(It was sweet, so sweet, the singing.)
But ever I hear the same low trill,
Of the song that shakes my heart with a thrill,
And goes forever winging.

LOVE DESPOILED

As lone I sat one summer's day,
With mien dejected, Love came by;
His face distraught, his locks astray,
So slow his gait, so sad his eye,
I hailed him with a pitying cry:

"Pray, Love, what has disturbed thee so?"
Said I, amazed. "Thou seem'st bereft;
And see thy quiver hanging low,—
What, not a single arrow left?
Pray, who is guilty of this theft?"

Poor Love looked in my face and cried:
"No thief were ever yet so bold
To rob my quiver at my side.
But Time, who rules, gave ear to Gold,
And all my goodly shafts are sold."

THE LAPSE

THIS poem must be done to-day;
Then, I 'll e'en to it.
I must not dream my time away,—
I 'm sure to rue it.
The day is rather bright, I know
The Muse will pardon
My half-defection, if I go
Into the garden.
It must be better working there,—
I 'm sure it 's sweeter:
And something in the balmy air
May clear my metre.

[*In the Garden.*]

Ah this is noble, what a sky!
What breezes blowing!
The very clouds, I know not why,
Call one to rowing.
The stream will be a paradise
To-day, I 'll warrant.
I know the tide that 's on the rise
Will seem a torrent;
I know just how the leafy boughs
Are all a-quiver;
I know how many skiffs and scows
Are on the river.
I think I 'll just go out awhile
Before I write it;
When Nature shows us such a smile,
We should n't slight it.
For Nature always makes desire
By giving pleasure;
And so 't will help me put more fire
Into my measure.

[*On the River.*]

The river 's fine, I 'm glad I came,
That poem 's teasing;
But health is better far than fame,
Though cheques are pleasing.

I don't know what I did it for,—
This air 's a poppy.
I 'm sorry for my editor,—
He 'll get no copy!

THE WARRIOR'S PRAYER

Long since, in sore distress, I heard one pray,
"Lord, who prevailest with resistless might,
Ever from war and strife keep me away,
My battles fight!"

I know not if I play the Pharisee,
And if my brother after all be right;
But mine shall be the warrior's plea to thee —
Strength for the fight.

I do not ask that thou shalt front the fray,
And drive the warring foeman from my sight;
I only ask, O Lord, by night, by day,
Strength for the fight!

When foes upon me press, let me not quail
Nor think to turn me into coward flight.
I only ask, to make mine arms prevail,
Strength for the fight!

Still let mine eyes look ever on the foe,
Still let mine armor case me strong and bright;
And grant me, as I deal each righteous blow,
Strength for the fight!

And when, at eventide, the fray is done,
My soul to Death's bedchamber do thou light,
And give me, be the field or lost or won,
Rest from the fight!

FAREWELL TO ARCADY

With sombre mien, the Evening gray
Comes nagging at the heels of Day,
And driven faster and still faster
Before the dusky-mantled Master,
The light fades from her fearful eyes,
She hastens, stumbles, falls, and dies.

Beside me Amaryllis weeps;
The swelling tears obscure the deeps
Of her dark eyes, as, mistily,
The rushing rain conceals the sea.
Here, lay my tuneless reed away,—
I have no heart to tempt a lay.

I scent the perfume of the rose
Which by my crystal fountain grows.
In this sad time, are roses blowing?
And thou, my fountain, art thou flowing,

While I who watched thy waters spring
Am all too sad to smile or sing?
Nay, give me back my pipe again,
It yet shall breathe this single strain:
Farewell to Arcady!

THE VOICE OF THE BANJO

In a small and lonely cabin out of noisy traffic's way,
Sat an old man, bent and feeble, dusk of face, and hair of gray,
And beside him on the table, battered, old, and worn as he,
Lay a banjo, droning forth this reminiscent melody:

" Night is closing in upon us, friend of mine, but don't be sad;
Let us think of all the pleasures and the joys that we have had.
Let us keep a merry visage, and be happy till the last,
Let the future still be sweetened with the honey of the past.

" For I speak to you of summer nights upon the yellow sand,
When the Southern moon was sailing high and silvering all the land;
And if love tales were not sacred, there 's a tale that I could tell
Of your many nightly wanderings with a dusk and lovely belle.

" And I speak to you of care-free songs when labour's hour was o'er,
And a woman waiting for your step outside the cabin door,
And of something roly-poly that you took upon your lap,
While you listened for the stumbling, hesitating words, 'Pap, pap.'

" I could tell you of a 'possum hunt across the wooded grounds,
I could call to mind the sweetness of the baying of the hounds,
You could lift me up and smelling of the timber that 's in me,
Build again a whole green forest with the mem'ry of a tree.

" So the future cannot hurt us while we keep the past in mind,
What care I for trembling fingers, — what care you that you are blind?

Time may leave us poor and stranded, circumstance may make us bend;
But they 'll only find us mellower, won't they, comrade? — in the end."

THE STIRRUP CUP

Come, drink a stirrup cup with me,
Before we close our rouse.
You 're all aglow with wine, I know:
The master of the house,
Unmindful of our revelry,
Has drowned the carking devil care,
And slumbers in his chair.

Come, drink a cup before we start;
We 've far to ride to-night.
And Death may take the race we make,
And check our gallant flight:
But even he must play his part,
And tho' the look he wears be grim,
We 'll drink a toast to him!

For Death,— a swift old chap is he,
And swift the steed He rides.
He needs no chart o'er main or mart,
For no direction bides.
So, come, a final cup with me,
And let the soldiers' chorus swell,—
To hell with care, to hell!

A CHOICE

They please me not — these solemn songs
That hint of sermons covered up.
'T is true the world should heed its wrongs,
But in a poem let me sup,
Not simples brewed to cure or ease
Humanity's confessed disease,
But the spirit-wine of a singing line,
Or a dew-drop in a honey cup!

HUMOUR AND DIALECT

THEN AND NOW

THEN

HE loved her, and through many years,
Had paid his fair devoted court,
Until she wearied, and with sneers
Turned all his ardent love to sport.

That night within his chamber lone,
He long sat writing by his bed
A note in which his heart made moan
For love; the morning found him dead.

NOW

Like him, a man of later day
Was jilted by the maid he sought,
And from her presence turned away,
Consumed by burning, bitter thought.

He sought his room to write — a curse
Like him before and die, I ween.
Ah no, he put his woes in verse,
And sold them to a magazine.

AT CHESHIRE CHEESE

WHEN first of wise old Johnson taught,
My youthful mind its homage brought,
And made the pond'rous crusty sage
The object of a noble rage.

Nor did I think (How dense we are!)
That any day, however far,
Would find me holding, unrepelled,
The place that Doctor Johnson held!

But change has come and time has moved,
And now, applauded, unreproved,
I hold, with pardonable pride,
The place that Johnson occupied.

Conceit! Presumption! What is this?
You surely read my words amiss;
Like Johnson I,— a man of mind!
How could you ever be so blind?

No. At the ancient "Cheshire Cheese,"
Blown hither by some vagrant breeze,
To dignify my shallow wit,
In Doctor Johnson's seat I sit!

MY CORN-COB PIPE

Men may sing of their Havanas, elevating to the stars
The real or fancied virtues of their foreign-made cigars;

But I worship Nicotina at a different sort of shrine,
And she sits enthroned in glory in this corn-cob pipe of mine.

It 's as fragrant as the meadows when the clover is in bloom;
It 's as dainty as the essence of the daintiest perfume;
It 's as sweet as are the orchards when the fruit is hanging ripe,
With the sun's warm kiss upon them — is this corn-cob pipe.

Thro' the smoke about it clinging, I delight its form to trace,
Like an oriental beauty with a veil upon her face;
And my room is dim with vapour as a church when censers sway,
As I clasp it to my bosom — in a figurative way.

It consoles me in misfortune and it cheers me in distress,
And it proves a warm partaker of my pleasures in success;
So I hail it as a symbol, friendship's true and worthy type,
And I press my lips devoutly to my corn-cob pipe.

IN AUGUST

When August days are hot an' dry,
When burning copper is the sky,
I 'd rather fish than feast or fly
In airy realms serene and high.

I 'd take a suit not made for looks,
Some easily digested books,
Some flies, some lines, some bait, some hooks,
Then would I seek the bays and brooks.

I would eschew mine every task,
In Nature's smiles my soul should bask,
And I methinks no more could ask,
Except — perhaps — one little flask.

In case of accident, you know,
Or should the wind come on to blow,
Or I be chilled or capsized, so,
A flask would be the only go.

Then could I spend a happy time,—
A bit of sport, a bit of rhyme
(A bit of lemon, or of lime,
To make my bottle's contents prime).

When August days are hot an' dry,
I won't sit by an' sigh or die,
I 'll get my bottle (on the sly)
And go ahead, and fish, and lie!

THE DISTURBER

OH, what shall I do? I am wholly upset;
I am sure I 'll be jailed for a lunatic yet.
I 'll be out of a job — it 's the thing to expect
When I 'm letting my duty go by with neglect.
You may judge the extent and degree of my plight
When I 'm thinking all day and a-dreaming all night,
And a-trying my hand at a rhyme on the sly,
All on account of a sparkling eye.

There are those who say men should be strong, well-a-day!
But what constitutes strength in a man? Who shall say?
I am strong as the most when it comes to the arm.
I have aye held my own on the playground or farm.
And when I 've been tempted, I have n't been weak;
But now — why, I tremble to hear a maid speak.
I used to be bold, but now I 've grown shy,
And all on account of a sparkling eye.

There once was a time when my heart was devout,
But now my religion is open to doubt.
When parson is earnestly preaching of grace,
My fancy is busy with drawing a face,
Thro' the back of a bonnet most piously plain;
'I draw it, redraw it, and draw it again.'
While the songs and the sermon unheeded go by,—
All on account of a sparkling eye.

Oh, dear little conjurer, give o'er your wiles,
It is easy for you, you 're all blushes and smiles:
But, love of my heart, I am sorely perplexed;
I am smiling one minute and sighing the next;
And if it goes on, I 'll drop hackle and flail,
And go to the parson and tell him my tale.
I warrant he 'll find me a cure for the sigh
That you 're aye bringing forth with the glance of your eye.

EXPECTATION

YOU 'LL be wonderin' whut 's de reason
I 's a grinnin' all de time,
An' I guess you t'ink my sperits
Mus' be feelin' mighty prime.

Well, I 'fess up, I is tickled
  As a puppy at his paws.
But you need n't think I 's crazy,
  I ain' laffin' 'dout a cause.

You 's a wonderin' too, I reckon,
  Why I does n't seem to eat,
An' I notice you a lookin'
  Lak you felt completely beat
When I 'fuse to tek de bacon,
  An' don' settle on de ham.
Don' you feel no feah erbout me,
  Jes' keep eatin', an' be ca'm.

Fu' I 's waitin' an' I 's watchin'
  'Bout a little t'ing I see —
D' othah night I 's out a walkin'
  An' I passed a 'simmon tree.
Now I 's whettin' up my hongry,
  An' I 's laffin' fit to kill,
Fu' de fros' done turned de 'simmons,
  An' de possum 's eat his fill.

He done go'ged hisse'f owdacious,
  An' he stayin' by de tree!
Don' you know, ol' Mistah Possum
  Dat you gittin' fat fu' me?
'T ain't no use to try to 'spute it,
  'Case I knows you 's gittin' sweet
Wif dat 'simmon flavoh thoo you,
  So I 's waitin' fu' yo' meat.

An' some ebenin' me an Towsah
  Gwine to come an' mek a call,
We jes' drap in onexpected
  Fu' to shek yo' han', dat 's all.
Oh, I knows dat you 'll be tickled,
  Seems lak I kin see you smile,
So pu'haps I mought pu'suade you
  Fu' to visit us a while.

LOVER'S LANE

SUMMAH night an' sighin' breeze,
  'Long de lovah's lane;
Frien'ly, shadder-mekin' trees,
  'Long de lovah's lane.
White folks' wo'k all done up gran'—
Me an' 'Mandy han'-in-han'
Struttin' lak we owned de lan',
  'Long de lovah's lane.

Owl a-settin' 'side de road,
  'Long de lovah's lane,
Lookin' at us lak he knowed
  Dis uz lovah's lane.
Go on, hoot yo' mou'nful tune,
You ain' nevah loved in June,
An' come hidin' f'om de moon
  Down in lovah's lane.

Bush it ben' an' nod an' sway,
  Down in lovah's lane,
Try'n' to hyeah me whut I say
  'Long de lovah's lane.
But I whispahs low lak dis,
An' my 'Mandy smile huh bliss —
Mistah Bush he shek his fis',
  Down in lovah's lane.

Whut I keer ef day is long,
  Down in lovah's lane.
I kin allus sing a song
  'Long de lovah's lane.
An' de wo'ds I hyeah an' say
Meks up fu' de weary day
W'en I 's strollin' by de way,
  Down in lovah's lane.

An' dis t'ought will allus rise
  Down in lovah's lane;
Wondah whethah in de skies
  Dey 's a lovah's lane.
Ef dey ain't, I tell you true,
'Ligion do look mighty blue,
'Cause I do' know whut I 'd do
  'Dout a lovah's lane.

PROTEST

Who say my hea't ain't true to you?
  Dey bettah heish dey mouf.
I knows I loves you thoo an' thoo
  In watah time er drouf.
I wush dese people 'd stop dey talkin',
Don't mean no mo' dan chicken's squawkin':
I guess I knows which way I 's walkin',
  I knows de norf f'om souf.

I does not love Elizy Brown,
  I guess I knows my min'.
You allus try to tek me down
  Wid evaht'ing you fin'.
Ef dese hyeah folks will keep on fillin'
Yo' haid wid nonsense, an' you 's willin'
I bet some day dey 'll be a killin'
  Somewhaih along de line.

O' cose I buys de gal ice-cream,
  Whut else I gwine to do?
I knows jes' how de t'ing 'u'd seem
  Ef I 'd be sho't wid you.
On Sunday, you 's at chu'ch a-shoutin',
Den all de week you go 'roun' poutin'—
I 's mighty tiahed o' all dis doubtin',
  I tell you cause I 's true.

HYMN

O li'l' lamb out in de col',
De Mastah call you to de fol',
    O li'l' lamb!
He hyeah you bleatin' on de hill;
Come hyeah an' keep yo' mou'nin' still,
    O li'l' lamb!

De Mastah sen' de Shepud fo'f;
He wandah souf, he wandah no'f,
    O li'l' lamb!
He wandah eas', he wandah wes';
De win' a-wrenchin' at his breas',
    O li'l' lamb!

Oh, tell de Shepud whaih you hide;
He want you walkin' by his side,
O li'l' lamb!
He know you weak, he know you so';
But come, don' stay away no mo',
O li'l' lamb!

An' af'ah while de lamb he hyeah
De Shepud's voice a-callin' cleah —
Sweet li'l' lamb!
He answah f'om de brambles thick,
" O Shepud, I 's a-comin' quick "—
O li'l' lamb!

LITTLE BROWN BABY

Little brown baby wif spa'klin' eyes,
Come to yo' pappy an' set on his knee.
What you been doin', suh — makin' san' pies?
Look at dat bib — you 's ez du'ty ez me.
Look at dat mouf — dat 's merlasses, I bet;
Come hyeah, Maria, an' wipe off his han's.
Bees gwine to ketch you an' eat you up yit,
Bein' so sticky an sweet — goodness lan's!

Little brown baby wif spa'klin' eyes,
Who 's pappy's darlin' an' who 's pappy's chile?
Who is it all de day nevah once tries
Fu' to be cross, er once loses dat smile?
Whah did you git dem teef? My, you 's a scamp!
Whah did dat dimple come f'om in yo' chin?
Pappy do' know you — I b'lieves you 's a tramp;
Mammy, dis hyeah 's some ol' straggler got in!

Let 's th'ow him outen de do' in de san',
We do' want stragglers a-layin' 'roun' hyeah;
Let's gin him 'way to de big buggah-man;
I know he 's hidin' erroun' hyeah right neah.
Buggah-man, buggah-man, come in de do',
Hyeah 's a bad boy you kin have fu' to eat.
Mammy an' pappy do' want him no mo',
Swaller him down f'om his haid to his feet!

Dah, now, I t'ought dat you 'd hug me up close.
Go back, ol' buggah, you sha'n't have dis boy.
He ain't no tramp, ner no straggler, of co'se;
He 's pappy's pa'dner an' playmate an' joy.

Come to you' pallet now — go to yo' res';
Wisht you could allus know ease an' cleah skies;
Wisht you could stay jes' a chile on my breas'—
Little brown baby wif spa'klin' eyes!

TIME TO TINKER 'ROUN'!

SUMMAH 's nice, wif sun a-shinin',
Spring is good wif greens and grass,
An' dey 's some t'ings nice 'bout wintah,
Dough hit brings de freezin' blas;
But de time dat is de fines',
Whethah fiel's is green er brown,
Is w'en de rain 's a-po'in'
An' dey 's time to tinker 'roun.

Den you men's de mule's ol' ha'ness,
An' you men's de broken chair.
Hummin' all de time you 's wo'kin'
Some ol' common kind o' air.
Evah now an' then you looks out,
Tryin' mighty ha'd to frown,
But you cain't, you 's glad hit 's rainin',
An' dey 's time to tinker 'roun'.

Oh, you 'ten's lak you so anxious
Evah time it so't o' stops.
W'en hit goes on, den you reckon
Dat de wet 'll he'p de crops.
But hit ain't de crops you 's aftah;
You knows w'en de rain comes down
Dat 's hit 's too wet out fu' wo'kin',
An' dey 's time to tinker roun'.

Oh, dey 's fun inside de co'n-crib,
An' dey 's laffin' at de ba'n;
An' dey 's allus some one jokin',
Er some one to tell a ya'n.
Dah 's a quiet in yo' cabin,
Only fu' de rain's sof' soun';
So you 's mighty blessed happy
W'en dey 's time to tinker 'roun'!

THE REAL QUESTION

FOLKS is talkin' 'bout de money, 'bout de silvah an' de gold;
All de time de season 's changin' an' de days is gittin' cold.
An' dey 's wond'rin' 'bout de metals, whethah we'll have one er two.
While de price o' coal is risin' an' dey 's two months' rent dat 's due.

Some folks says dat gold 's de only money dat is wuff de name,
Den de othahs rise an' tell 'em dat dey ought to be ashame,

An' dat silvah is de only thing to save us f'om de powah
Of de gold-bug ragin' 'roun' an' seekin' who he may devowah.

Well, you folks kin keep on shoutin' wif yo' gold er silvah cry,
But I tell you people hams is sceerce an' fowls is roostin' high.
An' hit ain't de so't o' money dat is pesterin' my min',
But de question I want answehed 's how to get at any kin'!

JILTED

LUCY done gone back on me,
  Dat 's de way wif life.
Evaht'ing was movin' free,
  T'ought I had my wife.
Den some dahky comes along,
Sings my gal a little song,
Since den, evaht'ing 's gone wrong,
  Evah day dey 's strife.

Did n't answeh me to-day,
  W'en I called huh name,
Would you t'ink she 'd ac' dat way
  W'en I ain't to blame?
Dat 's de way dese women do,
W'en dey fin's a fellow true,
Den dey 'buse him thoo an' thoo;
  Well, hit 's all de same.

Somep'n's wrong erbout my lung,
  An' I 's glad hit 's so.
Doctah says 'at I 'll die young,
  Well, I wants to go!
Whut 's de use o' livin' hyeah,
W'en de gal you loves so deah,
Goes back on you clean an' cleah —
  I sh'd like to know?

THE NEWS

WHUT dat you whisperin' keepin' f'om me?
Don't shut me out 'cause I 's ol' an' can't see.
Somep'n's gone wrong dat 's a-causin' you dread,—
Don't be afeared to tell — Whut! mastah dead?

Somebody brung de news early to-day,—
One of de sojers he led, do you say?
Did n't he foller whah ol' mastah lead?
How kin he live w'en his leadah is dead?

Let me lay down awhile, dah by his bed;
I wants to t'ink,— hit ain't cleah in my head: —
Killed while a-leadin' his men into fight,—
Dat 's whut you said, ain't it, did I hyeah right?

Mastah, my mastah, dead dah in de fiel'?
Lif' me up some,— dah, jes' so I kin kneel.
I was too weak to go wid him, dey said,
Well, now I 'll — fin' him — so — mastah is dead.

Yes, suh, I 's comin' ez fas' ez I kin,—
'T was kin' o' da'k, but hit 's lightah agin:
P'omised yo' pappy I 'd allus tek keer
Of you,— yes, mastah,— I 's follerin',— hyeah!

CHRISMUS ON THE PLANTATION

It was Chrismus Eve, I mind hit fu' a mighty gloomy day —
Bofe de weathah an' de people — not a one of us was gay;
Cose you 'll t'ink dat 's mighty funny 'twell I try to mek hit cleah,
Fu' a da'ky 's allus happy when de holidays is neah.

But we was n't, fu' dat mo'nin' Mastah 'd tol' us we mus' go,
He 'd been payin' us sence freedom, but he could n't pay no mo';
He wa'n't nevah used to plannin' 'fo' he got so po' an' ol',
So he gwine to give up tryin', an' de homestead mus' be sol'.

I kin see him stan'in' now erpon de step ez cleah ez day,
Wid de win' a-kind o' fondlin' thoo his haih all thin an' gray;
An' I 'membah how he trimbled when he said, " It 's ha'd fu' me,
Not to mek yo' Chrismus brightah, but I 'low it wa'n't to be."

All de women was a-cryin', an' de men, too, on de sly,
An' I noticed somep'n shinin' even in ol' Mastah's eye.
But we all stood still to listen ez ol' Ben come f'om de crowd
An' spoke up, a-try'n' to steady down his voice and mek it loud: —

" Look hyeah, Mastah, I 's been servin' you' fu' lo! dese many yeahs,
An' now, sence we 's got freedom an' you 's kind o' po', hit 'pears
Dat you want us all to leave you 'cause you don't t'ink you can pay.
Ef my membry has n't fooled me, seem dat whut I hyead you say.

"Er in othah wo'ds, you wants us to fu'git dat you 's been kin',
An' ez soon ez you is he'pless, we 's to leave you hyeah behin'.
Well, ef dat 's de way dis freedom ac's on people, white er black,
You kin jes' tell Mistah Lincum fu' to tek his freedom back.

"We gwine wo'k dis ol' plantation fu' whatevah we kin git,
Fu' I know hit did suppo't us, an' de place kin do it yit.
Now de land is yo's, de hands is ouahs, an' I reckon we 'll be brave,
An' we 'll bah ez much ez you do w'en we has to scrape an' save."

Ol' Mastah stood dah trimblin', but a-smilin' thoo his teahs,
An' den hit seemed jes' nachul-like, de place fah rung wid cheahs,
An' soon ez dey was quiet, some one sta'ted sof' an' low:
"Praise God," an' den we all jined in, "from whom all blessin's flow!"

Well, dey was n't no use tryin', ouah min's was sot to stay,
An' po' ol' Mastah could n't plead ner baig, ner drive us 'way,
An' all at once, hit seemed to us, de day was bright agin,
So evahone was gay dat night, an' watched de Chrismus in.

ANGELINA

When de fiddle gits to singin' out a ol' Vahginny reel,
An' you 'mence to feel a ticklin' in yo' toe an' in yo' heel;
Ef you t'ink you got 'uligion an' you wants to keep it, too,
You jes' bettah tek a hint an' git yo'self clean out o' view.
Case de time is mighty temptin' when de chune is in de swing,
Fu' a darky, saint or sinner man, to cut de pigeon-wing.
An' you could n't he'p f'om dancin' ef yo' feet was boun' wif twine,
When Angelina Johnson comes a-swingin' down de line.

Don't you know Miss Angelina? She 's de da'lin' of de place.
W'y, dey ain't no high-toned lady wif sich mannahs an' sich grace.
She kin move across de cabin, wif its planks all rough an' wo';
Jes' de same 's ef she was dancin' on ol' mistus' ball-room flo'.
Fact is, you do' see no cabin — evaht'ing you see look grand,
An' dat one ol' squeaky fiddle soun' to you jes' lak a ban';
Cotton britches look lak broadclof an' a linsey dress look fine,
When Angelina Johnson comes a-swingin' down de line.

Some folks say dat dancin 's sinful, an' de blessed Lawd, dey say,
Gwine to punish us fu' steppin' w'en we hyeah de music play.
But I tell you I don' b'lieve it, fu' de Lawd is wise and good,
An' he made de banjo's metal an' he made de fiddle's wood,
An' he made de music in dem, so I don' quite t'ink he 'll keer
Ef our feet keeps time a little to de melodies we hyeah.
W'y, dey 's somep'n' downright holy in de way our faces shine,
When Angelina Johnson comes a-swingin' down de line.

Angelina steps so gentle, Angelina bows so low,
An' she lif' huh sku't so dainty dat huh shoetop skacely show:
An' dem teef o' huh'n a-shinin', ez she tek you by de han'—
Go 'way, people, d' ain't anothah sich a lady in de lan'!
When she 's movin' thoo de figgers er a-dancin' by huhse'f,
Folks jes' stan' stock-still a-sta'-in', an' dey mos' nigh hol's dey bref;
An' de young mens, dey 's a-sayin', " I 's gwine mek dat damsel mine,"
When Angelina Johnson comes a-swingin' down de line.

FOOLIN' WID DE SEASONS

Seems lak folks is mighty curus
In de way dey t'inks an' ac's.
Dey jes' spen's dey days a-mixin'
Up de t'ings in almanacs.
Now, I min' my nex' do' neighbour,—
He 's a mighty likely man,
But he nevah t'inks o' nuffin
'Ceptin' jes' to plot an' plan.

All de wintah he was plannin'
How he 'd gethah sassafras
Jes' ez soon ez evah Springtime
Put some greenness in de grass.
An' he 'lowed a little soonah
He could stan' a coolah breeze
So 's to mek a little money
F'om de sugah-watah trees.

In de summah, he 'd be waihin'
Out de linin' of his soul,
Try 'n' ca'ci'late an' fashion
How he 'd git his wintah coal;
An' I b'lieve he got his jedgement
Jes' so tuckahed out an' thinned
Dat he t'ought a robin's whistle
Was de whistle of de wind.

Why won't folks gin up dey plannin',
An' jes' be content to know
Dat dey 's gittin' all dat 's fu' dem
In de days dat come an' go?
Why won't folks quit movin' forrard?
Ain't hit bettah jes' to stan'

An' be satisfied wid livin'
  In de season dat 's at han'?

Hit 's enough fu' me to listen
  W'en de birds is singin' 'roun',
'Dout a-guessin' whut 'll happen
  W'en de snow is on de groun'.
In de Springtime an' de summah,
  I lays sorrer on de she'f;
An' I knows ol' Mistah Wintah
  Gwine to hustle fu' hisse'f.

We been put hyeah fu' a pu'pose,
  But de questun dat has riz
An' made lots o' people diffah
  Is jes' whut dat pu'pose is.
Now, accordin' to my reas'nin',
  Hyeah 's de p'int whaih I 's arriv,
Sence de Lawd put life into us,
  We was put hyeah fu' to live!

MY SORT O' MAN

I DON'T believe in 'ristercrats
  An' never did, you see;
The plain ol' homelike sorter folks
  Is good enough fur me.
O' course, I don't desire a man
  To be too tarnal rough,
But then, I think all folks should know
  When they air nice enough.

Now there is folks in this here world,
  From peasant up to king,
Who want to be so awful nice
  They overdo the thing.
That 's jest the thing that makes me sick,
  An' quicker 'n a wink
I set it down that them same folks
  Ain't half so good 's you think.

I like to see a man dress nice,
  In clothes becomin' too;
I like to see a woman fix
  As women orter to do;
An' boys an' gals I like to see
  Look fresh an' young an' spry,—
We all must have our vanity
  An' pride before we die.

But I jedge no man by his clothes,—
  Nor gentleman nor tramp;
The man that wears the finest suit
  May be the biggest scamp,
An' he whose limbs air clad in rags
  That make a mournful sight,
In life's great battle may have proved
  A hero in the fight.

I don't believe in 'ristercrats;
  I like the honest tan
That lies upon the healthful cheek
  An' speaks the honest man;
I like to grasp the brawny hand
  That labor's lips have kissed,

For he who has not labored here
Life's greatest pride has missed:

The pride to feel that yore own strength
Has cleaved fur you the way
To heights to which you were not born,
But struggled day by day.
What though the thousands sneer an' scoff,
An' scorn yore humble birth?
Kings are but puppets; you are king
By right o' royal worth.

The man who simply sits an' waits
Fur good to come along,
Ain't worth the breath that one would take
To tell him he is wrong.
Fur good ain't flowin' round this world
Fur every fool to sup;
You 've got to put yore see-ers on,
An' go an' hunt it up.

Good goes with honesty, I say,
To honour an' to bless;
To rich an' poor alike it brings
A wealth o' happiness.
The 'ristercrats ain't got it all,
Fur much to their su'prise,
That 's one of earth's most blessed things
They can't monopolize.

POSSUM

Ef dey 's anyt'ing dat riles me
An' jes' gits me out o' hitch,
Twell I want to tek my coat off,
So 's to r'ar an' t'ar an' pitch,
Hit 's to see some ign'ant white man
'Mittin' dat owdacious sin —
W'en he want to cook a possum
Tekin' off de possum's skin.

W'y dey ain't no use in talkin',
Hit jes' hu'ts me to de hea't
Fu' to see dem foolish people
Th'owin' 'way de fines' pa't.
W'y, dat skin is jes' ez tendah
An' ez juicy ez kin be;
I knows all erbout de critter —
Hide an' haih — don't talk to me!

Possum skin is jes lak shoat skin;
Jes' you swinge an' scrope it down,
Tek a good sha'p knife an' sco' it,
Den you bake it good an' brown.
Huh-uh! honey, you 's so happy
Dat yo' thoughts is 'mos' a sin
When you 's settin' dah a-chawin'
On dat possum's cracklin' skin.

White folks t'ink dey know 'bout eatin',
An' I reckon dat dey do
Sometimes git a little idee
Of a middlin' dish er two;

But dey ain't a t'ing dey knows of
  Dat I reckon cain't be beat
W'en we set down at de table
  To a unskun possum's meat!

ON THE ROAD

I 's boun' to see my gal to-night —
  Oh, lone de way, my dearie!
De moon ain't out, de stars ain't bright —
  Oh, lone de way, my dearie!
Dis hoss o' mine is pow'ful slow,
But when I does git to yo' do'
Yo' kiss 'll pay me back, an' mo',
  Dough lone de way, my dearie.

De night is skeery-lak an' still —
  Oh, lone de way, my dearie!
'Cept fu' dat mou'nful whippo'-will —
  Oh, lone de way, my dearie!
De way so long wif dis slow pace,
'T 'u'd seem to me lak savin' grace
Ef you was on a nearer place,
  Fu' lone de way, my dearie.

I hyeah de hootin' of de owl —
  Oh, lone de way, my dearie!
I wish dat watch-dog would n't howl —
  Oh, lone de way, my dearie!
An' evaht'ing, bofe right an' lef',
Seem p'int'ly lak hit put itse'f
In shape to skeer me half to def —
  Oh, lone de way, my dearie!

I whistles so 's I won't be feared —
  Oh lone de way, my dearie!
But anyhow I 's kin' o' skeered,
  Fu' lone de way, my dearie.
De sky been lookin' mighty glum,
But you kin mek hit lighten some,
Ef you 'll jes' say you 's glad I come,
  Dough lone de way, my dearie.

A DEATH SONG

Lay me down beneaf de willers in de grass,
Whah de branch 'll go a-singin' as it pass.
  An' w'en I 's a-layin' low,
  I kin hyeah it as it go
Singin', " Sleep, my honey, tek yo' res' at las'."

Lay me nigh to whah hit meks a little pool,
An' de watah stan's so quiet lak an' cool,
  Whah de little birds in spring,
  Ust to come an' drink an' sing,
An' de chillen waded on dey way to school.

Let me settle w'en my shouldahs draps dey load
Nigh enough to hyeah de noises in de road;
  Fu' I t'ink de las' long res'
  Gwine to soothe my sperrit bes'
Ef I 's layin' 'mong de t'ings I 's allus knowed.

PAUL LAURENCE DUNBAR

A BACK-LOG SONG

De axes has been ringin' in de woods de blessid day,
An' de chips has been a-fallin' fa' an' thick;
Dey has cut de bigges' hick'ry dat de mules kin tote away,
An' dey 's laid hit down and soaked it in de crik.
Den dey tuk hit to de big house an' dey piled de wood erroun'
In de fiah-place f'om ash-flo' to de flue,
While ol' Ezry sta'ts de hymn dat evah yeah has got to soun'
When de back-log fus' commence a-bu'nin' thoo.

Ol' Mastah is a-smilin' on de da'kies f'om de hall,
Ol' Mistus is a-stannin' in de do',
An' de young folks, males an' misses, is a-tryin', one an' all,
Fu' to mek us feel hit 's Chrismus time fu' sho'.
An' ouah hea'ts are full of pleasure, fu' we know de time is ouahs
Fu' to dance er do jes' whut we wants to do.
An' dey ain't no ovahseer an' no othah kind o' powahs
Dat kin stop us while dat log is bu'nin thoo.

Dey 's a-wokin' in de qua'tahs a-preparin' fu' de feas',
So de little pigs is feelin' kind o' shy.
De chickens ain't so trus'ful ez dey was, to say de leas',
An' de wise ol' hens is roostin' mighty high.
You could n't git a gobblah fu' to look you in de face —
I ain't sayin' whut de tu'ky 'spects is true;
But hit 's mighty dange'ous trav'lin' fu' de critters on de place
F'om de time dat log commence a bu'nin' thoo.

Some one 's tunin' up his fiddle dah, I hyeah a banjo's ring,
An', bless me, dat 's de tootin' of a ho'n!
Now dey 'll evah one be runnin' dat has got a foot to fling,
An' dey 'll dance an' frolic on f'om now 'twell mo'n.
Plunk de banjo, scrap de fiddle, blow dat ho'n yo' level bes',
Keep yo' min' erpon de chune an' step it true.
Oh, dey ain't no time fu' stoppin' an' dey ain't no time fu' res',
Fu' hit 's Chrismus an' de back-log 's bu'nin' thoo!

LULLABY

Bedtime 's come fu' little boys.
Po' little lamb.
Too tiahed out to make a noise,
Po' little lamb.
You gwine t' have to-morrer sho'?
Yes, you tole me dat befo',
Don't you fool me, chile, no mo',
Po' little lamb.

You been bad de livelong day,
Po' little lamb.
Th'owin' stones an' runnin' 'way,
Po' little lamb.
My, but you 's a-runnin' wil',
Look jes' lak some po' folks chile;
Mam' gwine whup you atter while,
Po' little lamb.

Come hyeah! you mos' tiahed to def,
Po' little lamb.
Played yo'se'f clean out o' bref,
Po' little lamb.
See dem han's now — sich a sight!
Would you evah b'lieve dey's white?
Stan' still twell I wash 'em right,
Po' little lamb.

Jes' cain't hol' yo' haid up straight,
Po' little lamb.
Had n't oughter played so late,
Po' little lamb.
Mammy do' know whut she 'd do,
Ef de chillun's all lak you;
You 's a caution now fu' true,
Po' little lamb.

Lay yo' haid down in my lap,
Po' little lamb.
Y' ought to have a right good slap,
Po' little lamb.
You been runnin' roun' a heap.
Shet dem eyes an' don't you peep,
Dah now, dah now, go to sleep,
Po' little lamb.

THE PHOTOGRAPH

See dis pictyah in my han'?
Dat 's my gal;
Ain't she purty? goodness lan'!
Huh name Sal.
Dat 's de very way she be —
Kin' o' tickles me to see
Huh a-smilin' back at me.

She sont me dis photygraph
Jes' las' week;
An' aldough hit made me laugh —
My black cheek
Felt somethin' a-runnin' queer;
Bless yo' soul, it was a tear
Jes' f'om wishin' she was here.

Often when I 's all alone
Layin' here,
I git t'inkin' 'bout my own
Sallie dear;
How she say dat I 's huh beau,
An' hit tickles me to know
Dat de gal do love me so.

Some bright day I 's goin' back,
Fo' de la!

An' ez sho' 's my face is black,
  Ax huh pa
Fu' de blessed little miss
Who 's a-smilin' out o dis
Pictyah, lak she wan'ed a kiss!

JEALOUS

Hyeah come Cæsar Higgins,
Don't he think he 's fine?
Look at dem new riggin's
Ain't he tryin' to shine?
Got a standin' collar
An' a stove-pipe hat,
I 'll jes' bet a dollar
Some one gin him dat.

Don't one o' you mention,
Nothin' 'bout his cloes,
Don't pay no attention,
Er let on you knows
Dat he 's got 'em on him,
Why, 't 'll mek him sick,
Jes go on an' sco'n him,
My, ain't dis a trick!

Look hyeah, whut 's he doin'
Lookin' t' othah way?
Dat ere move 's a new one,
Some one call him, " Say! "
Can't you see no pusson —
Puttin' on you' airs,
Sakes alive, you 's wuss'n
Dese hyeah millionaires.

Need n't git so flighty,
Case you got dat suit.
Dem cloes ain't so mighty,—
Second hand to boot,
I 's a-tryin' to spite you!
Full of jealousy!
Look hyeah, man, I 'll fight
  you,
Don't you fool wid me!

PARTED

De breeze is blowin' 'cross de bay.
  My lady, my lady;
De ship hit teks me far away,
  My lady, my lady;
Ole Mas' done sol' me down de
  stream;
Dey tell me 't ain't so bad 's hit
  seem,
  My lady, my lady.

O' co'se I knows dat you 'll be
  true,
  My lady, my lady;
But den I do' know whut to do,
  My lady, my lady;
I knowed some day we 'd have to
  pa't,
But den hit put' nigh breaks my
  hea't,
  My lady, my lady.

De day is long, de night is black,
  My lady, my lady;
I know you 'll wait twell I come
  back,
  My lady, my lady;
I 'll stan' de ship, I 'll stan' de
  chain,

But I 'll come back, my darlin' Jane,
My lady, my lady.

Jes' wait, jes' b'lieve in whut I say,
My lady, my lady;
D' ain't nothin' dat kin keep me 'way,
My lady, my lady;
A man 's a man, an' love is love;
God knows ouah hea'ts, my little dove;
He 'll he'p us f'om his th'one above,
My lady, my lady.

TEMPTATION

I DONE got 'uligion, honey, an' I 's happy ez a king;
Evahthing I see erbout me 's jes' lak sunshine in de spring;
An' it seems lak I do' want to do anothah blessid thing
But jes' run an' tell de neighbours, an' to shout an' pray an' sing.

I done shuk my fis' at Satan, an' I 's gin de worl' my back;
I do' want no hendrin' causes now a-both'rin' in my track;
Fu' I 's on my way to glory, an' I feels too sho' to miss.
W'y, dey ain't no use in sinnin' when 'uligion 's sweet ez dis.

Talk erbout a man backslidin' w'en he 's on de gospel way;
No, suh, I done beat de debbil, an' Temptation 's los' de day.
Gwine to keep my eyes right straight up, gwine to shet my eahs, an' see
Whut ole projick Mistah Satan 's gwine to try to wuk on me.

Listen, whut dat soun' I hyeah dah? 'tain't no one commence to sing;
It 's a fiddle; git erway dah! don' you hyeah dat blessid thing?
W'y, dat 's sweet ez drippin' honey, 'cause, you knows, I draws de bow,
An' when music 's sho' 'nough music, I 's de one dat 's sho' to know.

W'y, I 's done de double shuffle, twell a body could n't res',
Jes' a-hyeahin' Sam de fiddlah play dat chune his level bes';
I could cut a mighty caper, I could gin a mighty fling
Jes' right now, I 's mo' dan suttain I could cut de pigeon wing.

Look hyeah, whut 's dis I 's been sayin'? whut on urf 's tuk holt o' me?
Dat ole music come nigh runnin' my 'uligion up a tree!

Cleah out wif dat dah ole fiddle,
don' you try dat trick agin;
Did n't think I could be tempted,
but you lak to made me sin!

POSSUM TROT

I 've journeyed 'roun' consid'able,
a-seein' men an' things,
An' I 've learned a little of the
sense that meetin' people
brings;
But in spite of all my travellin',
an' of all I think I know,
I 've got one notion in my head,
that I can't git to go;
An' it is that the folks I meet in
any other spot
Ain't half so good as them I
knowed back home in Possum
Trot.

I know you 've never heerd the
name, it ain't a famous
place,
An' I reckon ef you 'd search the
map you could n't find a trace
Of any sich locality as this I 've
named to you;
But never mind, I know the place,
an' I love it dearly too.
It don't make no pretensions to
bein' great or fine,
The circuses don't come that way,
they ain't no railroad line.
It ain't no great big city, where
the schemers plan an' plot,
But jest a little settlement, this
place called Possum Trot.

But don't you think the folks that
lived in that outlandish place
Were ignorant of all the things
that go for sense or grace.
Why, there was Hannah Dyer, you
may search this teemin' earth
An' never find a sweeter girl, er
one o' greater worth;
An' Uncle Abner Williams, a-
leanin' on his staff,
It seems like I kin hear him talk,
an' hear his hearty laugh.
His heart was big an' cheery as a
sunny acre lot,
Why, that 's the kind o' folks we
had down there at Possum
Trot.

Good times? Well, now, to suit
my taste,— an' I 'm some hard
to suit,—
There ain't been no sich pleasure
sence, an' won't be none to
boot,
With huskin' bees in Harvest time,
an' dances later on,
An' singin' school, an taffy pulls,
an' fun from night till
dawn.
Revivals come in winter time, bap-
tizin's in the spring,
You 'd ought to seen those people
shout, an' heerd 'em pray an'
sing;

You 'd ought to 've heard ole Parson Brown a-throwin' gospel shot
Among the saints an' sinners in the days of Possum Trot.

We live up in the city now, my wife was bound to come;
I hear aroun' me day by day the endless stir an' hum.
I reckon that it done me good, an' yet it done me harm,
That oil was found so plentiful down there on my ole farm.
We 've got a new-styled preacher, our church is new-styled too,
An' I 've come down from what I knowed to rent a cushioned pew.
But often when I 'm settin' there, it 's foolish, like as not,
To think of them ol' benches in the church at Possum Trot.

I know that I 'm ungrateful, an' sich thoughts must be a sin,
But I find myself a wishin' that the times was back agin.
With the huskin's an' the frolics, an' the joys I used to know,
When I lived at the settlement, a dozen years ago.
I don't feel this way often, I 'm scarcely ever glum,
For life has taught me how to take her chances as they come.
But now an' then my mind goes back to that ol' buryin' plot,
That holds the dust of some I loved, down there at Possum Trot.

DELY

Jes' lak toddy wahms you thoo'
Sets yo' haid a reelin',
Meks you ovah good and new,
Dat 's de way I 's feelin'.
Seems to me hit's summah time,
Dough hit 's wintah reely,
I 's a feelin' jes' dat prime —
An' huh name is Dely.

Dis hyeah love 's a cu'rus thing,
Changes 'roun' de season,
Meks you sad or meks you sing,
'Dout no urfly reason.
Sometimes I go mopin' 'roun',
Den agin I 's leapin';
Sperits allus up an' down
Even when I 's sleepin'.

Fu' de dreams comes to me den,
An' dey keeps me pitchin',
Lak de apple dumplin's w'en
Bilin' in de kitchen.
Some one sot to do me hahm,
Tryin' to ovahcome me,
Ketchin' Dely by de ahm
So 's to tek huh f'om me.

Mon, you bettah b'lieve I fights
(Dough hit 's on'y seemin');
I 's a hittin' fu' my rights
Even w'en I 's dreamin'.

But I 'd let you have 'em all,
Give 'em to you freely,
Good an' bad ones, great an' small,
So 's you leave me Dely.

Dely got dem meltin' eyes,
Big an' black an' tendah.
Dely jes' a lady-size,
Delikit an' slendah.
Dely brown ez brown kin be
An' huh haih is curly;
Oh, she look so sweet to me,—
Bless de precious girlie!

Dely brown ez brown kin be,
She ain' no mullatter;
She pure cullud,— don' you see
Dat 's jes' whut 's de mattah?
Dat 's de why I love huh so,
D' ain't no mix about huh,
Soon 's you see huh face you know
D' ain't no chanst to doubt huh.

Folks dey go to chu'ch an' pray
So 's to git a blessin'.
Oomph, dey bettah come my way,
Dey could lu'n a lesson.
Sabbaf day I don' go fu',
Jes' to see my pigeon;
I jes' sets an' looks at huh,
Dat 's enuff 'uligion.

BREAKING THE CHARM

Caught Susanner whistlin'; well,
It 's most nigh too good to tell.
'Twould 'a' b'en too good to see
Ef it had n't b'en fur me,
Comin' up so soft an' sly
That she didn' hear me nigh.
I was pokin' 'round that day,
An' ez I come down the way,
First her whistle strikes my ears,—
Then her gingham dress appears;
So with soft step up I slips.
Oh, them dewy, rosy lips!
Ripe ez cherries, red an' round,
Puckered up to make the sound.
She was lookin' in the spring,
Whistlin' to beat anything,—
"Kitty Dale" er "In the Sweet."
I was jest so mortal beat
That I can't quite ricoleck
What the toon was, but I 'speck
'T was some hymn er other, fur
Hymny things is jest like her.
Well she went on fur awhile
With her face all in a smile,
An' I never moved, but stood
Stiller 'n a piece o' wood —
Would n't wink ner would n't stir,
But a-gazin' right at her,
Tell she turns an' sees me — my!
Thought at first she 'd try to fly.
But she blushed an' stood her ground.
Then, a-slyly lookin' round,
She says: "Did you hear me, Ben?"
"Whistlin' woman, crowin' hen,"
Says I, lookin' awful stern.
Then the red commenced to burn
In them cheeks o' hern. Why, la!
Reddest red you ever saw —
Pineys wa'n't a circumstance.

You 'd 'a' noticed in a glance
She was pow'rful shamed an' skeart;
But she looked so sweet an' peart,
That a idee struck my head;
So I up an' slowly said:
"Woman whistlin' brings shore harm,
Jest one thing 'll break the charm."
"And what 's that?" "Oh, my!" says I,
"I don't like to tell you." "Why?"
Says Susanner. "Well, you see
It would kinder fall on me."
Course I knowed that she 'd insist,—
So I says: "You must be kissed
By the man that heard you whistle;
Everybody says that this 'll
Break the charm and set you free
From the threat'nin' penalty."
She was blushin' fit to kill,
But she answered, kinder still:
"I don't want to have no harm,
Please come, Ben, an' break the charm."
Did I break that charm?—oh, well,
There 's some things I must n't tell.
I remember, afterwhile,
Her a-sayin' with a smile:
"Oh, you quit,—you sassy dunce,
You jest caught me whistlin' *once*."
Ev'ry sence that when I hear
Some one whistlin' kinder clear,
I most break my neck to see
Ef it 's Susy; but, dear me,
I jest find I 've b'en to chase
Some blamed boy about the place.
Dad 's b'en noticin' my way,
An' last night I heerd him say:
"We must send fur Dr. Glenn,
Mother; somethin 's wrong with Ben!"

HUNTING SONG

Tek a cool night, good an' cleah,
Skiff o' snow upon de groun';
Jes' 'bout fall-time o' de yeah
W'en de leaves is dry an brown;
Tek a dog an' tek a axe,
Tek a lantu'n in yo' han',
Step light whah de switches cracks,
Fu' dey 's huntin' in de lan'.
Down thoo de valleys an' ovah de hills,
Into de woods whah de 'simmon-tree grows,
Wakin' an' skeerin' de po' whip-po'wills,
Huntin' fu' coon an' fu' 'possum we goes.

Blow dat ho'n dah loud an' strong,
Call de dogs an' da'kies neah;
Mek its music cleah an' long,
So de folks at home kin hyeah.

Blow it twell de hills an' trees
Sen's de echoes tumblin' back;
Blow it twell de back'ard breeze
Tells de folks we 's on de track.
Coons is a-ramblin' an' 'possums is out;
Look at dat dog; you could set on his tail!
Watch him now — steady,— min' — what you 's about,
Bless me, dat animal 's got on de trail!

Listen to him ba'kin now!
Dat means bus'ness, sho 's you bo'n;
Ef he 's struck de scent I 'low
Dat ere 'possum 's sholy gone.
Knowed dat dog fu' fo'teen yeahs,
An' I nevah seed him fail
W'en he sot dem flappin' eahs
An' went off upon a trail.
Run, Mistah 'Possum, an' run, Mistah Coon,
No place is safe fu' yo' ramblin' to-night;
Mas' gin' de lantu'n an' God gin de moon,
An' a long hunt gins a good appetite.

Look hyeah, folks, you hyeah dat change?
Dat ba'k is sha'per dan de res'.
Dat ere soun' ain't nothin' strange,—
Dat dog 's talked his level bes'.
Somep'n' 's treed, I know de soun'.
Dah now,— wha 'd I tell you? see!
Dat ere dog done run him down;
Come hyeah, he'p cut down dis tree.
Ah, Mistah 'Possum, we got you at las'—
Need n't play daid, laying dah on de groun';
Fros' an' de 'simmons has made you grow fas',—
Won't he be fine when he 's roasted up brown!

A LETTER

DEAR MISS LUCY: I been t'inkin' dat I 'd write you long fo' dis,
But dis writin' 's mighty tejous, an' you know jes' how it is.
But I 's got a little lesure, so I teks my pen in han'
Fu' to let you know my feelin's since I retched dis furrin' lan'.
I 's right well, I 's glad to tell you (dough dis climate ain't to blame),
An' I hopes w'en dese lines reach you, dat dey 'll fin' yo' se'f de same.
Cose I 'se feelin kin' o' homesick — dat 's ez nachul ez kin be,

W'en a feller 's mo'n th'ee thousand miles across dat awful sea.
(Don't you let nobidy fool you 'bout de ocean bein' gran';
If you want to see de billers, you jes' view dem f'om de lan'.)
'Bout de people? We been t'inkin' dat all white folks was alak;
But dese Englishmen is diffunt, an' dey 's curus fu' a fac'.
Fust, dey 's heavier an' redder in dey make-up an' dey looks,
An' dey don't put salt nor pepper in a blessed t'ing dey cooks!
W'en dey gin you good ol' tu'nips, ca'ots, pa'snips, beets, an' sich,
Ef dey ain't some one to tell you, you cain't 'stinguish which is which.
W'en I t'ought I 's eatin' chicken — you may b'lieve dis hyeah 's a lie —
But de waiter beat me down dat I was eatin' rabbit pie.
An' dey 'd t'ink dat you was crazy — jes' a reg'lar ravin' loon,
Ef you 'd speak erbout a 'possum or a piece o' good ol' coon.
O, hit 's mighty nice, dis trav'lin', an' I 's kin' o' glad I come.
But, I reckon, now I 's willin' fu' to tek my way back home.
I done see de Crystal Palace, an' I 's hyeahd dey string-band play,
But I has n't seen no banjos layin' nowhahs roun' dis way.
Jes' gin ol' Jim Bowles a banjo, an' he 'd not go very fu',
'Fo' he 'd outplayed all dese fiddlers, wif dey flourish and dey stir.
Evahbiddy dat I 's met wif has been monst'ous kin an' good;
But I t'ink I 'd lak it better to be down in Jones's wood,
Where we ust to have sich frolics, Lucy, you an' me an' Nelse,
Dough my appetite 'ud call me, ef dey was n't nuffin else.
I 'd jes' lak to have some sweet-pertaters roasted in de skin;
I 's a-longin' fu' my chittlin's an' my mustard greens ergin;
I 's a-wishin' fu' some buttermilk, an' co'n braid, good an' brown,
An' a drap o' good ol' bourbon fu' to wash my feelin's down!
An' I 's comin' back to see you jes' as ehly as I kin,
So you better not go spa'kin' wif dat wuffless scoun'el Quin!
Well, I reckon, I mus' close now; write ez soon 's dis reaches you;
Gi' my love to Sister Mandy an' to Uncle Isham, too.
Tell de folks I sen' 'em howdy; gin a kiss to pap an' mam;
Closin' I is, deah Miss Lucy,
Still Yo' Own True-Lovin' SAM.

P. S. Ef you cain't mek out dis
letter, lay it by erpon de she'f,
An' when I git home, I 'll read
it, darlin', to you my own se'f.

CHRISMUS IS A-COMIN'

Bones a-gittin' achy,
Back a-feelin' col',
Han's a-growin' shaky,
Jes' lak I was ol'.
Fros' erpon de meddah
Lookin' mighty white;
Snowdraps lak a feddah
Slippin' down at night.
Jes' keep t'ings a-hummin'
Spite o' fros' an' showahs,
Chrismus is a-comin'
An' all de week is ouahs.

Little mas' a-axin',
"Who is Santy Claus?"
Meks it kin' o' taxin'
Not to brek de laws.
Chillun 's pow'ful tryin'
To a pusson's grace
W'en dey go a pryin'
Right on th'oo you' face
Down ermong yo' feelin's;
Jes' 'pears lak dat you
Got to change you' dealin's
So 's to tell 'em true.

An' my pickaninny—
Dreamin' in his sleep!
Come hyeah, Mammy Jinny,
Come an' tek a peep.
Ol' Mas' Bob an' Missis
In dey house up daih
Got no chile lak dis is,
D' ain't none anywhaih.
Sleep, my little lammy,
Sleep, you little limb,
He do' know whut mammy
Done saved up fu' him.

Dey 'll be banjo pickin',
Dancin' all night thoo.
Dey 'll be lots o' chicken,
Plenty tukky, too.
Drams to wet yo' whistles
So 's to drive out chills.
Whut I keer fu' drizzles
Fallin' on de hills?
Jes' keep t'ings a-hummin'
Spite o' col' an' showahs,
Chrismus day 's a-comin',
An' all de week is ouahs

A CABIN TALE

THE YOUNG MASTER ASKS FOR A STORY

Whut you say, dah? huh, uh! chile,
You 's enough to dribe me wile.
Want a sto'y; jes' hyeah dat!
Whah' 'll I git a sto'y at?
Di'n' I tell you th'ee las' night?
Go 'way, honey, you ain't right.
I got somep'n' else to do,
'Cides jes' tellin' tales to you.
Tell you jes' one? Lem me see
Whut dat one 's a-gwine to be.

When you 's ole, yo membry fails;
Seems lak I do' know no tales.
Well, set down dah in dat cheer,
Keep still ef you wants to hyeah.
Tek dat chin up off yo' han's,
Set up nice now. Goodness lan's!
Hol' yo'se'f up lak yo' pa.
Bet nobidy evah saw
Him scrunched down lak you was
den —
High-tone boys meks high-tone
men.

Once dey was a ole black bah,
Used to live 'roun' hyeah some-
whah
In a cave. He was so big
He could ca'y off a pig
Lak you picks a chicken up,
Er yo' leetles' bit o' pup.
An' he had two gread big eyes,
Jes' erbout a saucer's size.
Why, dey looked lak balls o' fiah
Jumpin' 'roun' erpon a wiah
W'en dat bah was mad; an' laws!
But you ought to seen his paws!
Did I see 'em? How you 'spec
I 's a-gwine to ricollec'
Dis hyeah ya'n I 's try'n' to spin
Ef you keeps on puttin' in?
You keep still an' don't you cheep
Less I 'll sen' you off to sleep.
Dis hyeah bah 'd go trompin'
'roun'
Eatin' evahthing he foun';
No one could n't have a fa'm
But dat bah 'u'd do' em ha'm;
And dey could n't ketch de scamp.
Anywhah he wan'ed to tramp.
Dah de scoun'el 'd mek his track,
Do his du't an' come on back.
He was sich a sly ole limb,
Traps was jes' lak fun to him.

Now, down neah whah Mistah
Bah
Lived, dey was a weasel dah;
But dey was n't fren's a-tall
Case de weasel was so small.
An' de bah 'u'd, jes' fu' sass,
Tu'n his nose up w'en he 'd pass.
Weasels 's small o' cose, but my!
Dem air animiles is sly.
So dis hyeah one says, says he,
"I 'll jes' fix dat bah, you see."
So he fixes up his plan
An' hunts up de fa'merman.
When de fa'mer see him come,
He 'mence lookin' mighty glum,
An' he ketches up a stick;
But de weasel speak up quick:
"Hol' on, Mistah Fa'mer man,
I wan' 'splain a little plan.
Ef you waits, I 'll tell you whah
An' jes' how to ketch ol' Bah.
But I tell yow now you mus'
Gin me one fat chicken fus'."
Den de man he scratch his haid,
Las' he say, "I'll mek de trade."
So de weasel et his hen,
Smacked his mouf and says,
"Well, den,
Set yo' trap an' bait ternight,
An' I 'll ketch de bah all right."

Den he ups an' goes to see
Mistah Bah, an' says, says he:
" Well, fren' Bah, we *ain't* been fren's,
But ternight ha'd feelin' 'en's.
Ef you ain't too proud to steal,
We kin git a splendid meal.
Cose I would n't come to you,
But it mus' be done by two;
Hit 's a trap, but we kin beat
All dey tricks an' git de meat."
" Cose I 's wif you," says de bah,
" Come on, weasel, show me whah."
Well, dey trots erlong ontwell
Dat air meat beginned to smell
In de trap. Den weasel say:
" Now you put yo' paw dis way
While I hol' de spring back so,
Den you grab de meat an' go."
Well, de bah he had to grin
Ez he put his big paw in,
Den he juked up, but — kerbing!
Weasel done let go de spring.
" Dah now," says de weasel, " dah,
I done cotched you, Mistah Bah! "
O, dat bah did sno't and spout,
Try'n' his bestes' to git out,
But de weasel say, " Goo'-bye!
Weasel small, but weasel sly."
Den he tu'ned his back an' run
Tol' de fa'mer whut he done.
So de fa'mer come down dah,
Wif a axe and killed de bah.

Dah now, ain't dat sto'y fine?
Run erlong now, nevah min'.
Want some mo', you rascal, you?
No, suh! no, suh! dat 'll do.

AT CANDLE-LIGHTIN' TIME

WHEN I come in f'om de co'n-fiel' aftah wo'kin' ha'd all day,
It 's amazin' nice to fin' my suppah all erpon de way;
An' it 's nice to smell de coffee bubblin' ovah in de pot,
An' it 's fine to see de meat a-sizzlin' teasin'-lak an' hot.

But when suppah-time is ovah, an' de t'ings is cleahed away;
Den de happy hours dat foller are de sweetes' of de day.
When my co'ncob pipe is sta'ted, an' de smoke is drawin' prime,
My ole 'ooman says, " I reckon, Ike, it 's candle-lightin' time."

Den de chillun snuggle up to me, an' all commence to call,
" Oh, say, daddy, now it 's time to mek de shadders on de wall."
So I puts my han's togethah — evah daddy knows de way,—
An' de chillun snuggle closer roun' ez I begin to say: —

" Fus' thing, hyeah come Mistah Rabbit; don' you see him wo'k his eahs?

Huh, uh! dis mus' be a donkey,—
look, how innercent he 'pears!
Dah 's de ole black swan a-swimmin'— ain't she got a' awful neck?
Who 's dis feller dat 's a-comin'?
Why, dat 's ole dog Tray, I 'spec'!"

Dat 's de way I run on, tryin' fu' to please 'em all I can;
Den I hollahs, "Now be keerful — dis hyeah las' 's de buga-man!"
An' dey runs an' hides dey faces; dey ain't skeered — dey 's lettin' on:
But de play ain't raaly ovah twell dat buga-man is gone.

So I jes' teks up my banjo, an' I plays a little chune,
An' you see dem haids come peepin' out to listen mighty soon.
Den my wife says, "Sich a pappy fu' to give you sich a fright!
Jes, you go to baid, an' leave him: say yo' prayers an' say good-night."

WHISTLING SAM

I HAS hyeahd o' people dancin' an' I 's hyeahd o' people singin'.
An' I 's been 'roun' lots of othahs dat could keep de banjo ringin';
But of all de whistlin' da'kies dat have lived an' died since Ham,
De whistlin'est I evah seed was ol' Ike Bates's Sam.
In de kitchen er de stable, in de fiel' er mowin' hay,
You could hyeah dat boy a-whistlin' pu'ty nigh a mile er-way,—
Puck'rin' up his ugly features 'twell you could n't see his eyes,
Den you 'd hyeah a soun' lak dis un f'om dat awful puckah rise:

When dey had revival meetin' an' de Lawd's good grace was flowin'
On de groun' dat needed wat'rin' whaih de seeds of good was growin',
While de othahs was a-singin' an' a-shoutin' right an' lef',
You could hyeah dat boy a-whistlin' kin' o' sof' beneaf his bref:

At de call fu' colo'ed soldiers, Sam enlisted 'mong de res'
Wid de blue o' Gawd's great ahmy wropped about his swellin' breas',
An' he laffed an' whistled loudah in his youfful joy an' glee
Dat de govament would let him he'p to mek his people free.
Daih was lots o' ties to bin' him, pappy, mammy, an' his Dinah,—
Dinah, min' you, was his sweet-hea't, an' dey was n't nary finah;
But he lef' 'em all, I tell you, lak a king he ma'ched away,
Try'n' his level bes' to whistle, happy, solemn, choky, gay:

To de front he went an' bravely fought de foe an' kep' his sperrit,
An' his comerds said his whistle made 'em strong when dey could hyeah it.
When a saber er a bullet cut some frien' o' his'n down,
An' de time 'u'd come to trench him an' de boys 'u'd gethah 'roun',
An' dey could n't sta't a hymn-tune, mebbe none o' dem 'u'd keer,
Sam 'u'd whistle "Sleep in Jesus," an' he knowed de Mastah 'd hyeah.
In de camp, all sad discouraged, he would cheer de hea'ts of all,
When above de soun' of labour dey could hyeah his whistle call:

When de cruel wah was ovah an' de boys come ma'chin' back,
Dey was shouts an' cries an' blessin's all erlong dey happy track,
An' de da'kies all was happy; souls an' bodies bofe was freed.
Why, hit seemed lak de Redeemah mus' 'a' been on earf indeed.
Dey was gethahed all one evenin' jes' befo' de cabin do',
When dey hyeahd somebody whistlin' kin' o' sof' an' sweet an' low.
Dey could n't see de whistlah, but de hymn was cleah and ca'm,
An' dey all stood daih a-listenin' ontwell Dinah shouted, "Sam!"

An' dey seed a little da'ky way off
yandah thoo de trees
Wid his face all in a puckah mekin'
jes' sich soun's ez dese:

HOW LUCY BACKSLID

De times is mighty stirrin' 'mong
de people up ouah way,
Dey 'sputin' an' dey argyin' an'
fussin' night an' day;
An' all dis monst'ous trouble dat
hit meks me tiahed to tell
Is 'bout dat Lucy Jackson dat was
sich a mighty belle.

She was de preachah's favoured,
an' he tol' de chu'ch one
night
Dat she travelled thoo de cloud o'
sin a-bearin' of a light;
But, now, I 'low he t'inkin' dat she
mus' 'a' los' huh lamp,
Case Lucy done backslided an' dey
trouble in de camp.

Huh daddy wants to beat huh, but
huh mammy daihs him to,
Fu' she lookin' at de question f'om
a ooman's pint o' view;
An' she say dat now she would n't
have it diff'ent ef she could;
Dat huh darter only acted jes' lak
any othah would.

Cose you know w'en women argy,
dey is mighty easy led
By dey hea'ts an' don't go foolin'
'bout de reasons of de haid.
So huh mammy laid de law down
(she ain' reckernizin' wrong),
But you got to mek erlowance fu'
de cause dat go along.

Now de cause dat made Miss Lucy
fu' to th'ow huh grace away
I 's afeard won't baih no 'spection
w'en hit come to jedgement
day;
Do' de same t'ing been a-wo'kin'
evah sence de worl' began,—
De ooman disobeyin' fu' to 'tice
along a man.

Ef you 'tended de revivals which
we held de wintah pas',
You kin rickolec' dat convuts was
a-comin' thick an' fas';
But dey ain't no use in talkin', dey
was all lef' in de lu'ch
W'en ol' Mis' Jackson's dartah
foun' huh peace an' tuk de
chu'ch.

W'y, she shouted ovah evah inch
of Ebenezah's flo';
Up into de preachah's pulpit an'
f'om dah down to de do';
Den she hugged an' squeezed huh
mammy, an' she hugged an'
kissed huh dad,
An' she struck out at huh sistah,
people said, lak she was mad.

I has 'tended some revivals dat
was lively in my day,
An' I 's seed folks git 'uligion in
mos' evah kin' o' way;
But I tell you, an' you b'lieve me
dat I 's speakin' true indeed,
Dat gal tuk huh 'ligion ha'dah dan
de ha'dest yit I 's seed.

Well, f'om dat, 't was "Sistah
Jackson, won't you please do
dis er dat?"
She mus' allus sta't de singin'
w'en dey 'd pass erroun' de
hat,
An' hit seemed dey was n't nuffin'
in dat chu'ch dat could go by
'Dout sistah Lucy Jackson had a
finger in de pie.

But de sayin' mighty trufeful dat
hit easiah to sail
W'en de sea is ca'm an' gentle dan
to weathah out a gale.
Dat 's whut made dis ooman's
trouble; ef de sto'm had kep'
away,
She 'd 'a' had enough 'uligion fu'
to lasted out huh day.

Lucy went wid 'Lishy Davis, but
w'en she jined chu'ch, you
know
Dah was lots o' little places dat, of
cose, she could n't go;
An' she had to gin up dancin' an'
huh singin' an' huh play.—
Now hit 's nachul dat sich goin's-
on 'u'd drive a man away.

So, w'en Lucy got so solemn, Ike
he sta'ted fu' to go
Wid a gal who was a sinnah an'
could mek a bettah show.
Lucy jes' went on to meetin' lak
she did n't keer a rap,
But my 'sperunce kep' me t'inkin'
dah was somep'n' gwine to
drap.

Fu' a gal won't let 'uligion er no
othah so't o' t'ing
Stop huh w'en she teks a notion
dat she wants a weddin' ring.
You kin p'omise huh de blessin's
of a happy aftah life
(An' hit 's nice to be a angel), but
she 'd ravah be a wife.

So w'en Chrismus come an' mas-
tah gin a frolic on de lawn,
Did n't 'sprise me not de littlest
seein' Lucy lookin' on.
An' I seed a wa'nin' lightnin' go
a-flashin' f'om huh eye
Jest ez 'Lishy an' his new gal went
a-gallivantin' by.

An' dat Tildy, umph! she giggled,
an' she gin huh dress a flirt
Lak de people she was passin' was
ez common ez de dirt;
An' de minit she was dancin', w'y
dat gal put on mo' aihs
Dan a cat a-tekin' kittens up a
paih o' windin' staihs.

She could 'fo'd to show huh sma'tness, fu' she could n't he'p but know
Dat wid jes' de present dancahs she was ownah of de flo';
But I t'ink she 'd kin' o' cooled down ef she happened on de sly
Fu' to noticed dat 'ere lightnin' dat I seed in Lucy's eye.

An' she would n't been so 'stonished w'en de people gin a shout,
An' Lucy th'owed huh mantle back an' come a-glidin' out.
Some ahms was dah to tek huh an' she fluttahed down de flo'
Lak a feddah f'om a bedtick w'en de win' commence to blow.

Soon ez Tildy see de trouble, she jes' tu'n an' toss huh haid,
But seem lak she los' huh sperrit, all huh darin'ness was daid.
Did n't cut anothah capah nary time de blessid night;
But de othah one, hit looked lak could n't git enough delight.

W'en you keeps a colt a-stan'nin' in de stable all along,
W'en he do git out hit 's nachul he 'll be pullin' mighty strong.
Ef you will tie up yo' feelin's, hyeah 's de bes' advice to tek,
Look out fu' an awful loosin' w'en de string dat hol's 'em brek.

Lucy's mammy groaned to see huh, an' huh pappy sto'med an' to',
But she kep' right on a-hol'in' to de centah of de flo'.
So dey went an' ast de pastoh ef he could n't mek huh quit,
But de tellin' of de sto'y th'owed de preachah in a fit.

Tildy Taylor chewed huh hank'-cher twell she 'd chewed it in a hole,—
All de sinnahs was rejoicin' 'cause a lamb had lef' de fol',
An' de las' I seed o' Lucy, she an' 'Lish was side an' side:
I don't blame de gal fu' dancin', an' I could n't ef I tried.

Fu' de men dat wants to ma'y ain't a-growin' 'roun' on trees,
An' de gal dat wants to git one sholy has to try to please.
Hit 's a ha'd t'ing fu' a ooman fu' to pray an' jes' set down,
An' to sacafice a husban' so 's to try to gain a crown.

Now, I don' say she was justified in follerin' huh plan;
But aldough she los' huh 'ligion, yit she sholy got de man.
Latah on, w'en she is suttain dat de preachah 's made 'em fas'
She kin jes' go back to chu'ch an' ax fu'giveness fu' de pas'!

LYRICS OF LOVE AND LAUGHTER

TWO LITTLE BOOTS

Two little boots all rough an' wo',
Two little boots!
Law, I 's kissed 'em times befo',
Dese little boots!
Seems de toes a-peepin' thoo
Dis hyeah hole an' sayin' "Boo!"
Evah time dey looks at you —
Dese little boots.

Membah de time he put 'em on,
Dese little boots;
Riz an' called fu' 'em by dawn,
Dese little boots;
Den he tromped de livelong day,
Laffin' in his happy way,
Evaht'ing he had to say,
"My little boots!"

Kickin' de san' de whole day long,
Dem little boots;
Good de cobblah made 'em strong,
Dem little boots!
Rocks was fu' dat baby's use,
I'on had to stan' abuse
W'en you tu'ned dese champeens loose,
Dese little boots!

Ust to make de ol' cat cry,
Dese little boots;
Den you walked it mighty high,
Proud little boots!
Ahms akimbo, stan'in' wide,
Eyes a-sayin' "Dis is pride!"
Den de manny-baby stride!
You little boots.

Somehow, you don' seem so gay,
Po' little boots,
Sence yo' ownah went erway,
Po' little boots!
Yo' bright tops don' look so red,
Dese brass tips is dull an' dead;
"Goo'-by," whut de baby said;
Deah little boots!

Ain't you kin' o' sad yo'se'f,
You little boots?
Dis is all his mammy 's lef',
Two little boots.
Sence huh baby gone an' died.
Heav'n itse'f hit seem to hide
Des a little bit inside
Two little boots.

TO THE ROAD

Cool is the wind, for the summer is waning,
Who 's for the road?
Sun-flecked and soft, where the dead leaves are raining,
Who 's for the road?
Knapsack and alpenstock press hand and shoulder,
Prick of the brier and roll of the boulder;

This be your lot till the season grow older;
Who 's for the road?

Up and away in the hush of the morning,
Who 's for the road?
Vagabond he, all conventions a-scorning,
Who 's for the road?
Music of warblers so merrily singing,
Draughts from the rill from the roadside up-springing,
Nectar of grapes from the vines lowly swinging,
These on the road.

Now every house is a hut or a hovel,
Come to the road:
Mankind and moles in the dark love to grovel,
But to the road.
Throw off the loads that are bending you double;
Love is for life, only labor is trouble;
Truce to the town, whose best gift is a bubble:
Come to the road!

A SPRING WOOING

Come on walkin' wid me, Lucy; 't ain't no time to mope erroun'
W'en de sunshine 's shoutin' glory in de sky,
An' de little Johnny-Jump-Ups 's jes' a-springin' f'om de groun',
Den a-lookin' roun' to ax each othah w'y.
Don' you hyeah dem cows a-mooin'? Dat 's dey howdy to de spring;
Ain' dey lookin' most oncommon satisfied?
Hit 's enough to mek a body want to spread dey mouf an' sing
Jes' to see de critters all so spa'klin'-eyed.

W'y dat squir'l dat jes' run past us, ef I didn' know his tricks,
I could swaih he 'd got 'uligion jes' to-day;
An' dem liza'ds slippin' back an' fofe ermong de stones an' sticks
Is a-wigglin' 'cause dey feel so awful gay.
Oh, I see yo' eyes a-shinin' dough you try to mek me b'lieve
Dat you ain' so monst'ous happy 'cause you come;
But I tell you dis hyeah weathah meks it moughty ha'd to 'ceive
Ef a body's soul ain' blin' an' deef an' dumb.

Robin whistlin' ovah yandah ez he buil' his little nes';
Whut you reckon dat he sayin' to his mate?
He 's a-sayin' dat he love huh in de wo'ds she know de bes',
An' she lookin' moughty pleased at whut he state.
Now, Miss Lucy, dat ah robin sholy got his sheer o' sense,
An' de hen-bird got huh mothah-wit fu' true;
So I t'ink ef you 'll ixcuse me, fu' I do' mean no erfence,
Dey 's a lesson in dem birds fu' me an' you.

I 's a-buil'in' o' my cabin, an' I 's vines erbove de do'
Fu' to kin' o' gin it sheltah f'om de sun;
Gwine to have a little kitchen wid a reg'lar wooden flo',
An' dey 'll be a back verandy w'en hit 's done.
I 's a-waitin' fu' you, Lucy, tek de 'zample o' de birds,
Dat 's a-lovin' an' a-matin' evahwhaih.
I cain' tell you dat I loves you in de robin's music wo'ds,
But my cabin 's talkin' fu' me ovah thaih!

JOGGIN' ERLONG

De da'kest hour, dey allus say,
Is des' befo' de dawn,
But it 's moughty ha'd a-waitin'
W'ere de night goes frownin' on;
An' it 's moughty ha'd a-hopin'
W'en de clouds is big an' black,
An' all de t'ings you 's waited fu'
Has failed, er gone to wrack —
But des' keep on a-joggin' wid a little bit o' song,
De mo'n is allus brightah w'en de night 's been long.

Dey 's lots o' knocks you 's got to tek
Befo' yo' journey 's done,
An' dey 's times w'en you 'll be wishin'
Dat de weary race was run;
W'en you want to give up tryin'
An' des' float erpon de wave,
W'en you don't feel no mo' sorrer
Ez you t'ink erbout de grave —
Den, des' keep on a-joggin' wid a little bit o' song,
De mo'n is allus brightah w'en de night 's been long.

De whup-lash sting a good deal mo'
De back hit 's knowed befo',
An' de burden 's allus heavies'
Whaih hits weight has made a so';
Dey is times w'en tribulation
Seems to git de uppah han'
An' to whip de weary trav'lah
'Twell he ain't got stren'th to stan'—

But des' keep on a-joggin' wid a little bit o' song,
De mo'n is allus brightah w'en de night 's been long.

IN MAY

OH to have you in May,
To talk with you under the trees,
Dreaming throughout the day,
Drinking the wine-like breeze,

Oh it were sweet to think
That May should be ours again,
Hoping it not, I shrink,
Out of the sight of men.

May brings the flowers to bloom,
It brings the green leaves to the tree,
And the fatally sweet perfume,
Of what you once were to me.

DREAMS

WHAT dreams we have and how they fly
Like rosy clouds across the sky;
Of wealth, of fame, of sure success,
Of love that comes to cheer and bless;
And how they wither, how they fade,
The waning wealth, the jilting jade —
The fame that for a moment gleams,
Then flies forever,— dreams, ah — dreams!

O burning doubt and long regret,
O tears with which our eyes are wet,
Heart-throbs, heart-aches, the glut of pain,
The somber cloud, the bitter rain,
You were not of those dreams — ah! well,
Your full fruition who can tell?
Wealth, fame, and love, ah! love that beams
Upon our souls, all dreams — ah! dreams.

THE TRYST

DE night creep down erlong de lan',
De shadders rise an' shake,
De frog is sta'tin' up his ban',
De cricket is awake;
My wo'k is mos' nigh done, Celes',
To-night I won't be late,
I 's hu'yin' thoo my level bes',
Wait fu' me by de gate.

De mockin'-bird 'll sen' his glee
A-thrillin' thoo and thoo,
I know dat ol' magnolia-tree
Is smellin' des' fu' you;
De jessamine erside de road
Is bloomin' rich an' white,

My hea't 's a-th'obbin' 'cause it knowed
You 'd wait fu' me to-night.

Hit 's lonesome, ain't it, stan'in' thaih
Wid no one nigh to talk?
But ain't dey whispahs in de aih
Erlong de gyahden walk?
Don't somep'n kin' o' call my name,
An' say "he love you bes'"?
Hit 's true, I wants to say de same,
So wait fu' me, Celes'.

Sing somep'n fu' to pass de time,
Outsing de mockin'-bird,
You got de music an' de rhyme,
You beat him wid de word.
I 's comin' now, my wo'k is done,
De hour has come fu' res',
I wants to fly, but only run —
Wait fu' me, deah Celes'.

A PLEA

Treat me nice, Miss Mandy Jane,
Treat me nice.
Dough my love has tu'ned my brain,
Treat me nice.
I ain't done a t'ing to shame,
Lovahs all ac's jes' de same:
Don't you know we ain't to blame?
Treat me nice!

Cose I know I 's talkin' wild;
Treat me nice;
I cain't talk no bettah, child,
Treat me nice;
Whut a pusson gwine to do,
W'en he come a-cou'tin' you
All a-trimblin' thoo and thoo?
Please be nice.

Reckon I mus' go de paf
Othahs do:
Lovahs lingah, ladies laff;
Mebbe you
Do' mean all the things you say,
An' pu'haps some latah day
W'en I baig you ha'd, you may
Treat me nice!

THE DOVE

Out of the sunshine and out of the heat,
Out of the dust of the grimy street,
A song fluttered down in the form of a dove,
And it bore me a message, the one word — Love!

Ah, I was toiling, and oh, I was sad:
I had forgotten the way to be glad.
Now, smiles for my sadness and for my toil, rest
Since the dove fluttered down to its home in my breast!

A WARM DAY IN WINTER

" Sunshine on de medders,
  Greenness on de way;
Dat 's de blessed reason
  I sing all de day."
Look hyeah! Whut you axin'?
  Whut meks me so merry?
'Spect to see me sighin'
  W'en hit 's wa'm in Febawary?

'Long de stake an' rider
  Seen a robin set;
W'y, hit 'mence a-thawin',
  Groun' is monst'ous wet.
Den you stan' dah wond'rin',
  Lookin' skeert an' stary;
I 's a right to caper
  W'en hit 's wa'm in Febawary.

Missis gone a-drivin',
  Mastah gone to shoot;
Ev'ry da'ky lazin'
  In de sun to boot.
Qua'tah 's moughty pleasant,
  Hangin' 'roun' my Mary;
Cou'tin' boun' to prospah
  W'en hit 's wa'm in Febawary.

Cidah look so pu'ty
  Po'in' f'om de jug —
Don' you see it 's happy?
  Hyeah it laffin'— glug?
Now 's de time fu' people
  Fu' to try an' bury
All dey grief an' sorrer,
  W'en hit 's wa'm in Febawary.

SNOWIN'

Dey is snow upon de meddahs, dey is snow upon de hill,
An' de little branch's watahs is all glistenin' an' still;
De win' goes roun' de cabin lak a sperrit wan'erin' 'roun'.
An' de chillen shakes an' shivahs as dey listen to de soun'.
Dey is hick'ry in de fiahplace, whah de blaze is risin' high,
But de heat it meks ain't wa'min' up de gray clouds in de sky.
Now an' den I des peep outside, den I hurries to de do',
Lawd a mussy on my body, how I wish it would n't snow!

I kin stan' de hottes' summah, I kin stan' de wettes' fall,
I kin stan' de chilly springtime in de ploughland, but dat 's all;
Fu' de ve'y hottes' fiah nevah tells my skin a t'ing,
W'en de snow commence a-flyin', an' de win' begin to sing.
Dey is plenty wood erroun' us, an' I chop an' tote it in,
But de t'oughts dat I 's a t'inkin' while I 's wo'kin' is a sin.
I kin keep f'om downright swahin' all de time I 's on de go,
But my hea't is full o' cuss-wo'ds w'en I 's trampin' thoo de snow.

What you say, you Lishy Davis, dat you see a possum's tracks?
Look hyeah, boy, you stop yo' foolin', bring ol' Spot, an' bring de ax.
Is I col'? Go way, now, Mandy, what you t'ink I 's made of? — sho,
W'y dis win' is des ez gentle, an' dis ain't no kin' o' snow.
Dis hyeah weathah 's des ez healthy ez de wa'mest summah days.
All you chillen step up lively, pile on wood an' keep a blaze.
What 's de use o' gittin' skeery case dey 's snow upon de groun'?
Huh-uh, I 's a reg'lar snowbird ef dey 's any possum 'roun'.

Go on, Spot, don' be so foolish; don' you see de signs o' feet.
What you howlin' fu? Keep still, suh, cose de col' is putty sweet;
But we goin' out on bus'ness, an' hit 's bus'ness o' de kin'
Dat mus' put a dog an' dahky in a happy frame o' min'.
Yes, you 's col'; I know it, Spotty, but you des stay close to me,
An' I 'll mek you hot ez cotton w'en we strikes de happy tree.
No, I don' lak wintah weathah, an' I'd wush 't uz allus June,
Ef it was n't fu' de trackin' o' de possum an' de coon.

KEEP A SONG UP ON DE WAY

Oh, de clouds is mighty heavy
An' de rain is mighty thick;
  Keep a song up on de way.
An' de waters is a rumblin'
On de boulders in de crick,
  Keep a song up on de way.
Fu' a bird ercross de road
Is a-singin' lak he knowed
Dat we people did n't daih
Fu' to try de rainy aih
  Wid a song up on de way.

What 's de use o' gittin' mopy,
Case de weather ain' de bes'!
  Keep a song up on de way.
W'en de rain is fallin' ha'des',
Dey 's de longes' times to res'
  Keep a song up on de way.
Dough de plough 's a-stan'in' still
Dey 'll be watah fu' de mill,
Rain mus' come ez well ez sun
'Fo' de weathah's wo'k is done,
  Keep a song up on de way.

W'y hit 's nice to hyeah de showahs
Fallin' down ermong de trees:
  Keep a song up on de way.
Ef de birds don' bothah 'bout it,
But go singin' lak dey please,
  Keep a song up on de way.
You don' s'pose I 's gwine to see
Dem ah fowls do mo' dan me?
No, suh, I 'll des chase dis frown,
An' aldough de rain fall down,
  Keep a song up on de way.

THE TURNING OF THE BABIES IN THE BED

WOMAN 's sho' a cur'ous critter,
an' dey ain't no doubtin' dat.
She 's a mess o' funny capahs f'om
huh slippahs to huh hat.
Ef you tries to un'erstan' huh, an'
you fails, des' up an' say:
" D' ain't a bit o' use to try to
un'erstan' a woman's way."

I don' mean to be complainin', but
I 's jes' a-settin' down
Some o' my own obserwations,
w'en I cas' my eye eroun'.
Ef you ax me fu' to prove it, I
ken do it mighty fine,
Fu' dey ain't no bettah 'zample
den dis ve'y wife o' mine.

In de ve'y hea't o' midnight, w'en
I 's sleepin' good an' soun',
I kin hyeah a so't o' rustlin' an'
somebody movin' 'roun'.
An' I say, " Lize, whut you do-
in'? " But she frown an' shek
huh haid,
" Heish yo' mouf, I 's only tu'nin'
of de chillun in de bed.

" Don' you know a chile gits rest-
less, layin' all de night one
way?
An' you' got to kind o' 'range him
sev'al times befo' de day?
So de little necks won't worry, an'
de little backs won't break;
Don' you t'ink case chillun 's chil-
lun dey hain't got no pain an'
ache."

So she shakes 'em, an' she twists
'em, an' she tu'ns 'em 'roun'
erbout,
'Twell I don' see how de chillun
evah keeps f'om hollahin' out.
Den she lif's 'em up head down-
'ards, so 's dey won't git livah-
grown,
But dey snoozes des' ez peaceful
ez a liza'd on a stone.

W'en hit 's mos' nigh time fu'
wakin' on de dawn o' jedg-
ment day,
Seems lak I kin hyeah ol' Gab'iel
lay his trumpet down an' say,
" Who dat walkin' 'roun' so easy,
down on earf ermong de
dead? "—
'T will be Lizy up a-tu'nin' of de
chillun in de bed.

THE DANCE

HEEL and toe, heel and toe,
That is the song we sing;
Turn to your partner and curtsey
low,
Balance and forward and swing.
Corners are draughty and meadows
are white,
This is the game for a winter's
night.

Hands around, hands around,
Trip it, and not too slow;
Clear is the fiddle and sweet its sound,
Keep the girls' cheeks aglow.
Still let your movements be dainty and light,
This is the game for a winter's night.

Back to back, back to back,
Turn to your place again;
Never let lightness nor nimbleness lack,
Either in maidens or men.
Time hasteth ever, beware of its flight,
Oh, what a game for a winter's night!

Slower now, slower now,
Softer the music sighs;
Look, there are beads on your partner's brow
Though there be light in her eyes.
Lead her away and her grace requite,
So goes the game on a winter's night.

SOLILOQUY OF A TURKEY

Dey 's a so't o' threatenin' feelin' in de blowin' of de breeze,
An' I 's feelin' kin' o' squeamish in de night;
I 's a-walkin' 'roun' a-lookin' at de diffunt style o' trees,
An' a-measurin' dey thickness an' dey height.
Fu' dey 's somep'n mighty 'spicious in de looks de da'kies give,
Ez dey pass me an' my fambly on de groun,'
So it 'curs to me dat lakly, ef I caihs to try an' live,
It concehns me fu' to 'mence to look erroun'.

Dey 's a cu'ious kin' o' shivah runnin' up an' down my back,
An' I feel my feddahs rufflin' all de day,
An' my laigs commence to trimble evah blessid step I mek;
W'en I sees a ax, I tu'ns my head away.
Folks is go'gin' me wid goodies, an' dey 's treatin' me wid caih,
An' I 's fat in spite of all dat I kin do.
I 's mistrus'ful of de kin'ness dat 's erroun' me evahwhaih,
Fu' it 's jes' too good, an' frequent, to be true.

Snow 's a-fallin' on de medders, all erroun' me now is white,
But I 's still kep' on a-roostin' on de fence;
Isham comes an' feels my breas'-bone, an' he hefted me las' night,

An' he 's gone erroun' a-grinnin' evah sence.
'T ain't de snow dat meks me shivah; 't ain't de col' dat meks me shake;
'T ain't de wintah-time itse'f dat 's 'fectin' me;
But I t'ink de time is comin', an' I 'd bettah mek a break,
Fu' to set wid Mistah Possum in his tree.

W'en you hyeah de da'kies singin', an' de quahtahs all is gay,
'T ain't de time fu' birds lak me to be 'erroun';
W'en de hick'ry chips is flyin', an' de log 's been ca'ied erway,
Den hit 's dang'ous to be roostin' nigh he groun'.

Grin on, Isham! Sing on, da'kies! But I flop my wings an' go
Fu' de sheltah of de ve'y highest tree,
Fu' dey 's too much close ertention — an' dey's too much fallin' snow —
An' it 's too nigh Chris'mus mo'nin' now fu' me.

FISHING

W'en I git up in de mo'nin' an' de clouds is big an' black,
Dey 's a kin' o' wa'nin' shivah goes a-scootin' down my back;
Den I says to my ol' ooman ez I watches down de lane,
"Don't you so't o' reckon, Lizy, dat we gwine to have some rain?"

"Go on, man," my Lizy answah, "you cain't fool me, not a bit,
I don't see no rain a-comin', ef you 's wishin' fu' it, quit;
Case de mo' you t'ink erbout it, an de mo' you pray an' wish,
W'y de rain stay 'way de longah, spechul ef you wants to fish."

But I see huh pat de skillet, an' I see huh cas' huh eye
Wid a kin' o' anxious motion to'ds de da'kness in de sky;
An' I knows whut she 's a-t'inkin', dough she tries so ha'd to hide.
She 's a-sayin', "Would n't catfish now tas'e monst'ous bully, fried?"

Den de clouds git black an' blackah, an' de thundah 'mence to roll,
An' de rain, it 'mence a-fallin'. Oh, I 's happy, bless my soul!
Ez I look at dat ol' skillet, an' I 'magine I kin see
Jes' a slew o' new-ketched catfish sizzlin' daih fu' huh an' me.

'T ain't no use to go a-ploughin', fu' de groun' 'll be too wet,
So I puts out fu' de big house at a moughty pace, you bet,
An' ol' mastah say, "Well, Lishy, ef you t'ink hit 's gwine to rain,
Go on fishin', hit's de weathah, an' I 'low we cain't complain."

Talk erbout a dahky walkin' wid his haid up in de aih!
Have to feel mine evah minute to be sho' I got it daih;
En' de win' is cuttin' capahs an' a-lashin' thoo de trees,
But de rain keeps on a-singin' blessed songs, lak "Tek yo' ease."

Wid my pole erpon my shouldah an' my wo'm can in my han',
I kin feel de fish a-waitin' w'en I strikes de rivah's san';
Nevah min', you ho'ny scoun'els, need n' swim erroun' an' grin,
I 'll be grinnin' in a minute w'en I 'mence to haul you in.

W'en de fish begin to nibble, an' de co'k begin to jump,
I 's erfeahed dat dey 'll quit bitin', case dey hyeah my hea't go "thump,"
'Twell de co'k go way down undah, an' I raise a awful shout,
Ez a big ol' yallah belly comes a gallivantin' out.

Need n't wriggle, Mistah Catfish, case I got you jes' de same,
You been eatin', I 'll be eatin', an' we needah ain't to blame.
But you need n't feel so lonesome fu' I 's th'owin' out to see
Ef dey ain't some of yo' comrades fu' to keep you company.

Spo't, dis fishin'! now you talkin', w'y dey ain't no kin' to beat;
I don' keer ef I is soakin', laigs, an' back, an' naik, an' feet,
It 's de spo't I 's lookin' aftah. Hit 's de pleasure an' de fun,
Dough I knows dat Lizy 's waitin' wid de skillet w'en I 's done.

A PLANTATION PORTRAIT

Hain't you see my Mandy Lou,
Is it true?
Whaih you been f'om day to day,
Whaih, I say?
Dat you say you nevah seen
Dis hyeah queen
Walkin' roun' f'om fiel' to street
Smilin' sweet?

Slendah ez a saplin' tree;
Seems to me

W'en de win' blow f'om de bay
She jes' sway
Lak de reg'lar saplin' do
Ef hit 's grew
Straight an' graceful, 'dout a limb,
Sweet an' slim.

Browner den de frush's wing,
An' she sing
Lak he mek his wa'ble ring
In de spring;
But she sholy beat de frush,
Hyeah me, hush:
W'en she sing, huh teef kin show
White ez snow.

Eyes ez big an' roun' an' bright
Ez de light
Whut de moon gives in de prime
Harvest time.
An' huh haih a woolly skein,
Black an' plain.
Hol's you wid a natchul twis'
Close to bliss.

Tendah han's dat mek yo' own
Feel lak stone;
Easy steppin', blessid feet,
Small an' sweet.
Hain't you seen my Mandy Lou,
Is it true?
Look at huh befo' she 's gone,
Den pass on!

A LITTLE CHRISTMAS BASKET

De win' is hollahin' "Daih you" to de shuttahs an' de fiah,
De snow 's a-sayin' "Got you" to de groun',
Fu' de wintah weathah 's come widout a-askin' ouah desiah,
An' he 's laughin' in his sleeve at whut he foun';
Fu' dey ain't nobody ready wid dey fuel er dey food,
An' de money bag look timid lak, fu' sho',
So we want ouah Chrismus sermon, but we 'd lak it ef you could
Leave a little Chrismus basket at de do'.

Wha 's de use o' tellin' chillen 'bout a Santy er a Nick,
An' de sto'ies dat a body allus tol'?
When de harf is gray wid ashes an' you has n't got a stick
Fu' to warm dem when dey little toes is col'?
Wha 's de use o' preachin' 'ligion to a man dat 's sta'ved to def,
An' a-tellin' him de Mastah will pu'vide?
Ef you want to tech his feelin's, save yo' sermons an' yo' bref,
Tek a little Chrismus basket by yo' side.

'T ain't de time to open Bibles an' to lock yo' cellah do',

'T ain't de time to talk o' bein' good to men;
Ef you want to preach a sermon ez you nevah preached befo',
Preach dat sermon wid a shoat er wid er hen;
Bein' good is heap sight bettah den a-dallyin' wid sin,
An' dey ain't nobody roun' dat knows it mo',
But I t'ink dat 'ligion 's sweeter w'en it kind o' mixes in
Wid a little Chrismus basket at de do'.

THE VALSE

WHEN to sweet music my lady is dancing
My heart to mild frenzy her beauty inspires.
Into my face are her brown eyes a-glancing,
And swift my whole frame thrills with tremulous fires.
Dance, lady, dance, for the moments are fleeting,
Pause not to place yon refractory curl;
Life is for love and the night is for sweeting;
Dreamily, joyously, circle and whirl.

Oh, how those viols are throbbing and pleading;
A prayer is scarce needed in sound of their strain.
Surely and lightly as round you are speeding,
You turn to confusion my heart and my brain.
Dance, lady, dance to the viol's soft calling,
Skip it and trip it as light as the air;
Dance, for the moments like rose leaves are falling,
Strikes, now, the clock from its place on the stair.

Now sinks the melody lower and lower,
The weary musicians scarce seeming to play.
Ah, love, your steps now are slower and slower,
The smile on your face is more sad and less gay.
Dance, lady, dance to the brink of our parting,
My heart and your step must not fail to be light.
Dance! Just a turn — tho' the tear-drop be starting.
Ah — now it is done — so — my lady, good-night!

REPONSE

WHEN Phyllis sighs and from her eyes
The light dies out; my soul replies

With misery of deep-drawn breath,
E'en as it were at war with death.

When Phyllis smiles, her glance beguiles
My heart through love-lit woodland aisles,
And through the silence high and clear,
A wooing warbler's song I hear.

But if she frown, despair comes down,
I put me on my sack-cloth gown;
So frown not, Phyllis, lest I die,
But look on me with smile or sigh.

MY SWEET BROWN GAL

W'EN de clouds is hangin' heavy in de sky,
An' de win's 's a-taihin' moughty vig'rous by,
I don' go a-sighin' all erlong de way;
I des' wo'k a-waitin' fu' de close o' day.

Case I knows w'en evenin' draps huh shadders down,
I won' care a smidgeon fu' de weathah's frown;
Let de rain go splashin', let de thundah raih,
Dey 's a happy sheltah, an' I 's goin' daih.

Down in my ol' cabin wa'm ez mammy's toas',
'Taters in de fiah layin' daih to roas';
No one daih to cross me, got no talkin' pal,
But I 's got de comp'ny o' my sweet brown gal.

So I spen's my evenin' listenin' to huh sing,
Lak a blessid angel; how huh voice do ring!
Sweetah den a bluebird flutterin' erroun',
W'en he sees de steamin' o' de new ploughed groun'.

Den I hugs huh closah, closah to my breas'.
Need n't sing, my da'lin', tek you' hones' res'.
Does I mean Malindy, Mandy, Lize er Sal?
No, I means my fiddle — dat 's my sweet brown gal!

SPRING FEVER

GRASS commence a-comin'
Thoo de thawin' groun',
Evah bird dat whistles
Keepin' noise erroun';
Cain't sleep in de mo'nin',
Case befo' it 's light
Bluebird an' de robin,
Done begun to fight.

Bluebird sass de robin,
  Robin sass him back,
Den de bluebird scol' him
  'Twell his face is black.
Would n' min' de quoilin'
  All de mo'nin' long,
'Cept it wakes me early,
  Case hit 's done in song.

Anybody wo'kin'
  Wants to sleep ez late
Ez de folks 'll 'low him,
  An' I wish to state
(Co'se dis ain't to scattah,
  But 'twix' me an' you),
I could stan' de bedclothes,
  Kin' o' latah, too.

'T ain't my natchul feelin',
  Dis hyeah mopin' spell.
I stan's early risin'
  Mos'ly moughty well;
But de ve'y minute,
  I feel Ap'il's heat,
Bless yo' soul, de bedclothes
  Nevah seemed so sweet.

Mastah, he 's a-scol'in',
  Case de han's is slow,
All de hosses balkin',
  Jes' cain't mek 'em go.
Don' know whut 's de mattah,
  Hit 's a funny t'ing,
Less'n hit 's de fevah
  Dat you gits in spring.

THE VISITOR

Little lady at de do',
  W'y you stan' dey knockin'?
Nevah seen you ac' befo'
  In er way so shockin'.
    Don' you know de sin it is
    Fu' to git my temper riz
    W'en I 's got de rheumatiz
  An' my jints is lockin'?

No, ol' Miss ain't sont you down,
  Don' you tell no story;
I been seed you hangin' 'roun'
  Dis hyeah te'itory.
    You des come fu' me to tell
    You a tale, an' I ain'—well—
    Look hyeah, what is dat I smell?
  Steamin' victuals? Glory!

Come in, Missy, how you do?
  Come up by de fiah,
I was jokin', chile, wid you;
  Bring dat basket nighah.
    Huh uh, ain't dat lak ol' Miss,
    Sen'in' me a feas' lak dis?
    Rheumatiz cain't stop my bliss,
  Case I 's feelin' spryah.

Chicken meat an' gravy, too,
  Hot an' still a-heatin';
Good ol' sweet pertater stew;
  Missy b'lieves in treatin'.
    Des set down, you blessed chile,

Daddy got to t'ink a while,
Den a story mek you smile
W'en he git thoo eatin'.

SONG

WINTAH, summah, snow er shine,
Hit 's all de same to me,
Ef only I kin call you mine,
An' keep you by my knee.

Ha'dship, frolic, grief er caih,
Content by night an' day,
Ef only I kin see you whaih
You wait beside de way.

Livin', dyin', smiles er teahs,
My soul will still be free,
Ef only thoo de comin' yeahs
You walk de worl' wid me.

Bird-song, breeze-wail, chune er moan,
What puny t'ings dey 'll be,
Ef w'en I 's seemin' all erlone,
I knows yo' hea't 's wid me.

THE COLORED BAND

W'EN de colo'ed ban' comes ma'chin' down de street,
Don't you people stan' daih starin'; lif' yo' feet!
Ain't dey playin'? Hip, hooray!
Stir yo' stumps an' cleah de way,
Fu' de music dat dey mekin' can't be beat.

Oh, de major man 's a-swingin' of his stick,
An' de pickaninnies crowdin' roun' him thick;
In his go'geous uniform,
He 's de lightnin' of de sto'm,
An' de little clouds erroun' look mighty slick.

You kin hyeah a fine perfo'mance w'en de white ban's serenade,
An' dey play dey high-toned music mighty sweet,
But hit 's Sousa played in ragtime, an' hit 's Rastus on Parade,
W'en de colo'ed ban' comes ma'chin' down de street.

W'en de colo'ed ban' comes ma'chin' down de street
You kin hyeah de ladies all erroun' repeat:
"Ain't dey handsome? Ain't dey gran'?
Ain't dey splendid? Goodness, lan'!
W'y dey 's pu'fect f'om dey fo'-heads to dey feet!"
An' sich steppin' to de music down de line,

'T ain't de music by itself dat meks it fine,
Hit 's de walkin', step by step,
An' de keepin' time wid " Hep,"
Dat it mek a common ditty soun' divine.

Oh, de white ban' play hits music, an' hit 's mighty good to hyeah,
An' it sometimes leaves a ticklin' in yo' feet;
But de hea't goes into bus'ness fu' to he'p erlong de eah,
W'en de colo'ed ban' goes ma'ch-in' down de street.

TO A VIOLET FOUND ON ALL SAINTS' DAY

Belated wanderer of the ways of spring,
Lost in the chill of grim November rain,
Would I could read the message that you bring
And find in it the antidote for pain.

Does some sad spirit out beyond the day,
Far looking to the hours forever dead,
Send you a tender offering to lay
Upon the grave of us, the living dead?

Or does some brighter spirit, unforlorn,
Send you, my little sister of the wood,
To say to some one on a cloudful morn,
" Life lives through death, my brother, all is good? "

With meditative hearts the others go
The memory of their dead to dress anew.
But, sister mine, bide here that I may know,
Life grows, through death, as beautiful as you.

INSPIRATION

At the golden gate of song
Stood I, knocking all day long,
But the Angel, calm and cold,
Still refused and bade me, " Hold."

Then a breath of soft perfume,
Then a light within the gloom;
Thou, Love, camest to my side,
And the gates flew open wide.

Long I dwelt in this domain,
Knew no sorrow, grief, or pain;
Now you bid me forth and free,
Will you shut these gates on me?

MY LADY OF CASTLE GRAND

Gray is the palace where she dwells,
Grimly the poplars stand
There by the window where she sits,
My Lady of Castle Grand.

There does she bide the livelong day,
Grim as the poplars are,
Ever her gaze goes reaching out,
Steady, but vague and far.

Bright burn the fires in the castle hall,
Brightly the fire-dogs stand;
But cold is the body and cold the heart
Of my Lady of Castle Grand.

Blue are the veins in her lily-white hands,
Blue are the veins in her brow;
Thin is the line of her blue drawn lips,
Who would be haughty now?

Pale is the face at the window-pane,
Pale as the pearl on her breast,
" Roderick, love, wilt come again?
Fares he to east or west?"

The shepherd pipes to the shepherdess,
The bird to his mate in the tree,
And ever she sighs as she hears their song,
" Nobody sings for me."

The scullery maids have swains enow
Who lead them the way of love,
But lonely and loveless their mistress sits
At her window up above.

Loveless and lonely she waits and waits,
The saddest in all the land;
Ah, cruel and lasting is love-blind pride,
My Lady of Castle Grand.

DRIZZLE

Hit 's been drizzlin' an' been sprinklin',
Kin' o' techy all day long.
I ain't wet enough fu' toddy,
I 's too damp to raise a song,
An' de case have set me t'inkin',
Dat dey 's folk des lak de rain,
Dat goes drizzlin' w'en dey 's talkin',
An' won't speak out flat an' plain.

Ain't you nevah set an' listened
At a body 'splain his min'?

W'en de t'oughts dey keep on drappin'
  Was n't big enough to fin'?
Dem 's whut I call drizzlin' people,
  Othahs call 'em mealy mouf,
But de fust name hits me bettah,
  Case dey nevah tech a drouf.

Dey kin talk from hyeah to yandah,
  An' f'om yandah hyeah ergain,
An' dey don' mek no mo' 'pression,
  Den dis powd'ry kin' o' rain.
En yo' min' is dry ez cindahs,
  Er a piece o' kindlin' wood,
'T ain't no use a-talkin' to 'em,
  Fu' dey drizzle ain't no good.

Gimme folks dat speak out nachul,
  Whut 'll say des whut dey mean,
Whut don't set dey wo'ds so skimpy
  Dat you got to guess between.
I want talk des' lak de showahs
  Whut kin wash de dust erway,
Not dat sprinklin' convusation,
  Dat des drizzle all de day.

DE CRITTERS' DANCE

AIN'T nobody nevah tol' you not a wo'd a-tall,
'Bout de time dat all de critters gin dey fancy ball?
Some folks tell it in a sto'y, some folks sing de rhyme,
'Peahs to me you ought to hyeahed it, case hit 's ol' ez time.

Well, de critters all was p'osp'ous, now would be de chance
Fu' to tease ol' Pa'son Hedgehog, givin' of a dance;
Case, you know, de critters' preachah was de stric'est kin',
An' he nevah made no 'lowance fu' de frisky min'.

So dey sont dey inbitations, Raccoon writ 'em all,
" Dis hyeah note is to inbite you to de Fancy Ball;
Come erlong an' bring yo' ladies, bring yo' chillun too,
Put on all yo' bibs an' tuckahs, show whut you kin do."

W'en de night come, dey all gathahed in a place dey knowed,
Fu' enough erway f'om people, nigh enough de road,
All de critters had ersponded, Hop-Toad up to Baih,
An' I 's hyeah to tell you, Pa'son Hedgehog too, was daih.

Well, dey talked an' made dey 'bejunce, des lak critters do,
An' dey walked an' p'omenaded 'roun' an' thoo an' thoo;
Jealous ol' Mis' Fox, she whispah, " See Mis' Wildcat daih,
Ain't hit scan'lous, huh a-comin' wid huh shouldahs baih? "

Ol' man T'utle was n't honin' fu' no dancin' tricks,
So he stayed by ol' Mis' Tu'tle, talkin' politics;
Den de ban' hit 'mence a-playin' critters all to place,
Fou' ercross an' fou' stan' sideways, smilin' face to face.

'Fessah Frog, he play de co'net, Cricket play de fife,
Slews o' Grasshoppahs a-fiddlin' lak to save dey life;
Mistah Crow, 'he call de figgers, settin' in a tree,
Huh, uh! how dose critters sasshayed was a sight to see.

Mistah Possom swing Mis' Rabbit up an' down de flo',
Ol' man Baih, he ain't so nimble, an' it mek him blow;
Raccoon dancin' wid Mis' Squ'il squeeze huh little han',
She say, "Oh, now ain't you awful, quit it, goodness lan'!"

Pa'son Hedgehog groanin' awful at his converts' shines,
'Dough he peepin' thoo his fingahs at dem movin' lines,
'Twell he cain't set still no longah w'en de fiddles sing,
Up he jump, an' bless you, honey, cut de pigeon-wing.

Well, de critters lak to fainted jes' wid dey su'prise,
Sistah Fox, she vowed she was n't gwine to b'lieve huh eyes;
But dey could n't be no 'sputin' 'bout it any mo':
Pa'son Hedgehog was a-cape'in' all erroun' de flo.'

Den dey all jes' capahed scan'lous case dey did n't doubt,
Dat dey still could go to meetin'; who could tu'n 'em out?
So wid dancin' an' uligion, dey was in de fol',
Fu' a-dancin' wid de Pa'son could-n't hu't de soul.

WHEN DEY 'LISTED COLORED SOLDIERS

Dey was talkin' in de cabin, dey was talkin' in de hall;
But I listened kin' o' keerless, not a-t'inkin' 'bout it all;
An' on Sunday, too, I noticed, dey was whisp'rin' mighty much,
Stan'in' all erroun' de roadside w'en dey let us out o' chu'ch.
But I did n't t'ink erbout it 'twell de middle of de week,
An' my 'Lias come to see me, an' somehow he could n't speak.
Den I seed all in a minute whut he 'd come to see me for;—
Dey had 'listed colo'ed sojers an' my 'Lias gwine to wah.

Oh, I hugged him, an' I kissed him, an' I baiged him not to go;
But he tol' me dat his conscience, hit was callin' to him so,
An' he could n't baih to lingah w'en he had a chanst to fight
For de freedom dey had gin him an' de glory of de right.
So he kissed me, an' he lef' me, w'en I 'd p'omised to be true;
An' dey put a knapsack on him, an' a coat all colo'ed blue.
So I gin him pap's ol' Bible f'om de bottom of de draw',—
W'en dey 'listed colo'ed sojers an' my 'Lias went to wah.

But I t'ought of all de weary miles dat he would have to tramp,
An' I could n't be contented w'en dey tuk him to de camp.
W'y my hea't nigh broke wid grievin' 'twell I seed him on de street;
Den I felt lak I could go an' th'ow my body at his feet.
For his buttons was a-shinin', an' his face was shinin', too,
An' he looked so strong an' mighty in his coat o' sojer blue,
Dat I hollahed, "Step up, manny," dough my th'oat was so' an' raw,—
W'en dey 'listed colo'ed sojers an' my 'Lias went to wah.

Ol' Mis' cried w'en mastah lef' huh, young Miss mou'ned huh brothah Ned,
An' I did n't know dey feelin's is de ve'y wo'ds dey said
W'en I tol' 'em I was so'y. Dey had done gin up dey all;
But dey only seemed mo' proudah dat dey men had hyeahed de call.
Bofe my mastahs went in gray suits, an' I loved de Yankee blue,
But I t'ought dat I could sorrer for de losin' of 'em too;
But I could n't, for I did n't know de ha'f o' whut I saw,
'Twell dey 'listed colo'ed sojers an' my 'Lias went to wah.

Mastah Jack come home all sickly; he was broke for life, dey said;
An' dey lef' my po' young mastah some'r's on de roadside,—dead.
W'en de women cried an' mou'ned 'em, I could feel it thoo an' thoo,
For I had a loved un fightin' in de way o' dangah, too.
Den dey tol' me dey had laid him some'r's way down souf to res',
Wid de flag dat he had fit for shinin' daih acrost his breas'.

Well, I cried, but den I reckon dat 's whut Gawd had called him for,
W'en dey 'listed colo'ed sojers an' my 'Lias went to wah.

LINCOLN

HURT was the nation with a mighty wound,
And all her ways were filled with clam'rous sound.
Wailed loud the South with unremitting grief,
And wept the North that could not find relief.
Then madness joined its harshest tone to strife:
A minor note swelled in the song of life.
'Till, stirring with the love that filled his breast,
But still, unflinching at the right's behest,
Grave Lincoln came, strong handed, from afar,
The mighty Homer of the lyre of war.
'T was he who bade the raging tempest cease,
Wrenched from his harp the harmony of peace,
Muted the strings, that made the discord,— Wrong,
And gave his spirit up in thund'rous song.
Oh mighty Master of the mighty lyre,
Earth heard and trembled at thy strains of fire:
Earth learned of thee what Heav'n already knew,
And wrote thee down among her treasured few.

ENCOURAGEMENT

WHO dat knockin' at de do'?
Why, Ike Johnson,— yes, fu' sho!
Come in, Ike. I 's mighty glad
You come down. I t'ought you 's mad
At me 'bout de othah night,
An' was stayin' 'way fu' spite.
Say, now, was you mad fu' true
W'en I kin' o' laughed at you?
Speak up, Ike, an' 'spress yo'se'f.

'T ain't no use a-lookin' sad,
An' a-mekin' out you 's mad;
Ef you 's gwine to be so glum,
Wondah why you evah come.
I don't lak nobidy 'roun'
Dat jes' shet dey mouf an' frown,—
Oh, now, man, don't act a dunce!
Cain't you talk? I tol' you once,
Speak up, Ike, an' 'spress yo'se'f.

Wha 'd you come hyeah fu' to-night?
Body 'd t'ink yo' haid ain't right.
I 's done all dat I kin do,—

Dressed perticler, jes' fu' you;
Reckon I 'd 'a' bettah wo'
My ol' ragged calico.
Aftah all de pains I 's took,
Cain't you tell me how I look?
  Speak up, Ike, an' 'spress yo'se'f.

Bless my soul! I 'mos' fu'got
Tellin' you 'bout Tildy Scott.
Don't you know, come Thu'sday night,
She gwine ma'y Lucius White?
Miss Lize say I allus wuh
Heap sight laklier 'n huh;
An' she 'll git me somep'n new,
Ef I wants to ma'y too.
  Speak up, Ike, an' 'spress yo'se'f.

I could ma'y in a week,
Ef de man I wants 'ud speak.
Tildy's presents 'll be fine,
But dey would n't ekal mine.
Him whut gits me fu' a wife
'Ll be proud, you bet yo' life.
I 's had offers; some ain't quit;
But I has n't ma'ied yit!
  Speak up, Ike, an' 'spress yo'se'f.

Ike, I loves you,— yes, I does;
You 's my choice, and allus was.
Laffin' at you ain't no harm.—
Go 'way, dahky, whah 's yo' arm?
Hug me closer — dah, dat 's right!
Was n't you a awful sight,
Havin' me to baig you so?
Now ax whut you want to know,—
  Speak up, Ike, an' 'spress yo'se'f!

THE BOOGAH MAN

W'EN de evenin' shadders
  Come a-glidin' down,
Fallin' black an' heavy
  Ovah hill an' town,
Ef you listen keerful,
  Keerful ez you kin,
So 's you boun' to notice
  Des a drappin' pin;
Den you 'll hyeah a funny
  Soun' ercross de lan';
Lay low; dat 's de callin'
  Of de Boogah Man!

Woo-oo, woo-oo!
  Hyeah him ez he go erlong de way;
Woo-oo, woo-oo!
  Don' you wish de night 'ud tu'n to day?
Woo-oo, woo-oo!
  Hide yo' little peepers 'hind yo' han';
Woo-oo, woo-oo!
  Callin' of de Boogah Man.

W'en de win 's a-shiverin'
  Thoo de gloomy lane,
An' dey comes de patterin'
  Of de evenin' rain,
W'en de owl 's a-hootin',
  Out daih in de wood,
Don' you wish, my honey,
  Dat you had been good?
'T ain't no use to try to
  Snuggle up to Dan;
Bless you, dat 's de callin'
  Of de Boogah Man!

Ef you loves yo' mammy,
  An' you min's yo' pap,
Ef you nevah wriggles
  Outen Sukey's lap;
Ef you says yo' "Lay me"
  Evah single night
'Fo' dey tucks de kivers
  An' puts out de light,
Den de rain kin pattah
  Win' blow lak a fan,
But you need n' bothah
  'Bout de Boogah Man!

THE WRAITH

AH me, it is cold and chill
  And the fire sobs low in the grate,
While the wind rides by on the hill,
  And the logs crack sharp with hate.

And she, she is cold and sad
  As ever the sinful are,
But deep in my heart I am glad
  For my wound and the coming scar.

Oh, ever the wind rides by
  And ever the raindrops grieve;
But a voice like a woman's sigh
  Says, "Do you believe, believe?"

Ah, you were warm and sweet,
Sweet as the May days be;
Down did I fall at your feet,
  Why did you hearken to me?

Oh, the logs they crack and whine,
  And the water drops from the eaves;
But it is not rain but brine
  Where my dead darling grieves.

And a wraith sits by my side,
  A spectre grim and dark;
Are you gazing here open-eyed
  Out to the lifeless dark?

But ever the wind rides on,
  And we sit close within;
Out of the face of the dawn,
  I and my darling,—sin.

SILENCE

'TIS better to sit here beside the sea,
  Here on the spray-kissed beach,
In silence, that between such friends as we
  Is full of deepest speech.

WHIP-POOR-WILL AND KATY-DID

SLOW de night 's a-fallin',
An' I hyeah de callin,
  Out erpon de lonesome hill;
Soun' is moughty dreary,
Solemn-lak an' skeery,
  Sayin' fu' to "whip po' Will."

Now hit 's moughty tryin',
Fu' to hyeah dis cryin',
'Deed hit 's mo' den I kin stan';
Sho' wid all our slippin',
Dey 's enough of whippin'
'Dout a bird a'visin' any man.

In de noons o' summah
Dey 's anothah hummah
Sings anothah song instid;
An' his th'oat 's a-swellin'
Wid de joy o' tellin',
But he says dat "Katy did."

Now I feels onsuhtain;
Won't you raise de cu'tain
Ovah all de ti'ngs dat 's hid?
W'y dat feathahed p'isen
Goes erbout a-visin'
Whippin' Will w'en Katy did?

'LONG TO'DS NIGHT

DAIH 's a moughty soothin' feelin'
Hits a dahky man,
'Long to'ds night.
W'en de row is mos' nigh ended,
Den he stops to fan,
'Long to'ds night.
De blue smoke f'om his cabin is a-callin' to him "Come;"
He smell de bacon cookin', an' he hyeah de fiah hum;
An' he 'mence to sing, 'dough wo'kin' putty nigh done made him dumb,
'Long to'ds night.

Wid his hoe erpon his shouldah
Den he goes erlong,
'Long to'ds night.
An' he keepin' time a-steppin'
Wid a little song,
'Long to'ds night.
De restin'-time 's a-comin', an' de time to drink an' eat;
A baby's toddlin' to'ds him on hits little dusty feet,
An' a-goin' to'ds his cabin, an' his suppah 's moughty sweet,
'Long to'ds night.

Daih his Ca'line min' de kettle,
Rufus min' de chile,
'Long to'ds night;
An' de sweat roll down his forred,
Mixin' wid his smile,
'Long to'ds night.
He toss his piccaninny, an' he hum a little chune;
De wokin' all is ovah, an' de suppah comin' soon;
De wo'kin' time 's Decembah, but de restin' time is June,
'Long to'ds night.

Dey 's a kin' o' doleful feelin',
Hits a tendah place,
'Long to'ds night;

Dey 's a moughty glory in him
Shinin' thoo his face,
Long to'ds night.
De cabin 's lak de big house, an' de fiah's lak de sun;
His wife look moughty lakly, an' de chile de puttiest one;
W'y, hit 's blessid, jes' a-livin' w'en a body's wo'k is done.
'Long to'ds night.

A GRIEVANCE

W'EN de snow 's a-fallin'
An' de win' is col'.
Mammy 'mence a-callin',
Den she 'mence to scol',
" Lucius Lishy Brackett,
Don't you go out do's,
Button up yo' jacket,
Les'n you 'll git froze."

I sit at de windah
Lookin' at de groun',
Nuffin nigh to hindah,
Mammy ain' erroun';
Wish 't she would n' mek me
Set down in dis chaih;
Pshaw, it would n't tek me
Long to git some aih.

So I jump down nimble
Ez a boy kin be,
Dough I 's all a-trimble
Feahed some one 'll see;
Bet in a half a minute
I fly out de do'
An' I 's knee-deep in it,
Dat dah blessed snow.

Den I hyeah a pattah
Come acrost de flo'.
Den dey comes a clattah
At de cabin do';
An' my mammy holler
Spoilin' all my joy,
" Come in f'om dat waller,
Don't I see you, boy? "

W'en de snow 's a-sievin'
Down ez sof' ez meal,
Whut 's de use o' livin'
'Cept you got de feel
Of de stuff dat 's fallin'
'Roun' an' white an' damp,
'Dout some one a-callin',
" Come in hyeah, you scamp!

DINAH KNEADING DOUGH

I HAVE seen full many a sight
Born of day or drawn by night:
Sunlight on a silver stream,
Golden lilies all a-dream,
Lofty mountains, bold and proud,
Veiled beneath the lacelike cloud;
But no lovely sight I know
Equals Dinah kneading dough.

Brown arms buried elbow-deep
Their domestic rhythm keep,
As with steady sweep they go
Through the gently yielding dough.

Maids may vaunt their finer charms—
Naught to me like Dinah's arms;
Girls may draw, or paint, or sew —
I love Dinah kneading dough.

Eyes of jet and teeth of pearl,
Hair, some say, too tight a-curl;
But the dainty maid I deem
Very near perfection's dream.
Swift she works, and only flings
Me a glance — the least of things.
And I wonder, does she know
That my heart is in the dough?

TO A CAPTIOUS CRITIC

Dear critic, who my lightness so deplores,
Would I might study to be prince of bores,
Right wisely would I rule that dull estate —
But, sir, I may not, till you abdicate.

DAT OL' MARE O' MINE

Want to trade me, do you, mistah? Oh, well, now, I reckon not,
W'y you could n't buy my Sukey fu' a thousan' on de spot.
Dat ol' mare o' mine?
Yes, huh coat ah long an' shaggy, an' she ain't no shakes to see;
Dat 's a ring-bone, yes, you right, suh, an' she got a on'ry knee,
But dey ain't no use in talkin', she de only hoss fu' me,
Dat ol' mare o' mine.

Co'se, I knows dat Suke 's contra'y, an' she moughty ap' to vex;
But you got to mek erlowance fu' de nature of huh sex;
Dat ol' mare o' mine.
Ef you pull her on de lef' han'; she plum 'termined to go right,
A cannon could n't skeer huh, but she boun' to tek a fright
At a piece o' common paper, or anyt'ing whut's white,
Dat ol' mare o' mine.

W'en my eyes commence to fail me, dough, I trus'es to huh sight,
An' she 'll tote me safe an' hones' on de ve'y da'kes' night,
Dat ol' mare o' mine.
Ef I whup huh, she jes' switch huh tail, an' settle to a walk,
Ef I whup huh mo', she shek huh haid, an' lak ez not, she balk.

But huh sense ain't no ways lackin', she do evah t'ing but talk,
Dat ol' mare o' mine.

But she gentle ez a lady w'en she know huh beau kin see.
An' she sholy got mo' gumption any day den you or me,
Dat ol' mare o' mine.
She 's a leetle slow a-goin,' an' she moughty ha'd to sta't,
But we 's gittin' ol' togathah, an' she 's closah to my hea't,
An' I does n't reckon, mistah, dat she 'd sca'cely keer to pa't;
Dat ol' mare o' mine.

W'y I knows de time dat cidah 's kin' o' muddled up my haid,
Ef it had n't been fu' Sukey hyeah, I reckon I 'd been daid;
Dat ol' mare o' mine.
But she got me in de middle o' de road an' tuk me home,
An' she would n't let me wandah, ner she would n't let me roam,
Dat 's de kin' o' hoss to tie to w'en you 's seed de cidah's foam,
Dat ol' mare o' mine.

You kin talk erbout yo' heaven, you kin talk erbout yo' hell,
Dey is people, dey is hosses, den dey's cattle, den dey 's—well —
Dat ol' mare o' mine;
She de beatenes' t'ing dat evah struck de medders o' de town,
An' aldough huh haid ain't fittin' fu' to waih no golden crown.
D' ain't a blessed way fu' Petah fu' to tu'n my Sukey down,
Dat ol' mare o' mine.

IN THE MORNING

'Lias! 'Lias! Bless de Lawd!
Don' you know de day 's erbroad?
Ef you don' git up, you scamp,
Dey 'll be trouble in dis camp.
T'ink I gwine to let you sleep
W'ile I meks yo' boa'd an' keep?
Dat 's a putty howdy-do —
Don' you hyeah me, 'Lias — you?

Bet ef I come crost dis flo'
You won' fin' no time to sno'.
Daylight all a-shinin' in
W'ile you sleep — w'y hit 's a sin!
Ain't de can'le-light enough
To bu'n out widout a snuff,
But you go de mo'nin' thoo
Bu'nin' up de daylight too?

'Lias, don' you hyeah me call?
No use tu'nin' to'ds de wall;

I kin hyeah dat mattuss squeak;
Don' you hyeah me w'en I speak?
Dis hyeah clock done struck off six —
Ca'line, bring me dem ah sticks!
Oh, you down, suh; huh, you down —
Look hyeah, don' you daih to frown.

Ma'ch yo'se'f an' wash yo' face,
Don' you splattah all de place;
I got somep'n else to do,
'Sides jes' cleanin' aftah you.
Tek dat comb an' fix yo' haid —
Looks jes' lak a feddah baid.
Look hyeah, boy, I let you see
You sha' n't roll yo' eyes at me.

Come hyeah; bring me dat ah strap!
Boy, I 'll whup you 'twell you drap;
You done felt yo'se'f too strong,
An' you sholy got me wrong.
Set down at dat table thaih;
Jes' you whimpah ef you daih!
Evah mo'nin' on dis place,
Seem lak I mus' lose my grace.

Fol' yo' han's an' bow yo' haid —
Wait ontwell de blessin' 's said;
" Lawd, have mussy on ouah souls —"
(Don' you daih to tech dem rolls —)
" Bless de food we gwine to eat —"
(You set still — I *see* yo' feet;
You jes' try dat trick agin!)
" Gin us peace an' joy. Amen!"

THE POET

He sang of life, serenely sweet,
With, now and then, a deeper note.
From some high peak, nigh yet remote,
He voiced the world's absorbing beat.

He sang of love when earth was young,
And Love, itself, was in his lays.
But ah, the world, it turned to praise
A jingle in a broken tongue.

A FLORIDA NIGHT

Win' a-blowin' gentle so de san' lay low,
San' a little heavy f'om de rain,
All de pa'ms a-wavin' an' a-weavin' slow,
Sighin' lak a sinnah-soul in pain.
Alligator grinnin' by de ol' lagoon,
Mockin'-bird a-singin' to be big full moon,

'Skeeter go a-skimmin' to his fightin' chune
(Lizy Ann 's a-waitin' in de lane!).

Moccasin a-sleepin' in de cyprus swamp;
Need n't wake de gent'man, not fu' me.
Mule, you need n't wake him w'en you switch an' stomp,
Fightin' off a 'skeeter er a flea.
Florida is lovely, she 's de fines' lan'
Evah seed de sunlight f'om de Mastah's han',
'Ceptin' fu' de varmints an' huh fleas an' san'
An' de nights w'en Lizy Ann ain' free.

Moon 's a-kinder shaddered on de melon patch;
No one ain't a-watchin' ez I go.
Climbin' of de fence so 's not to click de latch
Meks my gittin' in a little slow.
Watermelon smilin' as it say, "I 's free;"
Alligator boomin', but I let him be,
Florida, oh, Florida 's de lan' fu' me—
(Lizy Ann a-singin' sweet an' low).

DIFFERENCES

My neighbor lives on the hill,
And I in the valley dwell,
My neighbor must look down on me,
Must I look up?—ah, well,
My neighbor lives on the hill,
And I in the valley dwell.

My neighbor reads, and prays,
And I—I laugh, God wot,
And sing like a bird when the grass is green
In my small garden plot;
But ah, he reads and prays,
And I—I laugh, God wot.

His face is a book of woe,
And mine is a song of glee;
A slave he is to the great "They say,"
But I—I am bold and free;
No wonder he smacks of woe,
And I have the tang of glee.

My neighbor thinks me a fool,
"The same to yourself," say I;
"Why take your books and take your prayers,
Give me the open sky;"
My neighbor thinks me a fool,
"The same to yourself," say I.

LONG AGO

De ol' time 's gone, de new time 's hyeah
Wid all hits fuss an' feddahs;

I done fu'got de joy an' cheah
We knowed all kin's o' weddahs,
I done fu'got each ol'-time hymn
We ust to sing in meetin';
I 's leahned de prah's, so neat an' trim,
De preachah keeps us 'peatin'.

Hang a vine by de chimney side,
An' one by de cabin do';
An' sing a song fu' de day dat died,
De day of long ergo.

My youf, hit 's gone, yes, long ergo,
An' yit I ain't a-moanin';
Hit 's fu' somet'ings I ust to know
I set to-night a-honin'.
De pallet on de ol' plank flo',
De rain bar'l und' de eaves,
De live oak 'fo' de cabin do',
Whaih de night dove comes an' grieves.

Hang a vine by de chimney side,
An' one by de cabin do';
An' sing a song fu' de day dat died,
De day of long ergo.

I 'd lak a few ol' frien's to-night
To come an' set wid me;
An' let me feel dat ol' delight
I ust to in dey glee.
But hyeah we is, my pipe an' me,
Wid no one else erbout;
We bofe is choked ez choked kin be,
An' bofe 'll soon go out.

Hang a vine by de chimney side,
An' one by de cabin do';
An' sing a song fu' de day dat died,
De day of long ergo.

A PLANTATION MELODY

De trees is bendin' in de sto'm,
De rain done hid de mountain's fo'm,
I 's 'lone an' in distress.
But listen, dah 's a voice I hyeah,
A-sayin' to me, loud an' cleah,
"Lay low in de wildaness."

De lightnin' flash, de bough sway low,
My po' sick hea't is trimblin' so,
It hu'ts my very breas'.
But him dat give de lightnin' powah
Jes' bids me in de tryin' howah
"Lay low in de wildaness."

O brothah, w'en de tempes' beat,
An' w'en yo' weary head an' feet
Can't fin' no place to res',
Jes' 'membah dat de Mastah 's nigh,
An' putty soon you 'll hyeah de cry,
"Lay low in de wildaness."

O sistah, w'en de rain come down,
An' all yo' hopes is 'bout to drown,
Don't trus' de Mastah less.
He smilin' w'en you t'ink he frown,
He ain' gwine let yo' soul sink down —
Lay low in de wildaness.

A SPIRITUAL

De 'cession 's stahted on de gospel way,
De Capting is a-drawin' nigh:
Bettah stop a-foolin' an' a-try to pray;
Lif' up yo' haid w'en de King go by!

Oh, sinnah mou'nin' in de dusty road,
Hyeah 's de minute fu' to dry yo' eye:
Dey 's a moughty One a-comin' fu' to baih yo' load;
Lif' up yo' haid w'en de King go by!

Oh, widder weepin' by yo' husban's grave,
Hit 's bettah fu' to sing den sigh:
Hyeah come de Mastah wid de powah to save;
Lif' up yo' haid w'en de King go by!

Oh, orphans a-weepin' lak de widder do,
An' I wish you 'd tell me why:
De Mastah is a mammy an' a pappy too;
Lif' up yo' haid w'en de King go by!

Oh, Moses sot de sarpint in de wildahness
W'en de chillun had commenced to die:
Some 'efused to look, but hit cuohed de res';
Lif' up yo' haid w'en de King go by!

Bow down, bow 'way down,
Bow down,
But lif' up yo' haid w'en de King go by!

THE MEMORY OF MARTHA

Out in de night a sad bird moans,
An', oh, but hit 's moughty lonely;
Times I kin sing, but mos' I groans,
Fu' oh, but hit 's moughty lonely!
Is you sleepin' well dis evenin', Marfy, deah?
W'en I calls you f'om de cabin, kin you hyeah?
'T ain't de same ol' place to me,
Nuffin' 's lak hit used to be,

W'en I knowed dat you was allus some'ers near.

Down by de road de shadders grows,
An', oh, but hit 's moughty lonely;
Seem lak de ve'y moonlight knows,
An', oh, but hit 's moughty lonely!
Does you know, I 's cryin' fu' you, oh, my wife?
Does you know dey ain't no joy no mo' in life?
An' my only t'ought is dis,
Dat I 's honin' fu' de bliss
Fu' to quit dis groun' o' worriment an' strife.

Dah on de baid my banjo lays,
An', oh, but hit 's moughty lonely;
Can't even sta't a chune o' praise,
An', oh, but hit 's moughty lonely!
Oh, hit's moughty slow a-waitin' hyeah below.
Is you watchin' fu' me, Marfy, at de do'?
Ef you is, in spite o' sin,
Dey 'll be sho' to let me in,
W'en dey sees yo' face a-shinin', den dey 'll know.

W'EN I GITS HOME

It's moughty tiahsome layin' 'roun'
Dis sorrer-laden earfly groun',
An' oftentimes I thinks, thinks I,
'T would be a sweet t'ing des to die,
An' go 'long home.

Home whaih de frien's I loved 'll say,
"We 've waited fu' you many a day,
Come hyeah an' res' yo'se'f, an' know
You 's done wid sorrer an' wid woe,
Now you 's at home."

W'en I gits home some blessid day,
I 'lows to th'ow my caihs erway,
An' up an' down de shinin' street,
Go singin' sof' an' low an' sweet,
W'en I gits home.

I wish de day was neah at han',
I 's tiahed of dis grievin' lan',
I 's tiahed of de lonely yeahs,
I want to des dry up my teahs,
An' go 'long home.

Oh, Mastah, won't you sen' de call?
My frien's is daih, my hope, my all.

I 's waitin' whaih de road is rough,
I want to hyeah you say,
"Enough,
Ol' man, come home!"

"HOWDY, HONEY, HOWDY!"

Do' a-stan'in' on a jar, fiah a-shinin' thoo,
Ol' folks drowsin' 'roun' de place, wide awake is Lou,
W'en I tap, she answeh, an' I see huh 'mence to grin,
"Howdy, honey, howdy, won't you step right in?"

Den I step erpon de log layin' at de do',
Bless de Lawd, huh mammy an' huh pap 's done 'menced to sno',
Now 's de time, ef evah, ef I 's gwine to try an' win,
"Howdy, honey, howdy, won't you step right in?"

No use playin' on de aidge, trimblin' on de brink,
W'en a body love a gal, tell huh whut he t'ink;
W'en huh hea't is open fu' de love you gwine to gin,
Pull yo'se'f togethah, suh, an' step right in.

Sweetes' imbitation dat a body evah hyeahed,
Sweetah den de music of a love-sick mockin'-bird,
Comin' f'om de gal you loves bettah den yo' kin,
"Howdy, honey, howdy, won't you step right in?"

At de gate o' heaven w'en de storm o' life is pas',
'Spec' I 'll be a-stan'in', 'twell de Mastah say at las',
"Hyeah he stan' all weary, but he winned his fight wid sin.
Howdy, honey, howdy, won't you step right in?"

THE UNSUNG HEROES

A song for the unsung heroes who rose in the country's need,
When the life of the land was threatened by the slaver's cruel greed,
For the men who came from the cornfield, who came from the plough and the flail,
Who rallied round when they heard the sound of the mighty man of the rail.

They laid them down in the valleys, they laid them down in the wood,
And the world looked on at the work they did, and whispered, "It is good."

They fought their way on the hillside, they fought their way in the glen,
And God looked down on their sinews brown, and said, "I have made them men."

They went to the blue lines gladly, and the blue lines took them in,
And the men who saw their muskets' fire thought not of their dusky skin.
The gray lines rose and melted beneath their scathing showers,
And they said, "'T is true, they have force to do, these old slave boys of ours."

Ah, Wagner saw their glory, and Pillow knew their blood,
That poured on a nation's altar, a sacrificial flood.
Port Hudson heard their war-cry that smote its smoke-filled air,
And the old free fires of their savage sires again were kindled there.

They laid them down where the rivers the greening valleys gem.
And the song of the thund'rous cannon was their sole requiem,
And the great smoke wreath that mingled its hue with the dusky cloud,
Was the flag that furled o'er a saddened world, and the sheet that made their shroud.

Oh, Mighty God of the Battles Who held them in Thy hand,
Who gave them strength through the whole day's length, to fight for their native land,
They are lying dead on the hillsides, they are lying dead on the plain,
And we have not fire to smite the lyre and sing them one brief strain.

Give, Thou, some seer the power to sing them in their might,
The men who feared the master's whip, but did not fear the fight;
That he may tell of their virtues as minstrels did of old,
Till the pride of face and the hate of race grow obsolete and cold.

A song for the unsung heroes who stood the awful test,
When the humblest host that the land could boast went forth to meet the best;
A song for the unsung heroes who fell on the bloody sod,

Who fought their way from night to day and struggled up to God.

THE POOL

By the pool that I see in my dreams, dear love,
I have sat with you time and again;
And listened beneath the dank leaves, dear love,
To the sibilant sound of the rain.

And the pool, it is silvery bright, dear love,
And as pure as the heart of a maid,
As sparkling and dimpling, it darkles and shines
In the depths of the heart of the glade.

But, oh, I 've a wish in my soul, dear love,
(The wish of a dreamer, it seems,)
That I might wash free of my sins, dear love,
In the pool that I see in my dreams.

POSSESSION

Whose little lady is you, chile,
Whose little gal is you?
What 's de use o' kiver'n up yo' face?
Chile, dat ain't de way to do.
Lemme see yo' little eyes,
Tek yo' little han's down nice,
Lawd, you wuff a million bills,
Huh uh, chile, dat ain't yo' price.

Honey, de money ain't been made
Dat dey could pay fu' you;
'T ain't no use a-biddin'; you too high
Fu' de riches' Jap er Jew.
Lemme see you smilin' now,
How dem teef o' yo'n do shine,
An' de t'ing dat meks me laff
Is dat all o' you is mine.

How 's I gwine to tell you how I feel,
How 's I gwine to weigh yo' wuff?
Oh, you sholy is de sweetes' t'ing
Walkin' on dis blessed earf.
Possum is de sweetes' meat,
Cidah is the nices' drink,
But my little lady-bird
Is de bes' of all, I t'ink.

Talk erbout 'uligion he'pin' folks
All thoo de way o' life,
Gin de res' 'uligion, des' gin me
You, my little lady-wife.
Den de days kin come all ha'd,
Den de nights kin come all black,

Des' you tek me by de han',
An' I 'll stumble on de track.

Stumble on de way to Gawd, my chile,
Stumble on, an' mebbe fall;
But I 'll keep a-trottin', while you lead on,
Pickin' an' a-trottin', dat 's all.
Hol' me mighty tight, dough, chile,
Fu' hit 's rough an' rocky lan',
Heaben 's at de en', I know,
So I 's leanin' on yo' han'.

THE OLD FRONT GATE

W'EN daih 's chillun in de house,
Dey keep on a-gittin' tall;
But de folks don' seem to see
Dat dey 's growin' up at all,
'Twell dey fin' out some fine day
Dat de gals has 'menced to grow,
W'en dey notice as dey pass
Dat de front gate 's saggin' low.

W'en de hinges creak an' cry,
An' de bahs go slantin' down,
You kin reckon dat hit 's time
Fu' to cas' yo' eye erroun',
'Cause daih ain't no 'sputin' dis,
Hit 's de trues' sign to show
Dat daih 's cou'tin' goin' on
W'en de ol' front gate sags low.

Oh, you grumble an' complain,
An' you prop dat gate up right;
But you notice right nex' day
Dat hit 's in de same ol' plight.
So you fin' dat hit 's a rule,
An' daih ain' no use to blow,
W'en de gals is growin' up,
Dat de front gate will sag low.

Den you t'ink o' yo' young days,
W'en you cou'ted Sally Jane,
An' you so't o' feel ashamed
Fu' to grumble an' complain,
'Cause yo' ricerlection says,
An' you know hits wo'ds is so,
Dat huh pappy had a time
Wid his front gate saggin' low.

So you jes' looks on an' smiles
At 'em leanin' on de gate,
Tryin' to t'ink whut he kin say
Fu' to keep him daih so late,
But you lets dat gate erlone,
Fu' yo' 'sperunce goes to show,
'Twell de gals is ma'ied off,
It gwine keep on saggin' low.

DIRGE FOR A SOLDIER

IN the east the morning comes,
Hear the rollin' of the drums
On the hill.
But the heart that beat as they beat
In the battle's raging day heat
Lieth still.
Unto him the night has come,
Though they roll the morning drum.

What is in the bugle's blast?
It is: "Victory at last!
Now for rest."
But, my comrades, come behold him,
Where our colors now enfold him,
And his breast
Bares no more to meet the blade,
But lies covered in the shade.

What a stir there is to-day!
They are laying him away
Where he fell.
There the flag goes draped before him;
Now they pile the grave sod o'er him
With a knell.
And he answers to his name
In the higher ranks of fame.

There 's a woman left to mourn
For the child that she has borne
In travail.
But her heart beats high and higher,
With the patriot mother's fire,
At the tale.
She has borne and lost a son,
But her work and his are done.

Fling the flag out, let it wave;
They 're returning from the grave —
"Double quick!"
And the cymbals now are crashing,
Bright his comrades' eyes are flashing
From the thick
Battle-ranks which knew him brave,
No tears for a hero's grave.

In the east the morning comes,
Hear the rattle of the drums
Far away.
Now no time for grief's pursuing,
Other work is for the doing,
Here to-day.
He is sleeping, let him rest
With the flag across his breast.

A FROLIC

Swing yo' lady roun' an' roun',
Do de bes' you know;
Mek yo' bow an' p'omenade
Up an' down de flo';
Mek dat banjo hump huhse'f,
Listen at huh talk:
Mastah gone to town to-night;
'T ain't no time to walk.

Lif' yo' feet an' flutter thoo,
Run, Miss Lucy, run;
Reckon you 'll be cotched an' kissed
'Fo' de night is done.
You don't need to be so proud —
I 's a-watchin' you,
An' I 's layin' lots o' plans
Fu' to git you, too.

Moonlight on de cotton-fiel'
Shinin' sof' an' white,
Whippo'will a-tellin' tales
Out thaih in de night;
An' yo' cabin 's 'crost de lot:
Run, Miss Lucy, run;
Reckon you 'll be cotched an' kissed
'Fo' de night is done.

NODDIN' BY DE FIRE

SOME folks t'inks hit 's right an' p'opah,
Soon ez bedtime come erroun',
Fu' to scramble to de kiver,
Lak dey 'd hyeahed de trumpet soun'.
But dese people dey all misses
Whut I mos'ly does desiah;
Dat 's de settin' roun' an' dozin',
An' a-noddin' by de fiah.

When you 's tiahed out a-hoein',
Er a-followin' de plough,
Whut 's de use of des a-fallin'
On yo' pallet lak a cow?
W'y, de fun is all in waitin'
In de face of all de tiah,
An' a-dozin' and a-drowsin'
By a good ol' hick'ry fiah.

Oh, you grunts an' groans an' mumbles
Case yo' bones is full o' col',
Dough you feels de joy a-tricklin'
Roun' de co'nahs of yo' soul.
An' you 'low anothah minute
'S sho to git you wa'm an' dryah,
W'en you set up pas' yo' bedtime,
Case you hates to leave de fiah.

Whut 's de use o' downright sleepin'?
You can't feel it while it las',
An' you git up feelin' sorry
W'en de time fu' it is pas'.
Seem to me dat time too precious,
An' de houahs too short entiah,
Fu' to sleep, w'en you could spen' 'em
Des a-noddin' by de fiah.

LOVE'S CASTLE

KEY and bar, key and bar,
Iron bolt and chain!
And what will you do when the King comes
To enter his domain?

Turn key and lift bar,
Loose, oh, bolt and chain!
Open the door and let him in,
And then lock up again.

But, oh, heart, and woe, heart,
Why do you ache so sore?
Never a moment's peace have you
Since Love hath passed the door.

Turn key and lift bar,
And loose bolt and chain;
But Love took in his esquire, Grief,
And there they both remain.

MORNING SONG OF LOVE

Darling, my darling, my heart is on the wing,
It flies to thee this morning like a bird,
Like happy birds in springtime my spirits soar and sing,
The same sweet song thine ears have often heard.

The sun is in my window, the shadow on the lea,
The wind is moving in the branches green,
And all my life, my darling, is turning unto thee,
And kneeling at thy feet, my own, my queen.

The golden bells are ringing across the distant hill,
Their merry peals come to me soft and clear,
But in my heart's deep chapel all incense-filled and still
A sweeter bell is sounding for thee, dear.

The bell of love invites thee to come and seek the shrine
Whose altar is erected unto thee,
The offerings, the sacrifice, the prayers, the chants are thine,
And I, my love, thy humble priest will be.

ON A CLEAN BOOK

TO F. N.

Like sea-washed sand upon the shore,
So fine and clean the tale,
So clear and bright I almost see,
The flashing of a sail.

The tang of salt is in its veins,
The freshness of the spray
God give you love and lore and strength,
To give us such alway.

TO THE EASTERN SHORE

I 's feelin' kin' o' lonesome in my little room to-night,
An' my min 's done los' de minutes an' de miles,
W'ile it teks me back a-flyin' to de country of delight,
Whaih de Chesapeake goes grumblin' er wid smiles.
Oh, de ol' plantation 's callin' to me, Come, come back,

Hyeah 's de place fu' you to labouh an' to res',
'Fu my sandy roads is gleamin' w'ile de city ways is black;
Come back, honey, case yo' country home is bes'.

I know de moon is shinin' down erpon de Eastern sho',
An' de bay 's a-sayin' "Howdy" to de lan';
An' de folks is all a-settin' out erroun' de cabin do',
Wid dey feet a-restin' in de silvah san';
An' de ol' plantation 's callin' to me, Come, oh, come,
F'om de life dat 's des' a-waihin' you erway,
F'om de trouble an' de bustle, an' de agernizin' hum
Dat de city keeps ergoin' all de day.

I 's tiahed of de city, tek me back to Sandy Side,
Whaih de po'est ones kin live an' play an' eat;
Whaih we draws a simple livin' f'om de fo'est an' de tide,
An' de days ah faih, an' evah night is sweet.
Fu' de ol' plantation 's callin' to me, Come, oh, come.
An' de Chesapeake 's a-sayin' "Dat 's de t'ing,"
W'ile my little cabin beckons, dough his mouf is closed an' dumb,
I 's a-comin, an' my hea't begins to sing.

RELUCTANCE

Will I have some mo' dat pie?
No, ma'am, thank-ee, dat is—I—
Bettah quit daihin' me.
Dat ah pie look sutny good:
How 'd you feel now ef I would?
I don' reckon dat I should;
Bettah quit daihin' me.

Look hyeah, I gwine tell de truf,
Mine is sholy one sweet toof:
Bettah quit daihin' me.
Yass'm, yass'm, dat 's all right,
I 's done tried to be perlite:
But dat pie 's a lakly sight,
Wha 's de use o' daihin' me?

My, yo' lips is full an' red,
Don't I wish you 'd tu'n yo' haid?
Bettah quit daihin' me.
Dat ain't faih, now, honey chile,
I 's gwine lose my sense erwhile
Ef you des set daih an' smile,
Bettah quit daihin' me.

Nuffin' don' look ha'f so fine
Ez dem teef, deah, w'en dey shine:
Bettah quit daihin' me.
Now look hyeah, I tells you dis;

I 'll give up all othah bliss
Des to have one little kiss,
  Bettah quit daihin' me.

Laws, I teks yo' little han',
Ain't it tendah? bless de lan'—
  Bettah quit daihin' me.
I 's so lonesome by myse'f,
'D ain't no fun in livin' lef';
Dis hyeah life 's ez dull ez def:
  Bettah quit daihin' me.

Why n't you tek yo' han' erway?
Yass, I 'll hol' it: but I say
  Bettah quit daihin' me.
Holin' han's is sholy fine.
Seems lak dat 's de weddin' sign.
Wish you 'd say dat you 'd be mine;—
  Dah you been daihin' me.

BALLADE

By Mystic's banks I held my dream.
  (I held my fishing rod as well,)
The vision was of dace and bream,
  A fruitless vision, sooth to tell.
  But round about the sylvan dell
Were other sweet Arcadian shrines,
  Gone now, is all the rural spell,
Arcadia has trolley lines.

Oh, once loved, sluggish, darkling stream,
  For me no more, thy waters swell,
Thy music now the engines' scream,
  Thy fragrance now the factory's smell;
  Too near for me the clanging bell;
A false light in the water shines
  While Solitude lists to her knell,—
Arcadia has trolley lines.

Thy wooded lanes with shade and gleam
  Where bloomed the fragrant asphodel,
Now bleak commercially teem
  With signs "To Let," "To Buy," "To Sell."
  And Commerce holds them fierce and fell;
With vulgar sport she now combines
  Sweet Nature's piping voice to quell.
Arcadia has trolley lines.

L'ENVOI.

Oh, awful Power whose works repel
  The marvel of the earth's designs,—
I 'll hie me otherwhere to dwell,
  Arcadia has trolley lines.

SPEAKIN' AT DE COU'T-HOUSE

Dey been speakin' at de cou't-house,
An' laws-a-massy me,
'T was de beatness kin' o' doin's
Dat evah I did see.
Of cose I had to be dah
In de middle o' de crowd,
An' I hallohed wid de othahs,
W'en de speakah riz and bowed.

I was kind o' disapp'inted
At de smallness of de man,
Case I 'd allus pictered great folks
On a mo' expansive plan;
But I t'ought I could respect him
An' tek in de wo'ds he said,
Fu' dey sho was somp'n knowin'
In de bald spot on his haid.

But hit did seem so't o' funny
Aftah waitin' fu' a week
Dat de people kep' on shoutin'
So de man des could n't speak;
De ho'ns dey blared a little,
Den dey let loose on de drums,—
Some one tol' me dey was playin'
" See de conkerin' hero comes."

" Well," says I, " you all is white folks,
But you 's sutny actin' queer,
What 's de use of heroes comin'
Ef dey cain't talk w'en dey 's here? "

Aftah while dey let him open,
An' dat man he waded in,
An' he fit de wahs all ovah
Winnin' victeries lak sin.

W'en he come down to de present,
Den he made de feathahs fly.
He des waded in on money,
An' he played de ta'iff high.
An' he said de colah question,
Hit was ovah, solved, an' done,
Dat de dahky was his brothah,
Evah blessed mothah's son.

Well he settled all de trouble
Dat 's been pesterin' de lan',
Den he set down mid de cheerin'
An' de playin' of de ban'.
I was feelin' moughty happy
'Twell I hyeahed somebody speak,
" Well, dat 's his side of de bus'-ness,
But you wait for Jones nex' week."

BLACK SAMSON OF BRANDYWINE

"In the fight at Brandywine, Black Samson, a giant negro armed with a scythe, sweeps his way through the red ranks. . . ." C. M. Skinner's *"Myths and Legends of Our Own Land."*

Gray are the pages of record,
Dim are the volumes of eld;
Else had old Delaware told us
More that her history held.

Told us with pride in the story,
  Honest and noble and fine,
More of the tale of my hero,
  Black Samson of Brandywine.

Sing of your chiefs and your nobles,
  Saxon and Celt and Gaul,
Breath of mine ever shall join you,
  Highly I honor them all.
Give to them all of their glory,
  But for this noble of mine,
Lend him a tithe of your tribute,
  Black Samson of Brandywine.

There in the heat of the battle,
  There in the stir of the fight,
Loomed he, an ebony giant,
  Black as the pinions of night.
Swinging his scythe like a mower
  Over a field of grain,
Needless the care of the gleaners,
  Where he had passed amain.

Straight through the human harvest,
  Cutting a bloody swath,
Woe to you, soldier of Briton!
  Death is abroad in his path.
Flee from the scythe of the reaper,
  Flee while the moment is thine,
None may with safety withstand him,
  Black Samson of Brandywine.

Was he a freeman or bondman?
  Was he a man or a thing?
What does it matter? His brav'ry
  Renders him royal — a king.
If he was only a chattel,
  Honor the ransom may pay
Of the royal, the loyal black giant
  Who fought for his country that day.

Noble and bright is the story,
  Worthy the touch of the lyre,
Sculptor or poet should find it
  Full of the stuff to inspire.
Beat it in brass and in copper,
  Tell it in storied line,
So that the world may remember
  Black Samson of Brandywine.

THE LOOKING-GLASS

DINAH stan' befo' de glass,
  Lookin' moughty neat,
An' huh purty shadder sass
  At huh haid an' feet.
While she sasshay 'roun' an' bow,
Smilin' den an' poutin' now,
An' de lookin'-glass, I 'low
  Say: " Now, ain't she sweet? "

All she do, de glass it see,
  Hit des see, no mo',
Seems to me, hit ought to be
  Drappin' on de flo'.
She go w'en huh time git slack,
Kissin' han's an' smilin' back,
Lawsy, how my lips go smack,
  Watchin' at de do'.

Wisht I was huh lookin'-glass,
W'en she kissed huh han';
Does you t'ink I 'd let it pass,
Settin' on de stan'?
No; I'd des' fall down an' break,
Kin' o' glad 't uz fu' huh sake;
But de diffunce, dat whut make
Lookin'-glass an' man.

A MISTY DAY

Heart of my heart, the day is chill,
The mist hangs low o'er the wooded hill,
The soft white mist and the heavy cloud
The sun and the face of heaven shroud.
The birds are thick in the dripping trees,
That drop their pearls to the beggar breeze;
No songs are rife where songs are wont,
Each singer crouches in his haunt.

Heart of my heart, the day is chill,
Whene'er thy loving voice is still,
The cloud and mist hide the sky from me,
Whene'er thy face I cannot see.
My thoughts fly back from the chill without,
My mind in the storm drops doubt on doubt,
No songs arise. Without thee, love,
My soul sinks down like a frightened dove.

LI'L' GAL

Oh, de weathah it is balmy an' de breeze is sighin' low.
Li'l' gal,
An' de mockin' bird is singin' in de locus' by de do',
Li'l' gal;
Dere 's a hummin' an' a bummin' in de lan' f'om eas' to wes',
I 's a-sighin' fu' you, honey, an' I nevah know no res'.
Fu' dey 's lots o' trouble brewin' an' a-stewin' in my breas',
Li'l' gal.

Whut 's de mattah wid de weathah, whut 's de mattah wid de breeze,
Li'l' gal?
Whut 's de mattah wid de locus' dat 's a-singin' in de trees,
Li'l' gal?
W'y dey knows dey ladies love 'em, an' dey knows dey love 'em true,
An' dey love 'em back, I reckon, des' lak I 's a-lovin' you;
Dat 's de reason dey 's a-weavin' an' a-sighin', thoo an' thoo,
Li'l' gal.

Don't you let no da'ky fool you 'cause de clo'es he waihs is fine,
Li'l' gal.
Dey 's a hones' hea't a-beatin' unnerneaf dese rags o' mine,
Li'l' gal.
C'ose dey ain' no use in mockin' whut de birds an' weathah do,
But I 's so'y I cain't 'spress it w'en I knows I loves you true,
Dat 's de reason I 's a-sighin' an' a-singin now fu' you,
Li'l' gal.

DOUGLASS

Ah, Douglass, we have fall'n on evil days,
Such days as thou, not even thou didst know,
When thee, the eyes of that harsh long ago
Saw, salient, at the cross of devious ways,
And all the country heard thee with amaze.
Not ended then, the passionate ebb and flow,
The awful tide that battled to and fro;
We ride amid a tempest of dispraise.

Now, when the waves of swift dissension swarm,
And Honor, the strong pilot, lieth stark,
Oh, for thy voice high-sounding o'er the storm,
For thy strong arm to guide the shivering bark,
The blast-defying power of thy form,
To give us comfort through the lonely dark.

WHEN SAM'L SINGS

Hyeah dat singin' in de medders
Whaih de folks is mekin' hay?
Wo'k is pretty middlin' heavy
Fu' a man to be so gay.
You kin tell dey 's somep'n special
F'om de canter o' de song;
Somep'n sholy pleasin' Sam'l,
W'en he singin' all day long.

Hyeahd him wa'blin' 'way dis mo'nin'
'Fo' 't was light enough to see.
Seem lak music in de evenin'
Allus good enough fu' me.
But dat man commenced to hollah
'Fo' he 'd even washed his face;
Would you b'lieve, de scan'lous rascal
Woke de birds erroun' de place?

Sam'l took a trip a-Sad'day;
Dressed hisse'f in all he had,
Tuk a cane an' went a-strollin',
Lookin' mighty pleased an' glad.

Some folks don' know whut de mattah,
But I do, you bet yo' life;
Sam'l smilin' an' a-singin'
'Case he been to see his wife.

She live on de fu' plantation,
Twenty miles erway er so;
But huh man is mighty happy
W'en he git de chanst to go.
Walkin' allus ain' de nices'—
Mo'nin' fin's him on de way —
But he allus comes back smilin',
Lak his pleasure was his pay.

Den he do a heap o' talkin',
Do' he mos'ly kin' o' still,
But de wo'ds, dey gits to runnin'
Lak de watah fu' a mill.
" Whut 's de use o' havin' trouble,
Whut 's de use o' havin' strife? "
Dat 's de way dis Sam'l preaches
W'en he been to see his wife.

An' I reckon I git jealous,
Fu' I laff an' joke an' sco'n,
An' I say, " Oh, go on, Sam'l,
Des go on, an' blow yo' ho'n."
But I know dis comin' Sad'day,
Dey 'll be brighter days in life;
An' I 'll be ez glad ez Sam'l
W'en I go to see my wife.

BOOKER T. WASHINGTON

THE word is writ that he who runs may read.
What is the passing breath of earthly fame?
But to snatch glory from the hands of blame —
That is to be, to live, to strive indeed.
A poor Virginia cabin gave the seed,
And from its dark and lowly door there came
A peer of princes in the world's acclaim,
A master spirit for the nation's need.
Strong, silent, purposeful beyond his kind,
The mark of rugged force on brow and lip,
Straight on he goes, nor turns to look behind
Where hot the hounds come baying at his hip;
With one idea foremost in his mind,
Like the keen prow of some onforging ship.

THE MONK'S WALK

IN this sombre garden close
What has come and passed, who knows?
What red passion, what white pain
Haunted this dim walk in vain?

Underneath the ivied wall,
Where the silent shadows fall,

Lies the pathway chill and damp
Where the world-quit dreamers tramp.

Just across, where sunlight burns,
Smiling at the mourning ferns,
Stand the roses, side by side,
Nodding in their useless pride.

Ferns and roses, who shall say
What you witness day by day?
Covert smile or dropping eye,
As the monks go pacing by.

Has the novice come to-day
Here beneath the wall to pray?
Has the young monk, lately chidden,
Sung his lyric, sweet, forbidden?

Tell me, roses, did you note
That pale father's throbbing throat?
Did you hear him murmur, "Love!"
As he kissed a faded glove?

Mourning ferns, pray tell me why
Shook you with that passing sigh?
Is it that you chanced to spy
Something in the Abbot's eye?

Here no dream, nor thought of sin,
Where no worldling enters in;
Here no longing, no desire,
Heat nor flame of earthly fire.

Branches waving green above,
Whisper naught of life nor love;
Softened winds that seem a breath,
Perfumed, bring no fear of death.

Is it living thus to live?
Has life nothing more to give?
Ah, no more of smile or sigh —
Life, the world, and love, goodbye.

Gray, and passionless, and dim,
Echoing of the solemn hymn,
Lies the walk, 'twixt fern and rose,
Here within the garden close.

LOVE-SONG

If Death should claim me for her own to-day,
And softly I should falter from your side,
Oh, tell me, loved one, would my memory stay,
And would my image in your heart abide?
Or should I be as some forgotten dream,
That lives its little space, then fades entire?
Should Time send o'er you its relentless stream,
To cool your heart, and quench for aye love's fire?

I would not for the world, love, give you pain,
Or ever compass what would cause you grief;

And, oh, how well I know that tears are vain!
But love is sweet, my dear, and life is brief;
So if some day before you I should go
Beyond the sound and sight of song and sea,
'T would give my spirit stronger wings to know
That you remembered still and wept for me.

SLOW THROUGH THE DARK

Slow moves the pageant of a climbing race;
Their footsteps drag far, far below the height,
And, unprevailing by their utmost might,
Seem faltering downward from each hard won place.
No strange, swift-sprung exception we; we trace
A devious way thro' dim, uncertain light,—
Our hope, through the long vistaed years, a sight
Of that our Captain's soul sees face to face.
Who, faithless, faltering that the road is steep,
Now raiseth up his drear insistent cry?
Who stoppeth here to spend a while in sleep
Or curseth that the storm obscures the sky?
Heed not the darkness round you, dull and deep;
The clouds grow thickest when the summit 's nigh.

THE MURDERED LOVER

Say a mass for my soul's repose, my brother,
Say a mass for my soul's repose, I need it,
Lovingly lived we, the sons of one mother,
Mine was the sin, but I pray you not heed it.

Dark were her eyes as the sloe and they called me,
Called me with voice independent of breath.
God! how my heart beat; her beauty appalled me,
Dazed me, and drew to the sea-brink of death.

Lithe was her form like a willow. She beckoned,
What could I do save to follow and follow,
Nothing of right or result could be reckoned;
Life without her was unworthy and hollow.

Ay, but I wronged thee, my brother, my brother;
    Ah, but I loved her, thy beautiful wife.
Shade of our father, and soul of our mother,
    Have I not paid for my love with my life?

Dark was the night when, revengeful, I met you,
    Deep in the heart of a desolate land.
Warm was the life-blood which angrily wet you
    Sharp was the knife that I felt from your hand.

Wept you, oh, wept you, alone by the river,
    When my stark carcass you secretly sank.
Ha, now I see that you tremble and shiver;
    'T was but my spirit that passed when you shrank!

Weep not, oh, weep not, 't is over, 't is over;
    Stir the dark weeds with the turn of the tide;
Go, thou hast sent me forth, ever a rover,
    Rest and the sweet realm of heaven denied.

Say a mass for my soul's repose, my brother,
    Say a mass for my soul, I need it.
Sin of mine was it, and sin of no other,
    Mine was it all, but I pray you not heed it.

PHILOSOPHY

I BEEN t'inkin' 'bout de preachah; whut he said de othah night,
    'Bout hit bein' people's dooty, fu' to keep dey faces bright;
How one ought to live so pleasant dat ouah tempah never riles,
    Meetin' evahbody roun' us wid ouah very nicest smiles.

Dat 's all right, I ain't a-sputin' not a t'ing dat soun's lak fac',
    But you don't ketch folks a-grinnin' wid a misery in de back;
An' you don't fin' dem a-smilin' w'en dey 's hongry ez kin be,
    Leastways, dat 's how human natur' allus seems to 'pear to me.

We is mos' all putty likely fu' to have our little cares,
    An' I think we 'se doin' fus' rate w'en we jes' go long and bears,

Widout breakin' up ouah faces in
a sickly so't o' grin,
W'en we knows dat in ouah in-
nards we is p'intly mad ez
sin.

Oh dey 's times fu' bein' pleasant
an' fu' goin' smilin' roun',
'Cause I don't believe in people
allus totin' roun' a frown,
But it 's easy 'nough to titter w'en
de stew is smokin' hot,
But hit 's mighty ha'd to giggle
w'en dey 's nuffin' in de
pot.

A PREFERENCE

MASTAH drink his ol' Made'a,
Missy drink huh sherry wine,
Ovahseah lak his whiskey,
But dat othah drink is mine,
Des' 'lasses an' watah, 'lasses
an' watah.

W'en you git a steamin' hoe-cake
On de table, go way, man!
'D ain but one t'ing to go wid it,
'Sides de gravy in de pan,
Dat 's 'lasses an' watah, 'lasses
an' watah.

W'en hit 's 'possum dat you eatin',
'Simmon beer is moughty sweet;
But fu' evahday consumin'
'D ain't no mo'tal way to beat
Des' 'lasses an' watah, 'lasses
an' watah.

W'y de bees is allus busy,
An' ain' got no time to was'?
Hit 's beca'se dey knows de honey
Dey 's a makin', gwine to tas'
Lak 'lasses an' watah, 'lasses
an' watah.

Oh, hit 's moughty mil' an'
soothin',
An' hit don' go to yo' haid;
Dat 's de reason I 's a-backin'
Up de othah wo'ds I said,
" Des 'lasses an' watah, 'lasses
an' watah."

THE DEBT

THIS is the debt I pay
Just for one riotous day,
Years of regret and grief,
Sorrow without relief.

Pay it I will to the end —
Until the grave, my friend,
Gives me a true release —
Gives me the clasp of peace.

Slight was the thing I bought,
Small was the debt I thought,
Poor was the loan at best —
God! but the interest!

ON THE DEDICATION OF DOROTHY HALL

TUSKEGEE, ALA., APRIL 22, 1901.

NOT to the midnight of the gloomy past,
Do we revert to-day; we look upon
The golden present and the future vast
Whose vistas show us visions of the dawn.

Nor shall the sorrows of departed years
The sweetness of our tranquil souls annoy,
The sunshine of our hopes dispels the tears,
And clears our eyes to see this later joy.

Not ever in the years that God hath given
Have we gone friendless down the thorny way,
Always the clouds of pregnant black were riven
By flashes from His own eternal day.

The women of a race should be its pride;
We glory in the strength our mothers had,
We glory that this strength was not denied
To labor bravely, nobly, and be glad.

God give to these within this temple here,
Clear vision of the dignity of toil,
That virtue in them may its blossoms rear
Unspotted, fragrant, from the lowly soil.

God bless the givers for their noble deed,
Shine on them with the mercy of Thy face,
Who come with open hearts to help and speed
The striving women of a struggling race.

A ROADWAY

LET those who will stride on their barren roads
And prick themselves to haste with self-made goads,
Unheeding, as they struggle day by day,
If flowers be sweet or skies be blue or gray:
For me, the lone, cool way by purling brooks,
The solemn quiet of the woodland nooks,
A song-bird somewhere trilling sadly gay,

A pause to pick a flower beside the way.

BY RUGGED WAYS

By rugged ways and thro' the night
We struggle blindly toward the light;
And groping, stumbling, ever pray
For sight of long delaying day.
The cruel thorns beside the road
Stretch eager points our steps to goad,
And from the thickets all about
Detaining hands reach threatening out.

"Deliver us, oh, Lord," we cry,
Our hands uplifted to the sky.
No answer save the thunder's peal,
And onward, onward, still we reel.
"Oh, give us now thy guiding light;"
Our sole reply, the lightning's blight.
"Vain, vain," cries one, "in vain we call;"
But faith serene is over all.

Beside our way the streams are dried,
And famine mates us side by side.
Discouraged and reproachful eyes
Seek once again the frowning skies.
Yet shall there come, spite storm and shock,
A Moses who shall smite the rock,
Call manna from the Giver's hand,
And lead us to the promised land!

The way is dark and cold and steep,
And shapes of horror murder sleep,
And hard the unrelenting years;
But 'twixt our sighs and moans and tears,
We still can smile, we still can sing,
Despite the arduous journeying.
For faith and hope their courage lend,
And rest and light are at the end.

LOVE'S SEASONS

When the bees are humming in the honeysuckle vine
And the summer days are in their bloom,
Then my love is deepest, oh, dearest heart of mine,
When the bees are humming in the honeysuckle vine.

When the winds are moaning o'er the meadows chill and gray,
And the land is dim with winter gloom,
Then for thee, my darling, love will have its way,
When the winds are moaning o'er the meadows chill and gray.

In the vernal dawning with the starting of the leaf,

In the merry-chanting time of spring,
Love steals all my senses, oh, the happy-hearted thief!
In the vernal morning with the starting of the leaf.

Always, ever always, even in the autumn drear,
When the days are sighing out their grief,
Thou art still my darling, dearest of the dear,
Always, ever always, even in the autumn drear.

TO A DEAD FRIEND

It is as if a silver chord
Were suddenly grown mute,
And life's song with its rhythm warred
Against a silver lute.

It is as if a silence fell
Where bides the garnered sheaf,
And voices murmuring, "It is well,"
Are stifled by our grief.

It is as if the gloom of night
Had hid a summer's day,
And willows, sighing at their plight,
Bent low beside the way.

For he was part of all the best
That Nature loves and gives,
And ever more on Memory's breast
He lies and laughs and lives.

TO THE SOUTH

ON ITS NEW SLAVERY

Heart of the Southland, heed me pleading now,
Who bearest, unashamed, upon my brow
The long kiss of the loving tropic sun,
And yet, whose veins with thy red current run.

Borne on the bitter winds from every hand,
Strange tales are flying over all the land,
And Condemnation, with his pinions foul,
Glooms in the place where broods the midnight owl.

What art thou, that the world should point at thee,
And vaunt and chide the weakness that they see?
There was a time they were not wont to chide;
Where is thy old, uncompromising pride?

Blood-washed, thou shouldst lift up thine honored head,
White with the sorrow for thy loyal dead

Who lie on every plain, on every hill,
And whose high spirit walks the Southland still:

Whose infancy our mother's hands have nursed.
Thy manhood, gone to battle unaccursed,
Our fathers left to till th' reluctant field,
To rape the soil for what she would not yield;

Wooing for aye, the cold unam'rous sod,
Whose growth for them still meant a master's rod;
Tearing her bosom for the wealth that gave
The strength that made the toiler still a slave.

Too long we hear the deep impassioned cry
That echoes vainly to the heedless sky;
Too long, too long, the Macedonian call
Falls fainting far beyond the outward wall,

Within whose sweep, beneath the shadowing trees,
A slumbering nation takes its dangerous ease;
Too long the rumors of thy hatred go
For those who loved thee and thy children so.

Thou must arise forthwith, and strong, thou must
Throw off the smirching of this baser dust,
Lay by the practice of this later creed,
And be thine honest self again indeed.

There was a time when even slavery's chain
Held in some joys to alternate with pain,
Some little light to give the night relief,
Some little smiles to take the place of grief.

There was a time when, jocund as the day,
The toiler hoed his row and sung his lay,
Found something gleeful in the very air,
And solace for his toiling everywhere.

Now all is changed, within the rude stockade,
A bondsman whom the greed of men has made
Almost too brutish to deplore his plight,
Toils hopeless on from joyless morn till night.

For him no more the cabin's quiet rest,
The homely joys that gave to labor zest;
No more for him the merry banjo's sound,
Nor trip of lightsome dances footing round.

For him no more the lamp shall glow at eve,
Nor chubby children pluck him by the sleeve;
No more for him the master's eyes be bright,—
He has nor freedom's nor a slave's delight.

What, was it all for naught, those awful years
That drenched a groaning land with blood and tears?
Was it to leave this sly convenient hell,
That brother fighting his own brother fell?

When that great struggle held the world in awe,
And all the nations blanched at what they saw,
Did Sanctioned Slavery bow its conquered head
That this unsanctioned crime might rise instead?

Is it for this we all have felt the flame,—
This newer bondage and this deeper shame?
Nay, not for this, a nation's heroes bled,
And North and South with tears beheld their dead.

Oh, Mother South, hast thou forgot thy ways,
Forgot the glory of thine ancient days,
Forgot the honor that once made thee great,
And stooped to this unhallowed estate?

It cannot last, thou wilt come forth in might,
A warrior queen full armored for the fight;
And thou wilt take, e'en with thy spear in rest,
Thy dusky children to thy saving breast.

Till then, no more, no more the gladsome song,
Strike only deeper chords, the notes of wrong;
Till then, the sigh, the tear, the oath, the moan,
Till thou, oh, South, and thine, come to thine own.

PAUL LAURENCE DUNBAR

THE HAUNTED OAK

Pray why are you so bare, so bare,
Oh, bough of the old oak-tree;
And why, when I go through the shade you throw,
Runs a shudder over me?

My leaves were green as the best, I trow,
And sap ran free in my veins,
But I saw in the moonlight dim and weird
A guiltless victim's pains.

I bent me down to hear his sigh;
I shook with his gurgling moan,
And I trembled sore when they rode away,
And left him here alone.

They 'd charged him with the old, old crime,
And set him fast in jail:
Oh, why does the dog howl all night long,
And why does the night wind wail?

He prayed his prayer and he swore his oath,
And he raised his hand to the sky;
But the beat of hoofs smote on his ear,
And the steady tread drew nigh.

Who is it rides by night, by night,
Over the moonlit road?
And what is the spur that keeps the pace,
What is the galling goad?

And now they beat at the prison door,
" Ho, keeper, do not stay!
We are friends of him whom you hold within,
And we fain would take him away

" From those who ride fast on our heels
With mind to do him wrong;
They have no care for his innocence,
And the rope they bear is long."

They have fooled the jailer with lying words,
They have fooled the man with lies;
The bolts unbar, the locks are drawn,
And the great door open flies.

Now they have taken him from the jail,
And hard and fast they ride,
And the leader laughs low down in his throat,
As they halt my trunk beside.

Oh, the judge, he wore a mask of black,
And the doctor cne of white,

And the minister, with his oldest son,
Was curiously bedight.

Oh, foolish man, why weep you now?
'T is but a little space,
And the time will come when these shall dread
The mem'ry of your face.

I feel the rope against my bark,
And the weight of him in my grain,
I feel in the throe of his final woe
The touch of my own last pain.

And never more shall leaves come forth
On a bough that bears the ban;
I am burned with dread, I am dried and dead,
From the curse of a guiltless man.

And ever the judge rides by, rides by,
And goes to hunt the deer,
And ever another rides his soul
In the guise of a mortal fear.

And ever the man he rides me hard,
And never a night stays he;
For I feel his curse as a haunted bough,
On the trunk of a haunted tree.

WELTSCHMERTZ

You ask why I am sad to-day,
I have no cares, no griefs, you say?
Ah, yes, 't is true, I have no grief —
But — is there not the falling leaf?

The bare tree there is mourning left
With all of autumn's gray bereft;
It is not what has happened me,
Think of the bare, dismantled tree.

The birds go South along the sky,
I hear their lingering, long good-bye.
Who goes reluctant from my breast?
And yet — the lone and wind-swept nest.

The mourning, pale-flowered hearse goes by,
Why does a tear come to my eye?
Is it the March rain blowing wild?
I have no dead, I know no child.

I am no widow by the bier
Of him I held supremely dear.
I have not seen the choicest one
Sink down as sinks the westering sun.

Faith unto faith have I beheld,
For me, few solemn notes have swelled;

Love bekoned me out to the dawn,
And happily I followed on.

And yet my heart goes out to them
Whose sorrow is their diadem;
The falling leaf, the crying bird,
The voice to be, all lost, unheard —

Not mine, not mine, and yet too much
The thrilling power of human touch,
While all the world looks on and scorns
I wear another's crown of thorns.

Count me a priest who understands
The glorious pain of nail-pierced hands;
Count me a comrade of the thief
Hot driven into late belief.

Oh, mother's tear, oh, father's sigh,
Oh, mourning sweetheart's last good-bye,
I yet have known no mourning save
Beside some brother's brother's grave.

ROBERT GOULD SHAW

Why was it that the thunder voice of Fate
Should call thee, studious, from the classic groves,
Where calm-eyed Pallas with still footstep roves,
And charge thee seek the turmoil of the state?
What bade thee hear the voice and rise elate,
Leave home and kindred and thy spicy loaves,
To lead th' unlettered and despised droves
To manhood's home and thunder at the gate?

Far better the slow blaze of Learning's light,
The cool and quiet of her dearer fane,
Than this hot terror of a hopeless fight,
This cold endurance of the final pain,—
Since thou and those who with thee died for right
Have died, the Present teaches, but in vain!

ROSES

Oh, wind of the spring-time, oh, free wind of May,
When blossoms and bird-song are rife;
Oh, joy for the season, and joy for the day,
That gave me the roses of life, of life,
That gave me the roses of life.

Oh, wind of the summer, sing loud in the night,
When flutters my heart like a dove;
One came from thy kingdom, thy realm of delight,
And gave me the roses of love, of love,
And gave me the roses of love.

Oh, wind of the winter, sigh low in thy grief,
I hear thy compassionate breath;
I wither, I fall, like the autumn-kissed leaf,
He gave me the roses of death, of death,
He gave me the roses of death.

A LOVE SONG

Ah, love, my love is like a cry in the night,
A long, loud cry to the empty sky,
The cry of a man alone in the desert,
With hands uplifted, with parching lips,

Oh, rescue me, rescue me,
Thy form to mine arms,
The dew of thy lips to my mouth,
Dost thou hear me?— my call thro' the night?

Darling, I hear thee and answer,
Thy fountain am I,
All of the love of my soul will I bring to thee,
All of the pains of my being shall wring to thee,
Deep and forever the song of my loving shall sing to thee,
Ever and ever thro' day and thro' night shall I cling to thee.
Hearest thou the answer?
Darling, I come, I come.

ITCHING HEELS

Fu' de peace o' my eachin' heels, set down;
Don' fiddle dat chune no mo'.
Don' you see how dat melody stuhs me up
An' baigs me to tek to de flo'?
You knows I 's a Christian, good an' strong;
I wusship f'om June to June;
My pra'ahs dey ah loud an' my hymns ah long:
I baig you don' fiddle dat chune.

I 's a crick in my back an' a misery hyeah
Whaih de j'ints 's gittin' ol' an' stiff,
But hit seems lak you brings me de bref o' my youf;
W'y, I 's suttain I noticed a w'iff.
Don' fiddle dat chune no mo', my chile,
Don' fiddle dat chune no mo';

I 'll git up an' taih up dis groun' fu' a mile,
An' den I 'll be chu'ched fu' it, sho'.

Oh, fiddle dat chune some mo', I say,
An' fiddle it loud an' fas':
I 's a youngstah ergin in de mi'st o' my sin;
De p'esent 's gone back to de pas'.
I 'll dance to dat chune, so des fiddle erway;
I knows how de backslidah feels;
So fiddle it on 'twell de break o' de day
Fu' de sake o' my eachin' heels.

TO AN INGRATE

This is to-day, a golden summer's day
And yet — and yet
My vengeful soul will not forget
The past, forever now forgot, you say.

From that half height where I had sadly climbed,
I stretched my hand,
I lone in all that land,
Down there, where, helpless, you were limed.

Our fingers clasped, and dragging me a pace,
You struggled up.
It is a bitter Cup,
That now for naught, you turn away your face.

I shall remember this for aye and aye.
Whate'er may come,
Although my lips are dumb,
My spirit holds you to that yesterday.

IN THE TENTS OF AKBAR

In the tents of Akbar
Are dole and grief to-day,
For the flower of all the Indies
Has gone the silent way.

In the tents of Akbar
Are emptiness and gloom,
And where the dancers gather,
The silence of the tomb.

Across the yellow desert,
Across the burning sands,
Old Akbar wanders madly,
And wrings his fevered hands.

And ever makes his moaning
To the unanswering sky,
For Sutna, lovely Sutna,
Who was so fair to die.

For Sutna danced at morning,
And Sutna danced at eve;

Her dusky eyes half hidden
  Behind her silken sleeve.

Her pearly teeth out-glancing
  Between her coral lips,
The tremulous rhythm of passion
  Marked by her quivering hips.

As lovely as a jewel
  Of fire and dewdrop blent,
So danced the maiden Sutna
  In gallant Akbar's tent.

And one who saw her dancing,
  Saw her bosom's fall and rise
Put all his body's yearning
  Into his lovelit eyes.

Then Akbar came and drove him —
  A jackal — from his door,
And bade him wander far and look
  On Sutna's face no more.

Some day the sea disgorges,
  The wilderness gives back,
Those half-dead who have wandered,
  Aimless, across its track.

And he returned — the lover,
  Haggard of brow and spent;
He found fair Sutna standing
  Before her master's tent.

" Not mine, nor Akbar's, Sutna! "
  He cried and closely pressed,
And drove his craven dagger
  Straight to the maiden's breast.

Oh, weep, oh, weep, for Sutna,
  So young, so dear, so fair,
Her face is gray and silent
  Beneath her dusky hair.

And wail, oh, wail, for Akbar,
  Who walks the desert sands,
Crying aloud for Sutna,
  Wringing his fevered hands.

In the tents of Akbar
  The tears of sorrow run,
But the corpse of Sutna's slayer,
  Lies rotting in the sun.

THE FOUNT OF TEARS

All hot and grimy from the road,
  Dust gray from arduous years,
I sat me down and eased my load
  Beside the Fount of Tears.

The waters sparkled to my eye,
  Calm, crystal-like, and cool,
And breathing there a restful sigh,
  I bent me to the pool.

When, lo! a voice cried: " Pilgrim, rise,
  Harsh tho' the sentence be,
And on to other lands and skies —
  This fount is not for thee.

" Pass on, but calm thy needless fears,
  Some may not love or sin,
An angel guards the Fount of Tears;
  All may not bathe therein."

Then with my burden on my back
  I turned to gaze awhile,
First at the uninviting track,
  Then at the water's smile.

And so I go upon my way,
  Thro'out the sultry years,
But pause no more, by night, by day,
  Beside the Fount of Tears.

LIFE'S TRAGEDY

It may be misery not to sing at all
  And to go silent through the brimming day.
It may be sorrow never to be loved,
  But deeper griefs than these beset the way.

To have come near to sing the perfect song
  And only by a half-tone lost the key,
There is the potent sorrow, there the grief,
  The pale, sad staring of life's tragedy.

To have just missed the perfect love,
  Not the hot passion of untempered youth,
But that which lays aside its vanity
  And gives thee, for thy trusting worship, truth —

This, this it is to be accursed indeed;
  For if we mortals love, or if we sing,
We count our joys not by the things we have,
  But by what kept us from the perfect thing.

DE WAY T'INGS COME

De way t'ings come, hit seems to me,
Is des' one monst'ous mystery;
De way hit seem to strike a man,
Dey ain't no sense, dey ain't no plan;
Ef trouble sta'ts a pilin' down,
It ain't no use to rage er frown,
It ain't no use to strive er pray,
Hit 's mortal boun' to come dat way.

Now, ef you 's hongry, an' yo' plate
Des' keep on sayin' to you, "Wait,"
Don't mek no diffunce how you feel,
'T won't do no good to hunt a meal,
Fu' dat ah meal des' boun' to hide
Ontwell de devil 's satisfied,
An' 'twell dey 's some'p'n by to cyave
You 's got to ease yo'se'f an' sta've.

But ef dey 's co'n meal on de she'f
You need n't bothah 'roun' yo'se'f,

Somebody 's boun' to amble in
An' 'vite you to dey co'n meal bin;
An' ef you 's stuffed up to be froat
Wid co'n er middlin', fowl er shoat,
Des' look out an' you 'll see fu' sho
A 'possum faint befo' yo' do'.

De way t'ings happen, huhuh, chile,
Dis worl' 's done puzzled me one w'ile;
I 's mighty skeered I 'll fall in doubt,
I des' won't try to reason out
De reason why folks strive an' plan
A dinnah fu' a full-fed man,
An' shet de do' an' cross de street
F'om one dat raaly needs to eat.

NOON

SHADDER in de valley
Sunlight on de hill,
Sut'ny wish dat locus'
Knowed how to be still.
Don't de heat already
Mek a body hum,
'Dout dat insec' sayin'
Hottah days to come?

Fiel' 's a shinin' yaller
Wid de bendin' grain,
Guinea hen a callin',
Now 's de time fu' rain;
Shet yo' mouf, you rascal,
Wha' 's de use to cry?
You do' see no rain clouds
Up dah in de sky.

Dis hyeah sweat 's been po'in'
Down my face sence dawn;
Ain't hit time we 's hyeahin'
Dat ah dinnah ho'n?
Go on, Ben an' Jaspah,
Lif' yo' feet an' fly,
Hit out fu' de shadder
Fo' I drap an' die.

Hongry, lawd a' mussy,
Hongry as a baih,
Seems lak I hyeah dinnah
Callin' evahwhaih;
Daih 's de ho'n a blowin'!
Let dat cradle swing,
One mo' sweep, den da'kies,
Beat me to de spring!

AT THE TAVERN

A LILT and a swing,
And a ditty to sing,
Or ever the night grow old;
The wine is within,
And I 'm sure 't were a sin
For a soldier to choose to be cold, my dear,
For a soldier to choose to be cold.

We 're right for a spell,
But the fever is — well,
No thing to be braved, at least;

So bring me the wine;
No low fever in mine,
For a drink is more kind than a priest, my dear,
For a drink is more kind than a priest.

DEATH

Storm and strife and stress,
Lost in a wilderness,
Groping to find a way,
Forth to the haunts of day

Sudden a vista peeps,
Out of the tangled deeps,
Only a point — the ray
But at the end is day.

Dark is the dawn and chill,
Daylight is on the hill,
Night is the flitting breath,
Day rides the hills of death.

NIGHT, DIM NIGHT

Night, dim night, and it rains, my love, it rains,
(Art thou dreaming of me, I wonder)
The trees are sad, and the wind complains,
Outside the rolling of the thunder,
And the beat against the panes.

Heart, my heart, thou art mournful in the rain,
(Are thy redolent lips a-quiver?)
My soul seeks thine, doth it seek in vain?
My love goes surging like a river,
Shall its tide bear naught save pain?

LYRICS OF LOVE AND SORROW

I

Love is the light of the world, my dear,
Heigho, but the world is gloomy;
The light has failed and the lamp down hurled,
Leaves only darkness to me.

Love is the light of the world, my dear,
Ah me, but the world is dreary;
The night is down, and my curtain furled
But I cannot sleep, though weary.

Love is the light of the world, my dear,
Alas for a hopeless hoping,
When the flame went out in the breeze that swirled,
And a soul went blindly groping.

II

The light was on the golden sands,
A glimmer on the sea;
My soul spoke clearly to thy soul,
Thy spirit answered me.

Since then the light that gilds the sands,
And glimmers on the sea,
But vainly struggles to reflect
The radiant soul of thee.

III

The sea speaks to me of you
All the day long;
Still as I sit by its side
You are its song.

The sea sings to me of you
Loud on the reef;
Always it moans as it sings,
Voicing my grief.

IV

My dear love died last night;
Shall I clothe her in white?
My passionate love is dead,
Shall I robe her in red?
But nay, she was all untrue,
She shall not go drest in blue;
Still my desolate love was brave,
Unrobed let her go to her grave.

V

There are brilliant heights of sorrow
That only the few may know;
And the lesser woes of the world, like waves,
Break noiselessly, far below.
I hold for my own possessing,
A mount that is lone and still —
The great high place of a hopeless grief,

And I call it my " Heart-break
Hill."
And once on a winter's midnight
I found its highest crown,
And there in the gloom, my soul
and I,
Weeping, we sat us down.

But now when I seek that summit
We are two ghosts that go;
Only two shades of a thing that
died,
Once in the long ago.
So I sit me down in the silence,
And say to my soul, " Be still,"
So the world may not know we
died that night,
From weeping on " Heart-break
Hill."

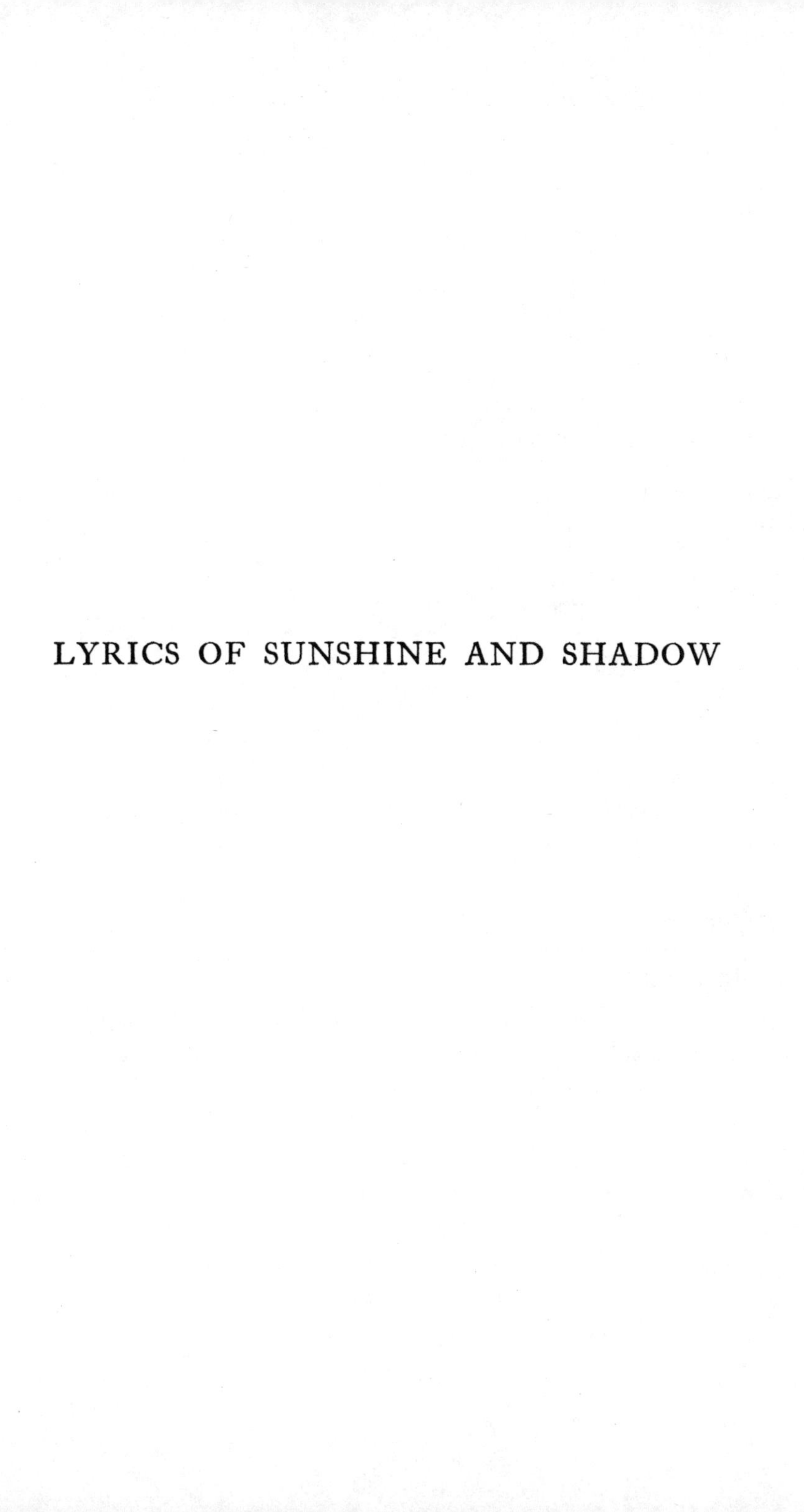

LYRICS OF SUNSHINE AND SHADOW

A BOY'S SUMMER SONG

'Tis fine to play
In the fragrant hay,
And romp on the golden load;
To ride old Jack
To the barn and back,
Or tramp by a shady road.
To pause and drink,
At a mossy brink;
Ah, that is the best of joy,
And so I say
On a summer's day,
What's so fine as being a boy?
Ha, Ha!

With line and hook
By a babbling brook,
The fisherman's sport we ply;
And list the song
Of the feathered throng
That flit in the branches nigh.
At last we strip
For a quiet dip;
Ah, that is the best of joy.
For this I say
On a summer's day,
What's so fine as being a boy?
Ha, Ha!

THE SAND-MAN

I know a man
With face of tan,
But who is ever kind;
Whom girls and boys
Leaves games and toys
Each eventide to find.

When day grows dim,
They watch for him,
He comes to place his claim;
He wears the crown
Of Dreaming-town;
The sand-man is his name.

When sparkling eyes
Troop sleepywise
And busy lips grow dumb;
When little heads
Nod toward the beds,
We know the sand-man's come.

JOHNNY SPEAKS

The sand-man he's a jolly old fellow,
His face is kind and his voice is mellow,
But he makes your eyelids as heavy as lead,
And then you got to go off to bed;
I don't think I like the sand-man.

But I've been playing this live-long day;
It does make a fellow so tired to play!
Oh, my, I'm a-yawning right here before ma,

I'm the sleepiest fellow that ever
you saw.
I think I do like the sand-man.

WINTER-SONG

Oh, who would be sad tho' the
sky be a-graying,
And meadow and woodlands are
empty and bare;
For softly and merrily now there
come playing,
The little white birds thro' the
winter-kissed air.

The squirrel's enjoying the rest
of the thrifty,
He munches his store in the old
hollow tree;
Tho' cold is the blast and the
snow-flakes are drifty
He fears the white flock not a
whit more than we.

Chorus:

Then heigho for the flying snow!
Over the whitened roads we go,
With pulses that tingle,
And sleigh-bells a-jingle
For winter's white birds here's a
cheery heigho!

A CHRISTMAS FOLKSONG

De win' is blowin' wahmah,
An hit's blowin' f'om de bay;
Dey's a so't o' mist a-risin'
All erlong de meddah way;
Dey ain't a hint o' frostin'
On de groun' ner in de sky,
An' dey ain't no use in hopin'
Dat de snow'll 'mence to fly.
It's goin' to be a green Christ-
mas,
An' sad de day fu' me.
I wish dis was de las' one
Dat evah I should see.

Dey's dancin' in de cabin,
Dey's spahkin' by de tree;
But dancin' times an' spahkin'
Are all done pas' fur me.
Dey's feastin' in de big house,
Wid all de windahs wide—
Is dat de way fu' people
To meet de Christmas-tide?
It's goin' to be a green Christ-
mas,
No mattah what you say.
Dey's us dat will remembah
An' grieve de comin' day.

Dey's des a bref o' dampness
A-clingin' to my cheek;
De aih's been dahk an' heavy
An' threatenin' fu' a week,
But not wid signs o' wintah,
Dough wintah'd seem so deah—
De wintah's out o' season,
An' Christmas eve is heah.
It's goin' to be a green Christ-
mas,
An' oh, how sad de day!
Go ax de hongry chu'chya'd,
An' see what hit will say.

Dey's Allen on de hillside,
An' Marfy in de plain;
Fu' Christmas was like springtime,
An' come wid sun an' rain.
Dey's Ca'line, John, an' Susie,
Wid only dis one lef':
An' now de curse is comin'
Wid murder in hits bref.
It's goin' to be a green Christmas —
Des hyeah my words an' see:
Befo' de summah beckons
Dey's many 'll weep wid me.

THE FOREST GREETING

Good hunting! — aye, good hunting,
Wherever the forests call;
But ever a heart beats hot with fear,
And what of the birds that fall?

Good hunting! — aye, good hunting,
Wherever the north winds blow;
But what of the stag that calls for his mate?
And what of the wounded doe?

Good hunting! — aye, good hunting;
And ah! we are bold and strong;
But our triumph call through the forest hall
Is a brother's funeral song.

For we are brothers ever,
Panther and bird and bear;
Man and the weakest that fear his face,
Born to the nest or lair.

Yes, brothers, and who shall judge us?
Hunters and game are we;
But who gave the right for me to smite?
Who boasts when he smiteth me?

Good hunting! — aye, good hunting,
And dim is the forest track;
But the sportsman Death comes striding on:
Brothers, the way is black.

THE LILY OF THE VALLEY

Sweetest of the flowers a-blooming
In the fragrant vernal days
Is the Lily of the Valley
With its soft, retiring ways.

Well, you chose this humble blossom
As the nurse's emblem flower,
Who grows more like her ideal
Every day and every hour.

Like the Lily of the Valley
In her honesty and worth,
Ah, she blooms in truth and virtue
In the quiet nooks of earth.

Tho' she stands erect in honor
When the heart of mankind bleeds,
Still she hides her own deserving
In the beauty of her deeds.

In the silence of the darkness
Where no eye may see and know,
There her footsteps shod with mercy,
And fleet kindness come and go.

Not amid the sounds of plaudits,
Nor before the garish day,
Does she shed her soul's sweet perfume,
Does she take her gentle way.

But alike her ideal flower,
With its honey-laden breath,
Still her heart blooms forth its beauty
In the valley shades of death.

ENCOURAGED

Because you love me I have much achieved,
Had you despised me then I must have failed,
But since I knew you trusted and believed,
I could not disappoint you and so prevailed.

TO J. Q.

What are the things that make life bright?
A star gleam in the night.
What hearts us for the coming fray?
The dawn tints of the day.
What helps to speed the weary mile?
A brother's friendly smile.
What turns o' gold the evening gray?
A flower beside the way.

DIPLOMACY

Tell your love where the roses blow,
And the hearts of the lilies quiver,
Not in the city's gleam and glow,
But down by a half-sunned river.
Not in the crowded ball-room's glare,
That would be fatal, Marie, Marie,
How can she answer you then and there?
So come then and stroll with me, my dear,
Down where the birds call, Marie, Marie.

SCAMP

AIN'T it nice to have a mammy
 W'en you kin' o' tiahed out
Wid a-playin' in de meddah,
 An' a-runnin' roun' about
Till hit's made you mighty hongry,
 An' yo' nose hit gits to know
What de smell means dat 's a-comin'
 F'om de open cabin do'?
  She wash yo' face,
  An' mek yo' place,
 You's hongry as a tramp;
Den hit's eat you suppah right away,
 You sta'vin' little scamp.

W'en you's full o' braid an' bacon,
 An' dey ain't no mo' to eat,
An' de lasses dat's a-stickin'
 On yo' face ta'se kin' o' sweet,
Don' you t'ink hit's kin' o' pleasin'
 Fu' to have som'body neah
Dat'll wipe yo' han's an' kiss you
 Fo' dey lif' you f'om you' cheah?
  To smile so sweet,
  An' wash yo' feet,
 An' leave 'em co'l an' damp;
Den hit's come let me undress you, now
 You lazy little scamp.

Don' yo' eyes git awful heavy,
 An' yo' lip git awful slack,
Ain't dey som'p'n' kin' o' weak-nin'
 In de backbone of yo' back?
Don' yo' knees feel kin' o' trimbly,
 An' yo' head go bobbin' roun',
W'en you says yo' "Now I lay me,"
 An' is sno'in on de "down"?
  She kiss yo' nose,
  She kiss yo' toes,
 An' den tu'n out de lamp,
Den hit's creep into yo' trunnel baid,
 You sleepy little scamp.

WADIN' IN DE CRICK

DAYS git wa'm an' wa'mah,
 School gits mighty dull,
Seems lak dese hyeah teachahs
 Mus' feel mussiful.
Hookey's wrong, I know it
 Ain't no gent'man's trick;
But de aih's a-callin',
 "Come on to de crick."

Dah de watah's gu'glin'
 Ovah shiny stones,
Des hit's ve'y singin'
 Seems to soothe yo' bones.
W'at's de use o' waitin'
 Go on good an' quick:
Dain't no fun lak dis hyeah
 Wadin' in de crick.

W'at dat jay-b'ud sayin'?
 Bettah shet yo' haid,
Fus' t'ing dat you fin' out,
 You'll be layin' daid.

Jay-bu'ds sich a tattlah,
Des seem lak his trick
Fu' to tell on folkses
Wadin' in de crick.

Willer boughs a-bendin'
Hidin' of de sky,
Wavin' kin' o' frien'ly
Ez de win' go by,
Elum trees a-shinin',
Dahk an' green an' thick,
Seem to say, "I see yo'
Wadin' in de crick."

But de trees don' chattah,
Dey des look an' sigh
Lak hit's kin' o' peaceful
Des a-bein' nigh,
An' yo' t'ank yo' Mastah
Dat dey trunks is thick
W'en yo' mammy fin's you
Wadin' in de crick.

Den yo' run behin' dem
Lak yo' scaihed to def,
Mammy come a-flyin',
Mos' nigh out o' bref;
But she set down gentle
An' she drap huh stick,—
An' fus' t'ing, dey's mammy
Wadin' in de crick.

THE QUILTING

Dolly sits a-quilting by her mother, stich by stitch,
Gracious, how my pulses throb, how my fingers itch,
While I note her dainty waist and her slender hand,
As she matches this and that, she stitches strand by strand.
And I long to tell her Life's a quilt and I'm a patch;
Love will do the stitching if she'll only be my match.

PARTED

She wrapped her soul in a lace of lies,
With a prime deceit to pin it;
And I thought I was gaining a fearsome prize,
So I staked my soul to win it.

We wed and parted on her complaint,
And both were a bit of barter,
Tho' I'll confess that I'm no saint,
I'll swear that she's no martyr.

FOREVER

I had not known before
Forever was so long a word.
The slow stroke of the clock of time
I had not heard.

'Tis hard to learn so late;
It seems no sad heart really learns,
But hopes and trusts and doubts and fears,
And bleeds and burns.

The night is not all dark,
Nor is the day all it seems,
But each may bring me this relief —
My dreams and dreams.

I had not known before
That Never was so sad a word,
So wrap me in forgetfulness —
I have not heard.

THE PLANTATION CHILD'S LULLABY

Wintah time hit comin'
Stealin' thoo de night;
Wake up in the mo'nin'
Evah t'ing is white;
Cabin lookin' lonesome
Stannin' in de snow,
Meks you kin' o' nervous,
W'en de win' hit blow.

Trompin' back from feedin',
Col' an' wet an' blue,
Homespun jacket ragged,
Win' a-blowin' thoo.
Cabin lookin' cheerful,
Unnerneaf de do',
Yet you kin' o' keerful
W'en de win' hit blow.

Hickory log a-blazin'
Light a-lookin' red,
Faith o' eyes o' peepin'
'Rom a trun'le bed,
Little feet a-patterin'
Cleak across de flo';
Bettah had be keerful
W'en de win' hit blow.

Suppah done an' ovah,
Evah t'ing is still;
Listen to de snowman
Slippin' down de hill.
Ashes on de fiah,
Keep it wa'm but low.
What's de use o' keerin'
Ef de win' do blow?

Smoke house full o' bacon,
Brown an' sweet an' good;
Taters in de cellah,
'Possum roam de wood;
Little baby snoozin'
Des ez ef he know.
What 's de use o' keerin'
Ef de win' do blow?

TWILIGHT

'Twixt a smile and a tear,
'Twixt a song and a sigh,
'Twixt the day and the dark,
When the night draweth nigh.

Ah, sunshine may fade
From the heavens above,
No twilight have we
To the day of our love.

CURIOSITY

Mammy's in de kitchen, an' de do' is shet;
All de pickaninnies climb an' tug an' sweat,

Gittin' to de winder, stickin' dah lak flies,
Evah one ermong us des all nose an' eyes.

"Whut's she cookin', Isaac?" "Whut's she cookin', Jake?"
"Is it sweet pertaters? Is hit pie er cake?"
But we couldn't mek out even whah we stood
Whut was mammy cookin' dat could smell so good.

Mammy spread de winder, an' she frown an' frown,
How de pickaninnies come a-tumblin' down!
Den she say: "Ef you-all keeps a-peepin' in,
How I'se gwine to whup you, my! 't 'ill be a sin!
Need n' come a-sniffin' an' a-nosin' hyeah,
'Ca'se I knows my business, nevah feah."
Won't somebody tell us — how I wish dey would! —
Whut is mammy cookin' dat it smells so good?

We know she means business, an' we dassent stay,
Dough it's mighty tryin' fuh to go erway;
But we goes a-troopin' down de ol' wood-track
'Twell dat steamin' kitchen brings us stealin' back,
Climbin' an' a-peepin' so's to see inside.
Whut on earf kin mammy be so sha'p to hide?
I'd des up an' tell folks w'en I knowed I could,
Ef I was a-cookin' t'ings dat smelt so good.

Mammy in de oven, an' I see huh smile;
Moufs mus' be a-wat'rin' roun' hyeah fuh a mile;
Den we almos' hollah ez we hu'ies down,
'Ca'se hit's apple dumplin's, big an' fat an' brown!
W'en de do' is opened, solemn lak an' slow,
Wisht you see us settin' all dah in a row
Innercent an' p'opah, des lak chillun should
W'en dey mammy's cookin' t'ings dat smell so good.

OPPORTUNITY

Granny's gone a-visitin',
 Seen huh git huh shawl
W'en I was a-hidin' down
 Hime de gyahden wall.
Seen huh put her bonnet on,
 Seen huh tie de strings,
An' I'se gone to dreamin' now
 'Bout dem cakes an' t'ings.

On de she'f behime de do'—
  Mussy, what a feas'!
Soon ez she gits out o' sight,
  I kin eat in peace.
I bin watchin' fu' a week
  Des fu' dis hyeah chance.
Mussy, w'en I gits in daih,
  I'll des sholy dance.

Lemon pie an' gingah-cake,
  Let me set an' t'ink —
Vinegah an' sugah, too,
  Dat'll mek a drink;
Ef dey's one t'ing dat I loves
  Mos' pu'ticlahly,
It is eatin' sweet t'ings an'
  A-drinkin' Sangaree.

Lawdy, won' po' granny raih
  W'en she see de she'f;
W'en I t'ink erbout huh face,
  I's mos' 'shamed myse'f.
Well, she gone, an 'hyeah I is,
  Back behime de do'—
Look hyeah! gran' 's done 'spected me,
  Dain't no sweets no mo'.

Evah sweet is hid erway,
  Job des done up brown;
Pusson t'ink dat someun t'ought
  Dey was t'eves erroun';
Dat des breaks my heart in two,
  Oh how bad I feel!
Des to t'ink my own gramma
  B'lieved dat I 'u'd steal!

PUTTIN' THE BABY AWAY

EIGHT of 'em hyeah all tol' an' yet
Dese eyes o' mine is wringin' wet;
My haht's a-achin' ha'd an' so',
De way hit nevah ached befo';
My soul's a-pleadin', "Lawd, give back
Dis little lonesome baby black,
Dis one, dis las' po' he'pless one
Whose little race was too soon run."

Po' Little Jim, des fo' yeahs ol'
A-layin' down so still an' col'.
Somehow hit don' seem ha'dly faih,
To have my baby lyin' daih
Wi'dout a smile upon his face,
Wi'dout a look erbout de place;
He ust to be so full o' fun
Hit don' seem right dat all's done, done.

Des eight in all but I don' caih,
Dey wa'nt a single one to spaih;
De worl' was big, so was my haht,
An' dis hyeah baby owned hit's paht;
De house was po', dey clothes was rough,
But daih was meat an' meal enough;
An' daih was room fu' little Jim;
Oh! Lawd, what made you call fu' him?

It do seem monst'ous ha'd to-day,
To lay dis baby boy away;
I'd learned to love his teasin' smile,
He mought o' des been lef' er-while;
You wouldn't t'ought wid all de folks,
Dat's roun' hyeah mixin' teahs an' jokes,
De Lawd u'd had de time to see
Dis chile an' tek him 'way f'om me.

But let it go, I reckon Jim,
'Ll des go right straight up to Him
Dat took him f'om his mammy's nest
An' lef' dis achin' in my breas',
An' lookin' in dat fathah's face
An' 'memberin' dis lone sorrerin' place,
He'll say, "Good Lawd, you ought to had
Do sumpin' fu' to comfo't dad!"

THE FISHER CHILD'S LULLABY

THE wind is out in its rage to-night,
And your father is far at sea.
The rime on the window is hard and white
But dear, you are near to me.
Heave ho, weave low,
Waves of the briny deep;
Seethe low and breathe low,
But sleep you, my little one, sleep, sleep.

The little boat rocks in the cove no more,
But the flying sea-gulls wail;
I peer through the darkness that wraps the shore,
For sight of a home set sail.
Heave ho, weave low,
Waves of the briny deep;
Seethe low and breathe low,
But sleep you, my little one, sleep, sleep.

Ay, lad of mine, thy father may die
In the gale that rides the sea,
But we'll not believe it, not you and I,
Who mind us of Galilee.
Heave ho, weave low,
Waves of the briny deep;
Seethe low and breathe low,
But sleep you, my little one, sleep, sleep.

FAITH

I's a-gittin' weary of de way dat people do,
De folks dat's got dey 'ligion in dey fiah-place an' flue;
Dey's allus somep'n comin' so de spit'll have to turn,

An' hit tain't no p'oposition fu' to
mek de hickory bu'n.
Ef de sweet pertater fails us an' de
go'geous yallah yam,
We kin tek a bit o' comfo't f'om
ouah sto' o' summah jam.
W'en de snow hit git to flyin',
dat's de Mastah's own desiah,
De Lawd'll run de wintah an' yo'
mammy'll run de fiah.

I ain' skeered because de win' hit
staht to raih and blow,
I ain't bothahed w'en he come er
rattlin' at de do',
Let him taih hisse'f an' shout, let
him blow an' bawl,

Dat's de time de branches shek an'
bresh-wood 'mence to fall.
W'en de sto'm er railin' an' de
shettahs blowin' 'bout,
Dat de time de fiah-place crack
hits welcome out.
Tain' my livin' business fu' to
trouble ner enquiah,
De Lawd'll min' de wintah an' my
mammy'll min' de fiah.

Ash-cake allus gits ez brown w'en
February's hyeah
Ez it does in bakin' any othah time
o' yeah.
De bacon smell ez callin'-like, de
kittle rock an' sing,
De same way in de wintah dat dey
do it in de spring;
Dey ain't no use in mopin' 'round
an' lookin' mad an' glum
Erbout de wintah season, fu' hit's
des plumb boun' to come;

An' ef it comes to runnin' t'ings
I's willin' to retiah,
De Lawd'll min' de wintah an'
my mammy'll min' de fiah.

THE FARM CHILD'S LULLABY

Oh, the little bird is rocking in
the cradle of the wind,
And it's bye, my little wee one,
bye;
The harvest all is gathered and
the pippins all are binned;
Bye, my little wee one, bye;
The little rabbit's hiding in the
golden shock of corn,
The thrifty squirrel's laughing
bunny's idleness to scorn;
You are smiling with the angels
in your slumber, smile till
morn;
So it's bye, my little wee one,
bye.

There'll be plenty in the cellar,
there'll be plenty on the
shelf;
Bye, my little wee one, bye;
There'll be goodly store of sweet-
ings for a dainty little elf;
Bye, my little wee one, bye.

The snow may be a-flying o'er the meadow and the hill,
The ice has checked the chatter of the little laughing rill,
But in your cosey cradle you are warm and happy still;
So bye, my little wee one, bye.

Why, the Bob White thinks the snowflake is a brother to his song;
Bye, my little wee one, bye;
And the chimney sings the sweeter when the wind is blowing strong;
Bye, my little wee one, bye;
The granary's overflowing, full is cellar, crib, and bin,
The wood has paid its tribute and the ax has ceased its din;
The winter may not harm you when you're sheltered safe within;
So bye, my little wee one, bye.

THE PLACE WHERE THE RAINBOW ENDS

THERE'S a fabulous story
Full of splendor and glory,
That Arabian legends transcends;
Of the wealth without measure,
The coffers of treasure,
At the place where the rainbow ends.

Oh, many have sought it,
And all would have bought it,
With the blood we so recklessly spend;
But none has uncovered,
The gold, nor discovered
The spot at the rainbow's end.

They have sought it in battle,
And e'en where the rattle
Of dice with man's blasphemy blends;
But howe'er persuasive,
It still proves evasive,
This place where the rainbow ends.

I own for my pleasure,
I yearn not for treasure,
Though gold has a power it lends;
And I have a notion,
To find without motion,
The place where the rainbow ends.

The pot may hold pottage,
The place be a cottage,
That a humble contentment defends,
Only joy fills its coffer,
But spite of the scoffer,
There's the place where the rainbow ends.

Where care shall be quiet,
And love shall run riot,

And I shall find wealth in my friends;
Then truce to the story,
Of riches and glory;
There's the place where the rainbow ends.

HOPE

De dog go howlin' 'long de road,
De night come shiverin' down;
My back is tiahed of its load,
I cain't be fu' f'om town.
No mattah ef de way is long,
My haht is swellin' wid a song,
No mattah 'bout de frownin' skies,
I'll soon be home to see my Lize.

My shadder staggah on de way,
It's monstous col' to-night;
But I kin hyeah my honey say
" W'y bless me if de sight
O' you ain't good fu' my so' eyes."
(Dat talk's dis lak my lady Lize)
I's so'y case de way was long
But Lawd you bring me love an' song.

No mattah ef de way is long,
An' ef I trimbles so'
I knows de fiah's burnin' strong,
Behime my Lizy's do'.
An' daih my res' an' joy shell be,
Whaih my ol' wife's awaitin' me —
Why what I keer fu' stingin' blas',
I see huh windah light at las'.

APPRECIATION

My muvver's ist the nicest one
'At ever lived wiz folks;
She lets you have ze mostes' fun,
An' laffs at all your jokes.

I got a ol' maid auntie, too,
The worst you ever saw;
Her eyes ist bore you through and through,—
She ain't a bit like ma.

She's ist as slim as slim can be,
An' when you want to slide
Down on ze balusters, w'y she
Says 'at she's harrified.

She ain't as nice as Uncle Ben,
What says 'at little boys
Won't never grow to be big men
Unless they're fond of noise.

But muvver's nicer zan 'em all,
She calls you, " precious lamb,"
An' let's you roll your ten-pin ball,
An' spreads your bread wiz jam.

An' when you're bad, she ist looks sad,
You fink she's goin' to cry;
An' when she don't you're awful glad,
An' den you're good, Oh, my!

At night, she takes ze softest hand,
An' lays it on your head,
An' says "Be off to Sleepy-Land
By way o' trundle-bed."

So when you fink what muvver knows
An' aunts an' uncle tan't,
It skeers a feller; ist suppose
His muvver 'd been a aunt.

A SONG

On a summer's day as I sat by a stream,
A dainty maid came by,
And she blessed my sight like a rosy dream,
And left me there to sigh, to sigh,
And left me there to sigh, to sigh.

On another day as I sat by the stream,
This maiden paused a while,
Then I made me bold as I told my dream,
She heard it with a smile, a smile,
She heard it with a smile, a smile.

Oh, the months have fled and the autumn's red,
The maid no more goes by;
For my dream came true and the maid I wed,
And now no more I sigh, I sigh,
And now no more I sigh.

DAY

The gray dawn on the mountain top
Is slow to pass away.
Still lays him by in sluggish dreams,
The golden God of day.

And then a light along the hills,
Your laughter silvery gay;
The Sun God wakes, a bluebird trills,
You come and it is day.

TO DAN

Step me now a bridal measure,
Work give way to love and leisure,
Hearts be free and hearts be gay —
Doctor Dan doth wed to-day.

Diagnosis, cease your squalling —
Check that scalpel's senseless bawling,
Put that ugly knife away —
Doctor Dan doth wed to-day.

'Tis no time for things unsightly,
Life's the day and life goes lightly;
Science lays aside her sway —
Love rules Dr. Dan to-day.

Gather, gentlemen and ladies,
For the nuptial feast now made is,
Swing your garlands, chant your lay
For the pair who wed to-day.

Wish them happy days and many,
Troubles few and griefs not any,
Lift your brimming cups and say
God bless them who wed to-day.

Then a cup to Cupid daring,
Who for conquest ever faring,
With his arrows dares assail
E'en a doctor's coat of mail.

So with blithe and happy hymning
And with harmless goblets brimming,
Dance a step — musicians play —
Doctor Dan doth wed to-day.

WHAT'S THE USE

WHAT'S the use o' folks a-frownin'
When the way's a little rough?
Frowns lay out the road fur smilin'
You'll be wrinkled soon enough.
What's the use?

What's the use o' folks a-sighin'?
It's an awful waste o' breath,
An' a body can't stand wastin'
What he needs so bad in death.
What's the use?

What's the use o' even weepin'?
Might as well go long an' smile.
Life, our longest, strongest arrow,
Only lasts a little while.
What's the use?

A LAZY DAY

THE trees bend down along the stream,
Where anchored swings my tiny boat.
The day is one to drowse and dream
And list the thrush's throttling note.
When music from his bosom bleeds
Among the river's rustling reeds.

No ripple stirs the placid pool,
When my adventurous line is cast,
A truce to sport, while clear and cool,
The mirrored clouds slide softly past.
The sky gives back a blue divine,
And all the world's wide wealth is mine.

A pickerel leaps, a bow of light,
The minnows shine from side to side.
The first faint breeze comes up the tide —
I pause with half uplifted oar,
While night drifts down to claim the shore.

ADVICE

W'EN you full o' worry
'Bout yo' wo'k an' sich,
W'en you kind o' bothered
Case you can't get rich,
An' yo' neighboh p'ospah
Past his jest desu'ts,
An' de sneer of comerds
Stuhes yo' heaht an' hu'ts,
Des don' pet yo' worries,
Lay 'em on de she'f,
Tek a little trouble
Brothah, wid yo'se'f.

Ef a frien' comes mou'nin'
'Bout his awful case,
You know you don' grieve him
Wid a gloomy face,
But you wrassle wid him,
Try to tek him in;
Dough hit cracks yo' features,
Law, you smile lak sin,
Ain't you good ez he is?
Don' you pine to def;
Tek a little trouble
Brothah, wid yo'se'f.

Ef de chillun pestahs,
An' de baby's bad,
Ef yo' wife gits narvous,
An' you're gettin' mad,
Des you grab yo' boot-strops,
Hol' yo' body down,
Stop a-tinkin' cuss-w'rds,
Chase away de frown,
Knock de haid o' worry,
Twell dey ain' none lef';
Tek a little trouble,
Brothah, wid yo'se'f.

LIMITATIONS

EF you's only got de powah fe' to blow a little whistle,
Keep ermong de people wid de whistles.
Ef you don't, you'll fin' out sho'tly dat you's th'owed yo' fines' feelin'
In a place dat's all a bed o' thistles.
'Tain't no use a-goin' now, ez sho's you bo'n,
A-squeakin' of yo' whistle 'g'inst a gread big ho'n.

Ef you ain't got but a teenchy bit o' victuals on de table,
Whut' de use a-claimin' hit's a feas'?
Fe' de folks is mighty 'spicious, an' dey's ap' to come a-peerin',
Lookin' fe' de scraps you lef' at leas'.
W'en de meal's a-hidin' f'om de meal-bin's top,
You needn't talk to hide it; ef you sta'ts, des stop.

Ef yo' min' kin only carry half a pint o' common idees,
Don' go roun' a-sayin' hit's a bar'l;

'Ca'se de people gwine to test you, an' dey'll fin' out you's a-lyin',
Den dey'll twis' yo' sayin's in a snarl.
Wuss t'ing in de country dat I evah hyahed —
A crow dot sat a-squawkin', " I's a mockin'-bird."

A GOLDEN DAY

I FOUND you and I lost you,
All on a gleaming day.
The day was filled with sunshine,
And the land was full of May.

A golden bird was singing
Its melody divine,
I found you and I loved you,
And all the world was mine.

I found you and I lost you,
All on a golden day,
But when I dream of you, dear,
It is always brimming May.

THE UNLUCKY APPLE

'TWAS the apple that in Eden
Caused our father's primal fall;
And the Trojan War, remember —
'Twas an apple caused it all.
So for weeks I've hesitated,
You can guess the reason why,
For I want to tell my darling
She's the apple of my eye.

THE DISCOVERY

THESE are the days of elfs and fays:
Who says that with the dreams of myth,
These imps and elves disport themselves?
Ah no, along the paths of song
Do all the tiny folk belong.

Round all our homes,
Kobolds and gnomes do daily cling,
Then nightly fling their lanterns out.
And shout on shout, they join the rout,
And sing, and sing, within the sweet enchanted ring.

Where gleamed the guile of moonlight's smile,
Once paused I, listening for a while,
And heard the lay, unknown by day,—
The fairies' dancing roundelay.

Queen Mab was there, her shimmering hair
Each fairy prince's heart's despair.
She smiled to see their sparkling glee,
And once I ween, she smiled at me.

Since when, you may by night or day,
Dispute the sway of elf-folk gay;
But, hear me, stay!

I've learned the way to find Queen
Mab and elf and fay.

Where e'er by streams, the moon-
light gleams,
Or on a meadow softly beams,
There, footing round on dew-lit
ground,
The fairy folk may all be found.

MORNING

THE mist has left the greening
plain,
The dew-drops shine like fairy
rain,
The coquette rose awakes again
Her lovely self adorning.
The Wind is hiding in the trees,
A sighing, soothing, laughing
tease,
Until the rose says "Kiss me,
please,"
'Tis morning, 'tis morning.

With staff in hand and careless-
free,
The wanderer fares right jauntily,
For towns and houses are, thinks
he,
For scorning, for scorning.
My soul is swift upon the wing,
And in its deeps a song I bring;
Come, Love, and we together sing,
"'Tis morning, 'tis morning."

THE AWAKENING

I DID not know that life could be
so sweet,
I did not know the hours could
speed so fleet,
Till I knew you, and life was sweet
again.
The days grew brief with love
and lack of pain —

I was a slave a few short days
ago,
The powers of Kings and Princes
now I know;
I would not be again in bondage,
save
I had your smile, the liberty I
crave.

LOVE'S DRAFT

THE draft of love was cool and
sweet
You gave me in the cup,
But, ah, love's fire is keen and
fleet,
And I am burning up.

Unless the tears I shed for you
Shall quench this burning flame,
It will consume me through and
through,
And leave but ash—a name.

A MUSICAL

Outside the rain upon the street,
The sky all grim of hue,
Inside, the music-painful sweet,
And yet I heard but you.

As is a thrilling violin,
So is your voice to me,
And still above the other strains,
It sang in ecstasy.

TWELL DE NIGHT IS PAS'

All de night long twell de moon goes down,
Lovin' I set at huh feet,
Den fu' de long jou'ney back f'om de town,
Ha'd, but de dreams mek it sweet.

All de night long twell de break of de day,
Dreamin' agin in my sleep,
Mandy comes drivin' my sorrers away,
Axin' me, "Wha' fu' you weep?"

All de day long twell de sun goes down,
Smilin', I ben' to my hoe,
Fu' dough de weddah git nasty an' frown,
One place I know I kin go.

All my life long twell de night has pas'
Let de wo'k come ez it will,
So dat I fin' you, my honey, at las',
Somewhaih des ovah de hill.

BLUE

Standin' at de winder,
Feelin' kind o' glum,
Listenin' to de raindrops
Play de kettle drum,
Lookin' crost de medders
Swimmin' lak a sea;
Lawd 'a' mussy on us,
What's de good o' me?

Can't go out a-hoein',
Wouldn't ef I could;
Groun' too wet fu' huntin',
Fishin' ain't no good.
Too much noise fo' sleepin',
No one hyeah to chat;
Des mus' stan' an' listen
To dat pit-a-pat.

Hills is gittin' misty,
Valley's gittin' dahk;
Watch-dog's 'mence a-howlin',
Rathah have 'em ba'k
Dan a-moanin' solemn
Somewhaih out o' sight;
Rain-crow des a-chucklin'—
Dis is his delight.

Mandy, bring my banjo,
Bring de chillen in,

Come in f'om de kitchen,
  I feel sick ez sin.
Call in Uncle Isaac,
  Call Aunt Hannah, too,
Tain't no use in talkin',
  Chile, I's sholy blue.

DREAMIN' TOWN

Come away to dreamin' town,
  Mandy Lou, Mandy Lou,
Whaih de skies don' nevah frown,
      Mandy Lou;
Whaih he streets is paved with
    gol',
Whaih de days is nevah col',
An' no sheep strays f'om de fol',
      Mandy Lou.

Ain't you tiahed of every day,
  Mandy Lou, Mandy Lou,
Tek my han' an' come away,
      Mandy Lou,
To the place whaih dreams is
    King,
Whaih my heart hol's everything,
An' my soul can allus sing,
      Mandy Lou.

Come away to dream wid me,
  Mandy Lou, Mandy Lou,
Whaih our hands an' hea'ts are
    free,
      Mandy Lou;
Whaih de sands is shinin' white,
Whaih de rivahs glistens bright,
      Mandy Lou.

Come away to dreamland town,
  Mandy Lou, Mandy Lou,
Whaih de fruit is bendin' down,
  Des fu' you.
Smooth your brow of lovin' brown,
An' my love will be its crown;
Come away to dreamin' town,
      Mandy Lou.

AT NIGHT

Whut time 'd dat clock strike?
    Nine? No — eight;
  I didn't think hit was so late.
Aer chew! I must 'a' got a cough,
  I raally b'lieve I did doze off —
Hit's mighty soothin' to de tiah,
  A-dozin' dis way by de fiah;
Oo oom — hit feels so good to
    stretch
  I sutny is one weary wretch!

Look hyeah, dat boy done gone to
    sleep!
  He des ain't wo'th his boa'd an'
    keep;
I des don't b'lieve he'd bat his
    eyes
  If Gab'el called him fo'm de
    skies!
But sleepin's good dey ain't no
    doubt —
  Dis pipe o' mine is done gone
    out.
Don't bu'n a minute, bless my soul,
  Des please to han' me dat ah
    coal.

You 'Lias git up now, my son,
Seems lak my nap is des begun;
You sutny mus' ma'k down de day
W'en I treats comp'ny dis away!
W'y, Brother Jones, dat drowse come on,
An' laws! I dremp dat you was gone!
You 'Lias, whaih yo' mannahs, suh,
To hyeah me call an' nevah stuh!

To-morrer mo'nin' w'en I call
Dat boy'll be sleepin' to beat all,
Don't mek no diffunce how I roah,
He'll des lay up an' sno' and sno'.
Now boy, you done hyeahed whut I said,
You bettah tek yo'se'f yo baid,
Case ef you gits me good an' wrong
I'll mek dat sno' a diffunt song.

Dis wood fiah is invitin' dho',
Hit seems to wa'm de ve'y flo'—
An' nuffin' ain't a whit ez sweet,
Ez settin' toastin' of yo' feet.
Hit mek you drowsy, too, but La!
Hyeah, 'Lias, don't you hyeah yo' ma?
Ef I gits sta'ted f'om dis cheah
I' lay, you scamp, I'll mek you heah!

To-morrer mo'nin' I kin bawl
Twell all de neighbohs hyeah me call;
An' you'll be snoozin' des ez deep
Ez if de day was made fu' sleep;
Hit's funny when you got a cough
Somehow yo' voice seems too fu' off—
Can't wake dat boy fu' all I say,
I reckon he'll sleep daih twell day!

KIDNAPED

I HELD my heart so far from harm,
I let it wander far and free
In mead and mart, without alarm,
Assured it must come back to me.

And all went well till on a day,
Learned Dr. Cupid wandered by
A search along our sylvan way
For some peculiar butterfly.

A flash of wings, a hurried dive,
A flutter and a short-lived flit;
This Scientist, as I am alive
Had seen my heart and captured it.

Right tightly now 'tis held among
The specimens that he has trapped,
And sings (Oh, love is ever young),
'Tis passing sweet to be kidnaped.

COMPENSATION

Because I had loved so deeply,
Because I had loved so long,
God in His great compassion
Gave me the gift of song.

Because I have loved so vainly,
And sung with such faltering breath,
The Master in infinite mercy
Offers the boon of Death.

WINTER'S APPROACH

De sun hit shine an' de win' hit blow,
Ol' Brer Rabbit be a-layin' low,
He know dat de wintah time a-comin',
De huntah man he walk an' wait,
He walk right by Brer Rabbit's gate —
He know —

De dog he lick his sliverin' chop,
An' he tongue 'gin' his mouf go flop, flop —
He —
He rub his nose fu' to clah his scent
So's to tell w'ich way dat cotton-tail went,
He —

De huntah's wife she set an' spin
A good wahm coat fu' to wrop him in
She —
She look at de skillet an' she smile, oh my!
An' ol' Brer Rabbit got to sholy fly.
Dey know.

ANCHORED

If thro' the sea of night which here surrounds me,
I could swim out beyond the farthest star,
Break every barrier of circumstance that bounds me,
And greet the Sun of sweeter life afar,

Tho' near you there is passion, grief, and sorrow,
And out there rest and joy and peace and all,
I should renounce that beckoning for to-morrow,
I could not choose to go beyond your call.

THE VETERAN

Underneath the autumn sky,
Haltingly, the lines go by.
Ah, would steps were blithe and gay,
As when first they marched away,
Smile on lip and curl on brow,—
Only white-faced gray-beards now,
Standing on life's outer verge,
E'en the marches sound a dirge.

Blow, you bugles, play, you fife,
Rattle, drums, for dearest life.
Let the flags wave freely so,
As the marching legions go,
Shout, hurrah and laugh and jest,
This is memory at its best.
(Did you notice at your quip,
That old comrade's quivering lip?)

Ah, I see them as they come,
Stumbling with the rumbling drum;
But a sight more sad to me
E'en than these ranks could be
Was that one with cane upraised
Who stood by and gazed and gazed,
Trembling, solemn, lips compressed,
Longing to be with the rest.

Did he dream of old alarms,
As he stood, "presented arms"?
Did he think of field and camp
And the unremitting tramp
Mile on mile — the lonely guard
When he kept his midnight ward?
Did he dream of wounds and scars
In that bitter war of wars?

What of that? He stood and stands
In my memory — trembling hands,
Whitened beard and cane and all
As if waiting for the call
Once again: "To arms, my sons,"
And his ears hear far-off guns,
Roll of cannon and the tread
Of the legions of the Dead!

YESTERDAY AND TO-MORROW

YESTERDAY I held your hand,
Reverently I pressed it,
And its gentle yieldingness
From my soul I blessed it.

But to-day I sit alone,
Sad and sore repining;
Must our gold forever know
Flames for the refining?

Yesterday I walked with you,
Could a day be sweeter?
Life was all a lyric song
Set to tricksy meter.

Ah, to-day is like a dirge,—
Place my arms around you,
Let me feel the same dear joy
As when first I found you.

Let me once retrace my steps,
From these roads unpleasant,
Let my heart and mind and soul
All ignore the present.

Yesterday the iron seared
And to-day means sorrow.
Pause, my soul, arise, arise,
Look where gleams the morrow.

THE CHANGE

Love used to carry a bow, you know,
But now he carries a taper;
It is either a length of wax aglow,
Or a twist of lighted paper.

I pondered a little about the scamp,
And then I decided to follow
His wandering journey to field and camp,
Up hill, down dale or hollow.

I dogged the rollicking, gay, young blade
In every species of weather;
Till, leading me straight to the home of a maid
He left us there together.

And then I saw it, oh, sweet surprise,
The taper it set a-burning
The love-light brimming my lady's eyes,
And my heart with the fire of yearning.

THE CHASE

The wind told the little leaves to hurry,
And chased them down the way,
While the mother tree laughed loud in glee,
For she thought her babes at play.

The cruel wind and the rain laughed loudly,
We'll bury them deep, they said,
And the old tree grieves, and the little leaves
Lie low, all chilled and dead.

SUPPOSE

If 'twere fair to suppose
That your heart were not taken,
That the dew from the rose
Petals still were not shaken,
I should pluck you,
Howe'er you should thorn me and scorn me,
And wear you for life as the green of the bower.

If 'twere fair to suppose
That that road was for vagrants,
That the wind and the rose,
Counted all in their fragrance;
Oh, my dear one,
By love, I should take you and make you,
The green of my life from the scintillant hour.

THE DEATH OF THE FIRST BORN

Cover him over with daisies white
And eke with the poppies red,
Sit with me here by his couch to-night,

For the First-Born, Love, is dead.

Poor little fellow, he seemed so fair
As he lay in my jealous arms;
Silent and cold he is lying there
Stripped of his darling charms.

Lusty and strong he had grown forsooth,
Sweet with an infinite grace,
Proud in the force of his conquering youth,
Laughter alight in his face.

Oh, but the blast, it was cruel and keen,
And ah, but the chill it was rare;
The look of the winter-kissed flow'r you've seen
When meadows and fields were bare.

Can you not wake from this white, cold sleep
And speak to me once again?
True that your slumber is deep, so deep,
But deeper by far is my pain.

Cover him over with daisies white,
And eke with the poppies red,
Sit with me here by his couch to-night,
For the First-Born, Love, is dead.

BEIN' BACK HOME

HOME agin, an' home to stay —
Yes, it's nice to be away.
Plenty things to do an' see,
But the old place seems to me
Jest about the proper thing.
Mebbe 'ts 'cause the mem'ries cling
Closer 'round yore place o' birth
'N ary other spot on earth.

W'y it's nice jest settin' here,
Lookin' out an' seein' clear,
'Thout no smoke, ner dust, ner haze
In these sweet October days.
What's as good as that there lane,
Kind o' browned from last night's rain?
'Pears like home has got the start
When the goal's a feller's heart.

What's as good as that there jay
Screechin' up'ards towards the gray
Skies? An' tell me, what's as fine
As that full-leafed pumpkin vine?
Tow'rin' buildin's — yes, they're good;
But in sight o' field and wood,
Then a feller understan's
'Bout the house not made with han's.

Let the others rant an' roam
When they git away from home;
Jest gi' me my old settee

An' my pipe beneath a tree;
Sight o' medders green an' still,
Now and then a gentle hill,
Apple orchards, full o' fruit,
Nigh a cider press to boot —

That's the thing jest done up brown;
D'want to be too nigh to town;
Want to have the smells an' sights,
An' the dreams o' long still nights,
With the friends you used to know
In the keerless long ago —
Same old cronies, same old folks,
Same old cider, same old jokes.

Say, it's nice a-gittin' back,
When yore pulse is growin' slack,
An' yore breath begins to wheeze
Like a fair-set valley breeze;
Kind o' nice to set aroun'
On the old familiar groun',
Knowin' that when Death does come,
That he'll find you right at home.

THE OLD CABIN

In de dead of night I sometimes,
Git to t'inkin' of de pas'
An' de days w'en slavery helt me
In my mis'ry — ha'd an' fas'.
Dough de time was mighty tryin',
In dese houahs somehow hit seem·
Dat a brightah light come slippin'
Thoo de kivahs of my dream.

An' my min' fu'gits de whuppins
Draps de feah o' block an' lash
An' flies straight to somep'n' joyful
In a secon's lightnin' flash.
Den hit seems I see a vision
Of a dearah long ago
Of de childern tumblin' roun' me
By my rough ol' cabin do'.

Talk about yo' go'geous mansions
An' yo' big house great an' gran',
Des bring up de fines' palace
Dat you know in all de lan'.
But dey's somep'n' dearah to me,
Somep'n' faihah to my eyes
In dat cabin, less you bring me
To yo' mansion in de skies.

I kin see de light a-shinin'
Thoo de chinks atween de logs,
I kin hyeah de way-off bayin'
Of my mastah's huntin' dogs,
An' de neighin' of de hosses
Stampin' on de ol' bahn flo',
But above dese soun's de laughin'
At my deah ol' cabin do'.

We would gethah daih at evenin',
All my frien's 'ud come erroun'
An' hit wan't no time, twell, bless you,
You could hyeah de banjo's soun'.
You could see de dahkies dancin'
Pigeon wing an' heel an' toe —

Joyous times I tell you people
Roun' dat same ol' cabin do'.

But at times my t'oughts gits saddah,
Ez I riccolec' de folks,
An' dey frolickin' an' talkin'
Wid dey laughin' an dey jokes.
An' hit hu'ts me w'en I membahs
Dat I 'll nevah see no mo'
Dem ah faces gethered smilin'
Roun' dat po' ol' cabin do'.

DESPAIR

Let me close the eyes of my soul
That I may not see
What stands between thee and me.

Let me shut the ears of my heart
That I may not hear
A voice that drowns yours, my dear.

Let me cut the cords of my life,
Of my desolate being,
Since cursed is my hearing and seeing.

CIRCUMSTANCES ALTER CASES

Tim Murphy's gon' walkin' wid Maggie O'Neill,
O chone!
If I was her muther, I 'd frown on sich foolin',
O chone!
I'm sure it's unmutherlike, darin' an' wrong
To let a gyrul hear tell the sass an' the song
Of every young felly that happens along,
O chone!

An' Murphy, the things that's be'n sed of his doin',
O chone!
'Tis a cud that no dacent folks wants to be chewin',
O chone!
If he came to my door wid his cane on a twirl,
Fur to thry to make love to you, Biddy, my girl,
Ah, wouldn't I send him away wid a whirl,
O chone!

They say the gossoon is indecent and dirty,
O chone!
In spite of his dressin' so.
O chone!
Let him dress up ez foine ez a king or a queen,
Let him put on more wrinkles than ever was seen,
You'll be sure he's no match for my little colleen,
O chone!

Faith the two is comin' back an' their walk is all over,
O chone!

'Twas a pretty short walk fur to take wid a lover,
O chone!
Why, I believe that Tim Murphy's a kumin' this way,
Ah, Biddy jest look at him steppin' so gay,
I'd niver belave what the gossipers say,
O chone!

He's turned in the gate an' he's coming a-caperin',
O chone!
Go, Biddy, go quick an' put on a clane apern,
O chone!
Be quick as ye kin fur he's right at the dure;
Come in, master Tim, fur ye're welcome I'm shure.
We were talkin' o' ye jest a minute before.
O chone!

TILL THE WIND GETS RIGHT

Oh the breeze is blowin' balmy
An the sun is in a haze;
There's a cloud jest givin' coolness
To the laziest of days.
There are crowds upon the lakeside,
But the fish refuse to bite,
So I'll wait and go a-fishin'
When the wind gets right.

Now my boat tugs at her anchor,
Eager now to kiss the spray,
While the little waves are callin'
Drowsy sailor come away,
There's a harbor for the happy,
And its sheen is just in sight,
But I won't set sail to get there,
Till the wind gets right.

That's my trouble, too, I reckon,
I've been waitin' all too long,
Tho' the days were always
Still the wind is always wrong.
An' when Gabriel blows his trumpet,
In the day o' in the night,
I will still be found waitin',
Till the wind gets right.

A SUMMER NIGHT

Summah is de lovin' time —
Do' keer what you say.
Night is allus peart an' prime,
Bettah dan de day.
Do de day is sweet an' good,
Birds a-singin' fine,
Pines a-smellin' in de wood,—
But de night is mine.

Rivah whisperin' "howdy do,"
Ez it pass you by —
Moon a-lookin' down at you,
Winkin' on de sly.
Frogs a-croakin' f'om de pon',
Singin' bass dey fill,
An' you listen way beyon'
Ol' man whippo'will.

Hush up, honey, tek my han',
  Mek yo' footsteps light;
Somep'n' kin' o' hol's de lan'
  On a summah night.
Somep'n' dat you nevah sees
  An' you nevah hyeahs,
But you feels it in de breeze,
  Somep'n' nigh to teahs.

Somep'n' nigh to teahs? dat's so;
  But hit's nigh to smiles.
An' you feels it ez you go
  Down de shinin' miles.
Tek my han', my little dove;
  Hush an' come erway —
Summah is de time fu' love,
  Night-time beats de day!

AT SUNSET TIME

Adown the west a golden glow
  Sinks burning in the sea,
And all the dreams of long ago
  Come flooding back to me.
The past has writ a story strange
  Upon my aching heart,
But time has wrought a subtle change,
  My wounds have ceased to smart.

No more the quick delight of youth,
  No more the sudden pain,
I look no more for trust or truth
  Where greed may compass gain.
What, was it I who bared my heart
  Through unrelenting years,
And knew the sting of misery's dart,
  The tang of sorrow's tears?

'Tis better now, I do not weep,
  I do not laugh nor care;
My soul and spirit half asleep
  Drift aimless everywhere.
We float upon a sluggish stream,
  We ride no rapids mad,
While life is all a tempered dream
  And every joy half sad.

NIGHT

Silence, and whirling worlds afar
  Through all encircling skies.
What floods come o'er the spirit's bar,
  What wondrous thoughts arise.

The earth, a mantle falls away,
  And, winged, we leave the sod;
Where shines in its eternal sway
  The majesty of God.

AT LOAFING-HOLT

Since I left the city's heat
For this sylvan, cool retreat,
High upon the hill-side here
Where the air is clean and clear,
I have lost the urban ways.

Mine are calm and tranquil days,
Sloping lawns of green are mine,
Clustered treasures of the vine;
Long forgotten plants I know,
Where the best wild berries grow,
Where the greens and grasses sprout,
When the elders blossom out.
Now I am grown weather-wise
With the lore of winds and skies.
Mine the song whose soft refrain
Is the sigh of summer rain.
Seek you where the woods are cool,
Would you know the shady pool
Where, throughout the lazy day,
Speckled beauties drowse or play?
Would you find in rest or peace
Sorrow's permanent release?—
Leave the city, grim and gray,
Come with me, ah, come away.
Do you fear the winter chill,
Deeps of snow upon the hill?
'Tis a mantle, kind and warm,
Shielding tender shoots from harm.
Do you dread the ice-clad streams,—
They are mirrors for your dreams.
Here's a rouse, when summer's past
To the raging winter's blast.
Let him roar and let him rout,
We are armored for the bout.
How the logs are glowing, see!
Who sings louder, they or he?
Could the city be more gay?
Burn your bridges! Come away!

WHEN A FELLER'S ITCHIN' TO BE SPANKED

W'EN us fellers stomp around, makin' lots o' noise,
Gramma says, "There's certain times come to little boys
W'en they need a shingle or the soft side of a plank;"
She says "we're a-itchin' for a right good spank."
An' she says, "Now thes you wait,
It's a-comin'— soon or late,
W'en a feller's itchin' fer a spank."

W'en a feller's out o' school, you know how he feels,
Gramma says we wriggle 'roun' like a lot o' eels.
W'y it's like a man that's thes home from out o' jail.
What's the use o' scoldin' if we pull Tray's tail?
Gramma says, tho', "Thes you wait,
It's a-comin'— soon or late,
You'se the boys that's itchin' to be spanked."

Cats is funny creatures an' I like to make 'em yowl,
Gramma alwus looks at me with a awful scowl
An' she says, "Young gentlemen, mamma should be thanked
Ef you'd get your knickerbockers right well spanked."

An' she says, "Now thes you wait,
It's a-comin'— soon or late,"
W'en a feller's itchin' to be spanked.

Ef you fin' the days is gettin' awful hot in school
An' you know a swimmin' place where it's nice and cool,
Er you know a cat-fish hole brimmin' full o' fish,
Whose a-goin' to set around school and wish?
'Tain't no use to hide your bait,
It's a-comin,— soon or late,
W'en a feller's itchin' to be spanked.

Ol' folks know most ever'thing 'bout the world, I guess,
Gramma does, we wish she knowed thes a little less,
But I alwus kind o' think it 'ud be as well
Ef they wouldn't alwus have to up an' tell;
We kids wish 'at they'd thes wait,
It's a-comin'— soon or late,
W'en a feller's itchin' to be spanked.

THE RIVER OF RUIN

ALONG by the river of ruin
They dally — the thoughtless ones,
They dance and they dream
By the side of the stream,
As long as the river runs.

It seems all so pleasant and cheery —
No thought of the morrow is theirs,
And their faces are bright
With the sun of delight,
And they dream of no night-brooding cares.

The women wear garlanded tresses,
The men have rings on their hands,
And they sing in their glee,
For they think they are free —
They that know not the treacherous sands.

Ah, but this be a venturesome journey,
Forever those sands are ashift,
And a step to one side
Means a grasp of the tide,
And the current is fearful and swift.

For once in the river of ruin,
What boots it, to do or to dare,
For down we must go
In the turbulent flow,
To the desolate sea of Despair.

TO HER

YOUR presence like a benison to me
  Wakes my sick soul to dreamful ecstasy,
I fancy that some old Arabian night
Saw you my houri and my heart's delight.

And wandering forth beneath the passionate moon,
  Your love-strung zither and my soul in tune,
We knew the joy, the haunting of the pain
  That like a flame thrills through me now again.

To-night we sit where sweet the spice winds blow,
  A wind the northland lacks and ne'er shall know,
With clasped hands and spirits all aglow
  As in Arabia in the long ago.

A LOVE LETTER

OH, I des received a letter f'om de sweetest little gal;
  Oh, my; oh, my.
She's my lovely little sweetheart an' her name is Sal:
  Oh, my; oh, my.
She writes me dat she loves me an' she loves me true,
  She wonders ef I'll tell huh dat I loves huh, too;
An' my heaht's so full o' music dat I do' know what to do;
  Oh, my; oh, my.

I got a man to read it an' he read it fine;
  Oh, my; oh, my.
Dey ain' no use denying dat her love is mine;
  Oh, my; oh, my.
But hyeah's de t'ing dat's puttin' me in such a awful plight,
I t'ink of huh at mornin' an' I dream of huh at night;
But how's I gwine to cou't huh w'en I do' know how to write?
  Oh, my; oh, my.

My heaht is bubblin' ovah wid de t'ings I want to say;
  Oh, my; oh, my.
An' dey's lots of folks to copy what I tell 'em fu' de pay;
  Oh, my; oh, my.
But dey's t'ings dat I's a-t'inkin' dat is only fu' huh ears,
An' I couldn't lu'n to write 'em ef I took a dozen years;
So to go down daih an' tell huh is de only way, it 'pears;
  Oh, my; oh, my.

AFTER MANY DAYS

I'VE always been a faithful man
  An' tried to live for duty,
But the stringent mode of life
  Has somewhat lost its beauty.

The story of the generous bread
  He sent upon the waters,
Which after many days returns
  To trusting sons and daughters,

Had oft impressed me, so I want
  My soul influenced by it,
And bought a loaf of bread and sought
  A stream where I could try it.

I cast my bread upon the waves
  And fancied then to await it;
It had not floated far away
  When a fish came up and ate it.

And if I want both fish and bread,
  And surely both I'm wanting,
About the only way I see
  Is for me to go fishing.

LIZA MAY

Little brown face full of smiles,
And a baby's guileless wiles,
    Liza May, Liza May.

Eyes a-peeping thro' the fence
With an interest intense,
    Liza May.

Ah, the gate is just ajar,
And the meadow is not far,
    Liza May, Liza May.

And the road feels very sweet,
To your little toddling feet,
    Liza May.

Ah, you roguish runaway,
What will toiling mother say,
    Liza May, Liza May?

What care you who smile to greet
Everyone you chance to meet,
    Liza May?

Soft the mill-race sings its song,
Just a little way along,
    Liza May, Liza May.

But the song is full of guile,
Turn, ah turn, your steps the while,
    Liza May.

You have caught the gleam and glow
Where the darkling waters flow,
    Liza May, Liza May.

Flash of ripple, bend of bough,
Where are all the angels now?
    Liza May.

Now a mother's eyes intense
Gazing o'er a shabby fence,
    Liza May, Liza May.

Then a mother's anguished face
Peering all around the place,
Liza May.

Hear the agonizing call
For a mother's all in all,
Liza May, Liza May.

Hear a mother's maddened prayer
To the calm unanswering air,
Liza May.

What's become of — Liza May?
What has darkened all the day?
Liza May, Liza May.

Ask the waters dark and fleet,
If they know the smiling, sweet
Liza May.

Call her, call her as you will,
On the meadow, on the hill,
Liza May, Liza May.

Through the brush or beaten track
Echo only gives you back,
Liza May.

Ah, but you were loving — sweet,
On your little toddling feet,
Liza May, Liza May.

But through all the coming years,
Must a mother breathe with tears,
Liza May.

THE MASTERS

Oh, who is the Lord of the land of life,
When hotly goes the fray?
When, fierce we smile in the midst of strife
Then whom shall we obey?

Oh, Love is the Lord of the land of life
Who holds a monarch's sway;
He wends with wish of maid and wife,
And him you must obey.

Then who is the Lord of the land of life,
At setting of the sun?
Whose word shall sway when Peace is rife
And all the fray is done?

Then Death is the Lord of the land of life,
When your hot race is run.
Meet then his scythe and pruning-knife
When the fray is lost or won.

TROUBLE IN DE KITCHEN

Dey was oncet a awful quoil 'twixt de skillet an' de pot;
De pot was des a-bilin' an' de skillet sho' was hot.
Dey slurred each othah's colah an' dey called each othah names,

W'ile de coal-oil can des gu-gled,
 po'in oil erpon de flames.

De pot, hit called de skillet des a
 flat, disfiggered t'ing,
An' de skillet 'plied dat all de pot
 could do was set an' sing,
An' he 'lowed dat dey was 'lusions
 dat he wouldn't stoop to mek
'Case he reckernize his juty, an' he
 had too much at steak.

Well, at dis de pot biled ovah, case
 his tempah gittin' highah,
An' de skillet got to sputterin',
 den de fat was in de fiah.
Mistah fiah lay daih smokin' an'
 a-t'inkin' to hisse'f,
W'ile de peppah-box us nudgin' of
 de gingah on de she'f.

Den dey all des lef' hit to 'im,
 'bout de trouble an' de talk;
An' howevah he decided, w'y dey
 bofe 'u'd walk de chalk;
But de fiah uz so 'sgusted how dey
 quoil an' dey shout
Dat he cooled 'em off, I reckon,
 w'en he puffed an' des went
 out.

CHRISTMAS

Step wid de banjo an' glide wid
 de fiddle,
Dis ain' no time fu' to pottah
 an' piddle;
Fu' Christmas is comin', it's right
 on de way,
An' dey's houahs to dance 'fo'
 de break o' de day.

What if de win' is taihin' an'
 whistlin'?
Look at dat fiah how hit 's
 spittin' an' bristlin'!
Heat in de ashes an' heat in de
 cindahs,
Ol' mistah Fros' kin des look
 thoo de windahs.

Heat up de toddy an' pas' de wa'm
 glasses,
Don' stop to shivah at blowin's
 an' blas'es,
Keep on de kittle an' keep it a-
 hummin',
Eat all an' drink all, dey's lots
 mo' a-comin'.
Look hyeah, Maria, don't open
 dat oven,
Want all dese people a-pushin'
 an' shovin'?

Res' f'om de dance? Yes, you
 done cotch dat odah,
Mammy done cotch it, an' law!
 hit nigh flo'd huh;
'Possum is monst'ous fu' mekin'
 folks fin' it!
Come, draw yo' cheers up, I 's
 sho' I do' min' it.
Eat up dem critters, you men folks
 an' wimmens,
'Possums ain' skace w'en dey's
 lots o' pu'simmons.

ROSES AND PEARLS

YOUR spoken words are roses fine and sweet,
The songs you sing are perfect pearls of sound.
How lavish nature is about your feet,
To scatter flowers and jewels both around.

Blushing the stream of petal beauty flows,
Softly the white strings trickle down and shine.
Oh! speak to me, my love, I crave a rose.
Sing me a song, for I would pearls were mine.

RAIN-SONGS

THE rain streams down like harp-strings from the sky;
The wind, that world-old harpist sitteth by;
And ever as he sings his low refrain,
He plays upon the harp-strings of the rain.

A LOST DREAM

AH, I have changed, I do not know
Why lonely hours affect me so.
In days of yore, this were not wont,
No loneliness my soul could daunt.

For me too serious for my age,
The weighty tome of hoary sage,
Until with puzzled heart astir,
One God-giv'n night, I dreamed of her.

I loved no woman, hardly knew
More of the sex that strong men woo
Than cloistered monk within his cell;
But now the dream is lost, and hell

Holds me her captive tight and fast
Who prays and struggles for the past.
No living maid has charmed my eyes,
But now, my soul is wonder-wise.

For I have dreamed of her and seen
Her red-brown tresses' ruddy sheen,
Have known her sweetness, lip to lip,
The joy of her companionship.

When days were bleak and winds were rude,
She shared my smiling solitude,
And all the bare hills walked with me
To hearken winter's melody.

And when the spring came o'er the land
We fared together hand in hand
Beneath the linden's leafy screen
That waved above us faintly green.

In summer, by the river-side,
Our souls were kindred with the tide
That floated onward to the sea
As we swept toward Eternity.

The bird's call and the water's drone
Were all for us and us alone.
The water-fall that sang all night
Was her companion, my delight,

And e'en the squirrel, as he sped
Along the branches overhead,
Half kindly and half envious,
Would chatter at the joy of us.

'Twas but a dream, her face, her hair,
The spring-time sweet, the winter bare,
The summer when the woods we ranged,—
'Twas but a dream, but all is changed.

Yes, all is changed and all has fled,
The dream is broken, shattered, dead.
And yet, sometimes, I pray to know
How just a dream could hold me so.

A SONG

THOU art the soul of a summer's day,
Thou art the breath of the rose.
But the summer is fled
And the rose is dead
Where are they gone, who knows, who knows?

Thou art the blood of my heart o' hearts,
Thou art my soul's repose,
But my heart grows numb
And my soul is dumb
Where art thou, love, who knows, who knows?

Thou art the hope of my after years —
Sun for my winter snows
But the years go by
'Neath a clouded sky.
Where shall we meet, who knows, who knows?

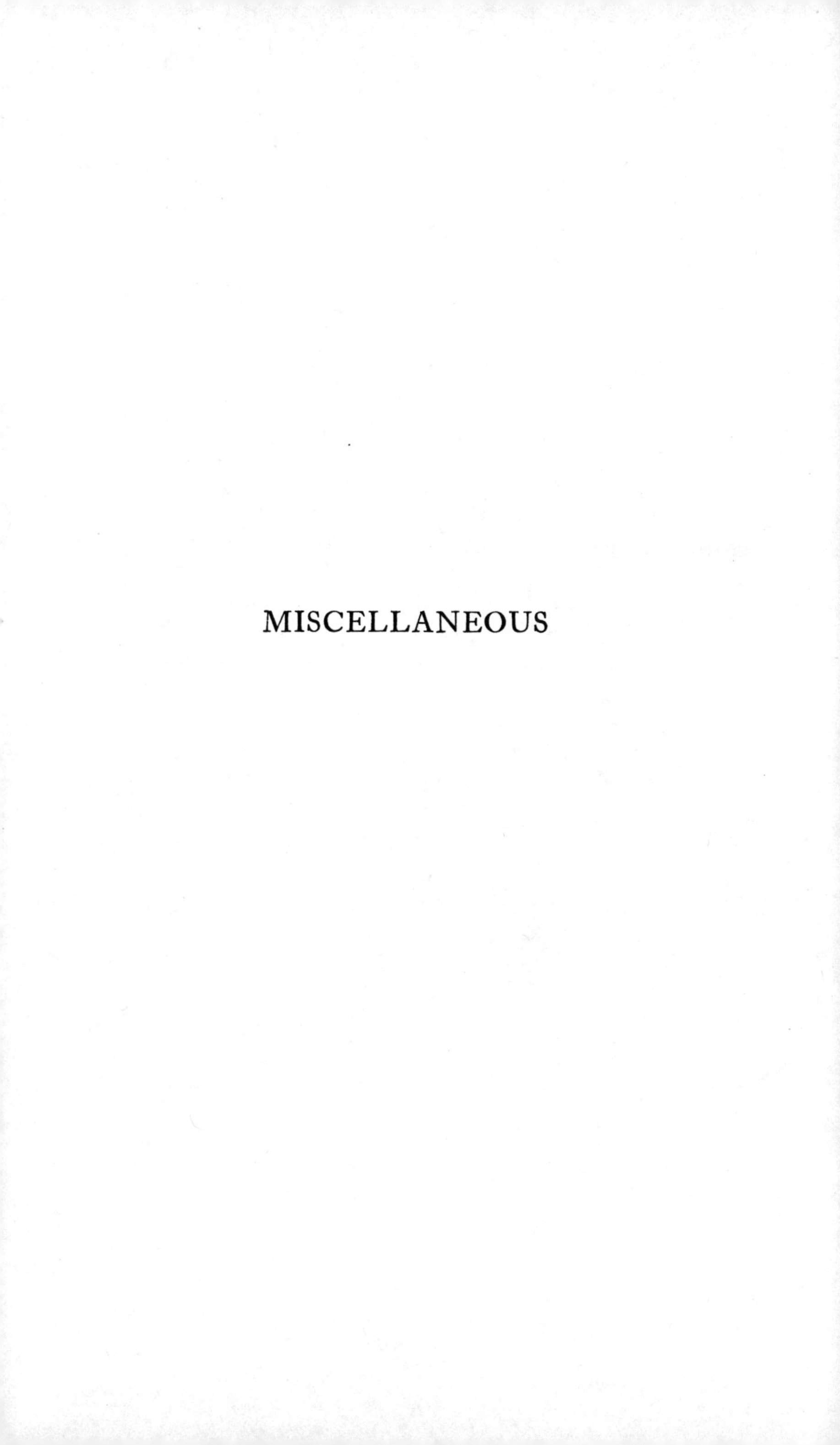

MISCELLANEOUS

THE CAPTURE

DUCK come switchin' 'cross de lot
Hi, oh, Miss Lady!
Hurry up an' hide de pot
Hi, oh, Miss Lady!
Duck's a mighty 'spicious fowl,
Slick as snake an' wise as owl;
Hol' dat dog, don't let him yowl!
Hi, oh, Miss Lady!

Th'ow dat co'n out kind o' slow
Hi, oh, Miss Lady!
Keep yo'se'f behin' de do'
Hi, oh, Miss Lady!
Lots o' food'll kill his feah,
Co'n is cheap but fowls is deah —
"Come, good ducky, come on heah."
Hi, oh, Miss Lady!

Ain't he fat and ain't he fine,
Hi, oh, Miss Lady!
Des can't wait to make him mine.
Hi, oh, Miss Lady!
See him waddle when he walk,
'Sh! keep still and don't you talk!
Got you! Don't you daih to squawk!
Hi, oh, Miss Lady!

WHEN WINTER DARKENING ALL AROUND

WHEN winter covering all the ground
Hides every sign of Spring, sir.
However you may look around,
Pray what will then you sing, sir?

The Spring was here last year I know,
And many bards did flute, sir;
I shall not fear a little snow
Forbid me from my lute, sir.

If words grow dull and rhymes grow rare,
I'll sing of Spring's farewell, sir.
For every season steals an air,
Which has a Springtime smell, sir.

But if upon the other side,
With passionate longing burning,
Will seek the half unjeweled tide,
And sing of Spring's returning.

FROM THE PORCH AT RUNNYMEDE

I STAND above the city's rush and din,
And gaze far down with calm and undimmed eyes,

To where the misty smoke wreath grey and dim
Above the myriad roofs and spires rise;

Still is my heart and vacant is my breath —
This lovely view is breath and life to me,
Why I could charm the icy soul of death
With such a sight as this I stand and see.

I hear no sound of labor's din or stir,
I feel no weight of worldly cares or fears,
Sweet song of birds, of wings the soothing whirr,
These sounds alone assail my listening ears.

Unwhipt of conscience here I stand alone,
The breezes humbly kiss my garment's hem;
I am a king — the whole world is my throne,
The blue grey sky my royal diadem.

EQUIPMENT

With what thou gavest me, O Master,
I have wrought.
Such chances, such abilities,
To see the end was not for my poor eyes,
Thine was the impulse, thine the forming thought.

Ah, I have wrought,
And these sad hands have right to tell their story,
It was no hard up striving after glory,
Catching and losing, gaining and failing,
Raging me back at the world's raucous railing.
Simply and humbly from stone and from wood,
Wrought I the things that to thee might seem good.

If they are little, ah God! but the cost,
Who but thou knowest the all that is lost!
If they are few, is the workmanship true?
Try them and weigh me, whate'er be my due!

EVENING

The moon begins her stately ride
Across the summer sky;
The happy wavelets lash the shore,—
The tide is rising high.

Beneath some friendly blade of grass
The lazy beetle cowers;
The coffers of the air are filled
With offerings from the flowers.

And slowly buzzing o'er my head
A swallow wings her flight;
I hear the weary plowman sing
As falls the restful night.

TO PFRIMMER

(Lines on reading "Driftwood.")

DRIFTWOOD gathered here and there
Along the beach of time;
Now and then a chip of truth
'Mid boards and boughs of rhyme;
Driftwood gathered day by day,—
The cypress and the oak,—
Twigs that in some former time
From sturdy home trees broke.
Did this wood come floating thick
All along down "Injin Crik?"
Or did kind tides bring it thee
From the past's receding sea
Down the stream of memory?

TO THE MIAMI

KISS me, Miami, thou most constant one!
I love thee more for that thou changest not.
When Winter comes with frigid blast,
Or when the blithesome Spring is past
And Summer's here with sunshine hot,
Or in sere Autumn, thou has still the pow'r
To charm alike, whate'er the hour.

Kiss me, Miami, with thy dewy lips;
Throbs fast my heart e'en as thine own breast beats.
My soul doth rise as rise thy waves,
As each on each the dark shore laves
And breaks in ripples and retreats.
There is a poem in thine every phase;
Thou still has sung through all thy days.

Tell me, Miami, how it was with thee
When years ago Tecumseh in his prime
His birch boat o'er thy waters sent,
And pitched upon thy banks his tent.
In that long-gone, poetic time,
Did some bronze bard thy flowing stream sit by
And sing thy praises, e'en as I?

Did some bronze lover 'neath this dark old tree
Whisper of love unto his Indian maid?
And didst thou list his murmurs deep,
And in thy bosom safely keep
The many raging vows they said?
Or didst thou tell to fish and frog and bird
The raptured scenes that there occurred?

But, O dear stream, what volumes thou couldst tell
To all who know thy language as I do,
Of life and love and jealous hate!
But now to tattle were too late,—
Thou who hast ever been so true.
Tell not to every passing idler here
All those sweet tales that reached thine ear.

But, silent stream, speak out and tell me this:
I say that men and things are still the same;
Were men as bold to do and dare?
Were women then as true and fair?
Did poets seek celestial flame,
The hero die to gain a laureled brow,
And women suffer, then as now?

CHRISTMAS CAROL

Ring out, ye bells!
All Nature swells
With gladness at the wondrous story,—
The world was lorn,
But Christ is born
To change our sadness into glory.

Sing, earthlings, sing!
To-night a King
Hath come from heaven's high throne to bless us.
The outstretched hand
O'er all the land
Is raised in pity to caress us.

Come at his call;
Be joyful all;
Away with mourning and with sadness!
The heavenly choir
With holy fire
Their voices raise in songs of gladness.

The darkness breaks
And Dawn awakes,
Her cheeks suffused with youthful blushes.
The rocks and stones
In holy tones
Are singing sweeter than the thrushes.

Then why should we
In silence be,

When Nature lends her voice to praises;
When heaven and earth
Proclaim the truth
Of Him for whom that lone star blazes?

No, be not still,
But with a will
Strike all your harps and set them ringing;
On hill and heath
Let every breath
Throw all its power into singing!

A SUMMER PASTORAL

It's hot to-day. The bees is buzzin'
Kinder don't-keer-like aroun'
An' fur off the warm air dances
O'er the parchin' roofs in town.
In the brook the cows is standin';
Childern hidin' in the hay;
Can't keep none of 'em a workin',
'Cause it's hot to-day.

It's hot to-day. The sun is blazin'
Like a great big ball o' fire;
Seems as ef instead o' settin'
It keeps mountin' higher an' higher.
I'm as triflin' as the children,
Though I blame them lots an' scold;
I keep slippin' to the spring-house,
Where the milk is rich an' cold.
The very air within its shadder
Smells o' cool an' restful things,
An' a roguish little robin
Sits above the place an' sings.
I don't mean to be a shirkin',
But I linger by the way
Longer, mebbe, than is needful,
'Cause it's hot to-day.

It's hot to-day. The horses stumble
Half asleep across the fiel's;
An' a host o' teasin' fancies
O'er my burnin' senses steals,—
Dreams o' cool rooms, curtains lowered,
An' a sofy's temptin' look;
Patter o' composin' raindrops
Or the ripple of a brook.

I strike a stump! That wakes me sudden;
Dreams all vanish into air.
Lordy! how I chew my whiskers;
'Twouldn't do fur me to swear.
But I have to be so keerful
'Bout my thoughts an' what I say;
Somethin' might slip out unheeded,
'Cause it's hot to-day.

Git up, there, Suke! you, Sal, git over!
Sakes alive! how I do sweat.
Every stitch that I've got on me,
Bet a cent, is wringin' wet.
If this keeps up, I'll lose my temper.

Gee there, Sal, you lazy brute!
Wonder who on airth this weather
Could 'a' be'n got up to suit?

You, Sam, go bring a tin o' water;
Dash it all, don't be so slow!
'Pears as ef you tuk an hour
'Tween each step to stop an' blow.
Think I want to stand a meltin'
Out here in this b'ilin' sun,
While you stop to think about it?
Lift them feet o' your'n an' run.

It ain't no use; I'm plumb fe-taggled.
Come an' put this team away.
I won't plow another furrer;
It's too mortal hot to-day.
I ain't weak, nor I ain't lazy,
But I'll stand this half day's loss
'Fore I let the devil make me
Lose my patience an' git cross.

IN SUMMER TIME

WHEN summer time has come, and all
The world is in the magic thrall
Of perfumed airs that lull each sense
To fits of drowsy indolence;
When skies are deepest blue above,
And flow'rs aflush,— then most I love
To start, while early dews are damp,
And wend my way in woodland tramp
Where forests rustle, tree on tree,
And sing their silent songs to me;
Where pathways meet and pathways part,—
To walk with Nature heart by heart,
Till wearied out at last I lie
Where some sweet stream steals singing by
A mossy bank; where violets vie
In color with the summer sky,—
Or take my rod and line and hook,
And wander to some darkling brook,
Where all day long the willows dream,
And idly droop to kiss the stream,
And there to loll from morn till night—
Unheeding nibble, run, or bite—
Just for the joy of being there
And drinking in the summer air,
The summer sounds, and summer sights,
That set a restless mind to rights
When grief and pain and raging doubt
Of men and creeds have worn it out;
The birds' song and the water's drone,
The humming bees' low monotone,
The murmur of the passing breeze,
And all the sounds akin to these,
That make a man in summer time

Feel only fit for rest and rhyme.
Joy springs all radiant in my breast;
Though pauper poor, than king more blest,
The tide beats in my soul so strong
That happiness breaks forth in song,
And rings aloud the welkin blue
With all the songs I ever knew.
O time of rapture! time of song!
How swiftly glide thy days along
Adown the current of the years,
Above the rocks of grief and tears!
'Tis wealth enough of joy for me
In summer time to simply be.

A THANKSGIVING POEM

THE sun hath shed its kindly light,
  Our harvesting is gladly o'er
Our fields have felt no killing blight,
  Our bins are filled with goodly store.

From pestilence, fire, flood, and sword
  We have been spared by thy decree,
And now with humble hearts, O Lord,
  We come to pay our thanks to thee.

We feel that had our merits been
  The measure of thy gifts to us,
We erring children, born of sin,
  Might not now be rejoicing thus.

No deed of ours hath brought us grace;
  When thou were nigh our sight was dull,
We hid in trembling from thy face,
  But thou, O God, wert merciful.

Thy mighty hand o'er all the land
  Hath still been open to bestow
Those blessings which our wants demand
  From heaven, whence all blessings flow.

Thou hast, with ever watchful eye,
  Looked down on us with holy care,
And from thy storehouse in the sky
  Hast scattered plenty everywhere.

Then lift we up our songs of praise
  To thee, O Father, good and kind;
To thee we consecrate our days;
  Be thine the temple of each mind.

With incense sweet our thanks ascend;

Before thy works our powers pall;
Though we should strive years without end,
We could not thank thee for them all.

NUTTING SONG

THE November sun invites me,
And although the chill wind smites me,
I will wander to the woodland
Where the laden trees await;
And with loud and joyful singing
I will set the forest ringing,
As if I were king of Autumn,
And Dame Nature were my mate,—

While the squirrel in his gambols
Fearless round about me ambles,
As if he were bent on showing
In my kingdom he'd a share;
While my warm blood leaps and dashes,
And my eye with freedom flashes,
As my soul drinks deep and deeper
Of the magic in the air.

There's a pleasure found in nutting,
All life's cares and griefs outshutting,
That is fuller far and better
Than what prouder sports impart.
Who could help a carol trilling
As he sees the baskets filling?
Why, the flow of song keeps running
O'er the high walls of the heart.

So when I am home returning,
When the sun is lowly burning,
I will once more wake the echoes
With a happy song of praise,—
For the golden sunlight blessing,
And the breezes' soft caressing,
And the precious boon of living
In the sweet November days.

LOVE'S PICTURES

LIKE the blush upon the rose
When the wooing south wind speaks,
Kissing soft its petals,
Are thy cheeks.

Tender, soft, beseeching, true,
Like the stars that deck the skies
Through the ether sparkling,
Are thine eyes.

Like the song of happy birds,
When the woods with spring rejoice,
In their blithe awak'ning,
Is thy voice.

Like soft threads of clustered silk
O'er thy face so pure and fair,
Sweet in its profusion,
Is thy hair.

Like a fair but fragile vase,
Triumph of the carver's art,
Graceful formed and slender,—
Thus thou art.

Ah, thy cheek, thine eyes, thy voice,
And thy hair's delightful wave
Make me, I'll confess it,
Thy poor slave!

THE OLD HOMESTEAD

'Tis an old deserted homestead
On the outskirts of the town,
Where the roof is all moss-covered,
And the walls are tumbling down;
But around that little cottage
Do my brightest mem'ries cling,
For 'twas there I spent the moments
Of my youth,—life's happy spring.

I remember how I used to
Swing upon the old front gate,
While the robin in the tree tops
Sung a night song to his mate;
And how later in the evening,
As the beaux were wont to do,
Mr. Perkins, in the parlor,
Sat and sparked my sister Sue.

There my mother — heaven bless her! —
Kissed or spanked as was our need,
And by smile or stroke implanted
In our hearts fair virtue's seed;
While my father, man of wisdom,
Lawyer keen, and farmer stout,
Argued long with neighbor Dobbins
How the corn crops would turn out.

Then the quiltings and the dances —
How my feet were wont to fly,
While the moon peeped through the barn chinks
From her stately place on high.
Oh, those days, so sweet, so happy,
Ever backward o'er me roll;
Still the music of that farm life
Rings an echo in my soul.

Now the old place is deserted,
And the walls are falling down;
All who made the home life cheerful,
Now have died or moved to town.
But about that dear old cottage
Shall my mem'ries ever cling,
For 'twas there I spent the moments
Of my youth,—life's happy spring.

ON THE DEATH OF W. C.

THOU arrant robber, Death!
Couldst thou not find
Some lesser one than he
To rob of breath,—
Some poorer mind
Thy prey to be?

His mind was like the sky,—
As pure and free;
His heart was broad and open
As the sea.
His soul shone purely through his face,
And Love made him her dwelling place.

Not less the scholar than the friend,
Not less a friend than man;
The manly life did shorter end
Because so broad it ran.

Weep not for him, unhappy Muse!
His merits found a grander use
Some other-where. God wisely sees
The place that needs his qualities.
Weep not for him, for when Death lowers
O'er youth's ambrosia-scented bowers
He only plucks the choicest flowers.

AN OLD MEMORY

How sweet the music sounded
That summer long ago,
When you were by my side, love,
To list its gentle flow.

I saw your eyes a-shining,
I felt your rippling hair,
I kissed your pearly cheek, love,
And had no thought of care.

And gay or sad the music,
With subtle charm replete;
I found in after years, love
'Twas you that made it sweet.

For standing where we heard it,
I hear again the strain;
It wakes my heart, but thrills it
With sad, mysterious pain.

It pulses not so joyous
As when you stood with me,
And hand in hand we listened
To that low melody.

Oh, could the years turn back, love!
Oh, could events be changed
To what they were that time, love,
Before we were estranged;

Wert thou once more a maiden
Whose smile was gold to me;
Were I once more the lover
Whose word was life to thee,—

O God! could all be altered,
The pain, the grief, the strife,
And wert thou — as thou shouldst be —
My true and loyal wife!

But all my tears are idle,
And all my wishes vain.
What once you were to me, love,
You may not be again.

For I, alas! like others,
Have missed my dearest aim.
I asked for love. Oh, mockery!
Fate comes to me with fame!

A CAREER

"Break me my bounds, and let me fly
To regions vast of boundless sky;
Nor I, like piteous Daphne, be
Root-bound. Ah, no! I would be free
As yon same bird that in its flight
Outstrips the range of mortal sight;
Free as the mountain streams that gush
From bubbling springs, and downward rush
Across the serrate mountain's side,—
The rocks o'erwhelmed, their banks defied,—
And like the passions in the soul,
Swell into torrents as they roll.
Oh, circumscribe me not by rules
That serve to lead the minds of fools!
But give me pow'r to work my will,
And at my deeds the world shall thrill.
My words shall rouse the slumb'ring zest
That hardly stirs in manhood's breast;
And as the sun feeds lesser lights,
As planets have their satellites,
So round about me will I bind
The men who prize a master mind!"

He lived a silent life alone,
And laid him down when it was done;
And at his head was placed a stone
On which was carved a name unknown!

ON THE RIVER

The sun is low,
The waters flow,
My boat is dancing to and fro.
The eve is still,
Yet from the hill
The killdeer echoes loud and shrill.

The paddles plash,
The wavelets dash,
We see the summer lightning flash;

While now and then,
In marsh and fen
Too muddy for the feet of men,

Where neither bird
Nor beast has stirred,
The spotted bullfrog's croak is heard.
The wind is high,
The grasses sigh,
The sluggish stream goes sobbing by.

And far away
The dying day
Has cast its last effulgent ray;
While on the land
The shadows stand
Proclaiming that the eve's at hand.

POOR WITHERED ROSE

A Song

Poor withered rose, she gave it me,
Half in revenge and half in glee;
Its petals not so pink by half
As are her lips when curled to laugh,
As are her cheeks when dimples gay
In merry mischief o'er them play.

Chorus

Forgive, forgive, it seems unkind
To cast thy petals to the wind;
But it is right, and lest I err
So scatter I all thought of her.

Poor withered rose, so like my heart,
That wilts at sorrow's cruel dart.
Who hath not felt the winter's blight
When every hope seemed warm and bright?
Who doth not know love unreturned,
E'en when the heart most wildly burned?

Poor withered rose, thou liest dead;
Too soon thy beauty's bloom hath fled.
'Tis not without a tearful ruth
I watch decay thy blushing routh;
And though thy life goes out in dole,
Thy perfume lingers in my soul.

WORN OUT

You bid me hold my peace
And dry my fruitless tears,
Forgetting that I bear
A pain beyond my years.

You say that I should smile
And drive the gloom away;
I would, but sun and smiles
Have left my life's dark day.

All time seems cold and void,
And naught but tears remain;
Life's music beats for me
A melancholy strain.

I used at first to hope,
But hope is past and gone;
And now without a ray
My cheerless life drags on.

Like to an ash-stained hearth
When all its fires are spent;
Like to an autumn wood
By storm winds rudely shent,—

So sadly goes my heart,
Unclothed of hope and peace;
It asks not joy again,
But only seeks release.

JAMES WHITCOMB RILEY

(From a Westerner's Point of View.)

No matter what you call it,
Whether genius, or art,
He sings the simple songs that come
The closest to your heart.
Fur trim an' skillful phrases,
I do not keer a jot;
'Tain't the words alone, but feelin's,
That tech the tender spot.
An' that's jest why I love him,—
Why, he's got sech human feelin',
An' in ev'ry song he gives us,
You kin see it creepin', stealin',
Through the core the tears go tricklin',
But the edge is bright an' smiley;
I never saw a poet
Like that poet Whitcomb Riley.

His heart keeps beatin' time with our'n
In measures fast or slow;
He tells us jest the same ol' things
Our souls have learned to know.
He paints our joys an' sorrers
In a way so stric'ly true,
That a body can't help knowin'
That he has felt them too.
If there's a lesson to be taught,
He never fears to teach it,
An' he puts the food so good an' low
That the humblest one kin reach it.
Now in our time, when poets rhyme
For money, fun, or fashion,
'Tis good to hear one voice so clear
That thrills with honest passion.
So let the others build their songs,
An' strive to polish highly,—
There's none of them kin tech the heart
Like our own Whitcomb Riley.

A MADRIGAL

DREAM days of fond delight and hours
As rosy-hued as dawn, are mine.

Love's drowsy wine,
Brewed from the heart of Passion flowers,
Flows softly o'er my lips
And save thee, all the world is in eclipse.

There were no light if thou wert not;
The sun would be too sad to shine,
And all the line
Of hours from dawn would be a blot;
And Night would haunt the skies,
An unlaid ghost with staring dark-ringed eyes.

Oh, love, if thou wert not my love,
And I perchance not thine—what then?
Could gift of men
Or favor of the God above,
Plant aught in this bare heart
Or teach this tongue the singer's soulful art?

Ah, no! 'Tis love, and love alone
That spurs my soul so surely on;
Turns night to dawn,
And thorns to roses fairest blown;
And winter drear to spring—
Oh, were it not for love I could not sing!

A STARRY NIGHT

A CLOUD fell down from the heavens,
And broke on the mountain's brow;
It scattered the dusky fragments
All over the vale below.

The moon and the stars were anxious
To know what its fate might be;
So they rushed to the azure op'ning,
And all peered down to see.

A LYRIC

My lady love lives far away,
And oh my heart is sad by day,
And ah my tears fall fast by night,
What may I do in such a plight.

Why, miles grow few when love is fleet,
And love, you know, hath flying feet;
Break off thy sighs and witness this,
How poor a thing mere distance is.

My love knows not I love her so,
And would she scorn me, did she know?
How may the tale I would impart
Attract her ear and storm her heart?

Calm thou the tempest in my breast,
Who loves in silence loves the best,
But bide thy time, she will awake,
No night so dark but morn will break.

But though my heart so strongly yearn,
My lady loves me not in turn,
How may I win the blest reply
That my void heart shall satisfy.

Love breedeth love, be thou but true,
And soon thy love shall love thee, too;
If Fate hath meant you heart for heart,
There's naught may keep you twain apart.

HOW SHALL I WOO THEE

How shall I woo thee to win thee, mine own?
Say in what tongue shall I tell of my love.
I who was fearless so timid have grown,
All that was eagle has turned into dove.
The path from the meadow that leads to the bars
Is more to me now than the path of the stars.

How shall I woo thee to win thee, mine own,
Thou who art fair and as far as the moon?
Had I the strength of the torrent's wild tone,
Had I the sweetness of warblers in June;
The strength and the sweetness might charm and persuade,
But neither have I my petition to aid.

How shall I woo thee to win thee, mine own?
How shall I traverse the distance between
My humble cot and your glorious throne?
How shall a clown gain the ear of a queen?
Oh teach me the tongue that shall please thee the best,
For till I have won thee my heart may not rest.

Added Poems

Jack Frost at Bedtime

Angels is a-mindin' you, my baby,
          Keep'n off de Bad Man in de night.
Whut de use o' bein' skeered o' nuffin'?
You don't fink de da'kness gwine to bite?
Whut de crackin' sound you hyeah erroun' you?
          Lawsy, chile, you tickles me to def—
Dat's de man what brings de frost', a-paintin'
          Picturs on de winder wid his bref.

Unidentified newspaper clipping, Henry Romeike clipping service, New York City, 1884. Copy courtesy of Paul Laurence Dunbar Collection, MSS 659, series 1, box 1, OHS.

Our Martyred Soldiers

In homes all green, but cold in death,
Robbed of the blessed boon of breath—
Resting in peace from field and fray,
Our martyred soldiers sleeping lay.

Beneath the dew, the rain, the snow,
They heed no more the bloody foe,
Their sleep is calm, to them alone
'Tis giv'n to lie without a moan.

The sun may shine in all his might—
They know no day, they know no night,
But wait a still more lasting ray,
The coming of eternal day.

No longer marches break their rest,
Or passioned hate thrills through the breast,
They lie all clothed in calm repose,
All safe from shots of lurking foes.

The grave's a sacred place where none
Of earth may touch the sleeping one;
Where silence reigns, enthroned, sedate,
An angel guarding heaven's gate.

The wind may blow, the hail may fall,
But at the tomb is silence all;
Man finds no nobler place to pray,
Then o'er a martyr's lifeless clay.

Sleep on, ye soldiers, men of God,
A nation's tears bedew the sod;
'Tis but a short, short time till ye
Shall through the shining portals flee.

And when this memory lost shall be,
We turn, oh Father, God, to thee!
Oh find in heaven some nobler thing
Than martyrs of which men can sing.

Dayton, Ohio, *Herald,* June 8, 1888. Copy courtesy of Paul Laurence Dunbar Collection, MSS 659, series 1, box 1, OHS.

Emancipation

Fling out your banners, your honors be bringing,
Raise to the ether your paeans of praise.
Strike every chord and let music be ringing!
Celebrate freely this day of all days.

Few are the years since that notable blessing,
Raised you from slaves to the powers of men.
Each year has seen you my brothers progressing,
Never to sink to that level again.

Perched on your shoulders sits Liberty smiling,
Perched where the eyes of the nations can see.
Keep from her pinions all contact defiling;
Show by your deeds what you're destined to be.

Press boldly forward nor waver, nor falter.
Blood has been freely poured out in your cause,
Lives sacrificed upon Liberty's altar.
Press to the front, it were craven to pause.

Look to the heights that are worth your attaining
Keep your feet firm in the path to the goal.
Toward noble deeds every effort be straining.
Worthy ambition is food for the soul!

Up! Men and brothers, be noble, be earnest!
Ripe is the time and success is assured;
Know that your fate was the hardest and sternest
When through those lash-ringing days you endured.

Never again shall the manacles gall you
Never again shall the whip stroke defame!
Nobles and Freemen, your destinies call you
Onward to honor, to glory and fame.

Dayton, Ohio, *Herald,* 1890. Copy courtesy of Paul Laurence Dunbar Collection, series 4, box 10, OHS.

Lager Beer

I lafs und sings, und shumps aroundt.
        Und somedimes acd so gueer.
You ask me vot der matter ish?
        I'm filled mit lager peer.

I hugs mine child, und giss mine vife.
        Oh, my dey was so dear;
Bot dot ish ven, you know, mire friend,
        I'm filled mit lager peer.

Eleetion gomes, I makes mire speech,
        Mine het it vas so glear:
De beoples laf, und say ha, ha,
        He's filled mit lager peer.

De oder night I got me mad,
De beoples run mit fear.
De bleeceman gome und took me down
All filled mit lager peer.

Next day I gomes pefore de judge,
Says he, "Eh heh, you're here!"
I gifs you yust five-fifty-five
For trinking lager peer.

I took mine bocket book qvick oud,
So poor I don't abbear;
Mine money all vas gone, mine friend
Vas gone in lager peer.

Und den dey dakes me off to shail,
To work mine sendence glear,
Und dere I shwears no more to be
Filled oup mit lager peer.

Und from dot day I drinks no more,
Yah, dat ish very gueer,
But den I found de tevil lifed
In dot same lager peer.

PFFENBERGER DEUTZELHEIM

Dayton, Ohio, *Tattler,* December 13, 1890. Copy courtesy of Paul Laurence Dunbar Collection, series 4, box 10, OHS.

My Best Girl

Her hair is a brilliant red, and her voice like a bumblebee's hum,
And this lovely young damsel is fed on the choicest of sweet chewing gum.
I have met her at church and at fair. How I love her no person can tell,
But the terrible hue of her hair has made me feel weary—ah, well,
But how can I justly complain? 'Tis the World with its sorrow and care,

And I'm not the first love-struck swain to be cursed with a girl with
red hair.
I called on her yesterday eve, and sweet were the words that I said.
I attempted when taking my leave to light my cigar on her head.
Poor damsel she stared and turned red till she looked like a full-
blown rose
But she murmured, "Don't worry, dear Ned. My hair corresponds to
your nose."
Then I swore in a still, silent way. That's the way those religious folk
swear,
For my nose, I am sorry to say, was as brilliantly red as her hair.
As I thought of her hair and my nose, and then of my nose and her
hair,
A stronger emotion arose, and I knelt on my knees then and there.
Dear hearers, I didn't propose, and to say what I said is a sin,
For I almost immediately rose. *Good heavens! I'd knelt on a pin!*

From *Tomfoolery,* Dayton, Ohio, 1890–91. Accompanied by hand-drawn cartoon. Copy courtesy of Blumenschien Collection, Dayton Public Library.

A Chappie

But a chappie needs diverting,
So her husband got to flirting,
But the lady couldn't stand for that, you know;
So she made an application
And she got a separation,
And since then she's married half a score or so;
But her alimony's faded,
And the stage she has invaded
And she's spreading golden butter on her bread.
Though her art is sadly lacking,
Yet she's got the best of backing—
And "She did it all herself," her mother said.

Circa 1890–91. Paul Laurence Dunbar Collection, series 4, box 10, OHS. Quoted by permission. (This poem also appears in Martin and Hudson's *Paul Laurence Dunbar Reader.*)

A Crumb, a Crumb, and a Little Seed

A crumb, a crumb, and a little seed,
And the bird will sing all day,
But the poet must have a gilded cage,
Or his songs are all laid away.

Circa 1890–91. Paul Laurence Dunbar Collection, MSS 659, series 1, box 1, OHS. Quoted by permission. (This poem also appears in Martin and Hudson's *Paul Laurence Dunbar Reader.*)

The Passage

FROM THE GERMAN OF UHLAND

I

Many a year is in its grave
Since I crossed this restless wave,
And the twilight, fair as ever,
Shines on ruin, rock, and river.

II

Then, in this same boat beside,
Sat two comrades, old and tried,
One with all a father's truth,
One with all the fire of youth.

III

One on earth in silence wrought,
And his grave in silence sought,
But the younger, brighter form
Passed in battle and in storm.

IV

So, when e'er I cast mine eye,
Back upon the days gone by,

Saddening thoughts of friends come o'er me,
Friends who closed their course before me.

V

But what binds us friend to friend,
Save that soul with soul may blend,
Soul-like were those days of yore,
Let us walk in soul once more.

VI

Take, oh boatman, thrice thy fee,
Take, I give it willingly;
For invisible to thee,
Spirits twain have crossed with me.

Paul Laurence Dunbar Collection, MSS 659, series 1, box 1, OHS. Quoted by permission. Martin and Hudson include this poem in the *Paul Laurence Dunbar Reader* and speculate that it may have been written sometime in 1890 or 1891, when Dunbar studied German in high school. Johann Ludwig Uhland (1787–1862) was a German poet who embraced folk materials in his writing.

Farewell Song

Why stirs, with sad alarm, the heart,
For all who meet must some day part?
So, let no useless cavil be,
True wisdom bows to God's decree.

Though lingers on the lid the tear,
'Tis one of sorrow, not of fear,
For well we know we cannot cling
Forever to the parent wing.

But not in vain our years were spent,
The mother kind gave nourishment,
And as the swift years rolled along,
We ever waxed more hale and strong.

And now, the world we fear no more,
As here we stand upon the shore,
Prepared to cast our moorings free,
And breast the waves of future's sea.

Our hearts are full, the prospect bright,
Our breasts are heaving at the sight,
While youthful joy o'erruns its cup,
And Hope's fair hand shall buoy us up.

The wind is fair, the sails are spread,
Let hearts be firm, "God Speed" is said;
Before us lies the untried way,
And we're impatient at the stay.

At last we move, how thrills the heart,
So long impatient for the start!
Now up o'er hill and down through dell,
The echoes bring our song—farewell.

The breezes take it up, and bear
The loud refrain on wings of air;
And to the skies, the sad notes swell,
Of this our last farewell, farewell!

Program, *Class of 1891, Commencement Exercises of Central High School at Grand Opera House,* June 16, 1891. Copy courtesy of Paul Laurence Dunbar Collection, MSS 659, series 1, box 1, OHS.

The Old High School and the New

We've all been off some little while—some one place, some another,
And coming back we thought to find a weeping widowed mother;
And now it seems the dear old girl forgot us while we tarried,
She dropped her weeds, came out in white and bless my soul! she's married.

Paul Laurence Dunbar

We left her lonely down the way clad in a somber gown,
But ah, she's wed a wealthy spouse, dressed up and moved up town.
She's lost her fine humility and timid bearing lately
And looms upon our dazzled gaze so dignified and stately
That we are prone to bend our ears to certain rumors shady
And really question of ourselves is this the same old lady?
You know when folks have been away and come back home it's
proper
To weep a little, gush some more, and casually to drop a
Word about "the dear old place" and other "memories tender,"
But oh! the chances here I find preeminently slender
For all the splendor round about my flow of memory hinders
And finery and newness knocks all memory to flinders.
I have searched about most carefully to find "the dear old place"
Where seniors shrieked the tenor out and juniors shouted bass.
But if there's any of it left I'm sure I haven't found it;
They've got a brand new singing hall with galleries around it;
I wish that classic hall was here where our ambitious feeling
Soared on the wings of paper wads and stuck against the ceiling.
I'd like to hear those boys again and all those maidens pretty
Who, standing on the old platform, waxed eloquent or witty,
Who sped their hits or rained the jokes as plentiful as manna,
I wonder if they're joking still about the old piano.
It seems that now some pretty tears the sentiment would garnish
But we're afraid to weep in here for fear we'll spoil the varnish.
So tearless, but with a regret, a deep one and a true one,
We'll bid the dear old school goodbye and welcome in the new one.
We've questioned her identity, of all this change abhorrent,
But on near view she warmer grows. She's not half bad I'll warrant.
She speaks and on her quivering lids the anxious tear drops glisten,
What can we do but pause awhile respectfully and listen?
"Don't let the thought that I have changed with stubborn hearts
imbue,
If you'll accept me, children dear, I'll be a mother to you."
We'll do it, won't we, girls and boys, excuse me, men and women,
We'll throw our arms about her neck in spite of all the trimmin',
We'll climb upon her ample lap, turn up our eager faces
And listen to her wisdom in the pause between embraces.
And while we toast the old that's gone, new joys shall make our pain
sweet

We'll take our love from Wilkinson and move it up to Main Street.
We'll bind this new'made mother's brow with every wreath and token
Of that deep love within our hearts that never can be spoken.
We'll love her as we loved the dear old school or very very near it,
For tho' she's thrown the dress away she's kept the same old spirit;
And of her present boys and girls we'll each prove a believer
That every year she'll turn them out as good and bright as we were.

September 1891. Paul Laurence Dunbar Collection, series 4, box 10, OHS. Quoted by permission. (This poem also appears in Martin and Hudson's *Paul Laurence Dunbar Reader.*)

The Concert

I

It was held in God's great temple
On a happy summer's day.
There was quite a host to hear it—
Old and youthful, grave and gray.

Mister Robin was conductor,
With an oak-twig in his hand
Held in readiness to signal
For the music of his band.

And the band was all attention,
All alert was every one.
Robin bowed and gave the signal
And the concert had begun.

Master Locust had his 'cello,
And the cricket played a fife;
While the bee held up a tuba,
Blowing it for dearest life.

Then a club of fine musicians—
Very famous—called "The Breeze"—
Charmed the hearts of all their hearers
With some wondrous symphonies.

II

And the "Tree Tops" bowed and nodded
Their approval in great haste,
For the symphonies were suited
To their strictly classic taste.

All the playing was delightful,
Both in point of time and tone;
And no instrument was louder
Than the Wood-Bird's xylophone.

There were vocalists in plenty,
All the noted ones were there;
E'en the River came to join them,
Gladly furnishing its share.

Why the tumult was stupendous
And was like to shake the place
When a Blue-Bird warbled treble
To the water's rolling bass.

Mrs. Katy-Did was present,
For her alto so well known;
Also Mr. Bull-Frog, famous
For his mellow baritone.

III

And the tenor of the concert
Was none other than our friend
G. Rass Hopper—why his encores
Seemed to me, they'd never end.

When the solos all were finished
And the orchestra was done,
Then they had the grand finale,
Which was joined by every one.

Locust, Bull-Frog, Cricket, Blue-Bird,
Katy-Did and Bumble Bee,
Blending all in Nature's chorus
In delightful harmony.

And the audiences who heard it,
All are willing to confess
That they never heard a concert
Which was such a grand success.

1892. Paul Laurence Dunbar Collection, series 4, box 10, OHS. Quoted by permission. (This poem also appears in Martin and Hudson's *Paul Laurence Dunbar Reader.*)

Come and Kiss Me Sweet and Twenty

Apple blossoms falling o'er thee,
        And the month is May,
Laden bows bend low before thee,
        With their gentle sway;
Look you where the thrush is swinging
        How his melody is ringing,
As he sings my heart is singing:—
        Come and kiss me sweet and twenty,
        Love blooms out with flowers a-plenty,
        Love me, love me without reason,
        Kiss me, now's the kissing season,
        White your cheek is as the blooms are,
        Sweet your breath as perfumes are,
        In this dolce far niente,
        Come and kiss me sweet and twenty.

Love is at thy window suing,
        All the live-long day,
Stay and listen to my wooing,
        Life shall all be May.
Love like mine can falter never,
        Naught from thee my heart can sever,
And my song shall be forever:—
        Come and kiss me sweet and twenty,
        Love blooms out with flowers a-plenty,
        Love me, love me without reason,
        Kiss me, now's the kissing season,

White your cheek is as the blooms are,
Sweet your breath is as perfumes are,
In this dolce far niente,
Come and kiss me sweet and twenty.

Circa 1892. Paul Laurence Dunbar Collection, series 4, box 10, OHS. Quoted by permission. (This poem also appears in Martin and Hudson's *Paul Laurence Dunbar Reader.*)

An Easter Ode

To the cold, dark grave they go
Silently and sad and slow,
From the light of happy skies
And the glance of mortal eyes.
In their beds the violets spring,
And the brook flows murmuring;
But at eve the violets die,
And the brook in the sand runs dry.

In the rosy, blushing morn,
See, the smiling babe is born;
For a day it lives, and then
Breathes its short life out again.
And anon gaunt-visaged Death,
With his keen and icy breath,
Bloweth out the vital fire
In the hoary-headed sire.

Heeding not the children's wail,
Fathers droop and mothers fail;
Sinking sadly from each other,
Sister parts from loving brother.
All the land is filled with wailing,—
Sounds of mourning garments trailing,
With their sad portent imbued,
Making melody subdued.

But in all this depth of woe
This consoling truth we know:
There will come a time of rain,
And the brook will flow again;
Where the violet fell, 'twill grow,
When the sun has chased the snow.
See in this the lesson plain,
Mortal man shall rise again.

Well the prophecy was kept;
Christ—"first fruit of them that slept"—
Rose with vic'try-circled brow;
So, believing one, shalt thou.
Ah! but there shall come a day
When, unhampered by this clay,
Souls shall rise to life newborn
On that resurrection morn.

Oak and Ivy (1893), p. 10.

To Dr. James Newton Matthews, Mason, Ill.

All round about, the clouds encompassed me;
        On every side I looked, my weary sight
        Was met by terrors of Plutonian night;
And chilling surges of a cruel sea
That beat against my stronghold ceaselessly,
        Roared rude derision at my hapless plight;
        And hope, which I had thought to hold so tight,
Slipped from my weak'ning grasp and floated free.

But when I thought to flee the unequal strife,
        As wearied out I could not bear it more,
        Fate gave the choicest gem of all her store,—
And noble Matthews came into my life.
        He warmed my being like a virile flame,
        And with his coming, light and courage came!

Oak and Ivy (1893), p. 13.

Paul Laurence Dunbar

Welcome Address

To the Western Association of Writers

"Westward the course of empire takes its way,"—
So Berkeley said, and so to-day
The men who know the world still say.
The glowing West, with bounteous hand,
Bestows her gifts throughout the land,
And smiles to see at her command
Art, science, and the industries,—
New fruits of new Hesperides.
So, proud are you who claim the West
As home land; doubly are you blest
To live where liberty and health
Go hand in hand with brains and wealth.
So here's a welcome to you all,
Whate'er the work your hands let fall,—
To you who trace on history's page
The footprints of each passing age;
To you who tune the laureled lyre
To songs of love or deeds of fire;
To you before whose well-wrought tale
The cheek doth flush or brow grow pale;
To you who bow the ready knee
And worship cold philosophy,—
A welcome warm as Western wine,
And free as Western hearts, be thine.
Do what the greatest joy insures,—
The city has no will but yours!

Oak and Ivy (1893), p. 25.

To Miss Mary Britton

When the legislature of Kentucky was discussing the passage of a separate-coach bill, Miss Mary Britton, a teacher in the schools of

Lexington, Kentucky, went before them, and in a ringing speech protested against the passage of the bill. Her action was heroic, though it proved to be without avail.

God of the right, arise
        And let thy pow'r prevail;
Too long thy children mourn
        In labor and travail.
Oh, speed the happy day
        When waiting ones may see
The glory-bringing birth
        Of our real liberty!

Grant thou, O gracious God,
        That not in word alone
Shall freedom's boon be ours,
        While bondage-galled we moan!
But condescend to us
        In our o'erwhelming need;
Break down the hind'ring bars,
        And make us free indeed.

Give us to lead our cause
        More noble souls like hers,
The memory of whose deed
        Each feeling bosom stirs;
Whose fearless voice and strong
        Rose to defend her race,
Roused Justice from her sleep,
        Drove Prejudice from place.

Let not the mellow light
        Of Learning's brilliant ray
Be quenched, to turn to night
        Our newly dawning day.
To that bright, shining star
        Which thou didst set in place,
With universal voice
        Thus speaks a grateful race:

"Not empty words shall be
Our offering to your fame;
The race you strove to serve
Shall consecrate your name.
Speak on as fearless still;
Work on as tireless ever;
And your reward shall be
Due meed for your endeavor."

Oak and Ivy (1893), p. 30.

The "Chronic Kicker"

It was at the town convention
Fur to nominate a mayor,
An' things had been progressin'
In a way both cool an' fair;
An' we thought that we had finished
In a manner mighty slick,
When up rose the chronic kicker
Fur to kick, kick, kick.

Then we felt our feathers fallin',
Nor we didn't laugh no more,
While some quite impatient fellers
Made a bee line fur the door;
An' we listened, an' we listened,
While the clock the hours ticked,
To that derned old chronic kicker
As he kicked, kicked, kicked.

Next we held a conf'rence meetin'
In our little mission church,—
Fur a cheap an' worthy pastor
We were in an earnest search;
We had jest made our agreement
(An' 'twas come to very quick),
When up rose the chronic kicker
Fur to kick, kick, kick.

An' we heard the birds a whistlin'
In the air so sweet an' cool,
While we all sat there a list'nin'
To that flambergasted fool;
But I'm sure the Lord was min'ful,
Fur no thorn our conscience pricked,
When we nodded while that kicker
Stood an' kicked, kicked, kicked.

Next 'twas a baseball battle,
Overlooked by boys in trees,
Where no act of bat or basement
Could this chronic kicker please,
Until weary with his yellin',
Some one hit him with a brick,
An' he lay down in the diamond
Fur to kick, kick, kick.

But Death, that great policeman,
By now frowns or kicks defied,
At last came up an' seized him,
An' so, with a kick, he died;
But he, jest before the fun'ral,
Made the undertaker sick,
As the coffin couldn't hold him
For that everlastin' kick.

Oak and Ivy (1893), p. 36.

Songs

I love the dear old ballads best,
That tell of love and death,
Whose every line sings love's unrest
Or mourns the parting breath.
I love those songs the heart can feel,
That make our pulses throb;

When lovers plead or contrites kneel
With choking sigh and sob.

God sings through songs that touch the heart,
And none are prized save these.
Though men may ply their gilded art
For fortune, fame, or fees,
The muse that sets the songster's soul
Ablaze with lyric fire,
Holds nature up, an open scroll,
And builds art's funeral pyre.

Oak and Ivy (1893), p. 37.

Memorial Day

Why deck with flow'rs these humble mounds?
Why gather round this fast decaying mold?
Why doth remembrance keep her solemn rounds
And wrap these sleepers in her loving fold?
Why kneel, ye silent mourners, here
To drop the reverential tear?
Flesh is but dust when parted from the breath.

Flesh is but dust, but worth of soul is gold!
'Tis not the dust we honor, but the brave
And noble spirits that it once did hold.
So kneel we weeping at the grave,
As at the door through which have passed,
To enter into mansions vast,
The heroes who have gone to meet
A dearer destiny than dirgeful death.

Oak and Ivy (1893), p. 43.

A Question

I wist not that I had the pow'r to sing,
    But here of late they say my songs are sweet.
Is it because my timid numbers ring
    With love's warm music that doth ever beat
Its melody within my throbbing heart?
    If so, what else can roguish Cupid do?
I know him master of the archer's art;
    Is he a trained musician too?

Oak and Ivy (1893), p. 46.

The Light

Once when my soul was newly shriven,
When perfect peace to me was given,
Pervading all in all with currents bright,
I saw shine forth a mighty Light;
And myriad lesser lights to this were joined,
Each light with every other light entwined;
And as they shone a sound assailed my ears,
Alike the mighty music of the spheres.
The greater light was Love and Peace and Law,
And it had power toward it the rest to draw;
It was the Soul of souls, the greatest One,
The Life of lives, of suns the Sun.
And floating through it all, my soul could see
The Christ-light, shining for humanity;
And silently I heard soft murmurs fall,
"Look up, earth child; the light is all."

Oak and Ivy (1893), p. 48.

Paul Laurence Dunbar

John Boyle O'Reilly

Of noble minds and noble hearts
    Old Ireland has goodly store;
But thou wert still the noblest son
    That e'er the Isle of Erin bore.
A generous race, and strong to dare,
    With hearts as true as purest gold,
With hands to soothe as well as strike,
    As generous as they are bold,—
This is the race thou lovedst so;
    And knowing them, I can but know
The glory thy whole being felt
    To think, to act, to be, the Celt!

Not Celt alone, America
    Her arms about thee hath entwined;
The noblest traits of each grand race
    In thee were happily combined.
As sweet of song as strong of speech,
    Thy great heart beat in every line.
No narrow partisan wert thou;
    The cause of all oppressed was thine!
The world is cruel still and cold,
But who can doubt thy life has told?
Though wrong and sorrow still are rife
Old Earth is better for thy life!

Oak and Ivy (1893), p. 49.

Confirmation

He was a poet who wrote clever verses,
    And folks said he had fine poetical taste;
But his father, a practical farmer, accused him
    Of letting the strength of his arm go to waste.

He called on his sweetheart each Saturday evening,
As pretty a maiden as man ever faced,
And there he confirmed the old man's accusation
By letting the strength of his arm go to *waist*.

Oak and Ivy (1893), p. 54.

Sympathy

The tear another's tears bring forth,
The sigh which answers sigh,
The pulse that beats at other's woes,
E'en though our own be nigh,

A balm to bathe the wounded heart
Where sorrow's hand hath lain,
The link divine from soul to soul
That makes us one in pain,—

Sweet sympathy, benignant ray,
Light of the soul doth shine;
In it is human nature giv'n
A touch of the divine.

Oak and Ivy (1893), p. 56.

My Love Irene

Farewell, farewell, my love Irene;
The pangs of sadness stir my breast;
Though many miles may intervene,
My soul's with thine, in East or West.
Go where thou wilt, to wealth or fame;
Win for thyself or praise or blame,—
My love shall ever be the same,
My love Irene.

Farewell, farewell, my love Irene;
Oh, sad decree, that we must part!
The wound is deep, the pain is keen
That agitates mine aching heart.
My feverish eyes burn up their tears;
I cannot still my doubts and fears;
And this one sigh the night wind hears,—
My love Irene.

Farewell, farewell, my love Irene;
The morning's gray now floods the sky;
The sun peeps from his misty screen;
Mine only love, good-bye, good-bye.
All love must fade, all life must die,
The smile must turn into the sigh.
Alas! how hard to say good-bye,
My love Irene.

Oak and Ivy (1893), p. 56.

Common Things

I like to hear of wealth and gold,
And El Doradoes in their glory;
I like for silks and satins bold
To sweep and rustle through a story.

The nightingale is sweet of song;
The rare exotic smells divinely;
And knightly men who stride along,
The role heroic carry finely.

But then, upon the other hand,
Our minds have got a way of running
To things that aren't quite so grand,
Which, maybe, we were best in shunning.

For some of us still like to see
The poor man in his dwelling narrow,
The hollyhock, the bumblebee,
The meadow lark, and chirping sparrow.

We like the man who soars and sings
With high and lofty inspiration;
But he who sings of common things
Shall always share our admiration.

Oak and Ivy (1893), p. 57.

Goin' Back

He stood beside the station rail,
A negro aged and bent and frail.
His palsied hands like the aspen shook,
And a mute appeal was in his look;
His every move was pained and slow,
And his matted hair was white as snow.
He noted our questioning looks, and said,
With a solemn shake of his hoary head:
"I reckon you're wonderin', an' well you may,
Whar an ol' man lak me's a goin' to-day.
I've lived in this town fur thirty years,
An' known alike my joys an' tears,
An' I've labored hard year out, year in;
But now I'm a goin' back agin
To the blue grass medders an' fiel's o' co'n
In the dear ol' State whar I was bo'n.
It's the same ol' tale that I have to tell,—
An' thar's few o' my race but knows it well,—
When fust the proclamation come
I felt too free to stay at home.
Freedom, it seemed, was a gift divine,
An' I thought the whole wide world was mine.
Then I was spry, an' my hair was black,

An' this troublesome crook wasn't in my back;
My soul was allus full o' song,
Fur my heart was light, an' my limbs was strong,
An' I wasn't afeared to show my face
To the sturdiest worker on the place.
Well, I caught the fever that ruled the day,
An', finally, northward made my way.
They said that things were better North,
An' a man was held at his honest worth.
Well, it may be so, but I have some doubt,
An' thirty years ain't wiped it out.
Thar was lots of things in the North to admire,
Though they hadn't the warmth an' passion an' fire
That all my life I'd been ust to seein'
An' thought belonged to a human bein'.
An' a thing I couldn't help but miss
Was the real ol' Southern heartiness.
But year after year I worried along,
While deep in my heart the yearnin' strong
Grew stronger an' fiercer to visit once more
The well loved scenes o' my native shore.
But money was skeerce, an' time went on,
Till now full thirty years have gone
Ere I turn my aged steps to roam
Back to my ol' Kaintucky home,
Back to the ol' Kaintucky sights,
Back to the scene o' my youth's delights,
Back whar my heart was full o' glee,
Back whar I fust found liberty.
E'en now as I think the ol' times should be o'er,
An' o' the joy they held in store,—
Yes, even now, on life's dark side,
My heart swells out with honest pride.
Oh, praise the Lamb, that I shall see
Once more the land so dear to me.
Don't mind an ol' man's tears, but say
It's joy, he's goin' back to-day."

Oak and Ivy (1893), p. 58.

Justice

Enthroned upon the mighty truth,
        Within the confines of the laws,
True Justice seeth not the man,
        But only hears his cause.

Unconscious of his creed or race,
She cannot see, but only weighs;
For Justice with unbandaged eyes
Would be oppression in disguise.

Oak and Ivy (1893), p. 59.

The Land o' Used to Be

There's a ripple of fountains
That rise in the mountains,
        And a murmur of rills
        That spring in the hills,
And the streams go on with a softer flow,
And the sun goes down with a warmer glow,
There's a smiling cot by a sparkling sea
In the dear old land o' Used to Be!

The skies there are bluer,
And fond hearts are truer,
        And love is the theme
        That mountain and stream
Sing to wood and sky as the days go by,
In a raptured voice that is sweet and high;
Oh, the days are bright and the nights care-free
In the dear old land o' Used to Be!

There's a smile in the shadows,
As over the meadows
        The wanderer springs
        While gayly he sings;

There's a kiss from mother who bides at the gate,
And a shy, glad glance from my wee winsome Kate—
Oh, there's light and there's love and there's life for me
In the dear old land o' Used to Be!

Munsey's Magazine 10 (February 1894): 516.

Old

I have seen peoples come and go
Alike the Ocean's ebb and flow;
I have seen kingdoms rise and fall
Like springtime shadows on a wall.
I have seen houses rendered great
That grew from life's debased estate,
And all, all, all is change I see,
So, dearest God, take me, take me.

Majors and Minors (1895), p. 71.

If I Could But Forget

If I could but forget
The fullness of those first sweet days,
When you burst sun-like thro' the haze
Of unacquaintance, on my sight,
And made the wet, gray day seem bright
While clouds themselves grew fair to see.
And since, no day is gray or wet,
But all the scene comes back to me,
If I could but forget.

If I could but forget
How your dusk eyes look into mine,
And how I thrilled as with strong wine
Beneath your touch; while sped amain

The quickened stream thro' ev'ry vein;
How near my breath fell to a gasp,
When for a space our fingers met
In one electric vibrant clasp,
If I could but forget.

If I could but forget
The months of passion and of pain,
And all that followed in their train—
Rebellious thoughts that would arise,
Rebellious tears that dimmed mine eyes,
The prayers that I might set love's fire
Aflame within your bosom yet—
The death at last of that desire—
If I could but forget.

Majors and Minors (1895), p. 75.

The Made to Order Smile

When a woman looks up at you with a twist about her eyes,
And her brows are half uplifted in a nicely feigned surprise
As you breathe some pretty sentence, though she hates you all the while,
She is very apt to stun you with a made to order smile.

It's a subtle combination of a sneer and a caress,
With a dash of warmth thrown in it to relieve its iciness,
And she greets you when she meets you with that look as if a file
Had been used to fix and fashion out the made to order smile.

I confess that I'm eccentric and am not a woman's man,
For they seem to be constructed on the bunko fakir plan,
And it somehow sets me thinking that her heart is full of guile
When a woman looks up at me with a made to order smile.

Now, all maidens, young and aged, hear the lesson I would teach—
Ye who meet us in the ballroom, ye who meet us at the beach—
Pray consent to try and charm us by some other sort of wile
And relieve us from the burden of that made to order smile.

Majors and Minors (1895), p. 126.

Parted

Beyond the cornfields and the wood,
    Nestling beneath the hill
In the old days a cottage stood,
    Beside a ruined mill.

And often on the edge of dark
    I lingered in the lane,
Until a candle's welcome spark
    Shone in the window pane.

Long years have gone, tonight once more
    Beside the foot-worn stile,
In the old lane as oft before
    I wait, and dream awhile.

Above the pines one lonely star
    Shines like her casement—lit
But far away—Alas! Too far
    For her to open it.

Fond dream! My longing eyes beguiled,—
    Yet must I turn again,
And like a little lonely child
    Stretch out my arms in vain!

The moon is but a clouded disc,
    Only the star shines bright,
To me it seems God's Asterisk
    Upon the page of night.

O love of happy days long past
My task is nearly done
Faithful to thee, till life at last
Be ended,—and begun!

Enclosed in a letter to Alice Ruth Moore dated May 23, 1897. Paul Laurence Dunbar Collection, series 10, box 22, OHS. Quoted by permission. (The letter is reproduced in full in Martin and Hudson's *Paul Laurence Dunbar Reader.*)

Oh little fledgling out of the nest

Oh little fledgling out of the nest—
Would you were cuddling here—close to my breast
Warming & melting my heart into song,
Then were the days not so lonesome & long.
Wildly the rain's falling blown from the west—
What a sweet time to be snug in the nest!
What a poor time to be waund'ring afar
Love where the winds & the bleak billows are.
Ah little lady-bird, soon let us sing
Our lay connubial here wing to wing.
Yearning is burning my heart with unrest—
Home be returning, sweet bird, to your nest!

Enclosed in a letter to Alice Dunbar dated August 10, 1898. Paul Laurence Dunbar Collection, series 10, box 22, OHS. Quoted by permission. (The letter is reproduced in full in Martin and Hudson's *Paul Laurence Dunbar Reader.*)

To Booker T. Washington

Beside our way the streams are dried,
And famine mates us side by side.
Discouraged and reproachful eyes
Seek once again, the frowning skies.
Yet shall there come spite storm and shock
A Moses who shall smite the rock,

Call manna from the Giver's hand,
And lead us to the promised land!

Program, Denver Minister's Alliance, Denver, Colorado, January 26, 1900. Copy courtesy of Paul Laurence Dunbar Collection, MSS 659, series 1, box 1, OHS.

The Old Story

I stand beside the window here
    And gaze at John and May,
As hand in hand, unheeding aught,
    They wend their wooing way;
And, oh, it brings me back the days,
    Ere age had changed my view,
And every tale I heard or told
    I still believed was new.

Go on, go on, my happy boy,
    And read your brief romance;
Youth is the time for love and rhyme,
    So do not lose your chance.
The joys that blessed my early days
    I would not keep from you;
For soon you'll find the happy tale
    Won't always seem so new.

We used to stroll, long years ago,
    About the same old way;
You were a blushing maiden then,
    And I a lover gay.
I told you how my heart was yours,
    And that I'd prove it true,
'Twas an old, old tale I told you, Kate,
    But, ah, we thought 'twas new.

And as I stand and watch them here
    It all comes back to me;

The shady walks, the loving talks,
            In days that used to be.
There they go walking slow, absorbed,
            Just as we used to do;
It's an old, old tale he's telling, Kate,
            But, ah, they think it new.

But can it be that I am wrong,
            Have I grown crabbed with age?
Let me turn back life's closing book,
            And view that older page.
I'm partly wrong, I'm partly right,
            Love's story's old, 'tis true;
But though 'twas born in earth's first morn,
            Love's self is ever new.

Good Housekeeping 30 (March 1900): 131.

Goin' Home

I wish de day was neah at han'
I'ze tiahed of dis grievin' lan'
I'ze tiahed of de lonely yeahs;
I want to des dry up my teahs
            An go 'long home.

Oh, Mastah, won't you sen' de call;
My frien's is daih, my hope, my all.
I'ze waitin' whaih de road is rough
I want to hyeah you say: "Enough,
            Ole man! Come home."

Weekly Bulletin, Auburn, New York, March 26, 1901.

Paul Laurence Dunbar

The Suitor

Miss Marfy sco'n young Issac so,
He swaih he sholy die;
He stan' befo huh cabin do',
An' hol' his hea't an' sigh.
Oh, swing yo' lady roun' and roun',
An' grant huh gent'man's grace;
Fu' dey's a smile behine de frown
On evah lady's face.

Miss Marfy cas' huh mantle down;
Young Issac tek it up.
De smile hit chase erway huh frown;
She ax him in to sup.
Miss Marfy drap huh han'kerchuh;
Young Issac pick it up.
He say he didn't need wid huh
No sugah in his cup.

Miss Marfy talk; young Issac smile,
An' mos' fu'git to eat,
An' kind o' back'ard aftahw'ile
He daihed to call huh sweet.

Young Issac ain't a-sighin' now,
He swaihs he nevah did;
He lookin' fu' a' o'ange bough
To deck Miss Marfy wid.
Oh, swing yo' lady roun' an' roun',
An' grant huh gent'man's grace;
Fu' dey's a smile behine de frown
On evah lady's face.

Mebbe some one comes to jine you;
Well, dat's good, but not de bes',
Less'n dat you's kind o' lonesome,
Er ain't honin' fu' de res'.
Den you wants to tell a sto'y,
Er you wants to hyeah de news

Kind o' hald tol', while you's stealin'
Ev'y now an' den a snooze.

W'en you's tiahed out a-hoein',
Er a-followin' de plow,
Whut's de use of des a-fallin'
On yo' pallet lak a cow?
W'y, de fun is all in waitin'
In de face of all de tiah,
An' a-dozin' an' a-drowsin'
By a good ol' hick'ry fiah.

Century Magazine 63 (November 1901): 22.

A Virginia Reel

De banjo done commence de shune,
You can't git on de flo' too soon;
Lead out yo' pa'dnah to de place,
Don' let de music go to was'e.

Now th'ow dem windows open wide,
An' fo'm a line f'om side to side;
Bow to de lef', bow to de right,
An' lif' yo' feet lak dy was light.

Now all togedah bow an' 'vance,
No draggin' feet in dis hyeah dance;
Lay all yo' sorrows on de she'f,
An' sta't in to enjoy yo'se'f.

Dah, Joe, you tek Miss Sally's han';
Don' be so lazy, goodness lan'!
A body'd t'ink dat you had foun'
A' int'rus' in a burying-groun'.

Come steppin' lively down de line;
Ef you got mannahs, show 'em fine;
Sasshay de lady, bow an' swing,
An' listen to dat banjo sing.

Now show de trim dat you is in
By shuffin' neatly back ergin;
Wipe all de shine f'om off yo' face,
An' swing yo' lady to huh place.

Now op'site ladies bow an' cross,
Dah ain't a minute to be los';
Jine han's, all tu'n yo' faces in,
An' tek yo' pa'dnahs back ergin.

Nex' couple forrard, do de same;
Ef you gits mixed, I ain't to blame;
Coime glidin' thoo, don' be so slow,
"T ain't no time 'fo' de cock'll crow.

Salute yo 'pa'dnahs ez befo',
Git out an 'taih up all dis flo';
Ef you's got feelin's, show you feel
By steppin' dis Vahginia reel.

Century Magazine 63 (November 1901): 22.

Lullaby

Kiver up yo' haid, my little lady,
        Hyeah de win' a-blowin' out o' do's.
Don' you kick, ner projick wid de comfo't,
        Less'n fros'll bite yo' little toes.
Shut yo' eyes, an' snuggle up to mammy;
        Gi' me bofe yo' han's, I hol' 'em tight;
Don' you be afeard, an' 'mence to trimble
        Des ez soon ez I blows out de light.

Angels is a-mindin' you, my baby,
Keepin' off de Bad Man in de night.
Whut de use o' bein' skeered o' nuffin'?
You don' fink de da'kness gwine to bite?
Whut de crackin' soun' you hyeah erroun' you?—
Lawsy, chile, you tickles me to def!—
Dat 's de man what brings de fros', a-paintin'
Picters on de winder wid his bref.

Mammy ain' afeard, you hyeah huh laffin'?
Go' way, Mistah Fros', you can't come in;
Baby ain' erceivin' folks dis evenin',
Reckon dat you'll have to call ag'in.
Curl yo' little toes up so, my possum—
Umph, but you's a cunnin' one fu' true!—
Go to sleep, de angels is a-watchin',
An' yo' mammy's mindin' of you, too.

Candle-Lightin' Time (1901), p. 91.

A Companion's Progress

My stock has gone down and my tailor has sent
To request that I settle my bill;
My landlady asks with a frown for her rent,
And there isn't a cent in the till.
The governor storms and my mother's in tears;
There's a coldness betwixt me and Nell,
But I'm utterly dead to regrets and to fears,
For my meerschaum is colouring well.

At first I had fears of what looked like a crack,
And my breath came in gasps of alarm,
But oh, how the joy of my heart flooded back
When I found that 'twas nothing to harm.
And so ever since I have nursed it with care,
With thrills that my heart cannot quell,

And I've bored all my friends to relate the affair
That my meerschaum is colouring well.

St. James Gazette, London, August 21, 1901. Clipping in Paul Laurence Dunbar Collection, MSS 659, series 1, box 1, OHS, from Henry Romeike clipping service, New York City. No page number given.

God Reigns

In ages past ere wisdom's height
Had sent its piercing ray
To cleave the heavy clouds of night
And usher in the day.
Men's minds were held in thralldom deep,
The slaves to one blind school,
Till reasons let this sentence sweep
"God reigns and right shall rule."

The war clouds heavy hung and dark,
The storm was swelling fast,
But over all the tumult—hark!
A voice comes down the blast
And, lo! the tempest is still,
And fiery passions cool;
As with a cry the earth is filled—
"God reigns and right shall rule."

Four million slaves in chains lay bound,
Harrassed by myriad woes—
The lash of whip, the chase of hound,
The curses of their foes.
But Lincoln came, and with a stroke
He broke the clanking chains
And unto all the world he spoke
Right rules, Jehovah reigns.

Today the skeptic wields his pen,
The infidel his tongue
The keen agnostic lureth men
His mazy ways among.
But let them talk and let them write—
O'er bigot, sage and fool,
There sways an arm of fearless might—
"God reigns and right shall rule."

The court may temper its decrees
To favor wealth or might;
The water of a thousand seas
May try to drown the right;
The king his agents may command,
And ply each royal tool,
But there is still the master hand—
"God reigns and right shall rule."

Yea, wrong may triumph for a day
With bold delusive power,
But, oh! how stormy is its sway,
And, oh! how brief its hour!
The hosts of sin are soon undone,
Peace flies on pinions cool;
The battle gained, the victory won—
"God reigns, and right shall rule."

Original manuscript in Dunbar's handwriting dated 1902 in Paul Laurence Dunbar Collection, MSS 659, series 1, box 1, OHS. Quoted by permission.

To Alice Dunbar

All the world is so sweet, dear
And matters so little to me—
You are the whole and the all, dear
The bride for eternity—

Life is so gray and so brief dear
And it is so hard to live
Why should we neighbor with grief, dear
Better to love and forgive.

E'en tho' I miss you today, dear
Miss you and pass like a breath—
Love is puissant in serving dear
Far past the portals of death.

Enclosed in a letter to Alice Dunbar dated February 2, 1903, Paul Laurence Dunbar Collection, series 8, box 22, OHS. Quoted by permission. (This letter is reproduced in Martin and Hudson's *Paul Laurence Dunbar Reader.*)

Summer in the South

The oriole sings in the greening grove
As if he were half-way waiting,
The rosebuds peep from their hoods of green,
Timid and hesitating.
The rain comes down in a torrent sweep
And the nights smell warm and piney,
The garden thrives, but the tender shoots
Are yellow-green and tiny.
Then a flash of sun on a waiting hill,
Streams laugh that erst were quiet,
The sky smiles down with a dazzling blue
And the woods run mad with riot.

Lippincott's Monthly Magazine 72 (September 1903): 378.

Charity

Now you, John Henry, 'tain't no use
To stan' up daih an' mak no 'scuse.
You need n't tink you foolin' me,
I sutny has got eyes to see!
Oh I's yo' sistah, yes, dat's true!
But den what good 's dat gwine to do?
Dey ain't no use in tellin' lies,
You look right sheepish f'om yo' eyes!

Let's see yo' han's, uh huh, I knowed
You washed 'em, but de traces showed.
Let's see yo' mouf; his looks lak ink—
Yo' sistah cain't tell 'serves, you t'ink.
Oh my, but yo 's a naughty chile,
I has to look at you one while;
You need n't twis' in all dem curves,
To tink you'd stole yo' ma's pusserves.

Ef I tol' ma I guess you'd git
The fines' whuppin' evah yit;
But guess I'll keep it to myse'f
Erbout dat jah erpon de she'f;
Case ma's des awful w'en she stahts,
An' my, oh, how a whuppin' smahts!
So you clomb up? Oh, she'd be madder!
Say, tell me whaih you put de ladder.

L'il' Gal (1904), p. 23.

Tuskegee Song

Tuskegee, thou pride of the swift growing South
        We pay thee our homage today,
For the worth of thy teaching, the joy of thy care;
        And the good we have known 'neath thy sway.

Oh, long-striving mother of diligent sons,
    And of daughters, whose strength is their pride.
We will love thee forever, and ever shall walk
    Thro' the oncoming years at thy side.

Thy hand we have held up the difficult steeps,
    When painful and slow was the pace,
And onward and upward we've labored with thee
    For the glory of God and our race.
The fields smile to greet us, the forests are glad,
    The ring of the anvil and hoe
Have a music as thrilling and sweet as a harp
    Which thou taught us to hear and to know.

Oh, Mother Tuskegee, thou shinest today
    As a gem in the fairest of lands;
Thou gavest the heav'n blessed power to see
    The worth of our minds and our hands.
We thank thee, we bless thee, we pray for thee years
    Imploring with grateful accord,
Full fruit for thy striving, time longer to strive,
    Sweet love and true labor's reward.

Words by Paul Laurence Dunbar; music by N. Clark Smith. Published in *Selected Songs Sung by Students at Tuskegee* (Tuskegee, Alabama: 1904).

For Theodore Roosevelt

There's a mighty sound a-comin'
From the East, and there's a hummin'
    And a bummin' from the bosom of the West,
While the North has given tongue
And the South will be among
    Those who holler that our Roosevelt is best.

We have heard of him in battle
And amid the roar and rattle
    When the foeman fled like cattle to their stalls;

We have seen him staunch and grim
When the only battle hymn
            Was the shrieking of the Spanish mauser balls.

Product of a worthy sireling,
Fearless, honest, brave, untiring—
            In the forefront of the firing there he stands;
And we're not afraid to show
That we all revere him so
            To dissentients of our own and other lands.

Now the fight is on in earnest,
And we care not if the sternest
            Of encounters try our valor or the quality of him,
For they're few who stoop to fear
As the glorious day draws near
            For you'll find him hell to handle when he gets in fightin'
                        trim.

Dayton, Ohio, *Daily News,* February 10, 1906.

Sling Along

Sling along, sling along, sling along,
            De moon done riz,
            Dem eyes o' his,
            Done sighted you,
            Where you stopped to woo.
Sling along, sling along,
            It ain't no use fu' to try to hide,
            De moonbeams allus at yo' side,
            He hang f'om de fence, he drap f'om de limb,
            Dey ain't no use bein' skeered o' him.
Sling along, sling along.

Sling along, sling along, sling along,
            De brook hit flow,
            Fu' to let you know,

Dat he saw dat kiss,
An' he know yo' bliss.
Sling along, sling along.
He run by yo' side,
An' he say howdydo,
He ain't gwine to tell but his eye's on you,
You can lay all yo' troubles on de very highest she'f,
Fu' de little ol' brook's jes' a talkin' to his se'f,
Sling along, sling along.

Sling along, sling along, sling along,
De 'possum grin,
But he run lak sin,
He know love's sweet,
But he prize his meat.
Sling along, sling along.
He know you'd stop fu' to hunt his hide,
If you los' a kiss and a hug beside,
But de feas' will come and de folks will eat,
When she tek yo' han' at de altah seat.
So sling along, sling along.

In *Joggin' Erlong* (New York: Dodd, Mead and Company, 1906), p. 16.

To Mary Church Terrell

Look hyeah, Molly, ain't it jolly
Jes' a loafin' roun'?
Tell the Jedge not to hedge
For I am still in town.

Quoted in Virginia Cunningham, *Paul Laurence Dunbar and His Song*, p. 257.

To a Poet and a Lady

You sing, and the gift of State's applause
        Is yours for the rune that is ringing.
But tell me truly, is that the cause?
        Don't you sing for the love of singing?

You think you are working for wealth and for fame,
        But ah, you are not, and you know it;
For wife is the sweetest and loveliest name,
        And every good wife is a poet!

Written to Lida Keck Wiggins and published in *The Life and Works of Paul Laurence Dunbar,* ed. Lida Keck Wiggins (Naperville, Ill., and Memphis: J. L. Nichols Co., 1907), pp. 116–17.

How Nathan Proposed

Nathan saw that his time had come. He sighed, cleared his throat and began: "Widder, I been thinkin' a good deal lately an' I been talkin' some with a friend o' mine." He felt guiltily conscious of what that friend had counseled him to keep back. "I've been greatly prospered in my day; in fact, 'my cup runneth over.' "

"You have been prospered Nathan."

"Seem's ef—seem's ef I'd ought to sheer it with somebody, don't it?"

"Well, Nathan, I do' know nobody that's more generous in givin' to the pore than you air."

"I don't mean jest exactly that way; I mean—widder, you're the morti—I mean the salvation of my soul. Could you—would you—er—do you think you'd keer to sheer my blessin's with me—an' add another one to 'em?"

The Widow Young looked at him in astonishment; then, as she perceived his drift, the tears filled her eyes and she asked, "Do you mean it, Nathan?"

"I wouldn't 'a' spent so much labor on a joke, widder."

"No, it don't seem like you would, Nathan. Well, it's sudden, mighty sudden, but I can't say no."

"Fur these an' all other blessin's make us truly thankful, oh Lord, we ask for His name's sake—Amen!" said Nathan devoutly. And he sat another hour with the widow making plans for the early marriage, on which he insisted.

Sacramento, California, *Record Union,* 1902. Paul Laurence Dunbar Collection, MSS 659, series 1, box 1, OHS, from Henry Romeike clipping service, New York City. No page number, date incomplete.

To Kelly Miller, Jr.

Dear Kelly, when I was a kid
I wrote this book: that's what I did.
When you grow up—I may be dead—
You allus think o' what I said,
Dat you gon' mek yo' ma'k fu' true,
Cos, Kelly M—, I bets on you.

Quoted by Benjamin Brawley in *Paul Laurence Dunbar: Poet of His People,* p. 62. Brawley indicates that the original autograph, dated January 1, 1898, was written on the flyleaf of a copy of *Oak and Ivy* presented to the young son of Professor Kelly Miller.

Song

De bee hit sip some honey f'om de matermony vine,
        De hummin'-bird hit lingahs roun' de rose.
De honey-suckle's sweetah dan de swetes' muscadine
        An' de mo'nin'-glory's tu'nin' up its nose.

De pinks is sayin' "pick us" ez de pansy meet dey eye,
        W'ile de pansies 's sayin' "look at us an' hush."
An' you'd hyeah de lily quoilin' w'en de two is passin' by
        Ef it wasn't fu' de wablin' of de frush.

In de fiel' de flags is wavin' in a tantalizin' way,
        Kin o' 'joicin' case de daisies all is daid.

But de fall flowehs come a-sayin' "needn't laugh, you've had yo' day
An' de fros' 'll lay de sod erpon yo' haid.

Oh, I know dey ain' no tulips an' de vi'lets died in May,
Deys lots o' folks dat miss 'em too, I 'low
But dey didn't have no pu'fume fu' to speak of anyway
So what's de use o' moanin' fu' 'em now.

De flowehs may die in Springtime an' de flowehs may die Fall,
An' people kin go cryin' 'bout dey def—
But sweetah dan de blossoms an' mo' fragrantah dan all
Is yo' lips my little lady an' yo' bref.

No date, Paul Laurence Dunbar Collection, series 4, box 10, OHS. Quoted by permission.

Comrade

Oh, comrade, comrade, I have missed you so!
The long, drear months still lagging come and go,
And I, I strive to fill them to the brim,
But still my heart cries out, But what of him?

To-night, I sat and pored o'er pages sere,
All filled with what we did and said last year;
And all the soul within me rose and cried,
And all the woman in me sobbed and sighed.

This day we sat beside a dimpling stream,
And hours flew by like moments in a dream;
And you and I, true comrades, laughed and played,
Nor deemed it long the while we fondly stayed.

These days we stood 'neath turquoise Western sky,
And breathed new life, sipped ozone from on high;
Did mem'ry ever smile and call to thee
Those long, sweet tramps of ours, of me and thee?

Then those long dreary hours you fought with death,
And I hung near and watched your feeble breath;
And those long evening hours you clasped my hand,
And watched the twilight creeping o'er the land.

We sat upon the shore and watched the sea,
Creep higher to the rocks e'er we did flee.
And erst we angled in the dimpling bay,
And proudly counted trophies, mind'st the day?

Oh, comrade, comrade, I have missed you so!
The long drear months still lagging come and go,
And I, I strive to fill them to the brim,
But still my heart cries out, But what of him?

We've lived through sorrow and we've lived through joy,
Sweets, sweets we've tasted to our senses' cloy;
And yet we've suffered sorrow to the deep,
Full bitterness of sorrow's deadly heap.

Dost mind the books we read in other days?
Dost mind the foolish cards and little plays?
Dost mind the lilting music of our song?
Dost mind the winter eves, so sweet and long?

There is no other heart to beat with mine,
There is no other soul attuned like thine;
I miss the quick return of kindred fire,
These duller minds, oh comrade, quickly tire.

The dreary days pass on, I smile and smile,
My heart a-heavy, and soul tired the while;
The dreary nights in sleepless mis'ry creep
My soul a-cry to thine in anguish deep.

Our paths have parted, ne'er perhaps, to meet,
Your way goes west, mine east. With slow-paced feet
I take my way; yet still, again, to-night,
I pause and sob before the dreary fight.

Oh, comrade, comrade, I have missed you so!
The long drear months still lagging come and go;
And I, I strive to fill them to the brim,
But still my heart cries out, But what of him?

No date. Paul Laurence Dunbar Collection, series 4, box 10, OHS. Quoted by permission.

Love Is a Star

ROUNDEAU

Love is a star that lights the night
Of life, and makes its fancies bright
As days of June with June's perfume;
A star that melts the clinging gloom
And makes the heart's dark chambers light.

To any depth, from any height
Its light doth leap; the dusk of doom
Could not its silver trace consume
Love is a star.

It shines undimmed, a beacon white
To Faith's unwavering, trustful sight.
'Mid warp and woof it findeth room
And weaves bright thoughts on Sorrow's loom
With lovestrung threads of pure delight.

Love is a star.

No date, Paul Laurence Dunbar Collection, series 4, box 10, OHS. Quoted by permission.

Paul Laurence Dunbar

Night on the Chesapeake

When night comes down upon the Chesapeake,
And on the bay the moon rides full and high;
Beside you I should dream nor care to speak,
Our hearts and souls should talk and make reply.

When on the shining track our eyes should roam,
Our thoughts go hand in hand the lambent way;
We'd turn no longing thoughts toward house or home—
Our dearer home is here beside the bay.

Raise me a tent beside this shining shore,
Whereon in storms the waves their vengeance wreak;
Give me my love and wave and forest-lore
And long sweet hours upon the Chesapeake.

No date, Paul Laurence Dunbar Collection, series 4, box 10, OHS. Quoted by permission.

A Matter of Locality

If I lived in sight of the lake
                                        I should make
A poem most exquisite, tender
Of its bosom at sunlight, its bosom in cloud
Of the gold of its eventide splendor.

If I lived in sound of the lake,
                                        I should break
The heads of the fishermen yelling;
With a whack for the lies they are dying to tell
And some more for the ones they are telling.

No date, Paul Laurence Dunbar Collection, series 4, box 10, OHS. Quoted by permission.

Home Longings

I've been here fur many days
Standin' in the city's maze,
Jumpin' out and skippin' in,
List'nin' to the roar an' din,
Gettin' hard an' keen an' cold
Growin' gray before I'm old;
I want home.

Home's the best place after all;
When the leaves begin to fall
An' the frosty atmosphere
Hints o' winter drawin' near,
Seems as ef yore mind goes back
Mighty swift along the track
'At leads home.

Want to see the ole house there,
Want to breathe a breath o' air
That ain't filled with dust or smoke,
Want to be where banks ain't broke,
Where yer treasure ends an' starts
In yer comrades' brimmin' hearts.
That's at home.

Want to see yer mother stand
In the door an' wave her hand
At you comin' up the road,
Want to shake off all the load—
Care an' pain, an' grief an' strife
'At beset a city life
An' git home.

Want to git back to the fields,
Where the hand o' nature yields
Due reward fur honest toil;
Want to tread the good ole soil
'At I ust to tread in glee—
Happy as I ust to be,
There at home.

Want to hear the cattle brown
Lowin' as the sun goes down,
Change these tracks an' rumblin' cars
Fur the sight o' paster bars,
Drop the pen an' take the plow
That's the thing to ketch me now
That—an' home.

Want some kale greens—smooth as silk,
Want to drink some buttermilk,
Want to eat some griddle cakes—
Them good kin', whut mother makes.
Want some butter, some 'at ain't
Made o' grease an' yaller paint.
Some from home.

Oh, the days grow sad an' long,
Life seems all a mournful song,
Nuthin' seems so fair er free
As it ust to seem to me.
Nuthin' ever will seem right
Tell I pack my grip an' light
Out fur home.

Unidentified, undated newspaper clipping. Copy courtesy of Paul Laurence Dunbar Collection, MSS 659, series 1, box 1, OHS.

Content

Give me no days more brilliant than I know,
The birth outside my window soothes my soul,
And even as the fleeting hours come and go,
Life's beauties to my wakened eyes unroll.

Give me no skies more beautiful than these,
'Neath which I sit beside you all elate,
All that I covet is life's warming breeze,
That leaves me breathless at the door of fate.

No date, Paul Laurence Dunbar Collection, series 4, box 10, OHS. Quoted by permission.

Too Busy

The Lord had a job for me, but I had so much to do,
I said, "You get somebody else—or wait 'till I get through."
I don't know how the Lord came out, but he seemed to get along;
But I felt kind o' sneakin' like; 'cause I knowed I done Him wrong.

One day I needed the Lord, needed Him right away—
And He never answered me at all, but I could hear Him say
Down in my accusin' heart, "Nigger, I's got too much to do.
You get somebody else—or wait 'till I get through."

Now, when the Lord has a job for me, I never tries to shirk;
I drops what I have on hand and does the good Lord's work;
And my affairs can run along, or wait 'till I get through.
Nobody else can do the work that God's marked out for you.

Homiletic Review 107 (March 1934): 243.

Appendix

Bibliography

Indexes

Appendix: Variants of Poems in The Complete Poems (1913)

POEM COLLECTIONS BY PAUL LAURENCE DUNBAR

Works are listed in the order of original publication.

Abbreviations

OI	Oak and Ivy (1893)
MM	Majors and Minors (1895)
LLi	Lyrics of Lowly Life (1896)
LH	Lyrics of the Hearthside (1899)
PCF	Poems of Cabin and Field (1899)
CLT	Candle-Lightin' Time (1901)
LLa	Lyrics of Love and Laughter (1903)
WMS	When Malindy Sings (1903)
LG	Li'l' Gal (1904)
HHH	Howdy, Honey, Howdy (1905)
LSS	Lyrics of Sunshine and Shadow (1905)

VARIANTS

Textual variants for all the poems in the 1913 *Complete Poems* are listed in the pages that follow. The page number after the poem title refers to the page on which the poem begins in that 1913 edition. Then follows a chronological list of all editions in which versions of the poem may be found. Variants are given below in italic type by line number.

ACCOUNTABILITY p. 5. In MM p. 6, HHH p. 29.
MM ln. 1: *aint . . . uthah*
ln. 2: *giv*
ln. 3: *grea'*
ln. 5: *diff'rent*
ln. 9: *cud fill*
ln. 16: *Viney*
HHH ln. 13: *W'en* you come to *t'ink*
ln. 14: *Nothin's*

AFTER A VISIT p. 42. In MM p. 124, LLi p. 91.
MM ln. 29: *jes*

AFTER THE QUARREL p. 40. In MM p. 63, LLi p. 88.
MM ln. 6: *best—*
ln. 10: *you,*
ln. 24: *Tho'*

ALICE p. 40. In MM p. 80, LLi p. 87.
MM ln. 1: *you winds*

AN ANTE-BELLUM SERMON p. 13. In MM p. 102, LLi p. 26.
MM ln. 1: *brothah,*
ln. 3: *Fer*
ln. 7: *Moses, Moses,*
ln. 16: *go.*
ln. 17: *An'*
ln. 24: *Ev'ry*
ln. 48: *I'se*
ln. 49: *a judgin'*
ln. 51: *a givin'*
ln. 52: *a handin'*
ln. 53: *believed*
ln. 60: *a worthy*
ln. 71: *bout*
ln. 73: *a comin,*
ln. 87: *reco'nized*

ANGELINA p. 138. In LH p. 153, HHH p. 49.
LH ln. 18: *purnish*
HHH ln. 1: *W'en*
ln. 4: *yo'se'f*
ln. 5: *W'en*
ln. 8: *W'en*
ln. 16: *W'en*
ln. 18: *purnish*
ln. 24: *W'en*
ln. 25: *step' . . . bow'*
ln. 29: *W'en*

BALLAD p. 58. In MM p. 80, LLi p. 135.
MM ln. 14: *spark—*

A BANJO SONG p. 20. In MM p. 105, PCF p. 107, LLi p. 42.
MM ln. 4: *roun',*
ln. 5: *'em—*

ln. 14: *fall—*
ln. 25: *all de chillun*
ln. 54: *Do'*
ln. 63: *F'um*

THE BARRIER p. 99. In LH p. 32, LSS p. 39.
LH ln. 19: *midnight*
LSS ln. 10: *love's*
ln. 11: *night*

BLACK SAMSON OF BRANDYWINE p. 205. In LLa, p. 120.
LLa epigraph: . . . sweeps his way *thro'*

BLUE p. 253. In LSS p. 54, LG p. 17.
LSS ln. 1: *stannin*
ln. 3: *listened*

A BORDER BALLAD p. 48. In MM p. 57, LLi p. 108.
MM ln. 9: *yesternight*

A BOY'S SUMMER SONG p. 235. In LSS p. 1.
LSS The final "Ha Ha" of each stanza does not stand as an independent line.

THE CHANGE HAS COME p. 58. In MM p. 19, LLi p. 136.
MM ln. 10: *to-morrow—*
ln. 12: *borrow?*

CHRISMUS IS A-COMIN' p. 153. In PCF p. 55, LH p. 201.
PCF ln. 11: *Chris'mus*
ln. 38: *th'oo*
ln. 40: *tu'ky*
ln. 47: *Chris'mus*

A CHRISTMAS FOLKSONG p. 236. In LSS p. 5, HHH p. 61.
HHH ln. 16: *fu'*

THE COLORED BAND p. 178. In WMS p. 31, LLa p. 44.
WMS and LLa ln. 28: *marchin'*

THE COLORED SOLDIERS p. 50. In MM p. 38, LLi p. 114.
MM ln. 21: *war*
ln. 37: *From the blaing breach of Wagner*
ln. 38: *To the*

ln. 45: *thy*
ln. 54: *night;*
ln. 73: *recond,*
ln. 78: *Sons*

COLUMBIAN ODE p. 47. In MM p. 27, LLi p. 105.
MM ln. 29: *deer haunts*
ln. 31: *bruin*

COMPARISON p. 59. In MM p. 43, LLi p. 137.
MM ln. 5: *over bright*

CONSCIENCE AND REMORSE p. 31. In MM p. 44, LLi p. 69.
MM ln. 4: *away,*
ln. 9: *conscience,*
ln. 11: *cannot,*

A CORN-SONG p. 59. In MM p. 58, LLi p. 137, LG p. 53, LSS p. 16.
MM This edition prints the four-line "song" only once; subsequently it merely says "Song—" in the appropriate place. Line numbers therefore refer to the text of *The Complete Poems.*
ln. 12: *head—*
ln. 13: *Tho'*
ln. 22: *burden full*
ln. 23: *clearer;*

THE CORN-STALK FIDDLE p. 16. In MM p. 116, LLi p. 33.
MM ln. 5: *heigho*
ln. 23: *twiddle,*

CURIOSITY p. 241. In LG p. 27, LSS p. 21.
LG ln. 2: *piccaninnies*
ln. 4: no stanza division before next line
ln. 5: *Whut* (twice)
ln. 10: *piccaninnies*
ln. 11: *you all keep*
ln. 12: *I's*
ln. 18: *fu'*
ln. 26: *fu'*
ln. 27: *almo'*
ln. 28: *hit*

CURTAIN p. 42. In MM p. 118, LLi p. 93.
MM ln. 5: *Scape-grace*
ln. 8: *ships*

DAT OL' MARE O' MINE p. 189. In CLT p. 21, LLa p. 76.
CLT ln. 13: . . . anyt'ing *dat's* white
ln. 18: *she'll*
ln. 19: *she'll*
ln. 20: *evah-ting*
ln. 27: *does n'* and *scarcely*
ln. 40: *dough*

DEACON JONES' GRIEVANCE p. 39. In MM p. 131, LLi p. 83.
MM ln. 18: *soon,*
ln. 28: *diddle*
ln. 36: *three-score*

DEAD p. 73. In MM p. 41, LLi p. 172.
MM ln. 3: *but ah*
ln. 14: *long,*

THE DELINQUENT p. 64. In LLi p. 151, HHH p. 23.
MM ln. 1: *Goo'by,*
ln. 6: *I'se*
ln. 11: *Jinks's*
ln. 16: *mawnin',*
ln. 17: *Dar's . . . dar*
refrain in every fifth line: *go long.*
HHH ln. 26: *'a' be'n*

THE DESERTED PLANTATION p. 67. In PCF p. 9, LLi p. 158.
PCF ln. 18: *ev'ry . . . ol'*
ln. 21: *ol'*
ln. 23: *ol'*
ln. 26: *ol'*
ln. 29: *ol'*
ln. 33: *ol'*
MM ln. 1: *Oh de grubbin-hoe's a rustin'*
ln. 2: *a tumblin' . . . fiel'—*
ln. 3: *a wailin' . . . mou'nah,*
ln. 4: *hawt*
ln. 7: *a bravin'*
ln. 8: *their*

ln. 14: *ah;*
ln. 16: *da*
ln. 17: *ust . . . a dancin',*
ln. 18: *Ebry*
ln. 19: *ust . . . a prancin',*
ln. 20: *a rollin'*
ln. 21: *de Uncle*
ln. 24: *ust*
ln. 25: *story.*
MM also consistently uses *wha'* and *wha's* for *whah* and *whah's.*

THE DILETTANTE: A MODERN TYPE p. 49. In MM p. 134, LLi p. 112.
MM ln. 3: *little—*
ln. 6: *roles,*

DIRGE p. 66. In MM p. 36, LLi p. 155.
MM ln. 10: *hour—*
ln. 13: *light.*
ln. 15: *me,*
ln. 17: *be,*

DISAPPOINTED p. 60. In MM p. 85, LLi p. 141.
MM ln. 2: *dew:*
ln. 3: *befriended*
ln. 16: *earth,*
ln. 17: *rain:*

DREAMIN' TOWN p. 254. In HHH p. 95.
HHH ln. 14: *everyt'ing*
ln. 19: *hahts*
ln. 24: *dreamin' town*

AN EASY-GOIN' FELLER p. 49. In MM p. 141, LLi p. 109.
MM ln. 5: *good*
ln. 10: stanza division at end of line
ln. 11: *a standin'*

ENCOURAGEMENT p. 184. In LLa p. 61, HHH p. 13.
HHH ln. 49: *whaih's*

ERE SLEEP COMES DOWN TO SOOTHE THE WEARY EYES p. 3. In MM p. 65, LLi p. 1.
MM ln. 7: *sighs;*

ln. 30: *Thro'*
ln. 34: *Till faint*
ln. 38: *soul—*
ln. 53: *thro'*

FAITH p. 244. In LSS p. 29, HHH p. 69.
HHH ln. 3: *somep'n'*
ln. 11: no stanza division after the end of the line. This reading seems more correct since the stanza division occurs in the middle of a sentence.
ln. 13: *st'om's er-railin'*

FISHING p. 172. In CLT p. 67, LLa p. 27.
CLT ln. 19: *think*
ln. 23: *Fu' de win'*
ln. 24: *blessid*
ln. 25: *wo'm-can*
ln. 30: *erfeared dey'll quit dey bitin'*
ln. 34: *needer*
ln. 36: *comerds*

FOOLIN' WID DE SEASONS p. 139. In LH p. 156, HHH p. 43.
HHH ln. 19: *try'n'*

FREDERICK DOUGLASS p. 6. In MM p. 17, LLi p. 8.
MM ln. 8: *love*
ln. 15: *pow'r*
ln. 20: *straight-forward*
ln. 22: *dark-hued*
ln. 27: *array—*
ln. 31: *him and*
ln. 37: *he—*
ln. 39: *talents and*
ln. 44: *pow'r*
ln. 47: *His*
ln. 51: *thro' out*
ln. 61: *And*

GOOD-NIGHT p. 61. In MM p. 79, LLi p. 144.
MM title: *Good Night*
ln. 3: *Sleep Love*
ln. 4: *Good night my love, good night, good night.*
ln. 5: *the sleep*

ln. 8: same as ln. 4 above
ln. 9: *well my love*
ln. 12: same as ln. 4 above

GROWIN' GRAY p. 80. In MM p. 127, LLi p. 192.
MM ln. 1: *a gittin'*
ln. 11: ust
ln. 14: *tho'*
ln. 25: *for*
ln. 26: *An' the night*

HE HAD HIS DREAM p. 61. In MM p. 33, LLi p. 143.
MM ln. 6: *barque*
(Note that this spelling is used throughout MM.)

"HOWDY, HONEY, HOWDY!" p. 196. In WMS p. 77, LLa p. 93, HHH p. 7.
HHH ln. 17: *sto'm*

HOW SHALL I WOO THEE p. 289. In MM p. 72.
MM ln. 1: *win the,*

HYMN ("When Storms Arise") p. 66. In MM p. 77, LLi p. 157.
MM ln. 3: *lower;*
(Note that MM does not indent the third and sixth line of each stanza as *The Complete Poems* does.)

IF p. 75. In MM p. 58, LLi p. 179.
MM ln. 4: *rhyme;*
ln. 12: *pain;*

INVITATION TO LOVE p. 61. In MM p. 76, LLi p. 142.
MM ln. 2: *is mellow*
ln. 7: *oh Love*
ln. 9: *oh love*
ln. 13: *grief,*
ln. 15: *leaf,*
ln. 19: *snows*

IONE p. 31. In MM p. 7, LLi p. 70.

Part I

MM ln. 1: *to still remember*
ln. 5: *And oh*

ln. 6: *pain,*
ln. 15: *could,*
ln. 16: *Ease . . . spurned,*
ln. 21: *passion:*
ln. 25: *"hasten,"*
ln. 39: *I too,*
ln. 44: *heart,*
ln. 52: *sphere*
ln. 56: *did*
ln. 64: *that*
ln. 70: *flow'r—,*
ln. 71: *pow'r*
ln. 79: *when*
ln. 82: *Ione:*
ln. 90: *act;*

Part II

ln. 4: *I;*
ln. 8: *claim,*
ln. 9: *others saw*
ln. 12: *bird*
ln. 14: *so,*
ln. 19: *story,*
ln. 25: *Who*
ln. 33: *oftimes*

Part III

ln. 6: *guest*
ln. 15: *wine—*
ln. 24: *sun—*
ln. 38: *But . . . right,*
ln. 42: *sound note . . . tone,*
ln. 57: *dearer,*
ln. 60: *so*
ln. 67: *well nigh*
ln. 72: *all.*
ln. 73: *all*
ln. 82: *Rome*
ln. 85: *gloom,*
ln. 87: *bow'r,*

THE LESSON p. 8. In MM p. 67, LLi p. 12.
MM ln. 4: *mocking bird's*
ln. 12: *art*
ln. 20: *Tho'*
ln. 21: *smile, . . . turn*

LINCOLN p. 184. In LLa p. 60.
LLa ln. 7: *Till*

LONESOME p. 79. In MM p. 113, LLi p. 189.
MM ln. 3: *agin;*
ln. 5: *ust*
ln. 10: *ust*
ln. 13: *holly-hocks*
ln. 15: *tho'*
ln. 23: *ust*
ln. 24: *Fore . . . a visitin'*
ln. 26: *sadder*
ln. 28: *blurred,*
ln. 29: *blue,*

'LONG TO'DS NIGHT p. 187. In WMS p. 137, LLa p. 69.
LLa ln. 28: *wo'kin'*

A LOVE LETTER p. 266. In LSS p. 91, HHH p. 77.
HHH ln. 3: *sweethaht*
ln. 7: *h'aht's*

THE LOVER AND THE MOON p. 29. In MM p. 45, LLi p. 66.
MM ln. 5: *"But*
ln. 6: *And*
ln. 9: *Oh*
ln. 14: *Oh guard . . . of mine.*
ln. 23: *joy,*
ln. 33: *ill-kept,*
ln. 38: *said,*
ln. 39: *men,*
ln. 40: *forth dear youth*
ln. 42: *Oh*
ln. 44: *soul sick*
ln. 50: *wind:*
ln. 54: *pierce:*

A LYRIC p. 288. In MM p. 69.
MM ln. 6: *feet:*

A MADRIGAL p. 287. In MM p. 20.
MM ln. 1: *hours,*
ln. 13: *love*
ln. 24: *Oh*

THE MASTER-PLAYER p. 17. In MM p. 62, LLi p. 35.
MM ln. 1: *play'd*
ln. 2: *fray'd*
ln. 3: *essay'd*
ln. 9: *song.*

THE MEADOW LARK p. 71. In MM p. 29, LLi p. 168.
MM ln. 3: *day*
ln. 17: *disaster;*

THE MYSTERY p. 17. In MM p. 81, LLi p. 36.
MM ln. 1: *hence,*
ln. 3: *Pow'r*
ln. 4: *pow'r*
ln. 12: *infinite,*
ln. 18: *roll on*

NATURE AND ART p. 52. In MM p. 48, LLi p. 118.
MM ln. 8: stanza separation before the next line
ln. 21: *wrought:*
ln. 22: *elf,*
ln. 23: *replies*
ln. 25: *"Oh, queen,"*

THE NEWS p. 136. In LH p. 147.
LH ln. 3: *Somep'n' 's*
ln. 7: *mastah led?*

NOT THEY WHO SOAR p. 18. In MM p. 62, LLi p. 37.
MM ln. 2: *unhelped*
ln. 4: *And*
ln. 7: *path,*
ln. 11: *share;*

ODE FOR MEMORIAL DAY p. 22. In MM p. 50, LLi p. 49.
MM ln. 3: *sweetly,*
ln. 16: *pain.*
ln. 18: *saber stroke . . . fell:*
ln. 22: *fight,*
ln. 27: *eternal,*
ln. 28: *Flowers that startle*
ln. 33: *So*

ODE TO ETHIOPIA p. 15. In MM p.23, LLi p. 30.
MM ln. 35: *labor's*

THE OL' TUNES p. 53. In MM p. 107, LLi p. 122.
MM ln. 3: *choir singin'*
ln. 9: *o' us*
ln. 10: *o' us*
ln. 12: *its complement*
ln. 15: *A singin'*
ln. 26: *in,*
ln. 29: *ust*
ln. 33: *agin to hear it,*
ln. 52: *shore;*
ln. 54: *o' endless*
ln. 55: *A singin'*

ONE LIFE p. 72. In MM p. 73, LLi p. 169.
MM ln. 1: *Love,*
ln. 20: *skyward soaring*
ln. 21: *born;*
ln. 26: *alone*
ln. 28: *mine,*
ln. 30: *me—'tis*

OPPORTUNITY p. 242. In LSS p. 24, HHH p. 105.
LSS ln. 29: *an' hyeah* (This reading is also found in HHH and would appear to be preferred.)
HHH ln. 7: *I's*

THE PARTY p. 83. In MM p. 89, LLi p. 199.
MM ln. 3: *invited*
ln. 4: *heahs*
ln. 5: *dere*
ln. 8: *a-shinin'*
ln. 10: *mustus,*

ln. 19: *would a noticed*
ln. 22: *"Oh*
ln. 23: *set down*
ln. 31: *'Oh*
ln. 33: *"Oh*
ln. 35: *now*
ln. 38: *youngsters*
ln. 40: *res',*
ln. 51: *tell he giv'*
ln. 58: *reckon*
ln. 65: *dough,*
ln. 71: *you'se . . . again*
ln. 72: *heah . . . 'Spose*
ln. 75: *d'want*
ln. 76: *I've*
ln. 77: *'pologizin'*
ln. 78: *Thompson*
ln. 80: *open—*
ln. 81: *hawts*
ln. 82: *yo'*
ln. 83: *twel*
ln. 85: *'roun'*
ln. 88: *'mounted*
ln. 94: *it,*
ln. 95: *lose*
ln. 100: *bahn-yard*

PASSION AND LOVE p. 11. In MM p. 56, LLi p. 21.
MM ln. 12: *tear*
ln. 13: *flow'r,—*

PHILOSOPHY p. 212. In LLa p. 138.
LLa 1n. 8: does not show stanza division after this line

PHYLLIS p. 74. In MM p. 70, LLi p. 177.
MM ln. 6: *May-day;*
ln. 8: *hey-day,*

THE PLANTATION CHILD'S LULLABY p. 241. In LG p. 13, LSS p. 19.
LG ln. 4: *ting*
ln. 20: *R'om*
LSS ln. 4: *ting*
ln. 20: *R'om*

THE POET AND HIS SONG p. 4. In MM p. 21, LLi p. 4.

MM ln. 1: *thing*
ln. 2: *sing.*
ln. 8: *song*
ln. 11: *still*
ln. 16: *song*
ln. 17: *ease,*
ln. 21: *hard*
ln. 26: *spot.*

POSSOM p. 141. In LH p. 163, HHH p. 39.

HHH ln. 10: *haht*
ln. 12: *paht*
ln. 25: *t'nk*
ln. 28: *miedlin'*

A PRAYER p. 11. In MM p. 76, LLi p. 20.

MM ln. 2: *feet;*
ln. 3: *Oh . . . smiles*
The third quatrain, which appears in LLi and *The Complete Poems,* does not appear here.

PREMONITION p. 23. In MM p. 49, LLi p. 51.

MM ln. 6: *"good-night.*
ln. 10: *telltale*
ln. 12: *But . . . good-night!*
ln. 18: *still, so*

PROMISE p. 12. In MM (as two separate poems entitled "Promise" and "Fulfillment," with only "Promise" listed in the Contents) p. 83, LLi (as "Promise and Fulfillment") p. 23.

MM ln. 1: *fair*
ln. 2: *And*
ln. 5: *And . . . bud,*
ln. 8: *it,*
ln. 11: *Then, . . . smiles,*
ln. 14: *it, . . . skies*
ln. 17: *flower*
ln. 18: stanza division after this line
ln. 19: *days,*
ln. 20: *flow'r.*
ln. 23: *Oh*
ln. 24: *but,*

PUTTIN' THE BABY AWAY p. 243. In LSS p. 26, HHH p. 83.
LSS ln. 19: *hy* haht
ln. 34: *'ll*
HHH ln. 35: nes'

RETORT p. 5. In MM p. 84, LLi 6.
MM ln. 4: *smart."*
ln. 9: *air;*
ln. 10: *Oh*

RETROSPECTION p. 24. In MM p. 60, LLi p. 52.
MM ln. 30: *in—*
ln. 35: *delight,*
ln. 52: *tears,*

RIDING TO TOWN p. 70. In MM p. 78, LLi p. 165.
MM ln. 20: *its*
ln. 27: *'mid*
ln. 30: *song,*
ln. 31: *way—*

RIGHT'S SECURITY p. 75. In MM p. 70, LLi p. 178.
MM ln. 4: *window-pane.*
ln. 14: *battle cry;*
ln. 17: *armors*
ln. 19: *Tho' single*

THE RISING OF THE STORM p. 8. In MM p. 51, LLi p. 13.
MM ln. 16: *water sprite*
ln. 18: *sea hymn's*
ln. 21: *loom:*
ln. 36: *earth*
ln. 38: *plies*
ln. 43: *rise*
ln. 46: *sweep*

THE RIVALS p. 27. In MM p. 134, LLi p. 61.
MM ln. 3: *hed*
ln. 8: *Joneses*
ln. 10: *wuz*
ln. 12: *fun.*
ln. 13: *Thet . . . hev*
ln. 16: *wuz*

ln. 22: *on us,*
ln. 35: *hed*
ln. 43: *Thro'*
ln. 71: *wuz*
ln. 87: *spile't*
ln. 88: *well*
ln. 103: *Lizy,*

THE SAND-MAN p. 235. In LSS p. 2.
LSS ln. 14: *Droop sleepywise*

SCAMP p. 239. In LSS p. 12, HHH p. 101.
LSS ln. 21: *yo*
HHH ln. 38: *trun'le*

THE SECRET p. 68. In MM p. 33, LLi p. 161.
MM ln. 6: *Good bye, good bye?"*

THE SEEDLING p. 12. In MM p. 30, LLi p. 22.
MM ln. 3: *a talking*
ln. 6: *can";*
ln. 14: *brother*

SHIPS THAT PASS IN THE NIGHT p. 64. In MM p. 47, LLi p. 150.
MM ln. 1: *massing,*
ln. 6: *eyes,*
ln. 10: *passing passing.*
ln. 11: *Oh . . . oh . . . oh*
ln. 12: *Oh . . . oh*
ln. 14: *bark,*

SIGNS OF THE TIMES p. 77. In MM p. 77, PCF p. 67, LLi p. 182.
PCF ln. 17: *Pum'Kin*
MM ln. 1: *a gittin'*
ln. 2: *a comin'*
ln. 9: *a squeakin'*
ln. 14: *a flyin'*
ln. 15: *Umph*
ln. 18: *Make*
ln. 19: *a lookin'*
ln. 20: *a la'in'*
ln. 29: *Heahs*
ln. 31: *min'*

ln. 32: *after*
ln. 35: *a cookin'*
ln. 37: *heah*
ln. 38: *larned*
ln. 40: *heah?*

SOLILOQUY OF A TURKEY p. 171. In LG p. 67, LLa p. 25.
LG and LLa: both show final eight lines as a single octave rather than two quatrains.

SONG p. 13. In MM p. 73, LLi p. 25.
MM ln. 5: *shade,*
ln. 6: *deep*

THE SPARROW p. 78. In MM p. 26, LLi p. 185.
MM ln. 4: *winsow pane*
ln. 11: *window sills*

SPEAKIN' O' CHRISTMAS p. 78. In MM p. 141, LLi p. 186.
MM ln. 14: *most nigh*
ln. 16: *ust to be.*
ln. 38: *all.*
ln. 41: *knee deep*
ln. 49: *An' when Christmas come, why, we*
ln. 58: *Chris'mus*
ln. 64: *She ust*
LLi ln. 38: *all.*

THE SPELLIN'-BEE p. 42. In MM p. 95, LLi p. 93.
MM Title is not hyphenated
ln. 2: *And*
ln. 9: *spellin' bee*
ln. 10: *meant*
ln. 11: *teens,*
ln. 16: *a drivin'*
ln. 18: *ears*
ln. 20: *wan't*
ln. 25: *Cause . . . wuz*
ln. 27: *wuz*
ln. 29: *Dobbses girl wuz*
ln. 37: *spellun' book*
ln. 45: *wuz . . . a livin',*
ln. 48: *wuzn't . . . wuz . . . stingy.*

ln. 49: *a smilin' an' a smirkin',*
ln. 50: *a workin'.*
ln. 51: *widower, he wuz*
ln. 52: *wuz . . . her'n*
ln. 53: *spellin' test*
ln. 56: *now-a-days*
ln. 60: *"charity,"*
ln. 61: *laffin's*
ln. 62: *'ud*
ln. 64: *kay . . . coquettin'.*
ln. 69: *Brown*
ln. 71: *a landin',*
ln. 72: *wuz*
ln. 75: *agin*
ln. 80: *a-shootin'*
ln. 83: *hymn*
ln. 91: *your'n by rights;"*

SPRING FEVER p. 176. In WMS p. 45, LLa p. 39.
WMS ln. 39: *Iess'n*

A SPRING WOOING p. 164. In CLT p. 37, LLa p. 5.
CLT ln. 23: *excuse*

A SUMMER NIGHT p. 262. In LSS p. 80, HHH p. 111.
HHH ln. 2: *Don 'keer*

A SUMMER'S NIGHT p. 64. In MM p. 72, LLi p. 64.
MM ln. 3: *breath,*
ln. 6: *hastening*

SUNSET p. 9. In MM p. 27, LLi p. 16.
MM ln. 6: *lay*
ln. 7: *day,—*
ln. 11: *space;*
ln. 13: *somber*

TO E. H. K. p. 97. In LH p. 24.
LH ln. 8: stanza division here, creating clear octave-sestet pattern.

TO THE MEMORY OF MARY YOUNG p. 81. In MM p. 41, LLi p. 193.
MM ln. 1: *we,*
ln. 3: *He,*

ln. 7: *unknown*
ln. 11: *eyes,*
ln. 27: *silence*
ln. 32: *sweet faith*

WADIN IN DE CREEK p. 239. In WMS p. 129, LSS p. 14.
WMS ln. 37: *you t'ank yo'*

WE WEAR THE MASK p. 71. In MM p. 21, LLi p. 167.
MM ln. 2: *eyes—*
ln. 4: *smile*
ln. 5: *subtleties,*
ln. 10: *but oh*
ln. 11: *Thee*
ln. 13: *mile,*

WHEN DE CO'N PONE'S HOT p. 57. In MM p. 111, LLi p. 132, LG p. 47.
MM ln. 1: *life,*
ln. 3: *a rattlin'*
ln. 8: *'Twel . . . slop.*
ln. 11: *ses*
ln. 23: *ses*
ln. 27: *chittlin's is a sputter'n'*
ln. 32: *its . . . very nigh,*
ln. 34: *Do*
ln. 35: *ses*
ln. 37: *heerd*
ln. 38: *heerd*
ln. 43: *hawt*
ln. 47: *ses*

WHEN DEY 'LISTED COLORED SOLDIERS p. 182. In CLT p. 77, LLa p. 56.
CLT title: *Listed*
ln. 2: *a-thinkin'*
ln. 5: *think*
ln. 17: *thought*
ln. 28: *heered*
ln. 34: *some'rs*
ln. 37: *some'rs*

WHEN MALINDY SINGS p. 82. In MM p. 138, LLi p. 195, WMS p. 9.
MM ln. 7: *de big*
ln. 20: *in in*

ln. 22: *hawt*
ln. 25: *heerd*
ln. 27: *heah,*
ln. 29: *heah*
ln. 33: *man,*
ln. 42: *heah*
ln. 44: *Timid-like*
ln. 51: *heah*
ln. 65: *heah*
ln. 67: *heah*
ln. 69: *heah*
LLi ln. 7: *de big*
WMS ln. 7: *de big*

WHIP-POOR-WILL AND KATY-DID p. 186. In LLa p. 68, LG p. 75.
LG ln. 2: *callin'*
LLa ln. 2: *callin'*

THE WIND AND THE SEA p. 69. In MM p. 53, LLi p. 162.
MM ln. 26: *eastern*

THE WOOING p. 55. In MM p. 115, LLi p. 128.
MM ln. 6: *hair—*
ln. 19: *not sir*
ln. 21: *your*
ln. 23: *myself*
ln. 29: *maiden*
ln. 33: *eyes*
ln. 39: *wed.*

Bibliography

SELECTED BOOKS BY PAUL LAURENCE DUNBAR

Oak and Ivy. Dayton, Ohio: Press of United Brethren Publishing House, 1893.

Majors and Minors: Poems. Toledo, Ohio: Hadley and Hadley, 1895; rpt. Miami: Mnemosyne Publishing Co., 1969.

Lyrics of Lowly Life. New York: Dodd, Mead and Company, 1896; London: Chapman & Hall, 1896.

Folks from Dixie. New York: Dodd, Mead and Company, 1898; London: Bowden, 1898.

The Uncalled: A Novel. New York: Dodd, Mead and Company, 1898; London: Service & Paton, 1899.

Lyrics of the Hearthside. New York: Dodd, Mead and Company, 1899.

Poems of Cabin and Field. New York: Dodd, Mead and Company, 1899.

The Love of Landry. New York: Dodd, Mead and Company, 1900.

The Strength of Gideon and Other Stories. New York: Dodd, Mead and Company, 1900.

Candle-Lightin' Time. New York: Dodd, Mead and Company, 1901.

The Fanatics. New York: Dodd, Mead and Company, 1901.

The Sport of Gods. New York: Dodd, Mead and Company, 1902; republished as *The Jest of Fate: A Story of Negro Life.* London: Jarrold, 1902.

In Old Plantation Days. New York: Dodd, Mead and Company, 1903.

Lyrics of Love and Laughter. New York: Dodd, Mead and Company, 1903.

When Malindy Sings. New York: Dodd, Mead and Company, 1903; rpt. New York: AMS Press, 1972.

The Heart of Happy Hollow. New York: Dodd, Mead and Company, 1904.

Li'l' Gal. New York: Dodd, Mead and Company, 1904; rpt. New York: AMS Press, 1972.

Howdy, Honey, Howdy. New York: Dodd, Mead and Company, 1905; rpt. New York: AMS Press, 1972.

Lyrics of Sunshine and Shadow. New York: Dodd, Mead and Company, 1905.

Joggin' Erlong. New York: Dodd, Mead and Company, 1906.

The Life and Works of Paul Laurence Dunbar, edited by Lida Keck Wiggins. Naperville, Ill., and Memphis: J. L. Nichols, 1907.

The Complete Poems of Paul Laurence Dunbar. New York: Dodd, Mead and Company, 1913.

Speaking of Christmas. New York: Dodd, Mead and Company, 1914.

The Best Stories of Paul Laurence Dunbar, edited by Benjamin Brawley. New York: Dodd, Mead and Company, 1938.

Little Brown Baby. New York: Dodd, Mead and Company, 1938.

The Paul Laurence Dunbar Reader, edited by Jay Martin and Gossie H. Hudson. New York: Dodd, Mead and Company, 1975.

SECONDARY SOURCES

Arnold, Edward F. "Some Personal Reminiscences of Paul Laurence Dunbar." *Journal of Negro History* 17 (October 1932): 400–408.

Bontemps, Arna. "The Relevance of Paul Laurence Dunbar." In *A Singer in the Dawn: Reinterpretations of Paul Laurence Dunbar,* edited by Jay Martin, pp. 45–54. New York: Dodd, Mead and Company, 1975.

Brawley, Benjamin. "Dunbar Thirty Years After." *Southern Workman* 59 (April 1930): 189–91.

———. *Paul Laurence Dunbar: Poet of His People.* Chapel Hill: University of North Carolina Press, 1936.

Bryfonski, Dedria, and S. K. Hall, eds. "Paul Laurence Dunbar." In *Twentieth-Century Literary Criticism,* vol. 2, pp. 127–34. Detroit: Gale Research, 1979.

Burch, Charles Eaton. "Dunbar's Poetry in Literary English." *Southern Workman* 50 (October 1921): 227–29.

Butcher, Philip. "Mutual Appreciation; Dunbar and Cable." *Free Lance* 4 (1957): 2–3.

Cunningham, Virginia. *Paul Laurence Dunbar and His Song.* New York: Dodd, Mead and Company, 1947.

Davis, Charles T. *Black Is the Color of the Cosmos: Essays on Black Literature and Culture, 1942–1981,* edited by Henry Louis Gates, Jr. New York: Garland Publishing, 1982.

Douglass, Frederick. *The Life of Frederick Douglass, an American Slave: Written by Himself.* 1845; rpt. Garden City, N.Y.: Doubleday and Company, 1963.

Du Bois, W. E. B. *The Souls of Black Folk.* 1903; rpt. New York: Signet, 1969.

Dunbar, Alice. "The Poet and His Song." *A.M.E. Review* 12 (October 1914): 121–35.

Emanuel, James A. "Racial Fire in the Poetry of Paul Laurence Dunbar." In *A Singer in the Dawn: Reinterpretations of Paul Laurence Dunbar,* edited by Jay Martin, pp. 75–93. New York: Dodd, Mead and Company, 1975.

Fuller, Sara S. *The Paul Laurence Dunbar Collection: An Inventory to the Microfilm Edition.* Columbus: Ohio Historical Society, 1972.

Gates, Henry Louis, Jr. "Dis and Dat: Dialect and the Descent." In *Afro-American Literature: The Reconstruction of Instruction,* edited by Robert Stepto and Daxter Fisher, pp. 88–117. New York: Modern Language Association, 1969.

———. *The Signifying Monkey: A Theory of Afro-American Literary Criticism.* New York: Oxford University Press, 1988.

Gayle, Addison, Jr. *Oak and Ivy: A Biography of Paul Laurence Dunbar.* Garden City, N.Y.: Anchor / Doubleday, 1971.

Giles, James R. "Paul Laurence Dunbar." In *Dictionary of Literary Biography: American Short Story Writers, 1880–1910,* edited by Bobby Kimbel, vol. 78. Detroit: Book Tower, 1989.

Giovanni, Nikki. Afterword to *A Singer in the Dawn: Reinterpretations of Paul Laurence Dunbar,* edited by Jay Martin, pp. 243–46. New York: Dodd, Mead and Company, 1975.

Gould, Jean. *That Dunbar Boy.* New York: Dodd, Mead and Company, 1958.

Harper, Michael S. "Paul Laurence Dunbar: 1872–1906." In *Nightmare Begins Responsibility,* p. 59. Urbana: University of Illinois Press, 1975.

Henry, Thomas Millard. "Old School of Negro 'Critics' Hard on Paul Laurence Dunbar." *Messenger* 6 (October 1924): 310–11.

Howells, William Dean. Introduction to Paul Laurence Dunbar's *Lyrics of Lowly Life.* New York: Dodd, Mead and Company, 1896.

———. "Life and Letters." *Harper's Weekly* 27 (June 27, 1896): 630.

Hughes, Langston. "The Negro Artist and the Racial Mountain." *Nation* 122 (June 28, 1926): 692–94.

Hull, Gloria T., ed. *Give Us This Day: The Diary of Alice Dunbar Nelson.* New York: W. W. Norton, 1984.

Lorde, Audre. *Sister Outsider: Essays and Speeches.* Trumansburg, N.Y.: Crossing Press, 1984.

Lucas, Doris M. "Patterns of Accommodation and Protest in the Fiction of Paul Laurence Dunbar." Ph.D. diss., University of Illinois, Urbana, 1973.

Lucas, Laryea Doris. "Paul Laurence Dunbar." In *Dictionary of Literary Biography: Afro-American Writers before the Harlem Renaissance,* edited by Trudier Harris, vol. 50. Detroit: Book Tower, 1986.

Martin, Jay, ed. *A Singer in the Dawn: Reinterpretations of Paul Laurence Dunbar.* New York: Dodd, Mead and Company, 1975.

Martin, Jay, and Gossie H. Hudson, eds. *Paul Laurence Dunbar Reader.* New York: Dodd, Mead and Company, 1975.

Metcalf, E. W. *Paul Laurence Dunbar: A Bibliography.* Metuchen, N.J.: Scarecrow Press, 1975.

Nettels, Elsa. *Language, Race, and Social Class in Howells's America.* Lexington: University Press of Kentucky, 1987.

Phillips, Waldo. "Paul L. Dunbar: A New Perspective." *Negro History Bulletin* 29 (October 1965): 8–9.

Poupard, Dennis, ed. "Paul Laurence Dunbar." In *Twentieth-Century Literary Criticism,* vol. 12. Detroit: Gale Research, 1984.

Revell, Peter. *Paul Laurence Dunbar.* Boston: Twayne Publishers, 1979.

———. "Paul Laurence Dunbar." In *Dictionary of Literary Biography: American Poets, 1880–1945,* edited by Peter Quartermain, vol. 54. Detroit: Book Tower, 1987.

Scarborough, W. S. "The Poet Laureate of the Negro Race." *A.M.E. Review* 31 (October 1914): 135–43.

Stronks, James B. "Paul Laurence Dunbar and William Dean Howells." *Ohio History Quarterly* 27 (1957): 95–108.

Turner, Darwin T. "Paul Laurence Dunbar: The Rejected Symbol," *Journal of Negro History* 52 (January 1967): 1–13.

Whittle, Gilberta S. "Paul Laurence Dunbar." *Philadelphia Times Book Review,* January 4, 1902. Clipping found in the Paul Laurence Dunbar Collection, MSS 659, series 1, box 1, Ohio Historical Society, Columbus; no page numbers.

Index of Titles of Poems in 1913 Edition

Index of Titles of Poems in 1913 Edition

Index of Titles of Poems in 1913 Edition

Index of Titles of Poems in 1913 Edition

Index of Titles of Poems in 1913 Edition

Index of Titles of Poems in 1913 Edition

Index of Titles of Poems in 1913 Edition

Index of Titles of Poems in 1913 Edition

Index of Titles of Added Poems

Poems not included in *The Complete Poems* (1913)

Index of First Lines of Poems in 1913 Edition

Index of First Lines of Poems in 1913 Edition

Index of First Lines of Poems in 1913 Edition

Index of First Lines of Poems in 1913 Edition

Index of First Lines of Poems in 1913 Edition

Index of First Lines of Poems in 1913 Edition

Index of First Lines of Poems in 1913 Edition

Index of First Lines of Poems in 1913 Edition

Index of First Lines of Poems in 1913 Edition

Index of First Lines of Poems in 1913 Edition

Index of First Lines of Poems in 1913 Edition

Index of First Lines of Poems in 1913 Edition

Index of First Lines of Poems in 1913 Edition

Index of First Lines of Added Poems

Poems not included in *The Complete Poems* (1913)